FREEDOM STRUGGLES

FREEDOM STRUGGLES

African Americans and World War I

—————

Adriane Lentz-Smith

HARVARD UNIVERSITY PRESS
Cambridge, Massachusetts
London, England
2009

Library of Congress Cataloging-in-Publication Data

Lentz-Smith, Adriane Danette.

Freedom struggles : African Americans and World War I / Adriane Lentz-Smith.

p. cm.

Includes bibliographical references and index.

ISBN 978-0-674-03592-8 (alk. paper)

1. World War, 1914–1918—Participation, African American. 2. United States.
Army—African American troops—History—20th century. 3. African American
soldiers—History—History—20th century. 4. African Americans—Social
conditions—20th century. 5. Racism—United States—History—20th century.
6. United States—Race relations. I. Title.

D639.N4L46 2009

940.4'03—dc22   2009017348

To Mom and Dad, with love.
And to Zora, whose story is just beginning.

Contents

Illustrations

FREEDOM STRUGGLES

Introduction: Studying War

I'm gonna lay down my burdens,
down by the riverside,
Down by the riverside, down by the riverside
I'm gonna lay down my burdens,
down by the riverside,
I ain't gonna study war no more,

I ain't gonna study war no more (chorus) . . .

I'm gonna lay down my sword and shield,
down by the riverside
Down by the riverside, down by the riverside
I'm gonna lay down my sword and shield,
down by the riverside
I ain't gonna study war no more

In 1918, as day turned to dusk, the sound of singing black soldiers wafted across Camp Gordon, Georgia. Situated on the edges of Atlanta, Camp Gordon housed almost 9,000 African American draftees during World War I, local men mostly, along with white recruits and draftees. These black Georgians wore the uniform of the United States Army, but military service had brought little of the honor and less of the glory that pro-war patriots had led them to expect. Instead, most of the African American troops labored as hard in camp as they did as civilians, maybe harder, toiling in labor battalions under white sergeants and commanding officers chosen because of their past experience as overseers of black work gangs. White military policemen were no kinder; they harassed black soldiers, provoking clashes that drew in soldiers as well as African American civilians. "Gonna lay down my burden, down by the riverside," black soldiers sang at the end of long days, "I ain't gonna study war no more."[1]

As he completed his book *American Negro Slavery,* white historian Ulrich Phillips could hear the soldiers singing. Phillips's wartime work with the Young Men's Christian Association (YMCA) had served to amplify his scholarly "conviction that Southern racial asperities are mainly superficial, and that the two great elements are fundamentally in accord." While listening to "Down by the Riverside," he wrote about the "harmony" evinced in the segregated camp and the shared local experience of hometown doughboys, black and white. A venerated scholar of the South, Phillips had long argued for the natural order of white supremacy and black inferiority. Watching the black soldiers in camp, he saw it again—"the same easy-going, amiable, serio-comic obedience and the same personal attachments to white men as well as the same sturdy light-heartedness" that he claimed "distinguished their forbears." He felt certain that "a generation of freedom has wrought less transformation in the bulk of blacks than might casually be supposed."[2]

Phillips heard the singing, but he did not actually listen. He recorded the refrain, "I ain't going to study war no more," but he paused to consider neither *what* burdens the soldiers might imagine laying down, nor *why* they would sing so "unmartial" a song. To truly hear African Americans, Phillips would have had to listen past his prejudices, to understand black people as fully human, and to see black troops as men, not children. A "generation of freedom" had also been a generation in citizenship, a status perpetually sought by black Americans and too often denied them. The system of Jim Crow that Phillips helped to construct had waged war on black citizenship since the late nineteenth century. The coming of the Great War both gave African Americans new weapons with which to fight and, by expanding and intensifying their struggle on fronts foreign as well as domestic, added to their already considerable burdens. "Down by the Riverside" may have rung out with hope, defiance, disgust, or despair, but it was never the unthinking, unchanging "old-time" song that Phillips imagined.[3]

I do not wish to tell a story of war; I wish to tell a story through war. *Freedom Struggles* asks a question that men like Ulrich Phillips never thought to consider: how did African Americans experience World War I? It takes as a given something Phillips rejected: that change, not stasis, marked the African American-experience in the Jim Crow years, just as it did the experience of all Americans. What changed because of World War I? The struggle for civil rights—indeed, in the words of some activists, human rights—did: in contours, strategies, and actors. During the second term of Woodrow

African American recruits at Camp Gordon. National Archives and Records Administration.

Wilson's presidency, as white southerners perfected a system of segregation and oppression and sought to export it beyond regional and national boundaries, many African Americans looked to use World War I to forestall white supremacy's ascent and to fulfill their quest for racial justice. For families and church groups, newspaper editors and organizations like the National Association for the Advancement of Colored People (NAACP), soldiers became emblems and agents in this struggle.[4]

This is a story of African American politics in the broadest sense. The black freedom struggle predated the end of the Civil War and has lasted long beyond the 1965 Voting Rights Act, with African Americans defining themselves in relation to community, state, and nation all the while. Stories of African American resistance are as old as stories of Africans in America. However, even within an understanding of African American history that takes assertions of self and citizenship as continual, certain moments emerge as particularly formative, or even transformative. The Great War stands as one of those transformative moments.

African Americans who supported mobilization went into the war thinking it would change them. It did, but not always in the manner they anticipated. World War I brought almost 400,000 African Americans into a military of four million and, by sending 200,000 of those men to Europe with the two-million-man American Expeditionary Forces (AEF), gave many black people their first taste of life outside the confines of American racial systems. At the same time, military discipline at home and abroad too often was enforced by Southern whites intent on making black soldiers servants of the state, rather than its agents. The great "war for democracy," as President Woodrow Wilson positioned it in his April 1917 speech on the floor of Congress, became in practice a war *over* democracy as white soldiers tried to carry Jim Crow to Europe and black soldiers fought against them. The resulting senses of entitlement and disillusion that developed would shape how African Americans approached the freedom struggle in ensuing decades and would inform critically their mobilization for the next world war twenty years after the first.[5]

It made sense that Jim Crow would travel abroad with the AEF; it headed toward hospitable terrain. The Great War had arisen from the rivalries of European powers jockeying for land in Africa and Asia, and Europeans' imperial dreams rested on a racial ideology that made it the white man's burden to subdue and civilize people of color. The system of white supremacy consolidating in the United States resonated with the racial systems of empire and colony. Indeed, as Americans increased their own overseas holdings in the 1890s and after, white supremacy and empire grew more densely intertwined.

As slaves, as freedmen, and as soldiers, African Americans had performed the bitter, often crushing, work of helping to build American nation and empire. In so doing, they helped to buttress and extend white supremacy. When they gave it any thought, most black people saw a trade-off: they would join themselves to the American national project in all its light and shadows in return for earning full citizenship rights. For African Americans, serving America meant establishing their central place in the national community and reaffirming their foundational place in the state. For African American soldiers, serving America also meant proving their manhood—asserting themselves as courageous and capable, independent and deserving of honor. This trade had never fully balanced out; the tally always added up to favor Jim Crow. By the end of World War I, many African Americans would decide the trade was no longer worth it.[6]

This book traces changes in political consciousness, collective and individual. African Americans retreated from their uneven bargain with the nation-state as they reformulated what they meant by manhood and nation, and reconsidered whether they needed to earn, or demand, full citizenship. This reformulation shifted what soldiers, in particular, saw when they viewed themselves as men and as citizens in relation to their home communities, their country, and the larger world. Reeling from the experience of war, they fought their battles over inclusion and equal rights through complex identities and on thick, contested terrain.[7]

Thinking about the transformation of black politics through World War I allows us to view African American history as international history. To do so, we must reconsider what we mean by "international." We could break it up into its component parts: between nations. Must this mean the interactions between nation-states and their representatives? Or can it describe, for example, the space occupied by African Americans in the Jim Crow era—struggling to assert their American-ness while defining a soul-sustaining blackness that could both enrich and provide a buffer from the experience of being American. We might think of the "inter" in "international" as its own word, signaling the ways in which some scholars run the risk of *burying* national histories and local complexities in their drive to create narratives of grand strategy where states and ideologies act with little connection to the particularities and people that generated them. The nuance is oft interred with the detail.[8]

If "geography is fate," as Ralph Ellison so famously concluded, then reading African American history as international history reminds us that geography, one's placement in the world, is itself fluid.[9] As descendants of varied nations scattered by the Atlantic slave trade, African Americans testify to this fluidity. Under Jim Crow especially, people found themselves constrained by local mores, local relationships, local taboos. Yet for all the lives lived locally, African Americans were, ontologically, global beings—linked to blacks across the diaspora through history and imagination. The movements spurred by war and migration altered African American identities and their fates.

Black soldiers offer a way to see the interconnections of history between local, national, and global scales. They are, after all, local people swimming in the currents of international affairs. Yet before African American soldiers could perceive those interconnections, before they could conceive of diasporic, pan-Africanist, or cosmopolitan identities, they needed to work through what it meant to be black men abroad in the service of America. First, black troops would have to develop an understanding of themselves as national subjects in an international world; they would have to locate themselves. Then they could devise strategies to bring that world back home with them. Even as overseas service cemented black troops' conviction that they had earned equal standing as Americans, it created room for African Americans to imagine emancipatory alternatives untethered from the nation. Unlike the black Army Regulars of the nineteenth century for whom imperialism and nationalism were of a piece, many members of the World War I cohort would begin to shape a sense of nation, rooted in their overseas experiences, that would allow for solidarity with subject people across national borders. This process was neither quick nor easy, but it was led by the civilians and soldiers who fought Jim Crow during World War I.

Even as this narrative stretches out beyond the territorially imagined space associated with nations, it also reaches down to the grounded places below. The engagement of individual African Americans with the nation and the federal government grew out of their participation in everyday politics in specific localities, experiences that shaped how black people viewed themselves as citizens and how they strategized to secure their rights. The alternatives they pursued in the international arena were informed by local experience as well. By exploring how some soldiers carried the burdens of home out into the world and how others disrupted Southern communities with their worldliness, *Freedom Struggles* nests the nation between international imaginaries and the groundedness of local place.

Manhood was the idiom of black soldiers' political discourse before and during the war. Black veterans of the Civil War and the turn of the century imperial wars had staked much of their claims to freedom and equality on their military service, and had cited it as a vindication of African American manhood. Figured as mastery and self-control, physical prowess and personal restraint, independence and honor, manhood formed the foundation of high political participation. In the New South it also formed the means by which white supremacists barred African American men from political sites. According to the ideological propositions of white supremacy—supported by the academic claims of scientific racism—African American men could not show independence or have dependents. They could not balance self-assertion with self-control. Whites often read their manifestations of physical prowess as brutishness. All men were created equal, Jim Crow's defenders conceded, but they did not count most African Americans as men.[10]

What the ideal of manhood meant to and for African Americans would change over the course of the war. How participants articulated the concept took forms as varied and complex as the backgrounds of the men who joined the Army and then continued to evolve as black soldiers labored and fought in Europe. Within the vast constellation of images and ideas from which soldiers' understandings of gender emerged, however, there moved a common belief that the war would make men of them and that from manhood would spring citizenship rights. This conviction would manifest itself in myriad ways, occasionally inspiring, sometimes exasperating, and too often tragic. As the promise of military service was ground beneath the heel of a Jim Crow army, soldiers began to reject the models of nation-based or romantic manhood that had previously sustained them. Their experiences in France altered how these soldiers saw themselves as citizens, workers, heroes, and lovers and transformed how they interpolated those identities into their worldview.

As soldiers redefined themselves, their civilian allies endeavored to make this new manhood a meaningful political identity for all African Americans. As scholar Martin Summers has cautioned, African American men did not simply react to white norms or state practices in formulating their sense of manhood; rather, their formations occurred "across a range of relationships, of which hegemonic masculinity versus marginalized masculinity is only one." Summers's theorizing serves as a reminder that black soldiers in World War I shaped their understanding of manhood in relation to the ideas and activism of black women, through the expectations of the civilian community, and through interactions with foreigners. Aware of their many audiences, black soldiers told their tales of transformed manhood through letters to the black press, in memoirs, and in fiction. Civilians spoke back to them through these same venues.[11]

Heeding Summers's call to interrogate "how black men engage in their gender identity formation through quotidian practices" such as "work, leisure . . . interactions with families and communities, and so forth," leads back to politics.[12] Even African American soldiers' most prosaic activities—how they spent their time off, whom they romanced, what they read—came under the watchful eye of powerful white Americans. The authority that African American men derived as uniformed representatives of the federal government posed a threat to Jim Crow at home, where they could inspire black civilians to push for their citizenship rights, and abroad, where foreigners might inspire them. Bureau of Investigation files, military intelligence reports, and court proceedings attest to the visibility of African Americans as well as the vigilance of the men who watched them. Black soldiers at war constructed and performed their masculinity in the glare of an attentive, scrutinizing state.[13]

If African Americans' status as soldiers threatened some white Americans, then their potential work as soldiers caused others to quake. Military service had the potential to legitimize black men as agents of violence. Bloodshed birthed Jim Crow, and segregationists sustained it through viciousness. Keeping up white supremacy's "social argument" required preserving the fiction that white folks alone could deploy mass violence, even as maintaining discipline within white supremacy's political program required the threat that some day African Americans might break out. In peacetime, white people could write off black resistance and rebellion as criminality, pathology, or isolated occurrences. Black self-defense, they thought, could be nullified with a noose. However, the world war required that tens of thousands of African American troops harness violence against white men in the service of a segregated state and contested nation.[14]

If respectability underlay most middle-class formulations of black gender roles, then violence and the capacity for violence offered African Americans one alternate way to frame manhood. Respectability and self-mastery had long vied with violence and aggression in making a man, just as strategies of uplifting the race sat in tension with challenging Jim Crow head on. The Great War amplified these tensions, granting violence an increased prominence and making it more acceptable to the black middle and laboring classes alike. Black warriors were heroes. African American women and men who weathered attacks from white supremacists during the war years imagined the days when black soldiers would come home, defend, and avenge them en masse.[15]

However, such celebrations of violence—in effect, of the brutalizing effect of war—could boomerang, and African American civilians often got the worst of it. White supremacists worried that once unleashed, black violence could not be contained. Wartime conflicts in the United States and abroad demonstrate the intensity with which white Americans sought to subdue black militancy and the extent to which they failed. Black and white soldiers did not leave brutality behind on the battlefield or limit it to army camp clashes. When black troops rioted in Houston, Texas, in 1917, for example, they collapsed the front and home front, setting their sights on the enemies of democracy at home. Still, after two decades of mostly declining numbers, lynchings rose steadily from thirty-six in 1917 to seventy-six in 1919, and the series of thirty-eight race riots that marked the Red Summer of 1919 would only add to the rolls. Violence, manhood, and white supremacy proved a potent mix.

Freedom Struggles does not aim to provide a comprehensive history of the African American experience in World War I. Rather, it situates World War I within the larger history of the black freedom struggle and places African Americans at the crossroads of social, military, and international histories. It chronicles a moment, particularly fraught and formative, in the ongoing fight against Jim Crow. The sons and grandsons of ex-slaves and Civil War veterans who joined the Army carried their communities' ambitions and expectations with them to camp, and they brought back home a new internationalized perspective and a renewed resolve. The rural traditions of resistance and armed self-defense that historians rightly argue sustained the struggle after World War II seem a continuation of the domestic battles that followed World War I, when African American civilians and veterans fought white Americans bent on reasserting white supremacy. Indeed, with military service in mind, traditions of resistance seem almost as cosmopolitan as they do rural; the Great War served as a crucible to fuse an indigenous militant black politics with a new, internationalized vision. Veterans of this war for democracy, domestic and European, carried this vision and their militancy through the interwar years and beyond.

How did African Americans experience World War I? The characters who populate this book help to answer that question by guiding readers through the many and varied facets of black humanity, fallibility, and hopefulness. These characters range from the eminent—academics and NAACP stalwarts like W. E. B. Du Bois, Rayford Logan, and Charles Hamilton Houston—to the lesser known, like middle-class clubwoman Kathryn Johnson and hard-headed, hardscrabble Texan Ely Green. Some, like the radical organizer Haywood Hall, chose to attack white supremacy from the outside; Hall first tried defiance and, later on, revolution. Others, like journalist and veteran Osceola McKaine, strove to undo segregation using the available tools of the American political system. Few of these people seem typical in the strictest sense, but together, they embody and typify a range of African American responses to the Great War.

The book tells the story through these characters and others like them. Chapter 1 uses the biographies of Kathryn Johnson and Ely Green to depict African American life on the eve of World War I, as American empire and white supremacy came of age. It recounts the efforts of African Americans to push back against an ascendant Jim Crow and explores how activists positioned themselves in relation to the coming conflict. Chapter 2 traces the Houston race riot of August 1917. Following the 24th Infantry of the regular army from service in the Philippines to conflict in Houston, it interrogates the relationship between nation and empire in black soldiers' formations of self.

Chapters 3 and 4 follow African Americans to France. Focusing on manhood and sexuality, Chapter 3 tracks the biographies of new inductees into the national army to illuminate how mobilization, service, memories of Houston, and encounters with black women in the United States and white women in France refined black soldiers' sense of themselves as men and citizens. Chronicling the violence and disillusion of military service, Chapter 4 begins with mobilization and the overseas journey to explore black soldiers' romance with the nation and to investigate the moments when that romance began to sour. Chapter 5 surveys the nascent and newfound worldliness of those people who began to see "the Negro problem" as part of a larger system of exploitation and inequality, and delineates the potential and limits of black internationalism in World War I years.

The final chapters return the soldiers home. Chapter 6 enters the postwar period by chronicling a criminal case involving a black soldier who shot and killed a streetcar conductor in Anniston, Alabama, ten days after the Armistice. His case went to the U.S. Supreme Court, sparking debate over federal citizenship, Jim Crow justice, and the limits of white supremacy in wartime. Chapter 7 looks ahead to the years between the two world wars, when African Americans learned to articulate and apply the lessons of the Great War. After World War I and in the lead-up to World War II, African American activists no longer tried to earn full citizenship rights; they started developing strategies to seize them.

The African Americans who served during World War I, or sent their loved ones to serve, packed their histories along with their hopes. To most Americans, wartime service felt at once monumental and mundane, as grand ideals of heroism and patriotism jockeyed with daily goals of subsistence and survival. Long after European soldiers had succumbed to the numbing senselessness of battle, American soldiers scurried to impart meaning to the conflict. How they found meaning depended on who they were and what they wanted; the nature of their journey changed with the baggage they brought. For black Americans, laden with the weight of a stillborn citizenship, the load sometimes felt too heavy to bear. They might have sung of laying down their burdens and setting aside their shield, but they would never stop thinking about the war. The Great War marked them, changed them, and readied them for a lifelong struggle. Ulrich Phillips heard the song in the distance, but he failed to grasp its portent.

I

World on Fire

Kathryn Johnson beat up the first person who ever called her "nigger." Growing up in Darke County, Ohio, in the 1880s, Johnson had plenty of experience negotiating the color line within her own community of free-born blacks and former slaves. After all, the oldest of her seven siblings had left home in protest when their widowed mother married a man they considered too dark to join their fair-skinned family. Still, the lines that Johnson's family drew inside their own community could never match the ones that white Ohioans drew around the race as a whole. Not until she ventured south of Darke County to attend school in New Paris, Preble County, did Johnson fully experience white people's contempt.[1]

Both Darke and Preble counties sat on Ohio's western border with Indiana, north of the Allegheny plateau that dipped between West Virginia and Kentucky but close enough to have connected down past those hills as a point on the underground railroad. Many of the people in Johnson's life had ties to the antebellum South—from her stepfather who had been born a slave in North Carolina to her mother's father who had escaped slavery and resettled in eastern Indiana near the Ohio line. Institutions like the Quaker-founded Union Literary School that her older brother Joseph attended also offered reminders of the region's antislavery past and of the persecution that many of local abolitionists had faced. Growing up between black settlements, former Indian communities, and a growing white population, Johnson knew more about the sustaining effect of race pride than the sting of racial discrimination, but she knew something of both. The shadow of the South hung over her, as it did the lives of all African Americans.[2]

When her *Eclectic Geography* primer informed Johnson and her white classmates that as a black person "the Ethiopian" belonged to "the most inferior race on the globe," she committed the lesson to memory. But she never quite believed it. Instead, when her elementary school classmate slung that slur at her, Johnson drew on different lessons: the memory of her maternal grandfather who had used his "fists and knives" to fight off slave catchers. Thus, after the white girl mocked her, Johnson "tumbled" her "to the gravel" and, she later recalled, "pummeled" her "with all my might."[3] Whatever gratification she derived from lashing out at her classmate, however, did not serve to allay her isolation; throughout school, Johnson continued to feel the aching gap that set her apart from her white classmates.[4] In New Paris, Ohio, in the 1890s, integration did not bespeak inclusion.

By the mid-1910s, even the lonely integration of Kathryn Johnson's high school years would have offered a respite for many African Americans. Between 1895 when Johnson graduated from high school and 1915 when she worked as the National Field Agent for the National Association for the Advancement of Colored People (NAACP), the world had closed in around black Americans. Historians refer to the period from the 1890s through World War I as the Progressive Era, a period that wedded the ambitions of myriad social reformers to the advocacy of an increasingly active state. Americans began to expect their elected officials to alleviate problems. These years also opened the age of segregation, when white Southerners came to believe that their elected officials had alleviated the Negro problem. Where Progressives sought to promote order, efficiency, and sometimes compassion in business, government, and society, segregationists organized government and social relations by regulating racial behavior.[5]

White supremacy, the system of social control and political order that undergirded segregation, came to govern African Americans' lives in the decades after the Civil War. From the 1890s on, it hardened from custom in most parts of the United States to law in most of the former Confederacy. Jim Crow, as folks popularly called it, made a ritual out of asserting the unequal citizenship of people of color and a virtue out of the exploitative behavior of white Americans. It dictated where people lived, whether they voted, whom they might love, and how they might work. Statutes required segregated public facilities as far west as Arizona and as far north as Wyoming and Indiana. Laws against miscegenation extended beyond the South to all the western states except Washington and New Mexico, and into the Midwest in Indiana and Nebraska. Other sanctions, both legal and social, governed how African Americans comported themselves in public, how they addressed white women and children, how they aspired to security or self-improvement.[6]

The conviction that people of color deserved less and, indeed, *were* less was not the exclusive provenance of white Americans. Even as Jim Crow swept the United States, an explicitly race-based colonialism swept the world. By the time the Great War began in 1914, most of the European combatants (and, increasingly, Japan) had staked colonial claims in all of Asia, except for Siam, and most of Africa, except for Ethiopia. The United States, too, had begun pursuing its own empire—focusing after the wars of 1898 on the Pacific and the Caribbean.[7] Just as Americans justified Jim Crow by likening the first generations out of slavery to children who lacked the mental and social development required for self-government, colonizers spoke of their *mission civilisatrice*—their obligation to elevate colonial subjects by suppressing them. In both the U.S. South and the global South, white people deployed these ideologies of development and uplift, predicated on racial hierarchy, to validate grabs for power, land, and resources.[8]

The Great War underscored the linkages between American-based and international systems of racialized oppression even as it drew people like Kathryn Johnson out of their national frameworks and impressed upon them their connection to the larger world. As early as 1915, Johnson's colleague at the NAACP, African American sociologist and writer W. E. B. Du Bois, linked the origins of the conflict to the problem of the color line. Writing in an American magazine on "The African Roots of the War," Du Bois argued that in Africa lay "hidden the roots, not simply of the war to-day but of the menace of wars to-morrow." As he saw it, Africa and other "darker nations" increasingly sustained the world's wealth as white European workers, less and less willing to toil for starvation wages, began to demand their just share of a wealth that, ironically, depended on injustice. Thus it was that a new compact between white men was born. "It is no longer . . . the employing class that is exploiting the world," Du Bois observed, "it is the nation; a new democratic nation comprised of united capital and labor."[9]

White supremacy secured the new industrial social compact. Ohio schoolgirls like Kathryn Johnson's classmate learned to call black children "nigger" not simply for the thrill of the insult but because they had already learned that asserting themselves as worthwhile required establishing themselves as not-black. It mattered little that neither white laborers nor white women would enjoy an expansive or total citizenship; their half-loaf looked abundant when set alongside black Americans' crumbs. For Du Bois, this pallid compact accounted for much of African Americans' changed circumstances since the end of Reconstruction. It explained how "the most rapid advance of democracy" could "go hand in hand with increased aristocracy and hatred of the darker races" in the United States and why imperialist countries, ones he characterized as "armed national associations of labor and capital," needed to mine "the wealth of the world." Even more, Du Bois's insight suggested that white supremacists may have caught themselves on the shoals of their own world war. If they wanted a viable, lasting peace, they would have to extend the new compact "to the yellow, brown, and black peoples" who lay outside of it. "We shall not drive war from this world," he warned, "until we treat them as free and equal citizens in a world-democracy of all nations."[10]

By war's end, both Kathryn Johnson and W. E. B. Du Bois would find themselves fighting in their own ways for a world democracy. As a camp volunteer for the Young Men's Christian Association (YMCA), Johnson would make the aspirations and insults of African American soldiers her own. Du Bois, through his association with the NAACP and its organ the *Crisis,* would attempt to shape a broad program for black involvement in the war and the subsequent peace. Like all the civilians and soldiers who engaged the war and, through it, the world, Johnson and Du Bois brought the whole of their past experiences to their wartime efforts. And, as with thousands of these others, the war would shape their subsequent politics and identities. In these early years before U.S. engagement, Du Bois realized, even as Johnson and others may not have, that the Great War had begun to touch African American lives long before it began to take any.

Generations

African Americans who looked back at the turn of the century from the other side of World War I would dub those early years "the long dark night."[11] In the 1890s, however, black people could barely divine from the clouds on the horizon the strength of the storms that lay ahead. Little by little the portents came: Plessy v. Ferguson, the 1896 Supreme Court ruling that upheld segregation; a growing number of white mobs and militias willing to murder in the name of white supremacy; the increasing currency of eugenics and racist social science that glossed race hatred with an academic veneer. The period from 1890 to 1917 saw African Americans buffeted by design and circumstance. Many of those later radicalized by World War I first expressed their racial politics in attempts to hold their ground in the new twentieth century.

For Kathryn Johnson the century dawned clear. Like many African American women of her station and educational background, she had gone to college to train as a teacher. After graduating from high school in 1895, Johnson attended Wilberforce University, the liberal arts college in her native Ohio run by the African Methodist Episcopal (AME) church. Wilberforce offered a revelation, an opportunity to immerse herself in an all-black life. W. E. B. Du Bois had taught there briefly while working on his Harvard dissertation, and Lieutenant Charles Young, a recent West Point graduate and the highest-ranking black officer in the U.S. Army, currently taught military science, math, and French. She shared classes with students from Africa and observed them "to see if they were in any way inferior" to white people, as her grade school textbook had claimed. They were not. Indeed, no one there appeared to be. With his keen mind and stately bearing, Lieutenant Young, especially, "gave an obvious lie" to white supremacy. Years later, Johnson easily recalled the sense of "pride" she derived from watching him, a fine soldier and good man, drilling a new generation of African American men.[12]

Images of black manhood and their evocations of black citizenship may well have steeled Johnson as she left the shelter of Wilberforce and Darke County for a position at the Elizabeth City Colored Normal and Industrial School in northeastern North Carolina.[13] Riding in the white train car because "no one seemed to recognize" her as "colored," Johnson could only partially envision the place she would find.[14] She had heard about the rebellious Old South from friends and family who had left there. With slavery ended and Reconstruction dead, she arrived in a New South where white men stood determined to reshape and redraw the boundaries of the nation as a whole.

Maritime North Carolina, with its oyster-shell-paved streets and newly codified segregation laws, seemed a sharp contrast to rural Ohio. White supremacy, a tacit assumption on the part of white Ohioans, rang as a battle cry from the mouths of white North Carolinians. When Johnson arrived in 1904, the state still seethed from the 1898 election season in which white Democrats had forcibly run members of the biracial Fusion Party from office. An alliance of white Populists—agrarian critics of the region's emerging industrial economy—and reformist Republicans both black and white, the Fusionists had swept state elections in 1896. Democrats responded in the 1898 campaigns by painting white Fusionists as more than dissenters: invoking the apocalyptic tones of American and European eugenicists, they excoriated their rivals as feeble, "degenerate sons of the white race."[15]

If a new social compact shaped the fates of Progressive Era Europeans and their colonial subjects, as Du Bois would later argue, North Carolina Democrats articulated that bargain in Southern vernacular. Led by party chair Furnifold Simmons and *Raleigh News & Observer* publisher Josephus Daniels, a coterie of enterprising Democrats made white supremacy the key to stifling agrarian discontent and guaranteeing the advance of an industrial economy. The Democrats strove to convince white voters that their identity as men (as all North Carolina voters were in 1898), and more specifically as white men, should override economic concerns or social critique. Figuring the American nation as explicitly "Anglo-Saxon," Simmons made loyalty to the Democratic party a test of white voters' "patriotism" as well as a testament "to their manhood, to their pride of race, to their immemorial custom and habit of ruling every other race with which they come into contact."[16]

Although Populists also had tried to rally voters around manhood, citing small farmers' increased subjection to a market economy as a threat to manly independence, Democrats stressed honor, rather than independence, as the measure of a man. By their zero-sum logic, black people's gains intrinsically dishonored and weakened white men, and weak patriarchs meant unprotected wives and children. Daniels amplified that argument in the pages of his newspaper by manufacturing a black-on-white rape scare that insistently linked "Negro Atrocities," as he called them, to the old bogey of Negro domination.[17]

To combat Negro domination, Democrats seized state offices through force. The Red Shirts—white supremacist shock troops who straddled the line between civic organization, lynch mob, and terrorist group—threatened Fusion candidates and intimidated black voters across the state. In Elizabeth City, they destroyed the local African American newspaper and ran Fusion candidates out of town. Most notoriously, south of Elizabeth City in Wilmington, the losing Democratic mayoral candidate Alfred Waddell led a mob of Red Shirts, National Guardsmen, and white citizens of all classes in an out-right coup d'état.[18]

Just days after the Fusionists defeated the Democrats in local elections, Waddell delivered on his campaign promise to "choke the current of the Cape Fear" river with African Americans' "carcasses" if necessary to gain the mayor's seat.[19] Rampaging whites targeted the economic infrastructure of Wilmington's African American community, murdered African Americans, and drove white Fusionists out of town. "There was not any rioting," an African American survivor wrote President William McKinley following the massacre, "[s]imply the strong slaying the weak."[20] At minimum, seven African Americans died (though estimates range up to 300), and countless others fled the state. Those left behind begged the McKinley administration to intervene, but to no avail. The federal government, which two decades before had ceased pressing for full African American citizenship, would no longer even endeavor to slow the ascent of white supremacy.

The government bowed to Jim Crow in the South because the nominally regional system performed crucial work for the country as a whole. Domestically, excising African Americans from the democratic process came easier than actually exercising true democracy, and it cleared the way for white men to come together across class and regional boundaries. Foreclosing black citizenship seemed a small price to pay for reunion between North and South, and between Northern capital and Southern capitalists. White supremacy served a second purpose, as well. The nationwide retreat from the ideal of universal rights—made official by the *Plessy* decision and confirmed by McKinley's indifference to the Wilmington coup—came as Americans routed the Spanish in the wars of 1898 and claimed dominion over Cuba, Puerto Rico, and the Philippines. Segregation strengthened, too, as the United States followed its quick victory over Spain in the Philippines with a protracted, brutal war to suppress Filipino freedom fighters, and then a five-decades-long occupation to hold on to its hard-won prize. As America hastened to join Europe in the scramble for empire, white supremacy provided a guide and justification for domesticating foreign people and lands.[21]

Although both Jim Crow and American empire existed prior to 1898, they came of age together. In the context of territorial expansion, white supremacy provided clarity. As a system of rule, it rationalized unequal power relations, giving a structure and coherence to day-to-day governance. As an ideological argument, it set the conceptual boundaries of the nation: whether white Americans pondered blacks in California, Creeks in Oklahoma, or mestizos in Puerto Rico, Jim Crow helped them imagine whom they might embrace—or reject—as their fellow citizens. Forming a frame both political and cultural, white supremacy joined together arguments justifying white America's hold on power with decisions about how, and over whom, it was to be exercised.

But white people had never built America alone, despite Southerners' shrill invocations of Anglo-Saxon conquest. Although Alfred Waddell might justify his insurrection by claiming descent from men "who stained with bleeding feet the snow of Valley Forge," African Americans could cite their own service in every war from the Revolution to the imperial wars of 1898 as grounds for civic access and inclusion.[22] Like the thriving black neighborhoods that rioters destroyed, or the black workers and voters that rioters murdered, black soldiers exposed the fictions cutting through the narrative of white supremacy. They "gave the lie," as Kathryn Johnson said of Charles Young. As the project of nation became more explicitly interlaced with the project of empire, maintaining those fictions required discounting the meaning of African American military service.

During the Spanish-Cuban and Philippine Wars, denying soldiers meant dishonoring them, as soldiers and as men. Fighting in Cuba in 1898, white troops showed less contempt for the white-skinned Spanish enemy before them than for the blacks battling alongside them. Writing a memoir of his exploits with the Rough Riders in Cuba, former Assistant Secretary of the Navy Theodore Roosevelt contrasted his self-described heroics on Kettle and San Juan hills with the cowardice of African American troops who, he claimed, tried to "shirk" their duty and slink behind the lines. Ever commanding, Roosevelt drew his pistol on the black troops and ordered them back to the front. Other Rough Riders had to inform him that the supposed shirkers actually had received orders to head back and restock tools and rations. The day after the battle, Roosevelt apologized to the African American troops he had insulted at gunpoint, but he was not too sorry to record his initial version of the story in the pages of *Scribner's* magazine one year later.[23]

Roosevelt glibly called upon tropes of black weakness to accentuate a picture of his own manly forcefulness.

As the turn-of-the-century wars brought more African Americans into the Army, Southern communities followed Roosevelt's lead in erasing or debasing black troops' service. Corporal C. W. Cordin stationed at Camp Haskell near Macon, Georgia, noticed that the local paper, the *Telegraph,* avoided any positive mention of African American troops.[24] Also in Macon, a streetcar conductor "shot and killed" a member of a black volunteer regiment from Virginia after he resisted riding in a Jim Crow car, and townspeople kept up signs in the local park saying, "Dogs and niggers not allowed here."[25] As an African American lieutenant lamented after mustering out of Camp Haskell in March 1899, it took more "forbearance" than some soldiers possessed to prove themselves "heroes" in Cuba only to come home and endure from white soldiers and civilians alike "the unprovoked and utter disregard of any but an old-time cotton field 'darkey.'"[26]

At Camp Shipp near Anniston, Alabama, the soldiers of the Third Alabama Colored Infantry abandoned their forbearance in the face of overwhelming hostility from other soldiers and the local white population. On their first night out of camp, the Third Alabama encountered the fury of a "howling, frantic mob" composed of "white soldiers and civilians" who assaulted them and drove them back to camp.[27] Although the men retained their composure that night, two more months of abuse finally wore them down. On Thanksgiving Day, 1898, the Third Alabama clashed with white soldiers in what would become known as "The Battle of Anniston." One black soldier and one white soldier died in the fray. Several soldiers and civilians were wounded.

Reaction to the Battle of Anniston revealed how Alabamans, and other Southerners, saw the interplay of military and civic participation during the wars for empire at the turn of the century and anticipated their response to mobilization for World War I. Senator John Tyler Morgan, an Alabama Democrat, pinned blame for the fight on African American military service. Tyler charged that "by putting guns in the hands of Negroes as soldiers and making them the peers of white men," state officials had caused "race conditions" to become "greatly exaggerated." Another concerned Alabaman, Anniston banker George Ide, viewed the African American soldiers as the "most dangerous element" still remaining at Camp Shipp in the spring of 1899. He worried that the soldiers would be mustered out of the Army in Anniston "just at the time" of a local election when they could "be easily purchased, either to register or to vote."[28] Having forcibly asserted their manhood while enlisted, veterans of the Third Alabama might threaten the balance of Anniston local politics once discharged. Although they refused to remove the troops from Anniston, federal government officials disbanded the unit before it saw service abroad. The ex-soldiers left town without incident.[29]

"The White South was no less active than the North was quiescent," a black reporter recalled, looking back at the turn of the century.[30] In the wake of the Wilmington Insurrection, the Battle of Anniston, and the imperial wars, Southern lawmakers moved to take the steps toward disenfranchisement and demobilization that the federal government had not. In Alabama in 1901, and in states across the South, white Democrats rewrote the Constitution to keep most African Americans from the polls, and concern about black veterans' effect on politics dissipated. In a special session following the end of the Spanish-Cuban and Philippine Wars, the Alabama state legislature also restructured the National Guard in a deliberate move to exclude black volunteers. A small company of African American guardsmen lingered in Montgomery for a few years, but by 1905, no African American militia units remained in Alabama to think themselves the peers of white men.[31] Legislatures across the South followed suit, disbanding their voluntary militias.[32] Although some black troops remained in the four segregated units left in the Regular Army, for symbolic and practical reasons, securing white supremacy required limiting African American military service.

No white Southerner wanted to see African Americans killing, not even in the service of the government. *Especially* not in the service of the government. The relationship between the nation as a "white man's country" and the state as arbiter and guarantor of its citizens' rights had blossomed into true romance since the federal government abandoned the democratic reforms of the Reconstruction Era. The romance, buoyed by idealizations of a commanding and courageous white male voter, relied in large part on the conviction that only white men could responsibly and justifiably wield violence. Indeed, from Teddy Roosevelt riding roughshod over black troops in Cuba to Josephus Daniels inciting his way to a post in the Wilson administration, white men's violence formed the heart of the nation-state union.[33] To African Americans like New York–raised teenager George Schuyler, black troops still "represented the power and authority of the United States," but to white supremacists, those remaining representatives stood as the remnants of a dying breed.[34] If, as contemporary philosophers argued, one could define the state by its claim to a legitimate monopoly on violence in a given territory, then Jim Crow's boosters had aligned the racial boundaries of the state with those of the nation.[35]

Little wonder, then, that racial violence occurred as regular as rain. White people argued with other Americans and amongst themselves about which violent acts counted as legitimate, but with ever more lurid lynchings and riots excused as a form of white home protection, Jim Crow was winning the debate. Lynchings of African Americans decreased in number over the first several years of the new century from more than 100 in 1900 to about 65 in 1916, but they increased in virulence.[36] To call it slaughter captures the fervor of the thousands who took part, but not the ritualistic nature of their crimes—the roasting of live men and women over bonfires or the carving off of noses, knuckles, ears for keepsakes.

The race riots that followed Wilmington in the years leading up to World War I also served as rites of community, with mobs sacrificing black bodies, institutions, and businesses to establish both political dominance and the sense of cultural solidarity.[37] In 1906, in "The City Too Busy to Hate," as Atlanta would later market itself, 10,000 white people paused long enough to lay waste to African American neighborhoods.[38] Black families fought to protect themselves and their homes. Thirteen-year-old Walter White's father handed him a rifle and told him to use it only if he needed it and, if it came to that, then not to miss, but the sidewalks of Atlanta still "ran red with the blood of dead and dying Negroes."[39] What white Georgia author John Temple Graves deemed a "lawless revolution," rioters on the ground simply called a move "to clean out the niggers."[40] Both phrases betrayed the speakers' sense of white entitlement to the state and nation. Similarly, when white mobs attacked African Americans in Springfield, Illinois, two years later, commentators blamed "the negroes' own misconduct, general inferiority, or unfitness for free institutions."[41] Although some white people might have claimed to deplore the racial slaughter of the times, few looked within when assigning blame for it.

Having relocated to Little Rock, Arkansas, in the fall of 1906, Kathryn Johnson came to understand riots and lynchings for what they were: semilegitimate forms of violence, tied to the state and claimed by white men as a necessary prerogative. Johnson had left North Carolina after the 1904–1905 school year, returning home to nurse her dying mother. Upon her mother's

passing, Johnson once again moved south—this time to become a dean at
Little Rock's AME-affiliated Shorter College. After living through a race riot
in Little Rock, she would observe bitterly that "it is the white people" who had
the bluntest instruments of state authority behind them, the "guns, ammunition, militia, etc." African Americans' comparative "helplessness" seemed to
her "pathetic."[42]

This lesson in pathos came in October 1906, when Johnson had barely
settled in to her new post. Trouble started in September after a white policeman killed a black man in a barroom brawl—a fight begun, Johnson later
heard whispered, "because of a colored woman."[43] During the inquest that
followed at the black-owned Colum Brothers funeral home, African American mourners clashed with "a number of white hoodlums."[44] In the fracas,
someone, most likely policeman Morton Lindsay, killed Robert Colum, one
of the three brothers who ran the funeral parlor. Neither the barroom shooter
nor Morton Lindsay were convicted of a crime.[45]

Four weeks later in early October, brothers Garrett and Charles Colum shot
down Morton Lindsay, wounding the policeman and killing his father as the
two passed in front of the funeral home. The Colums barricaded themselves
inside the funeral parlor, firing on the policemen who came to arrest them. The
brothers got their revenge, but at a high cost to the community. As they fled the
city—some guessed to Canada, others to the Philippines—"several hundred
armed [white] men" surged into the African American neighborhoods in north
Little Rock.[46] Members of the mob dynamited the Colum brothers' funeral
home and set the business district on fire, witnesses remembered, "the flames
reaching high toward the heavens." At Shorter, rioters shot at the women's dormitory to keep Kathryn Johnson and her charges inside while they doused the
steps of the men's dormitory with coal oil. As flames leapt "up to envelope the
building," the young college students inside had to choose between fleeing the
dorm and running the risk of getting shot or staying in the building and burning. When one of the male teachers ran over to save the dorm, someone turned
a shotgun on him. Somehow the building survived the night, as did its occu-
pants, but the assaults continued.[47]

Armed gangs occupied Shorter's neighborhood for another two days,
marching "up and down the streets with guns on their shoulders." Night
brought more violence. A lynch mob pulled a black man from the local jail,
strung him from a telegraph pole and "shot him full of holes."[48] On Monday,
teachers took in refugees too scared to stay alone at home while fielding rumors

that white folks planned to blow up one of the campus buildings. Black Arkansans sent a desperate plea for help to state troops, but none came. "We were," Kathryn Johnson felt, "at the mercy of the mob."[49]

What little protection they had seemed pitiful. Johnson had brought her brother's revolver with her to Arkansas when she made the trip from Ohio three weeks earlier, but sorely outnumbered and greatly outgunned, she worried what the mob would do to her if they found it. Secreting the pistol away, she opted instead for prayer. Still, though she and the other teachers put on their Sunday best, squared their shoulders, and forged ahead with Bible meetings, their nerves had worn so thin "that a pin drop sounded like a gunshot." Their faith and desperation mixed so thoroughly they could barely discern one from the other, and when they prayed for the Lord above to save them, Johnson clarified: "not particularly from our sins, but please save us from the white people."[50]

Two nights after mobs had started rampaging, the Little Rock police chief finally came by Shorter to promise them a guard. By then, Johnson had heard of eight people dead or wounded, and at least one of her co-workers had discounted the local police as "bloodthirsty beasts" in league with the rioters.[51] Johnson, though comforted by the police presence, kept returning to her community's stark vulnerability in the midst of the riot. Their posture as good, responsible citizens had not shielded them; if anything, rioters had zeroed in on the symbols of their ambition, like the college, or their prosperity, like the funeral home. Blacks in Little Rock had prayed, and they had endured. But praying felt like a half-measure and enduring, not enough. If North Carolina had given Kathryn Johnson her first direct exposure to Jim Crow, her experience at Shorter "changed the whole course" of her life.[52] After Little Rock, Johnson would fight often and endure little. Where once she had charted a path as a Race Woman—an unassailable exemplar of black rectitude and humanity—she now went forth as an activist.

After leaving Shorter at the end of the 1906–1907 school year, Johnson eventually found her way to the NAACP. Her path took her through Kansas, where she moved to teach at Kansas City's Sumner High School. She had barely been back in the Midwest a year when the Springfield race riot served notice, as Kentucky-born white Socialist William Walling warned, that demagogues like Mississippi's James Vardaman and South Carolina's Ben Tillman had just about "transferred the Race War to the North."[53] In 1909, to stave off the race war and secure African Americans "absolute political and social equality," Walling joined white journalist and social worker Mary White Ovington, W. E. B. Du Bois, black dynamo Ida Wells-Barnett, and others in founding the NAACP. A year later when Du Bois began publishing *Crisis,* the association's monthly magazine, Kathryn Johnson started distributing copies around Kansas City. Two years later, chafing against the "confinement" that teaching required, she left to take a job as a traveling *Crisis* agent and, later, as the national field organizer.[54]

Though barely three years old and ten branches strong when Johnson joined its staff in 1912, the NAACP had already come to symbolize a shift in the fight against Jim Crow away from the circumspect strategies of Booker T. Washington and his political machine. The principal of Alabama's Tuskegee Institute, Washington had become the most powerful African American in the United States by seeming to compromise with the architects and adherents of white supremacy. In his speech, both celebrated and reviled, at the Atlanta and Cotton States International Exposition in 1895, Washington had urged his fellow African Americans to stop openly resisting segregation and disfranchisement. Instead of striving for full citizenship, he advised African Americans to instead "cast down your buckets where you are," among the white folks of the industrializing South, and find a way to make themselves useful.[55] Focusing at Tuskegee on vocational instruction as self-help—he had little use for the classical education earned by students at schools like Wilberforce—Washington publicly framed "the Negro problem" as the *Negroes'* problem; when African Americans proved themselves worthy as workers and landowners, political rights might come to them like manna from a benevolent god. In the meantime, he prodded influential white people to draw on the most benign stores of their paternalism and shield black men and women from the worst excesses of racial violence.[56]

With his public renunciation of African American political rights, Washington became a kingmaker. Industrialists from Andrew Carnegie to William Baldwin swooned at his professed willingness to abide by the terms of the new social compact, and they rewarded Tuskegee with their philanthropy, making it one of the richest schools in the nation. Presidents Roosevelt and Taft delegated him the authority to choose plum federal patronage positions for black Republican stalwarts. Washington bought newspapers and bought off editors to propagate the Tuskegee line. Behind the scenes, he quietly financed legal challenges to disfranchisement and debt peonage, but he kept those cards close to his chest. On the public stage, he was "The Great Accommodator" and, to white people, the grand ambassador for the entire race.[57]

Some African Americans chose other political alliances in the fifteen years between the Atlanta Compromise and rise of the NAACP, but few managed to rival the Tuskegee machine. While Washington saw to the high-politicking, other reformers worked to build and enrich alternate public spheres using churches, schools, clubs, and businesses as material.[58] After the founding of the National Association of Colored Women (NACW) in 1896, for example, clubwomen constructed a politics of civic reform and mutual aid, and an ideology of uplift that bound African American strivers across class even as it recapitulated hierarchies of progress and development.[59] At the same time, in fraternal organizations like the Prince Hall Masons, black men both reconstituted the civic life denied them under Jim Crow and recast Victorian manhood to fit African American models of duty, respect-ability, and independence.[60] Such alternate sites of public engagement and political activity existed alongside Washington's machine, occasionally linked by membership and affinity but often pursuing different goals and paths.

Others did offer overt resistance to Tuskegee. Newspaperman T. Thomas Fortune's National Afro-American League, founded in 1887 and reconsti-tuted in 1898 as the National Afro-American Council, voiced a more aggres-sive line on citizenship rights and resistance to segregation than Washington publicly did. However, Fortune maintained so close a tie to Tuskegee that Washington's private secretary, Emmett Scott, boasted that "we control the Council" and assured his boss that Washington's "personality dominated ev-erything" therein.[61] Council member and clubwoman Ida B. Wells-Barnett, exiled to the North from Memphis because of her frank dissection of the myth of the black beast rapist, resisted Washington's influence and crusaded against lynching and for equality outside of Tuskegee's circle. In Boston, Monroe Trotter, the Harvard-educated founder of the National Independent Political League (NIPL; later the National Equal Rights League) took an unyielding, often incendiary stand for civil rights and against accommoda-tion. Within all this ferment, it took the idealistic, upstart NAACP to gather "the most courageous forces battling at that time for the Negro's civil rights," as Mary White Ovington described herself and her compatriots, and to add "new and valued recruits" to the ranks.[62]

As the association's National Field Agent, Kathryn Johnson performed what Ovington called the "difficult and even dangerous tasks" of bringing new recruits to the ranks.[63] Directed from New York by prominent African Americans and white stalwarts of the Progressive movement, the NAACP could come across as more alien and removed from most African Americans than Washington's deeply Southern, aggressively ingratiating Tuskegee. Armed with Du Bois's *Crisis* and an obdurate streak, however, Johnson canvassed to bring the NAACP out of its Manhattan offices and into the rural towns and growing cities of the South, mid-Atlantic, and midwest. Johnson relied on local members' judgment and preferences, working through black institutions like the church and neighborhood groups to build membership. In one year she helped double the number of branches; by 1914, the number reached 54, and by the time she left the NAACP in 1916, the number of branches had grown to 68. With every branch added, Johnson helped to make the NAACP more local and more vital. Over the years, it would develop a mass base that the Tuskegee machine never had.[64]

Within a year of Kathryn Johnson's signing on, NAACP secretary May Childs Nerney had written to express amazement at Johnson's "courage in spreading our militant propaganda."[65] Mobilizing people did require tremendous courage. Traveling to Jackson, Mississippi, Johnson discovered that although African Americans occasionally voted in the state capital, "many a colored man had been shot down for not voting as he was told." In the rural delta near the Arkansas line, she talked with a white man who wept as he remembered how his son "was killed" for "taking a truck-load of [black] voters to the polls to be registered." Arriving to speak in Caruthersville, Mississippi, Johnson heard that the last African American speaker before her "had been shot after he went to bed at night," and the hall where he had spoken, burned to the ground.[66] She got the message most clearly when she walked into a New Orleans museum during an organizing campaign. "The first thing" that she saw when she entered the vestibule was "a number of guns strung up by the side of the wall." The inscription above boldly announced them as "the guns with which we maintained white supremacy at the polls in Louisiana."[67] White supremacy had grown increasingly secure in the first thirteen years of the twentieth century, but no less vicious in its defenses.

In the ground that Kathryn Johnson covered in her travels, African Americans constantly had to choose between trying to survive white supremacy and trying to surmount it. Sometimes survival won out. Waxahachie, Texas, a railroad town not too far from Dallas, was deemed "too dangerous" to try to set up a branch when Johnson passed through in 1913. Johnson also tried and failed to organize a branch in New Iberia, Louisiana. When she traveled to Dallas in 1915 to protest residential segregation ordinances, the first minister that Johnson contacted, an old friend that she knew "very well," advised her not to come down from St. Louis and refused to let her use his church once she did.[68] To organize African Americans in the South and elsewhere, Johnson would have to overcome their fears about white supremacy's very real, and ever-growing, threat.

Still, some people fought without organizing. Kathryn Johnson and the NAACP offered a potentially powerful means of resisting white supremacy, but neither they nor the Tuskegee machine exhausted the possibilities of African American politics. During these years, when white supremacy had come to demarcate and warp the limits of social possibility, "politics" lay in how African Americans imagined themselves beyond those limits and how they pushed up against them. People need not possess the rhetorical skills of a minister or the education of an NAACP worker; they could act through daily choices—scrimping for money to educate their children, or daring to contradict a white man, or relocating in search of better opportunities. To claim more for oneself more than Jim Crow afforded was to commit a political act.

In Waxahachie, for example, the Texas town too dangerous for Kathryn Johnson to organize, chauffeur Elisha Green waged a tough and extended battle to claim the respect and prerogatives due him as a citizen. Neither a Bookerite toiler nor an NAACP campaigner, Green expressed his politics through his drive to call himself a man and not to back down when others claimed otherwise. Green followed no program save his own, but his biography—so different in background and tactics from Kathryn Johnson's—suggests the broad spectrum of African American politicization. Taken with Johnson's story, his biography also underscores the extent to which even oppositional politics drew on white Americans' norms of gender, civic status, and national belonging. In making his case for inclusion, Green simultaneously resisted and reinforced the underpinnings of white supremacy.

Elisha Green arrived in Waxahachie a year before Kathryn Johnson passed through, on the run from trouble. Born in Sewanee, Tennessee, in 1893 to an African American domestic and her prominent white employer, Green, called Ely by his friends and family, embodied many of the contradictions of the segregated South. Raised in the black community and granted the loose protection—if not the legitimacy—of association with his white family, Green remained nevertheless a "half-white" bastard to most of the black residents of Sewanee and a "nigger" to many of the whites.[69] Jim Crow argued for a world in which Green made no sense; he could traverse the line that divided black from white, but he seemed to belong on neither side. After his mother died, leaving him in the care of an ex-slave he called Mama Mat, Green took to spending most of his time alone in the hills surrounding Sewanee to avoid the isolation he felt among the people of the town. He was, as he described his alienation under Jim Crow, "a man without a country."[70]

Green saw his gender as the key to his self-preservation. The genteel paternalism that structured life in Sewanee made the Tennessee college town relatively safe for African Americans at the turn of the century, but precisely because of that paternalism, a black man could be a man "only with other Negroes." Green had seen his normally feisty grandfather Ned Green bow and scrape in the presence of white folks, and he understood their indulgent "Good old Ned" as the diminishment that it was.[71] Whereas Ned Green anesthetized his stunted pride with liquor, his grandson Ely resolved to protect his with his rifle and his fists. As a teenager, Ely vowed "not to let no one get by with nothing" when it came to him and his family. Be they black or white, Green announced to Mama Mat, "When they hurt me, I am going to hurt back." As she told him to hush, he persisted, "I am going to be a man."[72] Over his foster mother's protests, he went out and bought himself a rifle.

During his teenage years, Green strove to prove himself a man through his bearing and sexuality. He had learned from his grandfather three tenets of independence and authority: "protect everything you have, keep your money, don't be on your knees to nobody."[73] Although Ned Green had never managed to follow his own advice, Ely Green did. As he got older, Ely combined those rules with his passion for women—"little brown dolls"—and his eye for a good clean shot. By hunting in the mountains, he earned enough money to support himself and his family and sculpted a physique that added to his already striking good looks. Women loved him, and those men that did not respect him at least envied him a bit. He slept with the women who adored him, stood up to the men who tried to cheat him, and carried, coiled within himself, a knot of what he called "my grandfather's revenge as well as mine" against the world that had treated them so.[74]

By the time he left to join his foster sister's family in Waxahachie in 1912, he had worn out his welcome in Tennessee. Green had long drawn a sharp distinction between the law as the body of rules that governed social relations and the "the law" as the men who enforced those rules in the name of white supremacy. In a confrontation with the town constable and some white mountain farmers from nearby Tick Bush, Green defied both. The farmers had accused Green's hunting dogs of killing one of their sheep and had brought the town constable to put the dogs down. His gun trained on the white men, Green refused to let them near his animals. He repeated his vow to "protect every dam thing I own, law or no law" even as they threatened to kill him for disrupting Sewanee's racial code. When the men finally succeeded in disarming him, Green flew into a rage. He cursed the men and swore he would never stop until he killed them, adding "I don't want to live if I have to crawl to you poor white sager sons of bitches."[75] Although a bystander convinced the white men to leave without harming Ely, everyone knew they would return later for retribution. Even in Sewanee where they prided themselves on their civility, there existed some lines you could not cross. To avoid a lynching, Green's family snuck him aboard a train in the middle of the night. He headed for Waxahachie, Texas, where his foster sister and her husband had settled down.

The paternalism that guided race relations in Sewanee also set the slightly more ragged rhythms of Green's racial interactions in the Texas cotton belt. Employed as a chauffeur by a Republican judge, Oscar Dunlap, Green felt keenly the limits placed on African American men in Waxahachie and across the South.[76] Despite his affection for the Judge and the other Dunlaps, who insisted that they thought of him as family, Green understood his position in their household and in the community at large: he was, as even his white supporters characterized him, "Dunlap's nigger." Like every other "Negro," Green felt, he "had no right of law except where a white man protects him and gives him law through his prestige." Through his militancy and his manner, Green wanted to "win the respect of every white aristocrate in the United States" to fight for what he viewed as the fundamental prerogative of citizenship, an equal protection under the law.[77]

By 1913, equal protection almost seemed too much to ask. Ely Green moved to Texas just as Jim Crow's power began to reach its apex; by the mid 1910s, it seemed as entrenched and intractable as ever it would. Southern Democrats had been proselytizing their segregationist faith for well over two decades by then—"spreading the poison," an African American newspaperman bemoaned—and they had amassed a large following.[78] They had also gained a new leader; in

1912, Thomas Woodrow Wilson beat Republican incumbent William H. Taft and former President Theodore Roosevelt to become the first Southern Democrat to win a presidential election since 1848. Wilson's victory had made him the nation's most prominent Progressive. His New Freedom platform pledged to protect individual Americans from the heartlessness of modern society, to police corporations "to prevent the strong from crushing the weak," and to secure "a government devoted to the general interests and not to the special interests."[79] African Americans, however, did not fall under his protection. Within four years, Wilson's policies had earned him a reputation among civil rights advocates like Afro-American Council member and AME minister William Byrd as "an avowed enemy of the colored people."[80]

Woodrow Wilson did not preach white supremacy: he practiced it. Too restrained for the fire-eating theatrics of Jim Crow evangelists like South Carolina's Ben Tillman or Mississippi's James K. Vardaman, Wilson nevertheless shared their fundamental assumption that black people lacked a full capacity for self-government. Indeed, by definition, Wilson's conception of American politics excluded African Americans. The former political science professor saw American democracy as rooted in the "manly self-helping spirit of Saxon liberty," as he told members of the American Bible Society while governor of New Jersey. True politics came in the form of "men afraid of nobody, afraid of nothing but their own passions, on guard against being caught unaware by their own sudden impulses, and so getting their grapple upon life in firm-set institutions."[81] African Americans, particularly that first generation out of slavery, he long had viewed as "unschooled in liberty; unpracticed in self-control."[82] Disciplined Saxon liberty held little room for African Americans' wanton aspiration.

Born in Staunton, Virginia, and raised in Augusta, Georgia, Woodrow Wilson personified national reunion. He had commenced his undergraduate work at North Carolina's Davidson College and finished it in New Jersey, at Princeton. Returning to the South long enough to get a doctorate from Johns Hopkins, he left again to teach history and government at Bryn Mawr, Wesleyan, and Princeton. In 1902, he became president of Princeton—where he stopped accepting African Americans' applications, never mind African American applicants, so as to not discomfit white Southern students—and in 1910, he won election as governor of New Jersey by emphasizing morality and municipal reform.[83] A son of the South who had thrived in the North, Wilson could serve as ambassador for the legions of white people who saw segregation as the surest way of maintaining the marvelous peace regained in the healing heyday of the white supremacy campaigns.

Wilson had welcomed the new state constitutions that disfranchised the bulk of African Americans in the South and returned control to "whites who were the real citizens" of the Southern states.[84] Reflecting on Reconstruction in the pages of the *Atlantic Monthly,* Wilson characterized the Southern blacks who had tilled white planters' fields and raised slaveowners' children as laborers "never sobered by the discipline of self-support." He dismissed former bondsmen, people who had fought, prayed, pleaded, and fled to escape slavery, as naifs bewildered "by a freedom they did not understand."[85] Emphasizing manhood as shorthand for independence, self-possession, and civilization, he dismissed African Americans as "a host of dusky children untimely put out of school."[86] State disfranchisement and the federal government's acceptance of it signaled to the future President a return to the "normal balance" of the federal union and a "marvelous" indication of the "healing and oblivion peace has wrought."[87]

When Wilson entered the national scene, black and white Americans gambled on whether he would prove better or worse on the subject of race than his competition. Southern white supremacists sizing him up for a presidential bid expressed hope that Wilson would "take the aggressive for their political faith and ideals," as Asheville politico William Garrott Brown wrote to him in late 1911.[88] At the same time, Oswald Garrison Villard, publisher of the *Nation,* NAACP co-founder, and grandson of abolitionist William Lloyd Garrison, took Wilson at his word when the candidate pledged to rule impartially. Some African Americans, weary of the racial politics of candidates Taft and Roosevelt, took heart when Wilson assured AME minister Bishop Alexander Walters that he wished "to see justice done" to African Americans "in every matter." In a letter to Bishop Walters, Wilson noted that "colored people" had "made extraordinary progress towards self-support and usefulness," and he expressed a desire to encourage that progress in "every possible and proper way."[89] Roughly 100,000 African American voters read enough encouragement into Wilson's pledge to vote for him in the 1912 election, but in the end what seemed "possible and proper" to President Wilson would diverge widely from what African Americans deemed necessary or desirable.

Wilson's brand of Progressivism left a lasting mark on the country. The New Freedom brought more regulation of trusts, more oversight of finance, and increased protection of labor. With government help, the President ar-

gued, modern life had become more humane. Yet African Americans struggled to maintain their footing. "For the first time," an editor of the *Indianapolis
Freeman* lamented in the early months of Wilson's presidency, "the government
has taken an avowed stand in racial affairs," and that stand was squarely
against African Americans.[90] As the chair of the Republican National Committee put it when trying to woo African Americans back to the party of
Lincoln: President Wilson "preached the 'New Freedom,'" but he actually
"practised the 'New Bondage.'"[91]

Progressivism could cut several ways. It created openings for African American activists, as people like Kathryn Johnson and members of the NAACP
tapped the reform impulse to find common cause with white reformers or
push for racial justice. In contrast, Wilsonianism highlighted the compatibil-
ity between social reform and social control, Progressivism and Jim Crow.
The white Southerners in Wilson's administration, men like North Carolina's
Josephus Daniels as Secretary of the Navy and Texas segregationist Albert
Sydney Burleson as Postmaster General, had long intertwined Progressivism
and white supremacy. In Washington, it would be no different. Burleson,
Daniels, and Treasury Secretary William Gibbs McAdoo systematized Jim
Crow in the nation's capital and ensconced it. By September 1913, the Administration had segregated most federal departments, not simply placing African Americans in separate rooms but leaving them with harsher working
conditions, cramped quarters, and inadequate bathroom facilities.[92] When
pressed, Wilson admitted that he did in fact "approve of the segregation that
is being attempted in several departments," but he argued that it increased
the comfort of black and white people alike.[93]

"Instead of the condition of the Negro improving in a civic way during the
Wilson regime," a reporter declared in the first few months of the President's
second term, "it has been retarded."[94] The administration did soften its segregation orders in the face of powerful protest from African Americans, but it
had already set in motion a wave of activity. The effect extended beyond humiliation in D.C.'s executive offices. It affected people's livelihoods: Post Office and Treasury officials throughout the South downgraded or discharged
droves of black employees, and the Administration cleared African Americans
out of federal patronage positions across the country. It influenced other legislation: Wilson's stance "gave the cue," a bitter voice in the black press argued,
for cities like St. Louis and Dallas to press ahead with residential segregation
laws, and emboldened Southern congressmen to pursue legislation curtailing

black civil rights.[95] It drove foreign policy: in 1915 the U.S. Navy invaded Haiti and installed a white supremacist regime on the island, joining Jim Crow and empire more explicitly than ever. By the end of Wilson's first term in office, Wilsonianism had come to symbolize the triumph of Southern white supremacy in national politics and its expanding power abroad.

"World War for Humanity"

America's entry into World War I offered a crucial disruption of Jim Crow's ascendant power and a needed opportunity for African Americans to roll back the tide. The war had already spurred a dramatic demographic shift: decreased foreign immigration after the outbreak of hostilities in Europe in August 1914 led to a heightened demand for workers in American cities like Birmingham, Houston, Detroit, Chicago, and East St. Louis. African Americans weary of Jim Crow had responded by the hundreds of thousands, pouring out of the southern countryside—and out of the South—in a decades-long mass relocation that would come to be known as "The Great Migration." Between 1915 and 1921, roughly 700,000 African American men and women relocated from the South; by 1930, 1.5 million. Their departure worried white supremacists used to controlling black bodies and black labor, and it created new pockets of black political power in Northern and midwestern cities.[96]

After the United States joined the war in April 1917, mobilization further unsettled racial politics in the Jim Crow South and beyond. Segregationists' public pronouncements shifted from open anticipation of the moment when "the negro is actually eliminated from politics"—what the editors of the *Atlanta Constitution* framed as driving "the negro out of the country" in referring to black voters' dwindling ranks within the southern Republican party—to a heated debate over the meaning and potential rewards of African American military service.[97]

Black activists and segregationists both saw high stakes. As 200,000 black soldiers began traveling to Europe with the American Expeditionary Forces (AEF) and another 186,000 toiled in the United States or the Pacific, activists hastened to make President Wilson's "War for Democracy" abroad a tool for African American liberation at home. At the same time, white supremacists moved to protect their hard-won program by ensuring that Jim Crow also shipped out with the American army. The war and the world would supply new stages for the ongoing struggle between white supremacy and black equality.

Yet for all its import, an African American scholar would later claim, the Great War "came upon the United States as an unexpected bomb blast."[98] The war began in August 1914 as Europe's fight and Europe's folly; few Americans anticipated the extent to which the conflict would involve them. The first January of the war, President Wilson celebrated American neutrality, telling an Indiana crowd that "half the world is on fire,"—with America alone "free to govern her own life." Wilson urged the American people to maintain the "self-possession" of peace and the "exaltation of hope" so that they might succor war-devastated Europe in its "time of dismay."[99] Atlanta postmaster Bolling Jones sanguinely predicted that the South would not "be much affected by the war in the old country," save for higher cotton sales.[100] To Americans, the war seemed a foreign affair, "a spectacular concern" in the words of a British commentator, in which those in the United States might observe and even choose sides but not truly expect the conflict to breach their shores.[101]

W. E. B. Du Bois did publish his trenchant "African Roots of the War" in May 1915, but this one last time, though his power and health had begun to flag, Booker T. Washington got closer than Du Bois to reflecting the national temper. His reaction to the outbreak of war typified Americans' sense of watchful remove. Writing to Andrew Carnegie in August 1914, Washington professed bewilderment over "what [had] gotten into the people of Europe." Comparing the supposedly "civilized and cultured" belligerents across the ocean to black people in the United States, he found the Europeans sorely lacking. In a letter to another correspondent, Washington quipped that he would "have to wait until a majority of Europeans have succeeded in killing themselves off" before he could resume a planned trip to Europe. It could "be worth while," he added in a subsequent note, "to consider sending a group of black missionaries to Europe to see if something can be done for the white heathen."[102] In summer 1914, as Europeans marched giddily off to combat, the Tuskegee principal painted their Great War as farce.

By the end of 1915, Washington would be dead from heart disease, and the Great War would have grown more to tragedy than farce. The momentum that initially propelled Europeans into war had carried them to what one French legislator deemed a deadly, costly "equilibrium." Equilibrium meant "stagnation," creating a "war without end" and without victory. To "tilt the balance" in

France's favor, the legislator told the French Chamber of Deputies, they would have to wear down their enemy with numbers: they would have to mobilize their empire.[103] And mobilize they did. In addition to the 220,000 wartime laborers who came from Africa, the Americas, and Asia to work in France, over half a million colonial troops fought in the French army, with nearly 50,000 coming from Indochina and 450,000 from colonies in Africa.[104]

Not interested in civilized black missionaries to make men of white heathen, the French sought barbarians to vanquish the Huns. Where Booker T. Washington had used the occasion of war to lampoon European discourses of civilization and racial hierarchy, French authorities drew on those same discourses to structure and justify their use of *tirailleurs,* or soldiers from the colonies. The more than 150,000 troops who traveled to France from West Africa formed the heart of what French General Charles Mangin deemed a *Force Noire,* valued for their "rusticity, endurance, tenacity" as well as their "instinct for combat" and "incomparable power to shock."[105] Arguing for the use of colonial troops before the war and during, Mangin highlighted the invigorating effect on an effete France of African "primitives . . . whose young blood flows ardently, as if avid to be shed."[106] French racialism did not require that Army commanders like Mangin or General Hyppolite Langlois view *tirailleurs* as anything but "savage."[107] In depicting them as men so raw and elemental as to be almost beasts, French officials reinvigorated the trope of the noble savage, making African troops a vital corrective for the over-refined sensibility of the civilized French.

For commentators in the United States, the mobilization of African soldiers both underscored the affinities of American white supremacy and European colonial racism, and summoned the specter of black Americans in uniform. Like white Europeans, white Americans marveled when they read in the papers about the ferocious potential of troops of color who "less than a year" before had been "wild, untamed," and undisciplined.[108] If the tribulations of slavery had served as an intensive course in European civilization, as Woodrow Wilson intimated in 1901 by lamenting African Americans' untimely release from school, then the trials of war had served African soldiers much the same way. "No transformation from savagery to civilization" had ever occurred "with more thoroughness and speed" than colonial troops' rising to "Aryan courage" and order, a Southern reporter declared, comparing them to American "negro regiments" who fought under white officers in the Civil War.[109]

Yet such a great transformation carried certain dangers. German officials howled in protest that the French and English utilization of "men of the black and yellow races" would lead to a "tremendous restlessness" across "the entire colored world." Soldiers would return from Europe trained "to use the best of the white man's weapons" and with the conviction that "they must behave differently, make demands, remember that the future must belong to the colored man—Africa to the Africans, India to the Indians."[110] Although some Americans dismissed German concerns (as well as Germans' claims to civilization), those who heard echoes of their own race problem condemned the Allies for allowing "inferior races" to fight on European soil.[111]

As the war came home to the United States, the links between manhood and civilization, and between civilization and citizenship, proved too much for white supremacists like James Vardaman. Pressured by delegates from Africa and the Antilles, the French legislature had indeed granted rights— and, in parts of Senegal, citizenship—in exchange for military service. Neither insensate nor unsavvy, colonial troops parlayed their military service into an assertion of their humanity, a claim of comradeship with metropolitan French, and the potential for political standing.[112] Vardaman feared that blacks in the United States would stake similar claims. Once the federal government drafted the black man and "inflated his untutored soul with military airs," the Mississippi senator predicted while arguing against conscription two weeks into the war, only a few short steps would lead "to the conclusion that his political rights must be respected, even though it is necessary for him to give his life." Like the Germans who protested the Allies' use of troops from the colonies, Vardaman conjured the devil of black male militancy. He warned his fellow senators that "one of the horrible problems that will grow out of the war . . . is the training as a soldier that the Negro will receive."[113] Treat a Negro like a man, Vardaman cautioned his colleagues, and he will think himself a citizen.

Vardaman had cast the lone antiwar vote from a Southern Senator when, on April 2, 1917, President Wilson finally made the decision to go to war. Rather than maintain America's exalted neutrality, Wilson declared it time to "fight for the things we have always carried nearest in our hearts." Americans would go to war "for democracy," he declared, and the "right of those who submit to authority to have a voice in their own government."[114] As Vardaman and others recognized, Wilson's summons to the nation supplied blacks with the language and leverage they needed to bring issues of rights and citizenship to the fore. If America sought to redeem Europe's war by fighting for "rights and liberties" as a "concert of free peoples" and by constructing "a universal dominion of right" that would "make the world itself at last free," then black Americans could seek some of that much-vaunted freedom for themselves.[115] Although the President spoke specifically of European powers in the new world order, African Americans would extend his field to include the United States.

Mobilization became an occasion for all sorts of African Americans— enlisted soldiers, potential draftees, and engaged civilians—to articulate a relation to the nation, Jim Crow, and the potential for African American freedom. Black supporters of the war took what they saw as Woodrow Wilson's "lofty sentiments" and grounded them in domestic soil.[116] Down in Waxahachie, Ely Green decided to join the Army after hearing white planters assert that an African American was more "like a pig, cow, or horse" than a man and thus had "no right to fight." Still determined to secure "the right of law" for all the race, Green figured he could "enlist [as] a Negro of the South" and return as "an American and a representative of the Government of the United States."[117] Green had faith that war could give him the honor he sought and link him so inextricably to the state that even the lowest white man would have to concede his citizenship.

Kathryn Johnson argued something similar. "From its beginning," she wrote in a black women's monthly in June 1917, the Great War had "carried in its wake a wonderful opening of opportunities for the America Negro." As befitted her years of work in education, the NAACP, the club movement, and the AME church, Johnson framed her support for the war in terms of comportment and worth. Unlike Green she held little hope that African Americans would reach the battlefield, thinking it more "probable that the selective draft will select Colored men to do other things besides bear arms." However, she expected them to "bear their burden bravely" knowing "that the time will surely come that conduct and not color will be a measure of manhood in the world."[118]

In pulpits and papers from New York to California, pro-war African Americans elaborated on this belief that they could earn citizenship rights through exemplary service. Those who believed, as did Atlanta minister Reverend James Bond, that "the black man has nothing to lose and everything to gain" from wartime loyalty, all rushed to revivify the sense of African American military service as foundational to the nation. Delivering a

World War I poster. James Weldon Johnson Collection, Yale Collection of American Literature, Beinecke Rare Book and Manuscript Library, Yale University.

sermon improbably titled "Peace Through War," Bond informed his audience that "the black man has been true" in all past wars and would not begin to "sulk now" during this one. Instead, like Booker T. Washington at the Atlanta Exposition, he promised that African Americans would "make friends" through their "display of manly, heroic qualities." Waving an American flag above his pulpit, another Atlanta pastor, Henry Hugh Proctor, also declared his support for the "fight for human liberty" that the United States was undertaking. As Americans' nativist fervor marched in step with their growing support for the war, Proctor moved to position African Americans as more native than most. "We are Americans by birth and breeding, service and sympathy," he reminded his congregation, and he urged them to allow "no words of disloyalty fall" from their lips.[119]

Not everyone pledged their support so uncritically; some African American activists offered their loyalty without fully giving their trust. "The hearts of the colored people beat in unison with their President" when Wilson asked Congress for a declaration of war, the *Afro-American* wrote, but they doubted the breadth of his vision. Having "watched keenly" as France and England mobilized colonial troops and as Germany objected "on the grounds that this is a 'white man's war,'" black Americans wondered what place the administration would make for its own troops of color.[120] No matter how the administration might opt to use them, W. E. B. Du Bois believed there could be no denying that people of color had a role to play. "This is our War and not Woodrow Wilson's War," he wrote. African Americans would either "fight or work." If they fought, "they would learn the fighting game and cease to be so 'aisly lynched.'" Those who stayed would "learn the more lucrative trades and cease to be so easily robbed." Either way, he believed it would work to the detriment of white supremacy.[121]

The women and men of the all-black National Equal Rights League also balanced declarations of support with critiques of Jim Crow. The organization, whose leader Monroe Trotter once stood in the White House and rebuked Wilson for extending segregation in Washington, declared African Americans' "active loyalty" in this war, as in past ones. Nevertheless, they added, "Colored Americans" deeply resented "enforced segregation by city, state, or the federal government, whether in federal or military service." They called on white Americans to give "to white, to brown, to yellow, to black, Americans, all" the same rights to enlist, to rise on merit, and "the same right to civil service, and to civil rights without bar or segregation." The country was embarking on a "world war for humanity," and if America truly wanted to light the way, Wilson needed to see to it "that all shall have liberty within her borders."[122]

In less public fora, a few African Americans expressed far greater skepticism than the public figures who claimed to speak for them. "Some of our well educated negroes are touring the country encouraging our young race to be killed up like sheep, for nothing," an anonymous writer scoffed in a flyer circulated in the Mississippi delta. The circular went on, "Rather than fight I would rather commit self death."[123] A black man in Tampa, Florida, expressed a similar feeling. When interrogated about his patriotism by a white storeowner, the shopper flatly replied "that he would not fight for the United States" and that "no one could make him."[124] In Sweet Home, Texas, black resident Grant Dow went a step further, announcing that he "wish[ed] to God" that Germany would defeat the United States and that he was willing "to go over there and help them."[125]

Although white Southerners and government agents blamed German agents and outside agitators for most expressions of African Americans' wartime discontent, black people themselves cited more straightforward explanations. In a letter sent to Secretary of War Newton Baker, an African American conscript decried the race's state of suspended citizenship. One did not have to be a "slacker" or "traitor" to resent being drafted, the soldier told the Secretary, when "most Negroes" were "denied in a large measure the right to life, liberty, and the pursuit of happiness." The soldier wrote Baker to "protest" getting drafted after having felt "the sting of race prejudice and discrimination" in his failed attempts to *enlist* in the Army and Navy.[126] Asa Philip Randolph and Chandler Owen, Southern-born black socialists whose politics were a product, not a cause, of their commitment to equal rights, stated it boldly in the first issue of their monthly magazine, the *Messenger*. "Patriotism has no appeal for us," they wrote from New York, "justice has." Loyalty, without a worthy object of that loyalty, they declared "meaningless."[127]

For the 367,000 laborers, doctors, farmers, and lawyers called up in the June and September drafts in 1917, the question of loyalty would be subsumed within the larger reality of obligation. Whether they wished it or not, draftees joined the twelve hundred enlistees in the segregated Officers Training Camp at Fort Des Moines, Iowa, as well as the 10,000 members of the 9th and 10th Cavalries and 24th and 25th Infantry Regiments already in the Army. With National Guard units mobilized from the midwest, mid-Atlantic, and Ohio,

Illinois, New York, Maryland, Washington, D.C., Tennessee, and New England, African American soldiers numbered almost 400,000 in an army of 3.7 million men.[128] They had become uniformed representatives of the American state, and all of them—from the patriots dreaming of their manly heroics to the rebels thinking of their manhood rights—belied the notion that only white men had a legitimate monopoly on violence or that they could somehow place black Americans outside of politics.

White supremacists had worried about the link between military service and civic status in the turn-of-the-century wars; this time, a far more extensive military mobilization promised to bring thousands of African American men into the South to train for war and strain Jim Crow. Even reluctant soldiers understood the power of their mobilization. In the wake of a ghastly May 1917 lynching in Memphis, draftee Sydney Wilson wrote back to his Tennessee draft board from camp in Maryland promising that black soldiers planned to do "what little fighting we is going to do in this country and not France." Fully aware of the threat that thousands of armed black men posed to white supremacy, he added, "once we gets through with you all, you wont be quite so anshous to draft the nigroes in any more." In a separate letter he starkly challenged his draft board, "You low-down Mother Fuckers can put a gun in our hands, but who is able to take it out?" The war would not be over, he announced, "untill we straiten up" things back at home.[129]

The route between New Paris, Ohio, and Paris, France, was surprisingly direct. Over the next several years, African Americans would do their fighting both in the United States, as Sydney Wilson promised, and overseas, as Ely Green anticipated. This held true, not only for Kathryn Johnson, whose twenty-year journey from Ohio student to YMCA camp secretary in France would literally carry her down that road. It also held true for the domestic activists who hitched their local strategies for overcoming white supremacy to soldiers' service in a foreign war, and for the thousands of soldiers who went to France in search of freedom and found constraints as cruel and binding as any they had known at home. Jim Crow and the drive for civil rights were American phenomena, but race-based oppression and the drive for human rights were global ones. Questions of African Americans' nationalism and citizenship would prove inseparable from American's international experiences. And nowhere did the interplay of international experience and militant nationalism, military training, and black entitlement reveal itself as dramatically as it did in Houston in summer 1917.

2

Fighting the Southern Huns

"To hell with going to France," Corporal Larmon Brown called to fellow members of the 24th Infantry, "let's go clean up the god damn city."[1] In furious revolt, part mutiny and part riot, over one hundred soldiers in the all-black infantry's Third Battalion seized roughly 18,000 pounds of ammunition and arms from the supply tent in their camp, overpowered the white officers who tried to subdue them, and began what the *Houston Post* would luridly deem a "10-hour reign of terror." Army Regulars, some of the mutineers had served along the Mexico border in the 1916 Punitive Expeditions against Pancho Villa. Some had records that dated back to the turn-of-the-century Philippine War and subsequent occupation. By dawn on Friday August 24, 1917, these soldiers had killed seventeen white people in Houston and wounded eleven others. Two of their own lay dying. Contrary to the *Post* report, the violence lasted about three hours, but its effect lingered through the duration of the war and after.[2]

The summer of 1917 saw its fair share of racial violence. On a stormy May evening in Memphis, Tennessee, for example, a white mob lynched a black man and tossed his severed head down in the middle of the Beale Street, the city's "colored" business district. Six weeks later, further up the Mississippi, white men and women viciously beat, stoned, and burned African Americans in East St. Louis, Illinois, launching the infamous "pogrom" that killed roughly thirty-nine African Americans. Other race riots occurred in Chester, Pennsylvania, and Newark, New Jersey, other lynchings in Louisiana and Kentucky. Shocking though it was, the Houston mutiny marked but one in a series of racial conflagrations that ignited during the opening months of the War.[3]

Yet in a season marked by grisly conflicts, Houston stands out. A revolt of black soldiers against the strictures of Jim Crow, the riot, and the national response to it vividly illuminate the struggles over manhood and citizenship that informed African American politics—and American politics as a whole—during the early years of the twentieth century. The Houston riot came as African Americans took advantage of mobilization to renew their assault on Jim Crow. Against this backdrop of upheaval, all racial conflicts took on heightened political import, but the inversion evident in the soldiers' riot, as black men mercilessly shot down white men and women, made Houston a singular flashpoint.

Houston stood out, too, because of who the rioters were. The soldiers of the 24th Infantry held themselves up as ideals of African American manhood: masterful, courageous, and undeniably tied to the nation. By retaliating against the abuses heaped on them by white Houstonians, the soldiers saw themselves—and others saw them—as using manhood to claim their citizenship. Lamentable as other racial activists found the killing in Houston, they saw the soldiers' action as part of an ongoing war at home against Jim Crow.

Black women, especially, viewed the Houston riot as a vindication of their men's honor, and of their own. Doubly bound by a racial system that elevated man over woman as well as white over black, African American women understood events like those in Houston as attacks, first, on female bodies and security. For those women pushing at the confines, meaningful expressions of black manhood had to incorporate a mindfulness of women's trials and concerns. They lauded the soldiers as their champions and their equals, articulating a cooperative notion of manhood that fused the aspirations of African American men and women. The riot in Houston illuminated how other African Americans saw black soldiers—those who rioted and those who did not—as fighting a true "war for democracy."

Biggety Women and Colored Soldier Men

It all began with a woman. On Thursday August 23, Sara Travers stood iron-ing in her house in the predominantly black San Felipe district located in the fourth ward of Houston. She stepped outside, she would later recall, when she heard gunshots. As she stepped out, white city policeman Lee Sparks ap-proached the African American mother of five to demand whether she had seen "a nigger jumping over that yard" by her house. When she responded, "No, Sir," he ignored her and began searching inside her home.[4]

Travers called over her neighbor to find out what had happened. "I don't know," the neighbor replied. Explaining that Sparks and his partner were patrolling the streets in the fourth ward, she added, "I think they were shoot-ing at crap-shooters." Officer Sparks emerged from the house in time to hear the woman's explanation. In a flash of temper he called her a "god damn liar" and claimed to have shot only at the ground. As the two women exchanged glances, he added, "You all God damn nigger bitches. Since these God damn sons of bitches of nigger soldiers come here, you are trying to take the town."[5]

Sparks intended to demonstrate to the women of the fourth ward that the arrival of the 24th Infantry to guard Camp Logan had changed nothing for African American civilians in Houston. Accustomed to entering houses in the San Felipe district—"nigger dives" he later called them—at will, he re-turned to his search of Sara Travers's bedroom and kitchen.[6] When Mrs. Travers followed him inside to ask what he wanted, Sparks barked, "Don't you ask an officer what he want in your house." He informed her that in Fort Bend County where he came from, white men "don't allow niggers to talk back to us." Down there, he continued, "We generally whip them." As if to punctuate his statement, he lifted his hand and slapped her.[7]

As a Houston policeman, Sparks could spiff up his Fort Bend roughhand-edness with a thin coat of urban legal polish. Upon conferring with his part-ner Rufus Daniels about what to do with Travers, Sparks opted to "take and give her ninety days on the Pea Farm" as punishment for acting like what Daniels termed "one of these biggety nigger women." To Sparks and Daniels, Sara Travers's suggestion that access to her home was hers to control repre-sented a gross insult to Jim Crow. As white men, particularly as officers of the law, their rights of access to spaces in the fourth ward, public and pri-vate, went without question. By commenting on the police officers' behavior first in the streets in front of her house and then by questioning Sparks's right to search her house, Travers revealed herself to be a "biggety" woman, a troublemaker.[8]

Sparks and Daniels knew how to deal with such women. Just as they meant her arrest to send a message that their authority held sway over her domestic space, they manhandled Sara Travers to demonstrate that their power extended to her body itself. When she pleaded for time to put on something besides the "ol raggedy" slip and underwear that she later described herself as wearing, Sparks told her no. "We'll take you just as you are," he snarled at her, "If you was naked we'd take you." In a second, grand gesture of contempt, spectators later claimed, Sparks took the child that Travers reached for on her way out the door and threw it to the sidewalk. Rufe Daniels, the bigger of the two men, pulled Mrs. Travers away from her children and down the street with her arms pinned behind her back, warning that he would break both her arms if she did not come easily. The two policemen had effectively denied Sara Travers her status as lady or mother and reaffirmed their prerogatives as white men in the process.[9]

Once the conflict between "biggety" black women and white authority spilled out of Sara Travers's kitchen and into the neighborhood, however, the script changed. As the housewife and the two policemen waited at the call box for a paddy wagon to arrive, Travers recalled, "a crowd began a-coming"— a crowd led by "a colored soldier man." Leaving Travers by the call box, Sparks walked forward to meet the soldier.[10]

Sparks would later claim that 24th Infantry private, Alonzo Edwards, looked a little drunk, that the soldier came swaggering towards him "walking kind of in the street" with a mixed crowd of about "20 civilian negroes and women." Assessing the situation, the slender built Sparks quickly decided that he "was not going to wrestle with a big nigger" like Edwards. When the private boldly announced "that he wanted that woman," Sarah Travers, turned over to him, Sparks raised his pistol and struck him repeatedly. Avoiding a fair fight he knew he would not win, Sparks, in his own words, "hit" Edwards "until he got his heart right."[11]

Stunned, bystanders watched the scene unfold. Where Sparks saw a puffed-up soldier working other African Americans into a lather, eye witnesses saw a uniformed race man speaking up for an African American woman. They saw Private Edwards approach Sparks and Daniels and ask them to let Mrs. Travers dress, and they heard him request that the officers turn her over to his custody. As she donned an apron and a bonnet, emblems of respectability brought to her by "a lady friend," Sara Travers heard Sparks demand to know what business the whole thing was of Edwards. Then, she recalled, "he raised his six-shooter and he beat him—beat him *good*." Another witness saw both Sparks and Daniels knock Edwards to the ground. As one of the officers beat Edwards in the side with the muzzle of his gun, the witness heard Sparks reiterate the message that he and Rufe Daniels had given Sara Travers minutes earlier: that they were "running things, not the damned niggers."[12]

The arrival of Corporal Charles Baltimore a few hours after they sent Edwards and Travers off in a patrol wagon served as an unwelcome reminder that, with the 24th Infantry in Houston, the two policemen did not run things alone. They shared their jurisdiction with military policemen who performed provost guard duty in the neighborhoods frequented by African American soldiers. Although the MPs went unarmed in deference to white Houstonians' concerns about having armed black soldiers circulating in the city, their mere existence provoked white officers such as Sparks and Daniels. In a city with only two African Americans on the police force, the provost guard of the 24th Infantry signified unwelcome federal inversion of local racial mores.

Corporal Charles Baltimore had just climbed off a streetcar in the San Felipe district, he later testified, when he "met a boy of the 24th Battalion who told me a soldier had been beaten up by a policeman." Members of the civilian populace confirmed the soldier's story, saying that the police had taken Edwards and "beated him up pretty bad."[13] Trying to keep an open mind but determined to find out what had happened, he started down the street towards the call box where, hours earlier, the patrol wagon had come for Private Edwards and Mrs. Travers.

Baltimore encountered the two men near the scene of the morning's incident. Lee Sparks looked up to see a man he described as a big "ginger cake, a mulatto" coming at them.[14] He watched the uniformed soldier cross the street away from them as if reconsidering his approach. He then waited as Baltimore came back and started again in their direction. Witnesses could not hear what the men said once they got within speaking distance, but after a short exchange, one witness recalled, Sparks and Daniels raised their guns over Baltimore's head and "beat him, too."[15]

Sparks would later describe the encounter as a face-off. In his account, a confrontational Baltimore "came butting up . . . nearly rubbed his belly into mine" and addressed the two policemen in a "gross, grouchy way." Baltimore

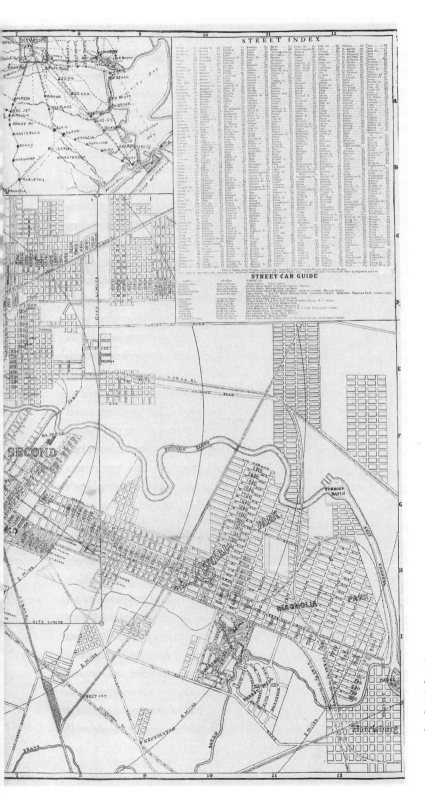

Houston street map, ca. 1913. Texas State Library and Archives Commission, Map 0435.

demanded to know "who whipped that soldier" earlier in the day. When Sparks claimed responsibility, the young corporal pressed to know "what the 'hell' he arrested a soldier for."[16]

"Who wants to know?" Sparks challenged.

Baltimore mustered all the weight imbued in his posting and uniform in his reply. "I am supposed to know," the soldier told the policeman.

Sparks brushed aside Baltimore's claims to authority as readily as he had Sara Travers's. Ignoring the agreement between the city and military police, he flatly told the corporal, "I don't report to no niggers."

Baltimore cursed him, Sparks later alleged, demanding to know, "Why the hell" the officers would not answer him. In the face of Sparks's defiance, Baltimore vowed, "By God, I will know about it." Riled by his tone, Sparks struck the soldier with his pistol.[17]

Baltimore recounted a different story. According to his version, he approached Sparks and Daniels with all the civility and decorum that their white officers had instructed the troopers to use when dealing with white Houstonians. He had prefaced his statement with "Sir" and respectfully asked Sparks whether he could "tell me what the trouble was." Sparks had been the one to curse, responding that they had taken in Private Edwards because he had interfered with Sara Travers's arrest and taunting, "By God, don't you like it?"[18]

The corporal futilely tried to keep the encounter from escalating. When Sparks cursed him, he cited his responsibility as a soldier: "Officer," he doggedly explained, "I am on duty on this street and when I return to camp I have to report."[19] Sparks supplied his characteristic response, knocking Baltimore on the head with the butt of his gun.

Baltimore "didn't have a gun" he later stated and "didn't care to get beat up."[20] Rather than take on two policemen alone, the soldier turned on his heel and—in Sparks's words—"ran like a greyhound."[21] As witnesses watched, Baltimore darted into a nearby house while Sparks "commenced firing at him—right at him."[22] After getting off a few shots, Sparks and Daniels followed Baltimore into the house, rustled him out from his hiding place under a bed and placed him under arrest.

Baltimore bled so much that witnesses in the crowd thought that Sparks had surely put a bullet in him. For his part, Sparks explained away the blood by saying that Baltimore "was so scared" coming out of the house that "he could not see the door" and cut himself "trying to make a hole through it."[23]

In contradiction, Baltimore claimed that he had taken another blow from the end of Sparks's pistol as the officer placed him under arrest. "He said he would kill me" the corporal recalled, "and I pleaded with him not to kill me."[24]

Whatever the cause, Sparks noted that Corporal Baltimore came out of the house so subdued "he didn't seem like the same nigger he was when he first came up to me." Thinking back on the encounter, Officer Sparks would later tell a municipal board of inquiry that he did not mind black military policemen, "as long as they would stay in their place."[25]

Place, Patriarchy, and Empire

During the age of Jim Crow, Lee Sparks's obsession with "place" was as southern as pecan pie. This central tenet of white supremacy did not simply draw a line between black and white; it structured relations across sex and class by assembling what one scholar has called "a stiff-sided box where southern whites expected African Americans to dwell."[26] Although poor white men could never aspire to the political influence of white male elites and poor white women would never truly stand on the pedestal reserved for the white ladies of the South, rigidity of place assured them a fixed position above even the most respectable African Americans. In turn, black men and women lived compressed lives, their public roles mortally constricted and their private spaces virtually unprotected. Place structured politics.

For African Americans, "place" allowed them to structure their world within that stiff-sided box as far removed from the hazards and indignities of Jim Crow as possible. During the war years and after, black people in Houston literally tried to "never get [themselves] in a place where" they would "have any trouble with" white people.[27] However, as Lee Sparks's rampage through the homes and streets of the fourth ward demonstrated, few such autonomous zones actually existed for African Americans. And as subsequent events would demonstrate, many African American men and women refused to remain within their stiff-sided box. Place always remained conceptual. In daily practice, the metaphor was continually undermined.

That logic of place rooted white patriarchy in black women's bodies. As an ideology and system of rule, white supremacy relied on the debasement of black women as much as it did the sanctification of white ones. White Southerners sought to teach African Americans that freedom had by no means brought self-possession, and they regularly abused black women's bodies to drive this lesson home. During Reconstruction, white vigilantes had used rape as one form of extralegal terror, and in those years and after, *legal* authorities also used sexualized assaults to enforce and embed the authority of white men. Assault was "commonplace," as South Carolina newspaperman John McCray recalled in the waning years of segregation. Many a community had its Lee Sparks and Rufe Daniels.[28]

West of Houston in Waxahachie, Ely Green referred to such officers as "the law that lurks in the dark." Green had long thought white lawmen "more enslaved to the propagander word white supremacy" than the white elites he knew who sat atop the economic and social totem, and he suspected that lower-class whites found their "self-apeasement" over their own foreshortened circumstances by seizing opportunities to "kick the Negro around." He had experienced his own run-ins with the local law, but in the fall of 1917, not long after Daniels and Sparks attacked Sarah Travers in Houston, Green discovered some sheriff's deputies trying to find their self-appeasement by assaulting black women teachers.[29]

Driving into the African American section of town one night in fall 1917, Green came across a gathering of "at least forty men," assembled on a street corner. The group of black men had just watched some sheriff's deputies arrest three black women schoolteachers on trumped up charges of prostitution. Calling the situation "a dam shame," the men anticipated that the deputies would "take" the school teachers "to the park and rape them." The deputies made no secret of their intentions—"they laugh about it in the barber shop," the gathered men told Green. Moreover, this was not the first time the deputies had committed such assaults. As the crowd lamented, they had "been doing this to cotton picking women for over a month."[30]

Green wasted no time on lamentations. Instead, he ran into the middle of the street and urged the black men of Waxahachie to help him "rescue those girls" from the law. Rescuing "those girls" would do far more than place three black professionals out of danger: as with Private Edwards's intercession on behalf of Sara Travers in Houston, rescue in Waxahachie offered the chance to challenge notions of place, to uphold black manhood, and to assert black male authority. For Green, fighting the rape was fighting the War. "You are going to fight for Democrasy," he appealed to a group of newly called draftees assembled with the rest of the men, "This is where you should start, at your own doorstep, to defend your women." In moving to save the teachers, Green did not break out of the confines of patriarchy; he took his stance within them.

Invoking his grandfather's lessons from his childhood, he had held on to the tenets of a heroic paternalism, that a real man protected his own and that only a man deserved the rights of citizenship: "If you haven't got guts enough to fight," he excoriated the gathering, "You dont need no Democracy."[31]

As a defining identity and motivating ideal, manhood had its limits. Green tried to convey to the men before him that by branding respectable women as prostitutes, raping them, and bragging about it in African American public spaces, the white deputies meant to strike a blow at black men and black women alike. The men in the crowd may have known this, probably knew it, but they did not budge. For them, the obligations of paternalism only extended so far. As one draftee put it in absolving himself from any but the most local of responsibilities, the teachers—who hailed from rural districts outside of Waxahachie—were decidedly "not our women." Another draftee flatly spurned the assumption that he needed to prove himself to anyone. "If you want to get killed," he dismissed Green, "you be the hero."

The only one of the forty who opted to accompany Green was the man he "least expected" to do so, a "listless downtrodden human" named Boomer Hines. Hines had no reputation, no white patrons to shield him, and most likely no bed or home to return to, but he responded to Green's call to defend the kidnapped teachers' "virtue" and, by extension, his own honor. They drove off in Green's car with the lights off and Green's gun out, ready to die if they had to.[32]

Like Green and Hines, the white deputies who abducted the three teachers saw the impending rape in terms of place and manhood. Pulling up behind the police car in the park, Green overheard the officers curse their struggling captives. "You high stepping bitches think what you got is for the nigger Doctors and the big rich," the deputy swore at the women, "but tonight we get it."[33] Lumping African American doctors with "the big rich" of indeterminate race, the deputy pointed to one of the many fissures in the metaphorical wall of white supremacy. Even moderate African American success gave the lie to assertions of inherent black inferiority and threatened to displace working class white men. By attacking teachers—symbols of black aspiration and achievement—the policemen attempted to reinforce the fixedness of place, combining a class resentment of elite white men's prerogatives with a race-based claim to those same privileges.

Green maneuvered layers of place and patriarchy to refuse the white lawmen the stature they sought. After securing Hines out of sight so that he could relay events to Green's employer, Judge Dunlap, if something went wrong, Green blinded the deputies with his headlights and ordered the men out of the car under threat of their lives. When they asked who he was, Green invoked the authority of his boss, replying, "Dunlap." Telling them that "this is one time a Negro will have the respect of the law," he instructed the deputies to take the teachers over to the jail in City Hall where they would be safe. Green followed behind them in his car, making sure to keep "out of pistol range." For further protection, he stopped on his way to the jail and asked two of his white supporters, both members of the Chamber of Commerce, to accompany him inside the building. Once in City Hall, his two patrons took over the work of getting the teachers safely home. Both courageous and tactical, Green had masterfully offset his fierce demonstration of his manhood with an ultimate deference to the racialized hierarchies that governed Waxahachie.[34]

Manipulating the racial codes in Waxahachie could only do so much for Green. Using white elites to discipline the white lawmen, Green had managed to save the three women without any lives lost, but in doing so, he made things impossible for himself. The marshal showed up at the Dunlap household the morning after the attempted rape to instruct that judge to "get rid of" Green if he did not "want him killed." Complaining that Green "had too much nerve to be a nigger," the marshal warned that members of the African American population might get themselves hurt trying to emulate him and his deputies might get hurt trying to control them.[35] The marshal and his men would kill Green before they saw that happen; big men's favor might protect him some of the time, but it could not shield him forever. After two more serious run-ins, this time with white elites who proved themselves as vicious in the protection of white supremacy as any working man, Green told himself that "it would be better to die in France as a man than to die in America as a nigger at the hands of a despicable evil white man."[36] By February, he had joined the Army.

There were other ways to challenge place besides with the barrel of a gun. For Officer Sparks in Houston, place had a spatial as well as social component, and shifting spaces undermined place and politics in the rapidly growing region. The section of the fourth ward that Lee Sparks and Rufus Daniels patrolled, along with other African American settlements in the third and fifth wards, rooted the metaphor of place in urban living patterns. White Houstonians thought they knew African Americans by the space they occupied. Thus, when Lee Sparks recounted his run-ins with Travers, Edwards, and Baltimore in the weeks after the riot, he only needed to tell his white audience that they took place in the San Felipe district. Listeners understood Sparks's implication that he had to act rough because the neighborhood on his beat was "rotten." Alone on patrol, district attorney John Crooker concurred with Sparks, a white man could find himself surrounded by "several hundred" black people in less than five minutes. As a police officer "you at times [had to] do things that you know aren't absolutely legal in order to keep the vicious negro from running over you."[37] In a place like San Felipe, safeguarding white manhood took precedence over obeying the law.

African Americans resisted Jim Crow by leaving the country for the city and the South for the North. Between 1900 and 1910, Houston's total population grew from 44,633 to 78,800, while the African American population grew from 14,608 to 23,929. Over the next ten years, those numbers would increase to 138,276 and 33,960, respectively. The 10,000 African Americans who flocked to the city between 1910 and war's end followed family, friends, educational opportunities, and jobs out of rural areas and into the neighborhoods that circled downtown Houston. Although the percentage of the blacks in the total population declined in this period, from 30.4 percent in 1910 to 24.6 percent in 1920, more African Americans walked the Houston streets than ever before.[38]

The net percentage declined because, as rural to urban migration swelled the numbers of African Americans in the city, the Great Migration to industrial centers in the North and West brought the numbers back down. While migrants from smaller towns and rural areas came to Houston to build themselves a life, other African American men and women "want[ed] to be direct about it and want[ed] to go" north as quickly as possible.[39] The influx of African Americans into Houston from more rural parts of Texas and Louisiana, along with a growing community of Mexican-born railroad workers recruited from San Antonio, made Houston's competitive job market even tighter. Because the World War had virtually cut off the supply of European-born laborers, Northern cities offered more jobs with higher wages than African Americans could find in the South.

More important to African Americans, the North seemed to promise an escape from the invasions and assaults of segregation. Migrants from Houston, grown tired of "this terrible state" in which Jim Crow held them, relocated by the thousands.[40] In pursuit of better wages, better job security, and a chance "to better" their "standing," they took their families and headed for their utopian North where, as one freight handler imagined it, "a man is a man."[41]

The impulse to find some place where a man could be a man, and the waves of movement of African American men and women responding to that impulse, challenged the foundations of the Southern caste system. "Place" denied the reality of African American mobility, either physical or social. It required and reinforced a static sense of Southern history, emphasizing continuity over change. In so doing, place bestowed upon white supremacy the luster of permanence. Place naturalized white supremacy—made it seem inevitable—by embedding it in the ground. Black mobility, however, revealed how fluid that ground actually was. Through their determination to reject place and better their status, African Americans disrupted the cultural imagination of white supremacy and threatened its stability as a political program.

Few groups appeared harder to pin down, spatially or psychically, than black Army Regulars. The frequent movement of the roughly 10,000 troops belied the illusion of fixedness created by place, even as their daily work helped to spread white supremacy to new locales. Since their consolidation in 1869 into the 9th and 10th Cavalry and the 24th and 25th Infantry Regiments, black Army Regulars had moved along the margins of the nation. In the decades between Reconstruction and the Spanish-Cuban and Philippines Wars, while North and South vied to define the national character, African American troops labored in the service of empire. Between 1869 and 1898, members of the 24th Infantry served in Texas, Indian Territory, the Dakotas, along the border in Arizona and New Mexico, and in Utah. They built roads, installed telegraph lines, conducted illegal raids across the Mexican border, and provided relief for the black cavalry troops battling to seize Native American lands in the Indian Wars.[42] Outside but not exempt from the boundaries of a maturing Jim Crow, African American soldiers "made the West"—as one member of the 10th Cavalry put it—to secure an equal footing back east.[43]

Unmoored from home and region, black troops espoused a vision of a broad civic nationalism that rested upon their own interpretation of manhood. As with Woodrow Wilson's Anglo-Saxon manhood, black soldiers' civic manhood drew on tropes of honor and valor, courage and skill. Membership in the Army proved they could serve without being servile. Fighting Native Americans and Mexicans showed they could harness violence in service of the state rather than of savagery. Having made the West in the image of the nation, they wanted their due as men and as citizens.

In appropriating the Anglo-Saxon model of civic manhood, African American troops absorbed its limits and embodied its contradictions. To install "a new civilization on the American frontier," African American soldiers had to perpetuate the very racial ideologies they sought to escape, even as they often had to impose civilization by barbaric means.[44] Like their white counterparts, many black troops saw the "pacification" of Native American tribes as a prerequisite to making "the land safe" for those they considered real Americans to settle.[45] Casting Native Americans as unruly or savage, African American soldiers set themselves in opposition: where Native Americans behaved as beasts, they acted as men; where Native Americans were obstacles to progress, they were part of the civilizing mission. By accepting conquest as the terms on which they had to prove their manhood, African American troops infused their *civic* nationalism with an *imperialist* nationalism grounded in racial hierarchies. Even as military service allowed black soldiers to evade or subvert the most virulent forms of white supremacy in the South, they carried the white man's burden to the Pacific Ocean and beyond.[46]

African American soldiers who served in the Philippines during and after the 1898 wars managed to sidestep the worst manifestations of Jim Crow even as their work seemed to ensure, as one soldier wrote back to Richmond, that "the future of the Filipino" would be "that of the Negro in the South."[47] Soldiers grown weary of the abuses heaped on them by an increasingly inhospitable military made bitter note when white soldiers "cursed" both blacks and Filipinos "as damn niggers."[48] By helping to pacify the Philippines, African American soldiers helped to put Filipinos in their place. They killed and died to subject the islands to what one soldier decried as white America's "diabolical race hatred, in all its home rancor."[49] And in extending white supremacy's reach into the Pacific, African American troops helped to strengthen its grip at home in the South. Black soldiers, intent on demonstrating their right to full citizenship through their commitment to American imperialism, found themselves caught, in the words of one soldier, "between 'the Devil and the Deep Blue.'"[50]

In the years after the turn-of-the-century wars, African American Regulars both supported and subverted white supremacy by learning to negotiate the spaces between nation and empire. Stationed in the Philippines from 1906 to 1908, soldiers in the 24th Infantry helped to squelch Filipino nationalist uprisings and maintain U.S. dominion over the island. During a subsequent posting, from 1911 to 1915, the infantry manned the institutions that propped up the U.S. occupation, even as many of them took Filipina girlfriends or wives and formed ties to Filipino families. Despite white officials' concerns that African American soldiers often appeared "in closer sympathy with the aims of the native population than they were with the white leaders and policy of the U.S.," most soldiers continued to align themselves with the American civilizing mission.[51]

Just as with the Indian Wars, service in the Philippines granted the men of the 24th an intermediate position below white soldiers and civilians but above other people of color. Ironically, despite ongoing disfranchisement campaigns at home and the Philippines' emerging position under U.S. occupation as "Jim Crow's Beach House," black troops posted on the island enjoyed a special status derived from their American citizenship.[52] Even if most white soldiers might dismiss African Americans as inferiors, they were inferiors in military uniforms who drew Army salaries. Among Filipinos, who regarded black troops as more "kindly and manly" in their execution of duty than white troops, the soldiers' resources as well as their comportment did much to ingratiate them.[53] Still, the dynamics of black-Filipino relationships, as soldiers wooed young women with gifts and food, reiterated their position as members of an occupying army. In the colonies, blacks counted as men. African American soldiers resisted white supremacy, but they did not reject the patriarchalism that underlay it.

Indeed, doing their duty as soldiers enhanced their standing as men back home. As Kathryn Johnson stated in an essay decrying the East St. Louis massacre, civilian activists' strategies of uplift and standards of behavior rested upon the belief that someday "conduct, character and culture, and not color, shall be the measure of [man]hood and womanhood."[54] Johnson and other like-minded African Americans had invited white people to take their measure as clubwomen and moral reformers, churchgoers and educators, but even their most dignified self-assertions contained a plea for white folks' recognition. The Army Regulars, in contrast, pled for nothing.

Even among the ever-increasing ranks of African American soldiers, the 9th and 10th Cavalries and 24th and 25th Infantries regarded themselves as elite. As a stevedore in France, Ely Green would soon note that his fellow soldiers who had transferred from the Regular Army were harsh and tyrannical. On separate occasions, he saw two men shot down by former Regulars who had joined overseas labor battalions. After the second murder, Green went to file charges against the shooter, a former member of the 24th, but found his word counted for little against a "regular Army man with years of seniority."[55] Back in Houston, E. O. Smith, black principal of Booker T. Washington High School, found that "many" members of the 24th Infantry stationed in Houston to provide security during Cam Logan's construction "had done service in the Philippines and Mexico" and "were proud of the records" of service to the nation.[56] They viewed their service as a rebuttal to white supremacists' images of African Americans as cowardly, childlike, or undisciplined, and they had internalized the "self respect," regard "for the uniform," and the "respect for the authority of the government" that Army officials would soon find volatile.[57]

Both the stature of the black Army Regulars and the tension with white Southerners increased with America's entry into the War. Like previous conflicts, World War I provided a grand avenue of entry for African American men by emphasizing the connection between soldiering and citizenship. The editor of the Galveston *New Idea* pressed this point, celebrating ten million African Americans as "brave and fearless, ready and willing to fight to the last ditch." He continued: "we are proud of our record as a soldier and law-abiding citizen. America should recognize us and accord us human rights."[58] Having served with honor in America's imperial adventures, African American men now demanded to be counted on the side of the civilizers. They refused to be seen as a "Negro problem"; rather, they had earned "human rights."

Black soldiers knew full well what they had earned, and Army life had honed their sense of honor. Lest the war intensify their militancy, the Army shipped most of its black Regulars far from the field of battle. The 25th went to Hawaii and the 10th to the Philippines. The 24th, however, broke into battalions and headed for posts in New Mexico and Texas. Assigned to Houston to guard over the construction of a National Guard training camp, the 645 members of the 24th Infantry's Third Battalion arrived in town on July 28, 1917, more seasoned, more traveled, and more entitled than any group of black folks that Houston had ever seen before.[59]

Houston at War

White Houstonians turned a wary eye on the troopers camped west of town. Few had forgotten what happened eleven years before in Brownsville when members of the 25th Infantry allegedly shot up the Texas border town, wounding one man and killing another. With no one admitting guilt, President Theodore Roosevelt had dishonorably discharged all 167 men stationed at Fort Brown and barred them from future military or civil service. Little matter that a Senate inquiry had concluded that the troopers in Brownsville had been framed by white residents who wanted them gone; reminding the white populace of the murderous potential of Negroes with guns gave moral reformers the ammunition they needed to crack down on Houston's black and mixed-race neighborhoods.[60] Anti-vice forces proved all too happy to resuscitate the memory in their temperance campaign, reminding readers of the *Houston Post* to "Remember Brownsville. Make Harris County Dry."[61] With the 24th in town, the attorney general ordered "something like 100 saloons in Houston closed." When the U.S. District Attorney later relaxed the rules, he still left closed the bars closest to the soldiers' encampment on the city's west side.[62]

To their frustration, white Houstonians' direct oversight of African Americans' body and behavior stopped at the gates of the military camps. White laborers who moved to restrict craps and card games on the grounds of Camp Logan found themselves stymied by federal law. Although illegal in Texas, the regiment's white commanders explained that nothing stopped U.S. soldiers from gambling on federal property.[63] Likewise, African American troops defied the Jim Crow labels on drinking troughs and clashed with racist white construction workers with little retribution from military authorities. Complaining that white men constructing the National Guard camp "couldn't resent insults without clashing with the armed authority of the United States," carpenter Tom Dixon revealed how black soldiers cloaked themselves in the mantle of the federal government.[64] When another white Texan complained that the 24th's white officers did "not have the proper comprehension and understanding of how to handle Negro soldiers," he meant that the regiment's commanders should have done more to strip them of the security of their federal citizenship.[65]

For white Houstonians, the women in and around the soldiers' encampment provided the surest signal that the soldiers had gotten out of hand. Everyone noticed them. While black civilians and military authorities described the combination of wives, girlfriends, and visiting families as resembling an "orderly . . . big picnic," scandalized whites visitors saw something else altogether.[66] They watched women piling into cars with members of the 24th, clucked at them frolicking in the dance hall that the soldiers had cajoled a local man into opening, gritted their teeth at them "laying around" the grounds with their male companions.[67] Some of the women might have been camp followers or women drawn by what black writer and reformer Alice Dunbar-Nelson gently called "the lure of the khaki," but many were just young women stepping out with their boyfriends.[68] To the scandalized white deliverymen, construction workers, and small businessmen who eyed them for weeks, however, the girls were all drunks and "dope fiends," denizens of the red light district who had set up satellite offices on army grounds.[69]

For many white people in Houston, the seemingly steady traffic of African American women into and out of the 24th's encampment signified all the things wrong with the regiment's coming to town. Despite the camp's welcome boost to the city's economy, it "wasn't fit for a white man, let alone a white woman" to breach the world where black soldiers courted black women with Jim Crow signs mockingly attached to their clothes.[70] After the riot finally came, many townspeople would point to the black women to show where things had gone awry.

"They sure have things their own way," a white salesman noted with consternation after glimpsing the social world fashioned by the 24th and their civilian friends.[71] To white Houstonians, it seemed that a bunch of "northern sons-of-bitches" had invaded their city and created a space on its outskirts where social order went flying out the window.[72] Despite the soldiers' largely Southern backgrounds and years of postings in the West, white Texans saw the men of the 24th as waging a War of Northern Aggression. With their self-assertion and unwillingness to keep in their place, the battalion gave white Houstonians little doubt that they "came South . . . looking for trouble" and that their girlfriends were helping them find it.[73] African American troops did more than deny Southern strictures of place: they turned place on its head by bringing their private affairs and foibles—their sexuality, their manhood and humanity—out into public view. Stationed on the edge of the cotton South, the soldiers sent to guard Camp Logan crossed the boundaries of Jim Crow in a manner that made white Houstonians "a little uneasy."[74]

The uneasiness, felt on both sides, festered during the first four weeks of the 24th's stay, from the end of July to the end of August. "A lot of men" in the 24th's Third Battalion reported verbal sallies with white workers who resented having to work near black servicemen, insults traded with local streetcar drivers who were used to strictly enforcing Jim Crow on their trolleys, and run-ins with the police who resented the competing authority of black

men in uniform.[75] When soldiers challenged the rootedness of place and refuted the notion that "the customs of the South are as fixed as the laws of the
land," as one Houstonian emphasized, white men invoked violence to bolster
their claims to white supremacy.[76] "Those niggers would look good with coils
around their necks," a workman said about soldiers working guard duty who
seemed too big for their britches.[77] Harris County sheriff's deputy Ed Sto-
ermer announced to a trolley full of people that he might "have to kill" a
member of Company I who deliberately sat in the front row of a streetcar. He
hit the soldier with his gun before he locked him in the county jail.[78] White
men in Houston saw nothing wrong in this; sometimes policemen just
had "to beat niggers" when they were "insolent."[79] And the men of the Third
Battalion were nothing if not insolent. Most galling to the local white police force was that the Army's "Negro police" guarding Camp Logan "were
usurping more power than they should be" by trying to assert jurisdiction
over their black troops. Before long, they guessed, "there would be a big
scrap."[80] On August 23, after Lee Sparks and Rufus Daniels attacked their
third African American, and second soldier, of the day, the big scrap finally
began.

Some people manage white supremacy as best they can, until they cannot
take it anymore. In the hours after Sparks beat up Baltimore, a woman, "presumably a colored woman on San Felipe Street," called to inform the company's white commander Major Kneeland Snow that trouble had occurred.[81]
Rumors circulated around the soldiers' encampment and half a mile over at
Camp Logan "that Corporal Baltimore had been shot through the head in
the San Felipe district" and left to lie "in the middle of the street with no one
to care for him."[82] The soldier and civilian who delivered the news to director
of the military police and Provost Marshall Captain Haig Shekerjian "were
sure" it had happened. They knew, they told him, "because they could see the
blood."[83] Although the white officers called down to the police station for a
more accurate version of the story, word rapidly spread over to Camp Logan
that "one of the damned policemen had shot up" one of their men. "And," a
trooper on guard duty defiantly told a sheriff's deputy, he and his comrades
were "not going to stand for it."[84] By time Shekerjian retrieved Baltimore
from the jail wounded but alive, both the soldiers' encampment and Camp
Logan were, according to a private in I Company, "in hell."[85]

The attack on Baltimore stoked the soldiers' growing fury over all of their
treatment at the hands of the police. "Major, what are we going to do," a

soldier asked Kneeland Snow, "when they . . . beat us up like this?"[86] Snow instructed his men to report all incidents to him, but enraged by the ongoing brutality in Houston and lacking "much confidence in Major Snow," some members of the Third Battalion had already voiced a desire to exact their own revenge.[87] Although the day's violence had begun in Sara Travers's kitchen, the soldiers would turn it into an affair between men. In the dance hall, a group of soldiers responded to the reports of the attack on Corporal Baltimore by telling their girlfriends that they had "better go home." If the girls "didn't go ahead" of the battalion, they "couldn't go behind them," troopers warned teenager Bessie Chaney and her younger sister Flossie, "because they were going to town to kill all these white policemen."[88]

For hours it simply sounded like idle talk. In Company I especially, men whiled away the afternoon "bunched and talking," spewing a rage as constant as the rain that fell with varying intensity throughout the afternoon.[89] In the encampment, soldiers readied their guns and announced to their female visitors that they planned to head downtown and "raise hell."[90] A few vented their anger by scaring off two white newspaper deliverers with the barrel of their guns.[91] For a few men, like Corporal James Wheatley, these half-hearted displays of aggression hardly seemed adequate. "If this was the 25th," Wheatley goaded his fellow soldiers with his mis-memory of Brownsville, "we would all be in town." He demanded they "run" all the women present "out of camp," so that the men could get down to business.[92]

Wheatley viewed violence not merely as legitimate but as necessary. A four-year veteran and former member of the 25th Infantry, Wheatley invoked Brownsville as triumph rather than tragedy and held the troopers in Brownsville up as models of courage and force. After announcing that "something should be done" about the law's treatment of Baltimore, Wheatley urged the men of the Third Battalion to preserve their dignity and sense of worth by retaliating as he imagined the 25th would have.[93] Such sentiments and comparison were not limited to the soldiers; like Corporal Wheatley, the African American civilians who circulated rumors of coming trouble saw the day's events as a test of the soldiers' manhood. According to camp laborer Robert Fitzsimmons, the soldiers complained that white folks in Houston "didn't know how to treat a northern man right." He claimed to have heard the soldiers declare their intention "to do like the 9th and 10th [*sic*] did in Brownsville."[94] Having established their civic manhood by fighting enemies outside the nation's borders, they would defend it by attacking the enemy within.

By day's end, emotions had grown so taut that Company I's Acting First Sergeant Vida Henry worriedly informed Major Snow that there was "going to be some trouble" later that night.[95] In response, Snow called all four companies in the battalion together, restricted them to base for the evening, ordered them disarmed, and considered the matter settled. But Sergeant Henry knew better. As a disciplinary officer and "a man that the men of the Company seemed to respect," the black noncom gauged the temper of the troops much more accurately than did his white superior officers.[96] Henry had spent the afternoon in a valiant effort to stave off the tempest brewing in the soldiers' encampment. After discussing the run-in with Sparks with the battered Corporal Baltimore, Henry had attempted to reassure the corporal that Captain Shekerjian had done "the best thing" in resolving the matter with the police.[97] Calm, Henry attempted to persuade the rest of the company to stay calm, too. Despite his status as someone other soldiers tended to "obey without question," he had little luck. When the storm finally broke later that evening, Henry could do nothing to stop it.

No one would ever find the words to describe adequately what happened over the next few hours. When Major Snow gave the order for the Battalion to surrender their weapons and ammunition, Companies K and L obeyed immediately. The men of Company I took longer as they tried to convey to Snow the load they bore in being "treated like dogs" by white Houstonians.[98] In Company M, the men launched a more dramatic protest, "bucking" on the first two orders to hand over their weapons. The soldiers' gradual compliance met with mixed reactions by the few who continued to defy Snow's order. Some holdouts denounced the rest as "cowards," while other grown men broke down in tears, weary "of seeing soldiers come in there with their heads beat up" and feeling that they had could nothing to stop it.[99] Turning over their rifles meant betraying their manhood, betraying themselves, and betraying each other.

As the soldiers struggled to decide whether or not to head over to Houston, sometime after 8 P.M., Houston appeared to come to them. The small dramas of defiance that wracked Companies I and M flared into outright mutiny amidst cries that a mob of white Houstonians had marched on the camp and begun to fire. Afterwards, no one could testify to having seen the mob, and witnesses would later debate whether there had been one, but in the initial cry, self-defense won out over discipline. Soldiers in all four companies rushed their supply tents to reclaim their weapons. Dozens of men scrambled out of camp—some in pursuit of, others in retreat from, shooters they could not see. Those who remained weathered a ten-minute volley as Companies I and M shot at one another through the rain, each mistaking the other for white mobbers. In Company K, the first sergeant watched his troops desert, "almost in a daze." Half crying, he could only say over and over, "This is awful. This is awful."[100] Career soldiers, black and white, watched as their battalion dissolved. "Hell," Kneeland Snow announced in a panicked phone call to the Houston chief of police, had "broken loose."[101]

In Company I, Sergeant Henry endeavored to regain order, but in the wake of the perceived attack he did so as mutineer rather than obedient soldier. Commanding in both stature and nature, Henry harshly ordered the men to fall in line and prepare to march on the Houston police station. To those who hesitated, he threatened, "I will kill."[102] With thirteen years in the 24th Infantry, the Kentucky native had served loyally while American forces spread Jim Crow through the Philippines, through the Army's betrayal of the 25th Infantry at Brownsville, and on into the beginning of the War. Yet when the storm broke in the soldiers' encampment, Henry broke with it. After an afternoon spent trying to preserve discipline, he now came down on the side of the rioters. "We are in it now," he told Sergeant William Fox when the shooting commenced. After the night's end, he predicted "there ain't going to be no camp."[103]

The older men knew better than most what sacrifices mutiny entailed. Sergeant Fox, himself a twenty-five-year veteran of the 24th and 25th Infantry Regiments, begged Henry to stay and protect the camp. Supply Sergeant Rhoden Bond, who had joined the regiment during the thick of the turn-of-the-century wars, echoed Fox. "I goes out after him," Bond recalled, "and tells him, 'I wouldn't do that. It is wrong; don't go away.'"[104] Bond considered himself an "old soldier" with primary responsibility to his wife, family, and the military. He refused to go "in for nothing like" revenge.[105] Many of those African Americans like Sergeants Fox and Bond who had built their lives around the Army—given over their lives to it—still saw duty as the ultimate mark of a man. The mutineers struck them, as they did Provost Sergeant Cecil Green, as "weak minded fellows" who "shattered" in a few short hours the "hard-earned reputation" that had taken the "older soldiers many years to build."[106]

Sergeant Henry, in contrast, behaved as though all his years of skills and training as a disciplinary officer were meant to carry him to the riot in Houston.

Marveling at how Henry "didn't seem to take any advice from no one but his own self," Sergeant Bond watched as the first sergeant arranged his men as deliberately as if he planned for them to march against the Kaiser.[107] Henry appointed Corporal Wheatley to the front of the line, Corporal Baltimore to the rear. He ordered them to kill any men who broke ranks, and he sent a former member of the 10th Cavalry, Corporal Larmon Brown, to recruit more soldiers from other companies. Henry reminded the men that they had "serious business" before them.[108] With the mutiny in full sway, they would not be able to turn back.

For the men who followed Vida Henry, self-defense pulled harder than duty. Although a few troopers returned to order after Rhoden Bond "commenced to holler at them to get back," most of the mutineers stuck to their guns.[109] The appeals "to their manhood," voiced by the older black noncommissioned officers and again by Major Kneeland Snow, were drowned beneath the din of "We have a job to do; let's do it."[110] The mutineers' manhood was not the same stuff as Rhoden Bond's; to them, forbearance and self-control, doing well and making good, all seemed inadequate for the situation in Houston. Their notion of manhood involved a different sort of control—disciplined rebellion, skilled aggression, and readiness to kill and die in the name of themselves, each other, and the race. Manhood as duty and self-defense long had existed in African American political tradition and likely had coexisted, competed, and connected within men like Vida Henry. Which impulse soldiers followed on the night of August 23 depended on how they measured character and conduct, and on what they felt they could bear.

As he pulled men into the ranks of mutineers, a solemn Corporal Larmon Brown tried to explain himself to his captain, Haig Shekerjian. Brown had recently written a letter to his mother in Atlanta expressing his heartfelt desire to head to the French front, but events in Houston had brought his war back home. "Captain," he quietly asked Shekerjian to understand his calibration of manhood, "We ain't going to be mistreated." Tears streaming down his cheeks, Brown rejoined Henry's column.[111] With members of the Battalion shouting "Stick by your race," the mutineers started down the road to Houston for the largest—and last—battle of their lives.[112]

The air, a reporter for the *Houston Chronicle* would write the next day, "was turgid." Black and thick as pitch, "the night was the kind that made one physically and mentally nervous and unstrung."[113] Soldiers who had broken camp after the initial panic entered Houston from the west, firing erratically as they charged through the all-white Brunner addition located in the sixth ward. From Camp Logan, a smaller group of guards abandoned their posts after the firing started. Cursing "god damn white people," they made their way north on Washington Avenue before heading east toward San Felipe.[114] In the shadows, soldiers who had been pulled into the riot at gunpoint slipped out of the column and took refuge in ditches, at Camp Logan, or in the woods that separated the soldiers' camp from the rest of town.[115] Some by choice, some coerced, Sergeant Henry's remaining men continued their march toward the police station.

To white Houston, it looked like war. As the men marched along, witness George Butcher could discern the outline of them coming four abreast, "marching all in line, marching, kinder trotting along." The soldiers mowed him down in the street.[116] Sitting on his porch, seventeen-year-old Willie Drucks watched them approach "as orderly as they could be." He assumed they were going on a hike until one soldier turned and shot off his arm.[117] Victim Fred Schofield recalled hearing the soldiers yell "On to victory!" after they drove a bayonet into his leg and fired three bullets into his friend's head.[118] O. H. Reichert heard them resolve to "show the white folks what we're made of." His daughter, Alma, heard nothing before a shot pierced the walls of the family grocery store and hit her in the stomach.[119]

As rioters of the Third Battalion wended their way east toward the fourth ward, they left a bloody trail behind them. Sergeant Henry's column killed Rufe Daniels, the mounted policemen who had roughed up Sara Travers for acting "biggety" earlier in the day. Daniels went down in a shootout near the corner of San Felipe and Wilson, not far from where the morning's events had transpired. Henry's men killed a second policeman in the same confrontation. A third died two weeks later from his wounds.

Few of the remaining victims ever had a chance to fight back. Some of the victims, the soldiers shot indiscriminately. Others simply got in the way. Willie Drucks lost his arm because a soldier tried to shoot out his porch light. He was lucky; a second bullet took the life of his half brother standing beside him. Stray bullets pierced the woodshed of a boarding house two blocks from camp and killed a Mexican laborer sleeping inside. Talking on the phone in her house one block from the soldier's camp, Madora Miller heard "one shot, then several," before a bullet struck her left hand.[120] Farther north on Washington, one soldier turned his gun on a white woman's dog, snarling "What are you barking at," as he shot it dead.[121]

"As I heard those shots," Brunner addition resident Fred Schneider recalled, "I said to my wife that the niggers and the whites were having at it." Schneider decided to sit at the window with his six shooter in hand. The first soldier that fired on his house, he planned "to kill."[122] All down Washington Avenue, clusters of white townspeople had the same idea. "Youthful, irresponsible crowds of eight or ten citizens," as the newspaper dubbed them, went running by with guns.[123] An Italian American immigrant and former member of the Italian cavalry recalled a white soldier appealing to him on the common ground of race: "Brother give me some gun because all the nigger soldiers are going to shoot up the white people."[124] Nearby, a crowd of 250 to 350 civilians and fifteen to twenty white soldiers tried to break into a hardware store and loot its stock of arms.[125] The prospect of race war brought together white Houstonians in a frenzy of "excitement such as had never before been experienced in Houston or any other Texas city."[126] Only intervention by an Illinois National Guard unit stationed in Houston kept the mob from invading the soldiers' encampment and attacking the men remaining inside.

Downtown, the riot continued. Stepping out on the street holding his .22 rifle, white civilian F. W. Sanker heard African American civilians applauding the rioting soldiers. One of them asked Sanker about his gun, "[W]hat could you do with that if those soldiers could see you?" The black man advised Sanker to go on home before he got killed.[127] Farther down San Felipe, Private Joseph Alexander recalled hearing a few onlookers in their yards cheering him on with a " 'All right boys, go ahead' " and "such things as that" as he passed with Sergeant Henry's column. When some asked to join the march, Alexander told them "that there was nothing they could do" for the soldiers, "unless they could pray for us." Voicing an acceptance of the column's coming fate, the private assured the people on San Felipe that, "we was going on."[128] Walking with him, soldier Henry Peacock concurred. "If we die," he saluted the spectators, "we die like men." The soldiers marched on, into another gun battle with policemen.[129]

Despite the continued determination of men like Private Alexander, Corporal Baltimore, and Sergeant Henry, the resolve of the rioters began to ebb. In the less organized columns, troopers simply fell out of ranks and started making their way back to camp. In Sergeant Henry's column, some soldiers stole away while the leaders fought with white civilians. Others begged to leave when the column veered off its course to rest and attend to the wounded. Ultimately, with the National Guard gathering and Henry nursing wounds in the hand and arm, even the most hardened leaders balked. Over Henry's protests, Corporals Baltimore and Wheatley sided with a contingent of rioters who opted to turn back.

In the end, only Vida Henry remained. Having found himself "in it" when the riot flared in camp, he had reconciled himself to staying in it for the duration. Bearing the weight of the mutiny he helped to lead, he accepted that there existed no camp, no army, no life to which he could return. Henry gave away his watch, saying "it wouldn't do him any good."[130] He shook hands with the men who had joined his rebellion, and he waited for them to depart. The following morning, two children found the first sergeant under a chinaberry tree near the turnaround of the Southern Pacific railroad. The whole top of his head "was blown off."[131] Some people speculated that white men had come across Henry and killed him, but most people thought it more likely that he had chosen to take his own life in his own way, rather than submit to a lynching at the hands of white Houstonians or the military that was sure to punish him.

Despotic Devil Democracy

Ten men probably "could not begin to tell the complete story of what took place that night," Army prosecutor Colonel John Hull would claim at the close of a long court martial.[132] Even if they could settle on the facts, they probably could not agree on their meaning. Hull painted a picture of a group of men beneath contempt. Sworn to "protect the life and property" of the United States, the soldiers of the 24th had betrayed their uniform.[133] In contrast, the rioters saw themselves as staying true to themselves as soldiers and men. Letting their rage burst through the barrel of their guns, they had forced white Houstonians to face the consequences of dishonoring the uniform and treating them as less than men. Even if they had not "straightened up the town" as they intended, the mutineers of the Third Battalion had followed through on their promise to "raise the devil."[134] In their two-hour riot, they had matched the terror of white supremacy with the terror of armed revolt.

In the wake of the riot, white men in Houston read the incident through a sexualized lens. Although the day's events had begun with white policemen roughhousing a black woman, white commentators quickly equated the soldiers' resistance with the threat of Negro domination. "These 24th infantry niggers and their white livered officers," white Houstonian W. R. Sinclair railed in a letter to his congressman, wanted "social equality a là Jack Johnson and his white Chicago wife."[135] Equating the soldiers of the 24th with Texas-born black heavyweight champion Jack Johnson, Sinclair made them the same type of men: masterful in their violence but anathema to Jim Crow.[136] By placing both Mrs. Johnson and the 24th's "white livered" officers outside Southern norms of gendered behavior, Sinclair also emphasized their alien-ness. Threats to white supremacy by white women who might cross the color line, or by military personnel who placed the Army before it, would gain no traction in the Bayou City.

Other white supremacists made more explicit the link between access and dominance. Writing in his diary the day after the riot, owner of the *Raleigh News & Observer* and Secretary of the Navy Josephus Daniels reduced the cause of the riot to a petty battle over public space—to a struggle over place in the most literal sense. Houston happened, he wrote, because the "Negro in uniform wants the whole sidewalk."[137] Daniels was no stranger to sidewalk stories; on the eve of the 1898 elections in North Carolina, he had broadcast stories of "impudent" Negro "wenches" attacking white women on sidewalks and in doing so helped to spark the Wilmington race riot.[138] Twenty years later, he was still using the same shorthand to describe African Americans' assertions of power.

Daniels was not alone in using sidewalk tussles as shorthand for assaults on Jim Crow. The Macon, Georgia, *Telegraph* claimed that "the Negro's way of asserting his conception of equality and equal rights is to jostle white people off the sidewalk" and "to force white women to take the mud puddles while he stands on dry ground."[139] "Sidewalk" had become a racial code word to imply that all the Negro wanted was to gain power over white women.

Power over white women implied a concomitant power over white men. Explicitly linking the riot to politics, the *Telegraph* underscored the incompatibility between Jim Crow and African American manhood. Mistaking the rioters for members of the Eighth Illinois National Guard, the paper used their supposed origins to observe that residence in the North made black men "unfit" to venture back into Dixie where white men would concede "neither political nor social recognition." The *Telegraph* argued that the combination of political power available to the African American man in the North "and the demeanor he absorbs" while up there could only lead to disaster when mixed with "the uniform of the American government" and "access to firearms." Echoing James Vardaman's Senate floor rant against conscription, the paper held that African Americans who bore themselves as men would bring a racial holocaust as more and more black soldiers came to bases in the South. "Surely," the paper appealed, "with a Southern man in the White House, a Southern man at the head of the navy and a Georgian guiding the treasury department," they could shore up white supremacy enough to forestall this outcome.[140]

All that white supremacy required, the *Nashville Banner* argued in counterpoint, was someone man enough to enforce it properly. Citing "pacivity [*sic*]" as "one of the distinguishing features" of the African American race, the *Banner* placed the onus on white men to rise to their responsibility. The paper reassured its readers that "Negroes kept under due control are tractable." Houston occurred because the 24th was not "kept under an authority" it could "fear and respect." In recounting the riot's cause, the *Banner* erased Sara Travers from its narrative and reasserted white men's place at the top of Southern hierarchy. According to the Nashville daily, the soldiers, who held "an undue estimation of their importance," ran amuck because they "had an idea" that "they were privileged to riot and that the government would protect them in what they did."[141]

The *Houston Chronicle* roundly concurred with the *Banner*'s assessment of "the Negro temperament" and the problems of black military service. Although the United States was engaged in a war to rid Europe from authoritarianism, the *Chronicle* saw no irony in arguing that African American troops required "absolutism" on the part of their command. After all, leniency had "led negro soldiers to believe that the government is in sympathy with their arrogance and impudence." If the South were going to survive the war intact, white men across the nation had to hold the line against African Americans in uniform. Repeating the call of the newspapers in Georgia and Tennessee, the *Houston Chronicle* urged the federal government to disabuse African American soldiers of the notion that government stood behind them.[142]

In the aftermath of the Houston riot, it looked as though the government was heeding the *Chronicle*'s advice. Military authorities quickly removed the Third Battalion from Houston, sending the accused to Fort Bliss in El Paso and the rest back to Columbus, New Mexico. They charged 63 members of the battalion with mutiny and moved them to Fort Sam Houston in San Antonio to await their November 1917 trial. The Army exerted its jurisdiction

First court
martial, San
Antonio, Texas,
November 1917.
National
Archives and
Records
Administration.

over the accused men in spite of white Houstonians desire to try them in civilian courts, but it offered locals the comfort that the military could mete out "justice" more swiftly than civil courts.

On December 8, 1917, under a blanket of silence, the Army sentenced Charles Baltimore, James Wheatley, Larmon Brown, and ten other men to death. Separated from the other fifty accused mutineers, the thirteen condemned men greeted the news with silence. William Nesbit wrote home to say, "Goodbye. I'm gone" and to tell his family he died "with a clean heart."[143] In his final letter, Charles Baltimore called the execution "God's will" and quoted John 3:16. He assured his brother that, although he had marched downtown, he was "innocent of shedding any blood."[144] At dawn on December 11, "in a wild grove of mesquite trees," the Army secretly hanged the thirteen soldiers.[145] A witness described their stance as "erect and unflinching" as they bade one another farewell. They wore their army khakis.[146]

In addition to those executed, forty-one men received life in prison. Another nine received shorter sentences, and five were acquitted altogether. In more rounds of courts martial early the next year, the Army tried another ninety-three men. They issued eleven more death sentences and eighteen more jail terms.

African Americans would go on fighting for the living. At the suggestion of Secretary of War Newton Baker, and under intense pressure from African American religious and civic groups including the National Association for the Advancement of Colored People (NAACP) and the more aggressive National Equal Rights League (NERL), President Woodrow Wilson eventually commuted ten of the death sentences to life imprisonment and made all subsequent military executions during the war subject to his review. Though some left through pardons and parole, most of the surviving mutineers languished in jail through the rest of the 1920s and into the 1930s.[147]

Many of those confined steadfastly maintained their innocence. Writing to the assistant to the Judge Advocate General, former private Douglass Lumpkins insisted that he "didn't take no part" in the Houston riot. Before the riot occurred, the twenty-year-old Kentucky native felt "eager to go to France and aid the country." He had desired only "to show the world at large" that he was "a useful and law abiding citizen." Wasting away from tuberculosis in Leavenworth, Lumpkins regretted his lost chance.[148] Also declaring himself innocent, Isaac Deyo demanded more than had Lumpkins. Quite certain that he had demonstrated himself a useful citizen during his eighteen years of military service, Deyo wanted the fair trial that the Constitution guaranteed him. "Humanely speaking," he wrote in protest of his incarceration, "it isn't a whole lot to ask in return for the many years of faithful service that have been rendered by the ex-members of the 24th Infantry." Put the "treasonable" Texans who incited the riot on trial, Deyo suggested, let him go home.[149]

The government's failure to punish treasonable Texans and its harsh punishments of the Houston mutineers broke black Americans' hearts. The condemned soldiers' fates seemed to presage the coming heartbreak of black servicemen in the overseas war. A grieving W. E. B. Du Bois emphasized the tragedy of the men who had "fought for a country which never was wholly theirs; men born to suffer ridicule, injustice, and, at last, death itself."[150] Alongside Du Bois, other "Men, strong men, bowed in grief" when they heard the news, claimed writers at the *Cleveland Advocate*. Gathered in "little assemblages" on city streets, they spoke of the hangings in hushed tones, like the sort that would characterize "a conversation in a friend's death chamber."[151] Their well of mourning sprang from the conviction that the federal government had "resolutely refused to protect" the 24th in the "rights and privileges which clearly belonged to men who were tendering their blood and lives to this country."[152] In the midst of wartime mobilization, the War Department had chosen racial nationalism over civic nationalism. It had carried forth what felt to the editors of one paper like a government-sponsored lynching.[153]

The government had also shown its contempt for African American manhood in doing so. If the troopers had "stood meekly by" and let Sparks "slap a Colored woman," the *Advocate* bitterly speculated, they could have passed their stay in Houston with no trouble from the Army. Expecting the regiment to function normally even as white Texans abused them, the government abandoned the 24th—and all black Houstonians—to the tender ministrations of the Houston police department. Worse, by executing the soldiers before anyone had time to review their sentence, the War Department betrayed the regiment and all African Americans who believed in the rule of law in order to slake white Texans' blood thirst.[154] With nothing to buffer them from the ritual abuses of Jim Crow, the *Savannah Tribune* grieved, the rioters of the 24th "were more sinned against than sinned."[155]

In countering the hostility evinced by Southern papers and the Wilson administration to African American manhood, their black defenders strove to portray the rioters of the 24th as "martyrs to the cause of liberty and self-preservation."[156] The *Cleveland Gazette* went so far as to kill off Baltimore in the initial confrontation with Lee Sparks. Like other papers, the *Gazette* saw the assault of Sara Travers "by a prejudiced white Southerner" as the initial affront to the soldiers' manhood. In their recounting of the ensuing fight, "a sergeant of the 24th regiment" grabbed the offending policeman, "knocked him down and beat him badly." As near as the *Gazette* could remember, after Baltimore gave the policeman "what he deserved for his unmanly act," a mob set upon him and killed him.[157]

Pulling their manhood back to the fore, African American commentators refused to let white Southerners control the narrative of the Houston riot. In an open letter published in the *Baltimore Afro American,* Bishop A. C. Smith of the African Methodist Episcopal Church described the soldiers as "too manly to submit to extreme brutal treatment."[158] His fellow pastor, the socialist Episcopalian George Frazier Miller, offered the men up to his congregation as sacrifices "on the infamous altar of Southern race prejudice." Unwilling to condemn the rioters, he urged his congregation to "copy their example of courage and fortitude."[159] Du Bois, like Miller, found it difficult to condemn the rioters. Indeed, he thought it "difficult for one of Negro blood to write of Houston" at all. In other accounts of racial violence, "it's SO MANY NEGROES killed, so many NEGROES wounded. But here, at last, at Houston is a change." In Houston, "white folk died. Innocent adventitious white folks, perhaps as innocent as the thousands of Negroes done to death in the last two centuries." Du Bois might regret the aftermath, but he could not find it in his heart to be sad about what the soldiers had done.[160]

As white and black men competed to shape the discourse of race, nation, and entitlement that grew out of the Houston riot, African American women worked to make their voices heard as well. For them, the riot's origins lay in Lee Sparks's and Rufe Daniels's assaults on Sara Travers, an assault they viewed as part of a larger attack on black women as well as black men. While they passionately joined in denunciations of the Army's "inhuman" treatment of the rioters, many black women hailed the soldiers specifically as "martyrs for the cause of colored womanhood."[161] Some of the fiercest champions of black manhood, female commentators on the riot emphasized the ties that bound together black womanhood and manhood.

Afro-Iowan Lillian Smith exalted the men of the 24th in response to a denunciation of them in the *Pueblo Chieftain.* The paper had conceded that the troopers' service in Cuba and "on the hot sands of the Mexico desert" gave them "a peculiar history in American national life." However, despite their contributions, the Colorado paper went on to argue, Americans could not overlook the regiments' crimes committed "under the influence of liquor" and "petty passions."[162] Lillian Smith thought otherwise. "It is hard for one of the negro extraction to write of Houston or any other Southern hellhole," she wrote in echo and extension of W. E. B. Du Bois's editorial on Houston. She persevered because she felt in necessary to remind the *Chieftain* that "these men were not young recruits." Rather, "they were disciplined men" who "had stood the insults of these ruffian police and other Southern huns until they said 'That is enough'" and stood them no more. Smith refuted the paper's allegations that the soldiers had acted under the influence of liquor. "They fought," she informed the paper, "because underneath that black skin flowed a wealth of good, red blood."[163]

Convinced that "what the American white man has sown, that he shall reap," Lillian Smith did not shy away from the riot's violence. She matter-of-factly noted that Officer Daniels "was dead and in hell, Thank God." Condemning Lee Sparks for entering "colored women's homes when they have been in their bath" and attacking African Americans with impunity, she lamented only that he had not joined his partner in the great beyond. To Smith, the Houston riot served as retribution for East St. Louis, for lynching, for all the violence endemic to white supremacy that put black men and women in peril. Smith predicted more bloodshed to come—"many Houstons"—until Southern "despotic, devil democracy" came to an end.[164]

Texas teacher Clara Threadgill-Dennis published an even more inflammatory response to the Houston riot. Writing in direct address to the soldiers, she told them, "Every woman in all this land of ours, who dares feel proud of the Negro blood that courses through her veins, reveres you." Although she regretted that the soldiers mutinied and "spilt innocent blood," the soldiers' actions were redeemed because they came in defense of black women. Writing in the midst of the court martial at Fort Sam Houston, in the pages of the San Antonio black newspaper the *Inquirer*, Threadgill-Dennis told them that African American women "would rather see you shot by the highest tribunal" of the Army "because you dared protect a Negro woman from the insult of a southern brute . . . than to have you forced to go to Europe to fight for a liberty you cannot enjoy."[165] As African American women would do throughout the war, and activists would learn to do in subsequent wars, Threadgill-Dennis collapsed the lines between front and homefront.

In her paean, Threadgill-Dennis used "the immortal 24th" to symbolize resistance to all the absurdities of Jim Crow. "I needed you in Austin this week," she wrote to them. If they had been with her in her home town, she "would not have been insulted by a street car conductor" when she requested a transfer. She and other African American teachers "would not have been insulted" by the Texas governor who could order them to buy Liberty Bonds to support the war while still under-funding their schools. With the 24th at her side, Threadgill-Dennis could have displayed her contempt for the notion of "fighting to make the world safe for a democracy" that the average African American "can't enjoy."[166]

A graduate of the Presbyterian Tillotson College, a homeowner and principal's wife, Clara Threadgill-Dennis was no radical.[167] Jim Crow, however, had made her militant. Wasting no sorrow on the fact that "southern policemen's bones now bleech [*sic*] in the graves of Houston," she infused the soldiers' action with almost spiritual import. For a man to die protecting his daughter, his wife, his mother, or his sister, she told them, was "the most sacred thing on earth." Through the language of sacrifice, Threadgill-Dennis washed the blood away. What truly mattered, by her reckoning, was the nobility of the mutineers' cause and the majesty of their deaths. She urged them to go with manly stoicism. "Be brave," she wrote in closing, "face death fearlessly."[168]

By joining the soldiers' humiliations to her own and their honor to her defense, Clara Threadgill-Dennis articulated a notion of black manhood that incorporated black womanhood in its core. Although she did not directly challenge the paternalism embedded in both white and black men's conceptions of civic manhood, Threadgill-Dennis refused to hide her own sense of entitled citizenship beneath manhood's cover. She broadened the discursive terrain through a move akin to Lee Sparks's associating biggety women and insolent Negroes—making the progress of black men connected to and contingent upon the protection and elevation of their female compatriots. Although the soldier offered a potent symbol of an entitled, empowered man, African Americans would have to use both their identities for mutual support to wage the war for democracy on American soil.

To many white Americans these women looked more than biggety; they looked incendiary. Just as white Houstonians quietly speculated that bad women helped encourage the soldiers to riot, federal authorities believed that militant women might spur further trouble. Both Clara Threadgill-Dennis and Lillian Smith ran afoul of federal agents who sensed danger in their discontent. Rather than publish Lillian Smith's letter, the editor of the *Pueblo Chieftain* passed it on to the U.S. attorney in Des Moines.[169] In San Antonio, agents from the Bureau of Investigation alerted Military Intelligence to Clara Threadgill-Dennis. Authorities arrested her, along with the *San Antonio Inquirer's* editor G. W. Bouldin and its contributing editor William Hegwood, and charged them all with violating the Espionage Act by inciting insubordination in military forces. Using the courts, federal authorities attempted to limit the ways African Americans conceptualized and asserted themselves— and each other—as citizens.

With G. W. Bouldin, it seemed to work. Although authorities did not pursue Clara Threadgill-Dennis for writing the letter, they eventually convicted the editor of the *Inquirer* for publishing it. During the trial Bouldin's attorney introduced evidence indicating that Threadgill-Dennis had spent time in the Texas state mental hospital, and he endeavored to distance his client from her letter by saying that Bouldin would not have printed it if he had read it first. Both the defense and the prosecution referred to Threadgill-Dennis as a "lunatic" and raving "maniac" over the course of the trial, alternately dismissing the validity of her lunatic article and, by using it as the basis of the espionage charge, taking it very seriously. Convicted of trying to incite soldiers to mutiny or insubordination, Bouldin spent a year total in Texas prisons and in Leavenworth.[170] Crazy or not, the government had expected African Americans to respond to the grievances and sentiment that Clara Threadgill-Dennis put forth. Even when it seemed a bit crazed, black rage and disillusion did not bode well for Jim Crow. Like their male counterparts, angry black women were dangerous.

Houston had laid bare the menace and promise of African American military service. African American soldiers were indeed dangerous, especially when they proved willing to fight for democracy at home. Houston revealed, too, the high costs of such a stance. African American men and women opened up new fronts in the fight for democracy and against white supremacy in the months after Houston and in the "many Houstons" that followed. Throughout the next few years, as black soldiers clashed with white civilians and soldiers in locales as far flung as Newport News, Virginia, and St. Nazaire, France, black civilians worked out new strategies to discuss and defend them, to make their violence something more than the act. In both offensive and defensive maneuvers, they deployed the language of manhood to press their case for full citizenship.

What both soldiers and civilians meant when they invoked manhood and citizenship would change, too, as black soldiers began sailing abroad. The Houston riot had demonstrated what happened when black agents of empire returned to claim their place in the nation; it had brought the 24th to the intersection of their domestic life and imperial dreams, with heartbreaking results. For soldiers in the American Expeditionary Forces, service in Europe would create a space between domestic realities and their international imaginations where they could forge new identities, new nationalisms, and new pictures of themselves of as men.

3

Men in the Making

Visiting Houston from Waxahachie in August 1917 before the soldiers' mutiny, Ely Green came across three members of the 24th Infantry in a pool hall. Over a quart of whiskey, he asked the men if they felt that "being a souldier gave them any respect." The men answered with a vehement "Hell, yes. When you are in uniform you are a man," and added, "You have to be to serve the Government." Green responded enthusiastically. He had spent his whole life rebelling against Jim Crow, trying to "take from [his] brow the emblem of slavery" that too often defined him. The soldiers affirmed his sense that Southern law treated them as slaves instead of men, but assured him that as servants of the federal government they "represent[ed] the greatest law of all." The Regulars explained to Green that their status as U.S. soldiers placed them outside the "dam law" of the "Southern Pecker woods" in Houston. If white Houstonians did not figure out that fact soon, Green recalled the Regulars boasting, the regiment would be more than happy to teach them. Listening to them talk, Green might not have guessed that the soldiers would soon launch a mutiny, but he did know that "it was a cinch" that he, too, "would be in uniform" before much longer.[1]

As the soldiers of the 24th made good on their threats to fight Jim Crow on the streets of Houston, Ely Green made plans to stand as a man on the streets of France. Honorable service in the world war, he anticipated, would garner him the "respect" and "right of law" denied him in civilian life. He planned to fight with the American Expeditionary Forces (AEF) in Europe and return home "an American and a representative of the Government of the United States." Embarking on "a one man mission" to "win my rights as a citizen," Green informed a white Army colonel that he was "going to France if I have to swim there." In spring 1918, when he finally did arrive in the Breton port town of Brest, Green proudly told himself, "I am now a man."[2]

One way to think about the African American experience in the war years is to consider the making and unmaking of black manhood. Culturally and socially constructed, what it meant to be an adult male drew on a suite of ideas, practices, and interpretations that embedded this form of identity in other social categories. Thus, as the war unfolded, the connections among manhood, citizenship, military service, and national belonging laid bare by the Houston riot took on heightened importance. Mobilization swelled the ranks of the U.S. National Guard and Regular Army from roughly 230,000 men at the time of America's entry to almost four million by the war's end, bringing all Americans into closer contact and negotiation with their government.[3] During the Progressive Era, when the federal government increasingly touched people's everyday lives, soldiers emerged as both its agents and its clients. For African American communities, this revitalized importance of soldiers as fact and symbol offered a way to reconceptualize and reassert black manhood to gain equal citizenship. As the Regulars in Houston had bragged to Ely Green, black soldiers' participation in a project above and beyond the confines of Jim Crow meant that they represented "the greatest law of all." In reflection and affirmation of this fact, they had to make their character fit their uniform. They had to act as men.

What did it mean to be a man in 1917? In the decades since Emancipation, global changes in marking time and measuring space wrought by industrialization, immigration, and empire had spawned new modes of work and forms of leisure. Vernacular expressions of white supremacy—Jim Crow in the United States and colonial regimes in European territories—had attempted to fix in place those lives and identities upended by modern change. Yet, for all the stability envisioned by white supremacists, identity could not be settled.

In the United States, racial and gender formations shifted with the tides of migration and urbanization, undermining the agrarian idyll that framed nineteenth-century manhood. The ability to do for oneself and decide for one's family took on different meanings as people moved from country to town, and as the mill encroached on the yeoman farm. Self-possession might imply rectitude, or it might mean rebellious autonomy. Refinement could connote a cultivation of the mind or a self-conscious physicality. Victorian ideals of manhood and mastery still held currency for people coming of age in the 1910s, but a new masculinity, linked to an urban, consumer economy and expressed through the body, had begun to take hold as well.[4]

For African Americans in particular, these broad changes and challenges came with an added burden. As an ideological system, Jim Crow tried to settle gender roles for white people by diminishing black humanity. It elevated white manhood by lowering African American men to the level of boys and beasts just as it reduced both black and white women to property to be protected or degraded. Whatever manhood might come to mean during the war or after, white supremacists insisted, the concept would never include African Americans. Neither, then, could full citizenship. In securing manhood for white men alone, Jim Crow also worked to secure the market, the bedroom, and the ballot.

World War I both revivified and revised popular notions of manhood. "This is the sort of thing that makes men," white North Carolinian Lennox McLendon wrote to his pregnant wife, Mary Aycock McLendon, in fall of 1917, "and I am determined to be a man worthy of you both." McLendon, who had earlier credited Mary's affection with empowering him to "fight [his] battles like a *real man,*" saw both love and war as ennobling. Both tested him, established his mastery, and "loosened," as he put it, his "energies." Married into one of North Carolina's leading Democrat families, McLendon celebrated the Anglo-Saxon model of manhood that had shaped the turn-of-the-century white supremacy campaigns Mary's father, Charles Aycock, had helped to lead. In letters home, he emphasized his martial skill, passionate patriotism, and devotion to his family, and he admonished his wife to behave as a model of stoic white womanhood. If she could "show the world that you can love and suffer with a smile," she would steel his "determination to come back a better man."[5]

Like Lennox McLendon, pro-war African Americans expected to come back from the Great War better men. Yet unlike McLendon, who expressed delight at finding "a real nigger porter" working on the military train during his tour with the AEF, black Americans expected the war to secure them a place as equals.[6] As Ely Green's conversation in the Houston pool hall indicated, African Americans looked to military service to clarify what it meant to be a man and to cull from among their numbers the best of their manhood. Whether they imagined dignity and self-restraint or ferocity and intimidation, African Americans trusted that war would showcase the New Negroes they had become.

Sexuality figured prominently in Americans' understandings of manhood and in African American soldiers' performance of it. The skirmishes over who got to call and consider themselves men signaled a larger clash over access, entitlement, and status. African Americans' service abroad stirred white supremacists' fears as fully as it did racial activists' hopes, and it spurred vicious attempts by white soldiers to extend and protect Jim Crow. As they did on the home front, white supremacists abroad framed the discourse of place, Negro domination, and black manhood in terms of sexuality and its political complement, social equality. Sex and the body came to overlay discussions about politics and the nation, and the menace of what Senator James K. Vardaman evocatively labeled "French-women-ruined Negroes" seemed self-evident to white soldiers who watched African Americans take French girlfriends or visit French brothels.[7] In the camps and civilian streets, African American soldiers threatened the spaces that white men had claimed as their own.

The danger of French-women-ruined Negroes came also from the women doing the ruining. Sustaining Jim Crow required that white women take their place in the social order, proscribed in the name of protection. Jim Crow's architects had defined white manhood with white women as counterpoint; thus did men like Lennox McLendon have to remind their wives to love and suffer and smile in support of their men. Yet if any woman, generally, might threaten white supremacy, French women, specifically, worried its defenders. Steeped in their own discourses of nation, race, and empire, women in France did not necessarily police the same borders as white people in the United States. As Americans prepared for war overseas, they braced themselves for the encounter between black manhood and French white womanhood—and for the resulting disruption in national purity. In France, the war for the American nation, bitterly fought in towns like Houston, extended to new fields of struggle.

Every Virile and Red-Blooded Son

African American women tried to keep black men's eyes on the true prize: civic, not social, equality. The Great War offered Kathryn Johnson, for example, an outlet both for her own ambitions and for those of the race. "What the colored people in this country need," she had written to the main office of the National Association for the Advancement of Colored People during her last days as a field agent, is something "which will imbue them with the sense that they are men and women." As an organizer, Johnson often expressed frustration with the timidity of black leadership in the local branches and with the internalized white supremacy that left many African Americans feeling that "the white man is a man" and the black man "only a Negro."[8] Cast adrift in 1916 when the NAACP replaced her with a field secretary more committed to interracialism, Johnson briefly worked for a middle-class black women's magazine, *Half-Century*. From its pages, she announced that the war "would mean nothing less than the purging and cleaning of the world." In this re-formed world, black soldiers—whom she had viewed in officers' training camp, "splendid in physique, masterly in intellect, and sober and clean in their lives"—would be the vanguard of black pride. They would lead African Americans into a new dawn where "conduct, character, and culture" proved the measure of African Americans' humanity.[9] War would prove the crucible, she imagined, that forged Negroes into men.

Johnson marched toward this new dawn, becoming what she and fellow activist Addie Waites Hunton called "crusaders for democracy."[10] If the oft-repeated clarion to "do your bit" urged "every virile and red-blooded son of a black mammy to war against intrenched prejudice," as Johnson's magazine argued in the first summer of the war, then it also spurred the women who nursed, supported, and struggled alongside those men to do the same. For, as Addie Hunton claimed, "colored women" realized that "what their men achieve in the war will be by virtue of their women."[11] She and Johnson both looked to war work as the most noble and pragmatic way to organize black womanhood and steer black manhood. Lobbying the Young Men's Christian Association (YMCA) to send them abroad as volunteers, Johnson and Hunton joined one other black woman aid worker, Helen Curtis, as stewards of African Americans' conduct, character, and culture in France.

Johnson and Hunton celebrated a respectable, middle-class version of manhood that black recruits and draftees adopted in pieces. Grammar school drop-

Addie Hunton with soldiers in France. Kautz Family YMCA Archives, University of Minnesota Libraries.

out Ely Green, for example, shared with the two college-educated clubwomen the conviction that manhood and nationhood were intertwined. But for the amateur boxer and hunter, conduct looked more rough than respectable, and courage seemed more salient than culture. Like the Army Regulars who believed that faithful service might win them civic stature, Green believed that manly behavior could gain him legal standing and the ability to protect himself. Moreover, he expected that his identity as a citizen would not simply eclipse but also erase his racial identity. Through manhood, he would "abolish the word Negro," which he considered a vestige of slavery no better than the word "nigger," and become instead "a man to the flag." Green anticipated that military service would free him from that soil, which represented the burdens of history and place, and link him to the State in all its modern, mobile glory.[12]

He had to go overseas to escape. Migration north, the only other alternative he could imagine in 1917, held little appeal for him. Green had tried it that summer, traveling to Chicago to see black life in the so-called "Negro heaven." He returned to Texas disappointed in the new paradise, and in the African Americans who had flocked to it.[13] Although he heard a number of migrants talking about the "freedom" they found in the North, what Green saw in black Chicago bore little resemblance to his own notions of freedom or manhood.

Where Green had appropriated the paternalism that created white men as citizens of the South and retooled it to develop American men as citizens in the nation, the black men he encountered in Chicago had little interest in performing civic manhood. They celebrated their ability to flash their money, to pursue leisure and entertainment, to "live nine days a week and every one Sunday." As they saw it, a man should have the freedom "to do anything he wants to do," even if what he wanted to do was nothing at all. Freedom did not necessarily imply citizenship, and it certainly did not imply responsibility as articulated in mainstream political discourse. The men Green met in Chicago wanted to live as black folks, with power to determine what that meant. Black migrants in Chicago had already begun a shift away from an identity defined by character, conduct, and culture and toward an ascendant masculinity defined by new forms of autonomy—in leisure, economics, and social mores. Theirs was a cultural resistance—because after all, as one historian noted, their Chicago was not so much a city as it "was a state of mind."[14]

Ely Green, heir to his grandfather's notions of honor and self-sufficiency, had not made such a journey; intellectually, he might be Johnson and

Hunton's rough-hewn cousin, but he was kin all the same. He aspired to be
"a man to the flag"; he could not separate his sense of freedom from his vision
of the nation, and he could divorce neither from the model of manhood
to which he was wedded. Without a country when it came to race, Green
thought the nation could give him a home. And between the disappoint-
ments of Chicago and the dangers of east Texas, he saw only one road to
home. By February 1918 Green had joined the Army. He shipped out several
weeks later from Newport News, Virginia.

The thousands of African American men who followed Ely Green's path
into the military defined the import of their service in ways most meaningful
to them. Some shared Green's pursuit of what one scholar would later call
"civil rights through carnage."[15] Others, such as Gulf Coast native Henry
Berry, simply saw enlisting as part of their duty as citizens. Like Green,
Henry Berry would eventually find himself in Newport News preparing to
ship out to Brest. And like Green, Berry thought it his duty to fight in the
War. Berry, however, identified with the ideals of the nation even more uncritically than did Green. Where Green was pragmatic, Berry was romantic.
Where Green anticipated that serving under the U.S. flag would allow African American men to grow into citizenship, Berry heard George Washington
and Abraham Lincoln "calling from their very graves" for him "to offer" himself "as a living sacrifice upon the altar of Democracy."[16] To Berry, the nation
"held a claim" on him "far greater" than that held by friends or family.[17] Pro-
fessing faith in a citizenship more spiritual than material, Berry signed up for
the National Army Training Detachment run out of the Tuskegee Institute
in Tuskegee, Alabama.

If Ely Green's biography offers insight into how experience and family
helped to form political identities from the ground up, then Henry Berry's
account of his war service illustrates how people on the ground internalized
high political rhetoric. Berry perceived himself as joining a war for democracy, becoming a "cog in the mighty machine that Uncle Sam was assembling to play such an important part," not merely in the fate of African
Americans, but "in the destiny of the world."[18] Flush with the promise and
possibility of the war, Berry shared the faith expressed by pro-war Progressives that it would prove "a great thing for the world to have such a war and a
still greater thing for the Negro to have been in it."[19] It would teach him discipline, sacrifice, and fraternity. It would spread the doctrine of American
liberal democracy to the furthest corners of Europe. Subsumed into the U.S.

military machine, Berry would become synonymous with the nation at its best and most expansive.

Berry's romance of the nation reinforced his romance of war. Even as European soldiers at the front divested themselves of their belief in the nobility of fighting and began to limit their loyalties and motivations to everyday survival, Berry framed the conflict in epic terms.[20] By enlisting, he could keep "blood-thirsty Huns" from crushing the "gallant Allies" in their quest for "world domination." He viewed the war as "a new and thrilling adventure" from which he "could never return except in honor."[21] The war would not simply make a man out of him; it would make a hero out of him. Anticipating the ennobling effects of the war, he saw his honor reflected in the proud expressions of his sisters and father as they sent him off to Tuskegee, and in the envy of his civilian brother as circumstance forced him to stay behind. Convinced of the force of moral principle and the grandeur of the war, Berry saw personal betterment as part of service.

Training at Tuskegee only intensified Berry's belief that the war would transform the world and that the Army would transform him. Indeed, the Army had formed its vocational training detachments with the express purpose of remaking men as soldiers. Although military officials originally had not intended to train African Americans, Emmett Scott, the Special Assistant to Secretary of War Newton Baker on racial matters and formerly Booker T. Washington's confidant at Tuskegee, convinced them to expand the industrial training program to black colleges. Tuskegee was one of thirteen schools— along with Atlanta University, Florida A&M, Hampton, Howard, and others—where black enlistees and draftees could learn skills from electrical work to carpentry to car repair. As a result, Emmett Scott wrote after war's end, soldiers came out with better work skills and, more importantly, with "a larger mental and moral endowment." To Scott and other African American Progressives, the enhanced fitness of African American men for public life constituted one of the greatest social triumphs of the war.[22]

For Henry Berry, the transformation would be more visceral than the abstracted republican virtue that Emmett Scott celebrated. Looking over his refined posture and "lithe, hard muscles" at the end of his time in the Army, Berry could see the results of military training inscribed on his person.[23] Initially "dazed" by the rigidity of life in the training camps, he ultimately came to appreciate that, as a result of Army training, he was "a boy no longer."[24] He bestowed credit on "Uncle Sam" who, he claimed, "has taught me to be a man and made a man of me."[25] As an outer manifestation of his mental and moral condition, his physical fitness placed on display the fortifying effects of participation in the body politic. His romance of war and the nation blossomed into a romance with manhood itself.

The idea that the war made men of African American "boys" did not belong solely to idealists like Berry or high-placed federal authorities like Emmett Scott. Hampton alumnus Joshua Blanton, the head of industrial education at the all-black Penn School on South Carolina's St. Helena Island, also argued that the African Americans who underwent military training were "Men in the Making."[26] Coming from a school that followed the Hampton and Tuskegee program of "health, thrift, perseverance, thoroughness, and morality" as the cornerstones of African American uplift, Blanton agreed with other pro-war Progressives that the military provided an excellent home for black citizens in training.[27] With the help of the YMCA secretaries assigned to the camps, Blanton marveled, the Army took African Americans "from all walks of life" and shaped each one of them into "a being trained to look out for himself." Indeed, he argued, if African Americans at home could become "as much improved in our physical bearing, in our mental ability, in financial ability, and in many other ways" as soldiers trained and sent abroad, "there'll be few excuses why democracy should deny us what it gives to the rest of the citizens of this country."[28] Despite having a white man warn him and other African Americans that, war or no, it remained "a white man's country and we expect to rule it," Blanton insisted that black manhood could overcome white supremacy.[29]

Far more African Americans could aspire to manhood than could agree on what it was. Blanton and Scott highlight ways in which black people continued to define manhood through uplift and republican virtue, independent bearing and developed character, but as Ely Green had discovered in Chicago, manhood had also gained a swagger and some fire. The older "canon of manliness," as one historian has called it, held limited appeal for soldiers oriented toward freedom, physicality, and fighting.[30] Some soldiers, like Ely Green, would oscillate between traditional manliness and emergent masculinity.

Others, like nineteen-year-old Nebraskan Haywood Hall, would reject tradition altogether. Hall joined the National Guard during World War I because the life of a soldier intrigued him, but he had none of Henry Berry's interest in noble sacrifice or Ely Green's conflicted nationalism. Indeed, looking back on his reasons for signing up with the 8th Illinois National Guard while working in Chicago, Hall recalled that patriotism "was the least" of his motives. The teenaged Hall instead responded to the prospect of "romance, adventure, travel," and most importantly, France's promise of "escape from the inequities and oppression that was the lot of Blacks in the U.S."[31]

Along with the four Regular Army regiments, the National Guard had provided African Americans entry into military service in the years leading up to World War I. During the Spanish-Cuban and Philippine Wars at the end of the nineteenth century, eight states had called up militia units of African American troops, with Illinois, Kansas, and North Carolina—states where African Americans held sway in local politics—supplying units headed by African American officers.[32] In the new century, amid the pall of disfranchisement and glow of national reunion, most states disbanded their African American militia units, and the states of the Deep South barred black men from membership in the newly organized National Guard.[33] By 1917, small companies of black guardsmen remained in Washington, D.C., Connecticut, Maryland, Massachusetts, Tennessee, and Ohio. A new unit, the 15th Regiment of New York, formed in time for the war, but only the 8th Illinois could boast of two decades with a full roster of African American officers.

The 8th Illinois drew in Haywood Hall. Inspired by the exploits of the 10th Cavalry and their pursuit of Pancho Villa along the Mexico border, Hall thought the military would allow him to walk tall alongside other African Americans who seemed proud, unafraid, and filled with "racial solidarity." For him, the all-black National Guard unit with its celebrated coterie of black officers seemed more like "a big social club of fellow race-men" than it did a bid for civic inclusion.[34]

Hall's sense of racial solidarity led him to see his wartime service in light of the riots of the summer of 1917. He knew something of racial violence from both personal experience and family lore. After killing a Klansman in self-defense during Reconstruction, his paternal grandfather, the senior Haywood Hall, had been forced to flee the Tennessee plantation where he had worked as a slave and freedman. His father, too, had run afoul of white men in Hall's hometown of South Omaha, Nebraska. Rather than stay and fight, Hall's father had abandoned the family home and uprooted Haywood, his siblings, and his mother to move to Minneapolis, Minnesota. As contemptuous of his father's "timidity" as he was proud of his grandfather's gumption, Hall vowed never to be cowed into submission.[35]

Not surprisingly, Hall respected the Regulars of the 24th for the stand they had taken in Houston in August 1917. Traveling south two months later to join the rest of his regiment training at Camp Logan, Hall could not help but feel "angry and apprehensive" at the thought of arriving in Houston on their heels. The government's harsh treatment of the mutineers left Hall and his fellow National Guardsmen "brooding" and bitter, and their passage through riot-devastated East St. Louis only fanned their anger. Treating their trip as an incursion into enemy territory, they turned on their "provocative best."[36]

While some recollections of the 8th Illinois's journey from Chicago to Houston depicted the journey as stately and "uneventful," Hall and others emphasized the soldiers' militancy and sexuality.[37] Pulling into Jonesboro, Arkansas, Guardsmen taunted white people gathered at the train station with the bugbear of social equality by catcalling and blowing kisses to white women assembled on the platform. At the same time they gleefully provoked white men, leaning out the train windows to call them "peckerwood mother-fuckers." One friendly spectator who asked where the soldiers were headed got the hostile reply, "To see your momma, you cracker son-of-a-bitch." Another member of the regiment declined to say exactly what happened to the "poor cracker" who "cussed out one of the 8th boys," but he assured readers of the *Chicago Defender* that the man and his family would never forget the lesson soldiers taught him. "That man's relatives," the Guardsman wrote with satisfaction, "will remember the Eighth regiment until the 73d day of Juvember, 2001 1/2."[38] Uninterested in behaving as upright men to the flag or Uncle Sam's sacrificial lambs, the Guardsmen wanted people to know that they were nothing to mess with.

Setting their rifles within view of spectators and maliciously flirting with white ladies, the soldiers emphasized a model of manhood defined by their defiance and aggression. Hall and his friends played at being bad men. They ransacked a general store in Jonesboro whose proprietor had refused to let "niggahs" drink their cokes on his premises. While Hall and others pulled merchandise off the shelves, one of his buddies angrily took a coke bottle and knocked the storeowner "out cold."[39] The soldiers repeated their behavior in the towns that ran alongside the tracks. In Pine Bluff, they wrecked a restaurant that refused to serve them. When the members of the 8th finished, one of the Guardsmen commented, it looked like the place "had been bombed, burned out, and then swept by a hurricane and flood."[40]

In Tyler, Texas, soldiers left a trail of bottles and wrappers that ran from a pillaged store straight back to the train. When the town's sheriff tried to board the train and search the soldiers, the train's guard, "a mean, grey-eyed

Men lining up to join the 8th Illinois National Guard, Chicago. National Archives and Records Administration.

light-skinned" soldier named Bland, informed the sheriff that he had no authority on a military train and pushed him back with the barrel of his rifle.
Bland "threw the bolt" of his rifle "and ejected a bullet" to let the sheriff
know who had the upper hand. When the sheriff retreated, the entire train
car "let out a tremendous roar" of triumph.[41] Although their officers docked
their pay to cover the damage they had done on the way down, Hall found
the punishment worth the boost in morale their behavior had given them.
Protected by their uniform as they ran amok along the railroad line, the
soldiers gleefully embodied white supremacists' greatest fears.[42]

     After their raucous trip south, the 8th Illinois went on to spend five "pleas-
ant" months in Houston before proceeding to the port of embarkation in
Newport News. W. S. Braddan, the black chaplain of the regiment, recalled
that members of Houston's African American community embraced the soldiers and "tried to outdo each other" in making them "feel welcome."[43]
Memories of the summer's riot initially kept the white community at arms'
length, but Reverend Braddan claimed that the 8th's demonstrations of "loyalty, discipline and Patriotism" eventually converted "the whites of Houston
from hate to love."[44]

     Although Braddan credited the soldiers' rock-solid "appearance and
discipline"—their performance of middle-class manliness—with winning
over the people of Houston, Haywood Hall had a different theory.[45] Hall attributed much of the change in the city to the 24th's mutineers scaring the
police into submission and the black civilians of Houston out of it. As black
Houstonians pointed out where some notorious policemen had "got his"
or where other gun battles took place, Hall sensed that the town's African
Americans, "the girls" in particular, seemed inspired and emboldened by
what the mutineers had done. He sensed, also, that he should carry their
mantle: when an elderly washwoman solemnly offered him Corporal Baltimore's unclaimed khakis, he took them and wore them as his own.[46] Encouraged by girlfriends and others, he used the example of the 24th to mold his
identity as a soldier.

     From Newport News, Haywood Hall, Ely Green, Henry Berry, and thou-
sands of other African Americans would board ship to cross the Atlantic. In
some ways, Newport News—"a place of a thousand prejudices," as Reverend
Braddan bitterly dubbed it—seemed a fitting point of departure for African
American troops.[47] There, Henry Berry's heart sank upon arrival because he
"had heard that Camp Hill, New Port News was the home of the labor

battalions." His heart sank lower when he saw the laborers clad in blue denim and "working to beat the band." Until then, he had imagined "that a soldier always wore his uniform and looked snappy" and that "all he was supposed to do was drill and fight."[48]

Berry's heart would have dropped to his feet if he had known of the conditions under which black labor battalions toiled in Newport News. The camps near the city constituted "little hells," one soldier lamented, "set up to torment colored men who would be something if they were allowed to rise." Enlisted in the Navy, the soldier sent an anonymous letter to the Baltimore *Afro-American* comparing the atmosphere in the camp to "the spirit of slavery."[49] Things were little better in the Army. The denim Henry Berry noticed upon his arrival, called "old Civil War blue" by other Army men, became the de facto uniform of black laborers in camp.[50] Other troops mocked the labor battalions when they marched past in denims, but having even the humiliating blue marked a vast improvement over previous circumstances: from October 1917, when they first arrived at Camp Hill, until January 1918, the incoming laborers had no uniforms issued to them. All they had to wear was the clothing they had on when they came to Camp.[51]

The Army's decision to clothe black laborers in work clothes helped to underscore the fact that African Americans' "manpower was wanted but not their manhood," as one soldier bitterly noted, but clothing was the least of the laborers' difficulties.[52] Laboring men had no barracks, few tents, fewer outhouses, and nowhere to bathe. Some slept outdoors, under trees and around fires. Down the road in Camp Humphreys, black laborers bathed in the Potomac River once a week because they had no showers and ate outside because they had no mess hall. Unclean and underfed, they just had work—and plenty of it. Most of the laborers in the camps around Newport News worked every day of the week, without any time off for illness or holidays.[53] Their only military training "consisted in marching to and from work with hoes, shovels, and picks on our shoulders," as one man sardonically commented to an investigator into the conditions of black troops.[54] For the African American men who served as noncombatants rather than as fighting troops, Army life held more toil than glory.

Assigned to the medical detachment of the 301st Labor Battalion, Henry Berry avoided the most abysmal of the experiences that befell stateside laborers. As part of a specially trained detachment within the battalion, he spent only a couple of weeks in Newport News before shipping overseas. He left behind roughly 180,000 black conscripts and volunteers, men who the staff officers of the Army War Plans Division considered "nothing more than laborers in uniform."[55]

Some 200,000 black men sailed with the AEF, 42,000 of them combat troops, and they all had to contend with the hostility of white civilians and soldiers. For Haywood Hall, Newport News provided an apt point of departure because the civilians he came across embodied the ugly racism he was all too happy to leave behind. Confronted by soldiers whom they could not deride as conscripted labor, "local crackers and the police"—as Hall contemptuously identified them—sought to keep them in their place all the same.[56] Civilian police and many white MPs came down hard on the men of the 8th Illinois after hearing rumors that they had caused the trouble at Camp Logan and planned to raise more hell in Newport News upon their arrival in March 1918.[57] The men of the 8th Illinois, newly designated the 370th Infantry of the 93rd Combat Division, stoked that concern by arguing with conductors on segregated streetcars and engaging in "small scale fighting" downtown, as Lieutenant Rayford Logan remembered it. Logan, who was waiting to disembark from Camp Stuart as part of the segregated 372nd Infantry, recalled his white commanding officer ordering them not to follow the "evil example" of the 370th and to obey all local laws.[58]

Just as it had for the 24th Infantry and Ely Green in Texas, following the law in Virginia required that African American soldiers accept law enforcement's role in perpetuating Jim Crow through violence. Haywood Hall recalled the hostility that civilian police displayed toward his combat unit. Taunting them and asking, "Why don't you darkies stay in camp," the police arrested some of the first of his regiment to venture out from Camp Stuart and drove others to the outskirts of town. When a number of soldiers returned to Hall's barracks, "some of them badly beaten," Hall and his fellow soldiers nearly marched on Newport News in a self-conscious "repetition of the Houston riot." Only the appeals of a respected officer "not to play into the hands of these crackers" kept them from taking their guns and breaking camp.[59] After the initial clashes downtown, the regiment had all leaves cancelled until they made their "get-a-way" aboard the USS *George Washington*.[60] As they marched toward the ship on the morning of April 6, 1918, Hall and his friends took a moment to rough up some white men watching them embark. Hall did not even know who they were: "probably dockworkers," he surmised. He just knew that "applying" his newfound "skills of close order

combat" made him feel better about the beating doled out to his fellow soldiers a few days earlier.[61]

Ely Green would have his last hurrah in Newport News as a lover, not a
fighter. Bidding his steady girlfriend adieu at a train stop in Waxahachie, he
began his final flirtations with American women on the journey to Virginia.
For Green, loving women was as much a part of manhood as protecting
women, and it could be just as troublesome. At the depot in Bristol, Virginia,
a young Red Cross worker—a "pretty young brunette"—approached Green
and asked, "Are they going to take you over there?" When Green told her yes,
she responded, "I wish they would leave you with me." The woman offered
him some cake and hot chocolate, explaining, "we don't serve it to Negroes";
black soldiers only got cigarettes. Faced with the Red Cross's discrimination,
Green opted to "let a Negro be served" this one time. He went ahead and
passed as white until a white soldier signaled to the aid worker that Green
was, in fact, black. The woman stepped back "looking," Green recalled, "like
she had seen a ghost."[62] Green proceeded on to Newport News bemused by
his flirtation across the color line and by his new realization that "the Northern white man supported white supremisy" as much as any Southerner."[63]

If Green's confusing collision with the Red Cross worker served to pique
his curiosity about interracial liaisons, the warning issued by Army higher-
ups temporarily helped to tamp it down. The day before his unit shipped to
France, one of the chaplains brought three soldiers suffering from venereal
disease before Green and other African American soldiers and, as Green said,
"made a show of them." Warning the soldiers that "this will be *your* reward"
if they fooled around with white women in France, the chaplain counseled
them to steer clear. Green later realized that the officer's warning "was the
beginning of a segregation move that would confront" him and his fellow
soldiers over and over again in France. At the time, however, he simply resolved to go out and "hold a little brown baby once more" before he left Virginia because he did not know when he would get to do so again.[64] Whatever
excitement France might hold, it also promised danger.

Black Virus in the Body Politic

American men's uneven embrace of visceral masculinity distressed proponents of a more duty-bound manliness. The Army's focus on "social hygiene,"
as reformers began to label it in the early years of the twentieth century,

sprang from a larger concern during the Progressive Era over order, personal behavior, and sexuality. In the realm of public health, both in the United States and elsewhere, modern medicine collided with Victorian morality to construct sexually transmitted diseases as social diseases—ones that could unravel marriages, families, and the very fabric of race and nation.[65] Lurking undetected, diseases such as syphilis and gonorrhea could cause developmental disorders in infants and infertility in women; corrupt behavior could lead to corrupted bodies. To protect women, white Progressive reformers called on men to curb their innate passions. Similarly, they implored women to guard their chastity to protect themselves and their children-to-be, configured in the writing of medical professionals as "our future citizenship."[66] Sexual responsibility, then, became public responsibility: as Kentucky-born crusader and dermatologist Prince Morrow wrote in his 1904 book, *Social Disease and Marriage,* "Public hygiene . . . in its highest expression is inseparable from public morality."[67]

Campaigns to eradicate social disease grew in prominence and stridence during the Progressive Era so that by World War I, a soldier's commitment to sexual hygiene could become the litmus for his patriotism. With the help of groups such as the American Red Cross and the YMCA, military and civilian authorities focused on "the protection and control of girls and women among the civil population," framing soldiers as simultaneously dangerous to and threatened by civilian women.[68] In training camps soldiers received brochures put together by civilian welfare organizations under the auspices of the Commission on Training Camp Activities (CTCA). The CTCA pamphlets asked them whether they dared "look the flag in the face" when they "were dirty with gonorrhea?"[69] Overseas, AEF commander General John J. Pershing informed American troops that "a soldier who contracts a venereal disease . . . fails in his duty to his country and his comrades."[70]

Protecting one's body marked the first step in protecting the nation. The doctors of the American Social Hygiene Association identified the "young men in the prime of life" as the "trustees of at least five hundred thousand combinations of character units which future generations should receive and mould for the nation's further progress." Secretary of the Navy Josephus Daniels echoed the Hygiene Association and spelled out the dire consequences. Arguing that "men must live straight if they would shoot straight," Daniels told a gathering of doctors in 1918 that reformers had to protect soldiers "from that contamination of their bodies which will not only impair their military efficiency but blast their lives for the future and return them to their homes a source of danger to their families and the community at large."[71]

One of the chief propagandists of the white supremacy campaigns in North Carolina, Daniels had long connected sexual behavior with home protection and linked the women in the home to nation and state making. During the late 1890s, from the pages of his newspaper, the *Raleigh News and Observer,* he repeatedly drew links between black voting and the "Negro atrocities" allegedly committed against white women.[72] If the miscegenated politics of the Populist era had created the conditions in which African American sexual aggression thrived, Daniels and his fellow Democrats argued, then there could be only one solution; "the safety of the home," as their slogan read during the 1898 elections, required what Daniels called "good government by the party of the white man."[73] Twenty years later, he once again argued for a protective paternalism. This time, however, he called upon the federal government to teach young men to suppress their passions as thoroughly as white men of his generation had suppressed African Americans in the South.

In the minds of many reformers, the danger of venereal disease was primarily one of racial degeneration—a weakening of Northern European stock by ailments thought common in African Americans, Slavs, and other supposedly lesser peoples. White Progressive reformers borrowed from the millenarian language of eugenicists to argue that neglect of social hygiene could herald the onset of "race suicide" as diseased-compromised, native-born whites might begin to produce fewer and less healthy babies.[74] In this scenario, women could either be the nation's salvation or its undoing. By demanding, as Josephus Daniels had, that white men stay healthy for the sake of their homes and that they remain free from the contagion of racial or ethnic others for the sake of their communities, reformers portrayed women as both potential victim and potential menace.

During World War I, *French* women, in particular, posed a danger. Unconcerned about the composition of America's "future citizenship" and unschooled in the tenets of American white supremacy, they could pollute the American citizenry by mixing indiscriminately with soldiers of all races. To white people concerned with racial purity, both gonorrhea and black aspiration were sexually transmitted diseases; responsible white men and women needed to guard against the black virus in the body politic.

Manhood, of course, never involved men alone. From the 8th Illinois's train-side catcalls to ideologues' clamoring about race suicide and social disease, women shaped how men spoke about and presented themselves, and—by extension—how they conceived of the American nation. The patriarchalism that undergirded both white supremacy and the African American struggle against it situated women as objects. In France, as in the United States, women became a means through which both black and white Americans expressed their thinking about manhood and civil rights. Because sex figured so prominently in white Americans' understanding of equality, attempts to circumscribe black soldiers' sexual behavior also represented attempts to limit African American troops' self-conceptions and projected images.

French women, and through them France itself, loomed in the American imagination as egalitarian threats. As tensions mounted between black and white soldiers in the American camps, a utopian France came to represent, emotionally and discursively, all that the United States denied African Americans. White supremacists deplored this ideal France, but African Americans held fast to the belief that black soldiers fought among a French populace who "know no color line," as two members of the 372nd marveled to a crowd in Missouri.[75]

Essential to African American's emotional and rhetorical emphasis on French egalitarianism was the thrill of social equality. White supremacists on the front and home front had sounded the alarm bells so stridently for so long that black soldiers, too, came to see interracial liaisons as a way of exhibiting manly prerogative. As increasing numbers of African American soldiers arrived in France in 1918 and began to interact with the French, their white counterparts reinforced the color line. Writing home from France, for example, a white lieutenant in the 142nd Field Artillery called political equality between the races "dangerous" and vowed that social equality would "never be."[76] Such a vow denied the reality of conditions in France (and, as the biracial Ely Green could testify, in the United States), buffering Jim Crow by denying its subversions.

Viewing the American "Negro problem" from foreign soil amplified the contrasts between white supremacy and an idealized democracy, but it also strengthened segregationist resolve. Although the lieutenant from the 142nd Field Artillery conceded that it sounded "illogical to talk of a 'world safe for democracy' and discriminate against any race," he nevertheless felt that "the belief and necessity for white supremacy" was "fundamental" to "Americanism as originally practised." America could survive with a stunted democracy, but without the white man as "guardian" of the country's "civilization," the nation might cease to exist.[77]

The crisis of white supremacy required action as well as argument. To protect white privilege in an increasingly international world, Jim Crow's defenders worked hard to cart it to France. "Soldat noir-vilain," a pair of French girls informed Kathryn Johnson when she met them while touring the Alps. The two girls had learned the lesson, that black soldiers were scoundrels, from white soldiers who had passed through the mountain area on leave months earlier.[78] Officially, the Army did not bother trying to scare off French women; they simply ordered black troops like the 804th Pioneers "not to talk to or be in company with any white woman, regardless of whether the women solicit their company or not."[79] Similarly, while stationed near Verdun, Lieutenant Rayford Logan heard from Suzanne Lemercier, his French language practice partner, that his regiment's white colonel "had drafted an order to the French people" telling them that "women were not to associate" with the African American troops. The townspeople ignored the company commander's statement, but the colonel continued to police his troops by sending men—Logan among them—to spy on soldiers in bars.[80]

Training in the Haute Marne, Lieutenant Howard Long and his men in the 368th Regiment were placed under what he labeled a "racial quarantine." Long, a former teacher at Howard University, recalled that the men of his unit "were forbidden to return to the village" located a quarter of a mile from their drill ground, and when townspeople came out to visit, the soldiers were "prohibited from meeting and talking with them." One of his fellow officers got arrested at bayonet point after a commanding officer saw him exchange notes with a white woman. Another was arrested and demoted to the labor battalions for greeting an acquaintance with a kiss on the cheek.[81] In short, as Matthew Bullock, a black YMCA worker serving among black troops in Bordeaux, observed with consternation, "The boys cannot 'look at' a French woman without getting into trouble."[82]

For their parts, Kathryn Johnson and Addie Hunton decried the propaganda and persecution used by the Army to keep black soldiers away from French civilians and French women in particular. Yet the two black women also hastened to distinguish black soldiers' chafing under military restrictions from any actual preference for white French women. Indeed, they claimed, one of their chief lessons as YMCA workers was that "colored men loved their own women as they could love no other women in the world." Addie Hunton characterized soldiers' reverence toward her, Johnson, and Helen Curtis as "bordering on worship," and a black soldier later echoed that sentiment by

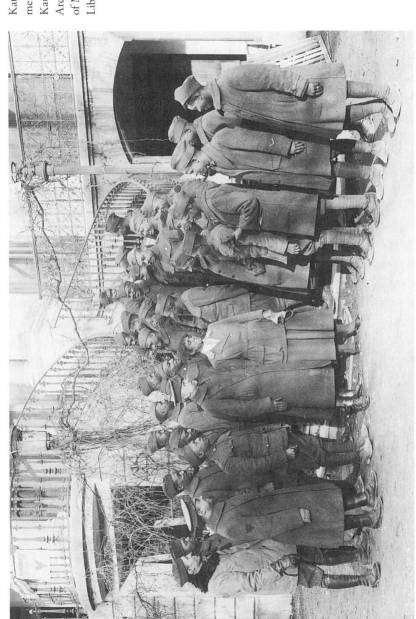

Kathryn Johnson with members of the AEF. Kautz Family YMCA Archives, University of Minnesota Libraries.

calling Hunton "the most dearly beloved woman in the AEF."[83] Kathryn Johnson remembered a man in St. Nazaire so "overcome" with seeing her that he "could not keep the tears back." Seeing the black women, a soldier explained to Hunton, took him "back home." Whatever attraction French women might hold, the two women argued, they could not match the enduring tie that held black men and women together.[84]

Johnson and Hunton intervened in the discourse of manhood, sex, and nation by stressing the link between black manhood and black womanhood and tethering black members of the AEF back to the country they had left behind. From her lessons on the causes of the war and reasons for military service to her reading drills for illiterate soldiers, Johnson used her YMCA work to underscore for soldiers that they fought for the community as a whole, and that black women worked alongside them.[85] Black soldiers could tussle with white men over relations with French women, but by serving as mother figures—the "trusted guardian[s]" of the "home back in America," as Hunton dubbed them—or even as occasional "surrogate sweetheart[s]" for black soldiers in France—as one scholar characterized them—Johnson and Hunton helped remind soldiers of their responsibilities to their communities on the home front.[86] Still, the black female YMCA workers numbered three among 200,000 African American troops. For all Hunton and Johnson's emphasis on black men's love of the women left behind, it would be an abstract French womanhood who appeared to most threaten white men's democracy.

French-Women-Ruined Nations

Traveling on the Paris metro during a short trip away from her YMCA camp, Kathryn Johnson observed a Senegalese military officer offer his seat to a "white-haired French woman" who had boarded the subway. The woman accepted the seat, gave "a gracious bow," and kissed the African man on his hand. Johnson watched with interest, remarking to herself that if the same scene had played out back in America, "someone would probably have set a bomb under the coach."[87] The French, she surmised, had different rules of conduct.

Such conduct infuriated white New Yorker Fred Parker. Complaining in a letter to his parents that it "cut might hard to see a white woman with a big black boy," the officer cited such relations as both cause and symptom of the coming trouble. He added, "They would never think of doing it back in the States." In his opinion, the problem arose because "the uneducated" French treated African Americans "just the same as if they were white and many times even better." Still, Parker observed, American white men were doing their part to maintain social order. About a week earlier, he mentioned in his letter, they had "strung up one of the colored boys who was accused of rape."[88]

In time, American authorities appealed to the French military to convince its civilians to follow Jim Crow's rules. W. E. B. Du Bois made infamous the confidential memo written by Colonel Linard, a French military officer attached to the AEF, by publishing it in the pages of the *Crisis*. In his memo "On the Subject of Black American Troops," Colonel Linard explained to French Army officers that white Americans thought they might succumb to racial degeneration if they did not draw an impassable line between black and white. Because such a danger "did not exist for the French race," Linard observed, "French civilians had indulged" African American troops and, in so doing, possibly "inspired in them intolerable pretensions." He urged French officers and civilians to avoid upsetting white Americans by forgoing any semblance of intimacy with African American soldiers.[89]

Despite Colonel Linard's claim that the French did not comprehend the racial tensions in the United States, many members of the "French race," to use Linard's term, actually shared white Americans' concerns over degeneration and contamination. Just as segregationists escalated rhetoric about the danger that French women and "French-women-ruined Negroes" posed to America, French demographers in the metropole and authorities in the colonies invoked similar discourses of sex and nation. Both Jim Crow America and Imperial France policed their borders using *métissage,* national and cultural intermixture through marriage and reproduction, as a metonym for authoritarian rule.[90] Where men like Jospehus Daniels decried the dangers of miscegenation, French reformers turned their baleful gaze on *métissage.* However, with the male population dramatically decreased by several years of war, and French observers bemoaning the resultant "family and repopulation crisis" for women of reproductive age, the French could little afford to reject all forms of intermixture. Instead, commentators turned their attention to *how* women mixed and with whom.[91]

As an encounter that troubled national boundaries, *métissage* had to be managed. Social theorists assumed that French wives of foreign immigrants could offset the diluting effect of immigration and integration by teaching their spouses and children what it meant to be properly, culturally French. As wives and mothers, they would transmit French "language, mores, traditions, and even . . . national prejudices" to the immigrants they might marry, one journalist wrote.[92] However, commentators agreed that some mixtures worked better than others. Most agreed with the author of *Hygienic Control of French Immigrants,* who argued that white races could join the French national body more naturally than "exotics of the black race, or yellow-skinned people with thick lips and slanty eyes."[93] Consequently, women had to act as selective, responsible wives and mothers. Like white women in America, their roles were circumscribed either to protecting the nation or to tainting it.

Understandings of the nation and national purity could not be extricated from the experience of French colonialism. Black "exotics" and "yellow-skinned people with thick lips" were French subjects as well, and the migrations spurred by the Great War brought them and the "tensions of empire" home to the metropole.[94] Unlike in the colonies where debates over *métissage* tended to emphasize white men's sexual relations with women of color, attention in wartime France was focused on white French women's interactions with nonwhite men.

Over one million men of color came to France from Africa, Southeast Asia, and North America—half of them from French colonies—to work and fight.[95] The military tried to keep a tight rein on these new arrivals. Soldiers from Indochina, for example, were court-martialed, transferred, or stripped of rank when civilians reported their relationships with French women.[96] Additionally, authorities attempted to police French women's interactions with colonial troops by extending the metaphor of the household in such a way that *temporarily* incorporated men from the colonies—without bringing them too close. Like other French troops, colonial troops found themselves adopted by *marraines de guerres*—literally wartime godmothers—who sent them gifts, wrote them letters, and sometimes brought them into their homes. Organized and administered through the French military, *marrainage* made foster sons of troops who had no one to watch over them on the homefront. Military officials warned these matrons of the motherland to keep colonials at arm's length lest the contact with supposedly less civilized peoples lead to what one functionary labeled "the depravity of French women."[97]

Attempts to construct and restrict white women as pure, republican mothers met with as much difficulty in France as they did in the American South. In port cities like Brest, the multinational and multiracial concentration of men—"not simply Americans, but also Russian, Portuguese, and Kabyle soldiers," as a French historian noted—caused an "extraordinary" wartime spike in the number of prostitutes, women more concerned with commerce than racial bias. Thousands more women came into contact with colonial subjects in factories, where they labored in ever-increasing numbers. All in all, nearly 700,000 working-class women fell outside the domestic constraints developed by French state authorities and social engineers.[98]

Moreover, contemporary observers claimed that the middle-class women who did sign on as *marraines de guerre* did so less out of a patriotic maternalism than out of a desire for romance.[99] Looking back on the war from the end of the 1920s, German sociologist, self-described "sexologist," and sexual reformer Magnus Hirschfeld asserted that the "erotic temperament of the French woman" had caused *marrainage* to devolve into sexual flirtation. Upon discovering the object of her flirtation to be "a particularly black Congo" or "an Indo-Chinese," Hirschfeld argued, the sentimental *marraine* abandoned her flirtation, and with it the lonely soldier, so that the entire program "gradually decayed." As he saw it, by transgressing racial boundaries, unwittingly or no, these women ultimately damaged the fighting spirit of France.[100]

Despite Hirschfeld's claims, not all *marraines* abandoned their flirtations upon realizing that they were writing to colonial troops. Senegalese veteran Mbaye Diagne recalled that, after meeting and interacting with Senegalese troops, "some *marraines de guerre* fell in love with the soldiers they invited home." The troops he knew often used the term *marraines* when they spoke of their girlfriends. Although Diagne made a point of emphasizing that he meant "girls of good families" rather than prostitutes, boundary-crossing *marraines* destabilized state discourses of gender and nation as surely as did prostitutes and working-class women.[101]

Jim Crow had its analog in French racial thinking, but for the French, trying to manage *métissage* equaled trying to contain the empire.[102] Thus, African American soldiers could influence French debates on intermixture and national character by sleeping with, dating, and sometimes marrying French women, but rarely could they engage those debates directly. In the complex French taxonomy of race, African Americans in the AEF belonged on the side of the exotics. However, as *Americans*—so wrapped up in their own domestic struggles over race and access—they confounded French nationalism less than did French colonial subjects. For American troops, intimate relations with French women primarily served to extend the debate over entitlement and access begun on American soil.

For Ely Green and the black stevedores in St. Nazaire, for instance, liaisons with French women defied taboo and bolstered their masculinity. In a segregated bar during a rare pass from their camp in St. Nazaire, one of Green's fellow soldiers spent his evening flirting with an elderly French woman "so wrinkled" that a nonplussed Green "couldnt tell where her lips started or ended." When Green asked his friend why he did not pursue one of the younger or more attractive women, the soldier replied, "She's white isn't she?" The soldier felt that fact alone worked "ninety per cent in her favor." Green noted that most of the men in his platoon "hadn't as much as shaken hands" with a white woman, much less been "entertained by one," and their new interactions both unnerved and excited them. In the five clubs that lined the only block in St. Nazaire where African American troops were allowed, they could flout the color line all they wished.[103]

Green remembered the bar proprietress as an Englishwoman who went by the name Big Fat Mama with the Meat Shaking on Her Bones. The name came from blues songs that celebrated sex, excess, and the charms of the women at hand. "I'm a big fat mama, got the meat shakin on my bones," the most common version of the song went, "And every time I shake, some skinny gal loses her home."[104] Texas or Chicago could not have seemed farther away than it did when black soldiers embraced the entertainments offered in the portside bars. Whether chosen by Big Fat Mama herself, bestowed on her by soldiers in the wartime Services of Supply (SOS), or refracted through Green's memory as he recalled his time in France, Big Fat Mama's name deftly captured the charge and transgression of social interactions in her club.

Big Fat Mama and her girls did not figure into the most exalted pronouncements of African Americans. For the loftiest rhetoricians, the "love" that existed between black men and white French women remained purely platonic, "too grand and beautiful to describe," in the words of Lieutenant Sylvanus Brown. A member of the 92nd Combat Division, Brown assured the readers of the *Cleveland Advocate* that the love he mentioned was "of such a nature that the sweethearts of our boys at home" would heartily approve.[105] He presented the women of France as sacrificing mothers and wives, figures whose loss made them all the more ready to recognize black soldiers as "great leaders of men."[106]

His portrait of a bereaved French womanhood allowed Brown to position African American troops as "true sons of France." Away from America, "minus the ball room and sin scarred women," black soldiers learned about "being a man . . . and performing the duties thereof." For Brown, the intimacy between black men and French women was born of the French nation's need for protection and regeneration, and stood as a symbol of African American vigor and capability. In Brown's words, by giving "back to these people what is left of their manhood and youth," African Americans established their own worth.[107]

Less sentimental than Brown, other soldiers commented on the prevalence of interracial liaisons, both romantic and civic. Many reveled in the way that black soldiers' social relations with French women upended racist discourses of attraction and repulsion. Returned soldiers boasted that "French girls . . . were carried away with the American Negroes."[108] Young soldiers wrote letters home unabashedly admitting that they "like[d] the girls in France."[109] Some of the girls liked them back. Ely Green swore that one of the first women that he met after his arrival in France embraced him and announced that she wanted him "to be her fiancé." When the white soldier with Green protested, the German prisoner of war acting as their interpreter chastised the white American for trying to impose segregation on Europeans. Green took the German's statement as proof that Europeans had avoided the taint of white supremacy.[110] Back at home, the most incendiary members of the black press crowed that "the experience of the war has been that the French girls are just as anxious to have colored troopers make love to them as white troopers."[111] In the bedroom, as on the battlefield, boosters of black manhood saw their cause vindicated.

Crossing racial boundaries allowed African American men in the AEF to show their contempt not only for white supremacy but also for its practitioners. Stationed in a town near Verdun, for example, Rayford Logan forged a flirtation with Suzanne Lemercier. When a white suitor called on the young woman during one of her and Logan's language lessons, Lieutenant Logan felt no compunction about excluding the white soldier from the all-French conversation until the other man grew uncomfortable and left.[112] As time passed Logan became more confrontational. Demoted from combat to heading a labor battalion in Bordeaux, he took his then girlfriend to a restaurant where white American officers had balked repeatedly at his presence. He recalled that when he showed up with the white French woman, white Americans responded with "fury." The restaurant manager considered evicting Logan and his date to appease the white troops, but Logan's girlfriend warned that she "would have 'her friend the mayor' close the establishment" if he did so.[113] In that one confrontation, Logan and his date won out.

To protect Jim Crow from French women, the U.S. Army tried to teach white supremacy to them. These white supremacists failed as teachers not because France was a land "that knew no color line," as its fans claimed, but rather because the French were too busy drawing *their own* color lines—between colony and metropole—to commit themselves to the American Negro problem. For Americans in France, then, the mire of their own white supremacy so fully obscured the landscape that most of them could not see the ground beneath their feet. That ideal France invoked by black soldiers and decried by white supremacists did not actually exist. Like its American ally, France was mundane, flawed, complex. And the white women who populated France were no more, or less, threatening to white supremacy than the white women of the U.S. South.

Yet France did serve the African American freedom movement by allowing black soldiers to conceive of a life unfettered by segregation. African American soldiers focused on the relative fluidity of their relations with white French men and women, and contrasted those relations with the rigid rituals of Jim Crow. The France of their cultural and political imaginations reflected black fury with the America that excluded them rather than their engagement with the racial politics of the country that temporarily took them in.

Gable Finley, a former chauffeur stationed at Camp Lee, Virginia, claimed that his training with the 349th Field Artillery gave him "improved health and mind" and "taught [him] to be a better man."[114] But Finley, who remained stateside, missed the two-front struggle that marked black soldiers' experiences overseas. The two wars for democracy—against the Central Powers and within the AEF—would do much to shape their sense of manhood. As James Vardaman feared, these soldiers were indeed ruined, if by "ruined" we mean "made militant." And it was not the sex alone that turned aspiring black men into militant New Negroes. Rather, African American soldiers found strength in their disillusion with an army that sought to deny them full humanity, much less equal citizenship. And they drew from their military service a willingness to fight for a democracy that they could imagine but did not have. The AEF camps, not the battlefield, would be the true crucible of the New Negro.

4

At War in the Terrestrial Heaven

"Raise a ruckus tonight," Haywood Hall sang out as he marched through northeastern France as part of the 370th Infantry. With their walking sticks offsetting their overstuffed backpacks and their overcoats left partly open, the members of the former 8th Illinois easily blended in with the French combat division to which they were attached. Country folk in the Meuse-Argonne mistook the African Americans for *tirailleurs,* colonial troops. Moroccan or Sudanese, maybe; their browns varied too much in hue for them to pass for the Senegalese who, Hall noted, "were practically all black." Most likely those country people on the roadside could not make out the soldiers' words as they sang to themselves and each other, "Get on board on down the river flow, gonna' raise a ruckus tonight."[1]

"Lost children," the French called the four infantry regiments—the 369th, 370th, 371st, and 372nd—that made up the 93rd Combat Division. Commander of the American Expeditionary Forces (AEF), General John J. Pershing, had given the division over to the French Army for the war's duration. Although a sympathetic white officer complained that Pershing had foisted off the troops like a "black orphan in a basket," Hall and his friends found much to like in their new posting.[2] French soldiers treated them like comrades, giving the first casualty of their unit "a hero's burial" and expressly thanking the black troops for their service. French civilians treated them well, too, impressing Hall with their "hospitality and kindness." For sex, African American troops visited the legal brothels near their leave areas, but the locals in town also invited them to come back after war's end and choose among their "pick of French girls" to marry. Hall figured the offer was extended "half-jokingly," but took the jest as a sign of the town's high regard for black troops.[3]

In spite of the respite provided by mixing with the French, Hall and other black American soldiers kept running up against reminders that they "had not escaped the long arm of American racism." Upon arriving in a small town in the Lorraine region, for example, Hall's battalion commander lined his men up and warned them that a black member of a labor battalion recently had been hanged in the same square where the unit now assembled. Someone had accused the laborer of raping a village girl, but villagers expressed doubts that an assault had actually occurred. The Army declared the soldier guilty and, after the hanging, had displayed his body for a day before cutting him down. "As a result," the battalion commander informed the soldiers lined up before him, "you . . . are to conduct yourselves as gentlemen" and to stick close to barracks. Hall noticed the major's voice drop as he muttered, "This is what I have been told to tell you."[4]

The major's message underscored the promise and perils of black soldiers' adventures abroad. The idea of France functioned as an imaginary—a bundle of expectations, associations, and encounters onto which African Americans tied their aspirations for liberation and civil rights. Encounters across both national boundaries and the color line served to shape this imaginary.[5] On the one hand, black soldiers' ability to bask in French hospitality or masquerade as Sudanese soldiers loosed them from the bonds of nation that had previously defined their military service. But on the other hand, white soldiers and the Army leadership gripped African Americans with the long arm of racism, creating extraterritorial spaces where Jim Crow still ruled. More often than not, the American camps functioned as Southern outposts on French soil.

If manhood and its attendant hopes offer one way to think about African Americans in World War I, then focusing on the disillusion of black soldiers' service in the AEF offers another. Looking at men in the making served to highlight the ways in which African Americans spawned the New Negro from their own aspirations. Revisiting the same ground with an emphasis on the workaday realities of life in the AEF illuminates how interracial conflicts shaped this New Negro and the extent to which fury and disillusion sharpened soldiers' politics. The American camps felt like "penal institution[s]," one black soldier commented, where white soldiers ferociously regulated their labor and movements, and the force and venom of white repression escalated with black soldiers' performances of loyalty, desirability, or worth.[6] World War I may not have begun as a two-front battle for the mass of African American soldiers, but it became one as white supremacists repeatedly demonstrated that they would not cede ground to African Americans without a fight.

The majority of those fights would take place in the labor battalions since most of the African Americans who served in the military during World War I would never see action on the front lines. Of the 200,000 black soldiers who began shipping out to Europe in the second half of 1917, almost 160,000 would work in labor units that came to be known by war's end as the Services of Supply (SOS).[7] Despite African Americans' rhetorical emphasis on the trenches during and after the war, combat troops numbered only 42,000—roughly 20 percent of the black soldiers overseas and only 11 percent of the African Americans in the entire wartime Army. They worked as stevedores in western and southern French ports such as Brest, St. Nazaire, Bordeaux, Marsailles, and Le Havre and in engineer and labor battalions that built warehouses, roads, and railroads near the ports and in the French interior.[8] Members of the Pioneer Infantry battalions had more technical skills and received some combat training, but like other members of the SOS, they mostly supplied cheap manpower. Rather than fighting on the front, black men made up a third of the Army's labor force.

Fighting troops felt the burden, too. Influenced by the rhetoric of both racial activists and white supremacists, African American combat troops first crossed the Atlantic with visions of French liberty, equality, and fraternity dancing in their heads. Many of them returned home feeling much the same way, imbued with a sense of themselves as new men—tested by war and aglow with the fortifying effects of French good will. Yet along with their fond memories of France came a renewed bitterness about their treatment at the hands of their fellow Americans. "To put it all in a nutshell," First Sergeant Louis H. Pontlock wrote to *Crisis* editor W. E. B. Du Bois, "the American Negro soldier in France was treated" by the American military "with the same contempt and undemocratic spirit as the American Negro citizen is

Soldiers building a railroad in France. National Archives and Records Administration.

treated in the United States."[9] This realization would have a profound effect on how black soldiers saw themselves in relation to each other and the American nation. For longshoremen and infantrymen alike, the disillusion of wartime encounters would feed the transformation of black soldiers' political consciousnesses.

Choosing Camps

American ships carried more than just soldiers. Jim Crow sailed to Europe on the same tankers that transported African American noncombatant troops from Hoboken and Newport News, where they shipped out, to the European ports on the Atlantic Coast, where they landed. Jim Crow traveled, too, with the members of the 92nd and 93rd Infantry Divisions, the segregated combat divisions put together from black National Guard units, black volunteers and draftees, white superior officers, and the 639 graduates of the African American officers training camp in Des Moines, Iowa. Soldiers disembarking in French ports swapped tales of the "many unkindnesses" as one sailor understated it, that they experienced en route "on account of color."[10] Black officers, especially, felt the sting of the discrimination, as their white counterparts hastened to demonstrate that rank did not confer status. "Among the first orders issued" aboard the converted passenger vessel that transported medical officer Lieutenant William Dyer "were those barring Colored officers from the same toilets," barbershop, or gymnasium as whites. In the 317th Ammunition Train, Dyer's unit in the 92nd Division, "that feeling of prejudice" arose from the very start.[11]

The soldiers who made up the 92nd and 93rd Divisions knew segregation. Southerners made up a large portion of the African American population in the Army, and though the South lay claim to it, Jim Crow had long since outgrown the eleven states of the old Confederacy. William Dyer, for instance, had come of age in Lincoln, Illinois, where one white native son recalled that the only things white folks "were . . . willing to share with the colored people were the drinking water and the cemetery."[12] Dyer had done well for himself nevertheless, going off to Kansas City to earn a medical degree. When the United States joined the war, he was thirty years old, a newly minted doctor, and he joined a medical detachment training in Fort Des Moines, Iowa.[13]

Fort Des Moines also housed the segregated Officer's Training Camp, where 1,250 volunteered for military service. The camp was pro-war African

Americans' concession to Jim Crow. Volunteers believed that the opportunity to serve as commissioned officers in charge of African American troops offset the insult of a segregated camp. They "made the best of it," said veteran Charles Hamilton Houston, because "it was better to go to war as infantry officers than to be drafted as privates in labor battalions." As part of the Central Committee of Negro College Men, Houston petitioned the Wilson administration for training and canvassed African American fraternities and other institutions of black civic life for volunteers.[14] In supporting the camp, they followed W. E. B. Du Bois and white NAACP board chair (and Army captain serving in military intelligence) Joel Spingarn, who urged African Americans to make peace with their "damnable dilemma" by earning commissions.[15] Not everyone agreed with the tradeoff, however. The editors of the *Chicago Defender, Cleveland Gazette,* and *Boston Guardian* all flayed the camp's proponents for compromising on segregation.[16] Disagreement over the training camp echoed the larger debate over the meaning, potential, and terms of African American participation in the war.

African Americans found themselves largely disillusioned by the Army's treatment of black officers. They had some inkling of the disappointment in store when the Wilson administration forcibly retired Lieutenant Colonel Charles Young, Kathryn Johnson's hero from Wilberforce, rather than let him command white officers or lead a black combat division. Young had earned laurels in the Philippine War and in the Punitive Expeditions into Mexico and had risen through the ranks, remaining the most senior African American in the Army. Although Army officials cited Young's frail health—a point Young disputed by riding a horse from Ohio to Washington, D.C.—his friend W. E. B. Du Bois believed that the colonel was kept home because "if he had gone to Europe he could not have been denied the stars of a General."[17] The Army promoted Young to a full colonel when they removed him from active duty, but neither Young nor other African Americans derived much comfort from the gesture. For black Californian, and future Communist, William Patterson, the Army's treatment of Colonel Young cemented his "conviction that the war was a white man's war."[18]

If Charles Young's forced retirement did not deflate black trainees' spirits, then the Army's ongoing contempt for them did. Twenty-one years after his service ended, Charles Hamilton Houston still could pinpoint the moment when "morale at Fort Des Moines" finally "died." It came in the wake of the 24th's mutiny at Camp Logan, when the Army's Inspector General traveled up to Des Moines to make clear to trainees that the Army would not "have its war effort crippled by racial disorders." With no mention of how white soldiers often inflamed those disorders, Houston felt the that Inspector General had "in substance prohibited us from protecting ourselves against the aggressions of others." As the administration's attitude sunk in, and as the original three months' training dragged out into five, a number of candidates "lost all confidence in the Government's intention to give the Negro a square deal" and tendered their resignations.[19]

Houston's own father, D.C. lawyer William Houston, advised him to give up on "getting across the ocean" much less seeing battle. "The colored troops that are officered by white officers may get to the trenches," the senior Houston predicted, but not the ones with black officers.[20] Charles Houston soldiered on anyway, as did his fellow Howard University instructor Howard Long, who would go on to become first African American to earn an Ed.D. from the Harvard Education School. Although he remained at Fort Des Moines, Long described training methods as "jejune" and the material as "utterly useless." And though the Army surprised the Houstons by sending black officers to France, Long would find that racial tensions undercut the fighting troops' effectiveness. In the 368th Infantry where he was a liaison officer, Long found that many of the white "field officers seemed far more concerned with reminding their Negro subordinates that they were Negroes than they were with having an effective unit."[21]

Lieutenant Rayford Logan would lose heart when tasting the same bitter pill. As a senior at Williams College, Logan had viewed the war as an opening, a "far-flung front of democracy's battleline." In a speech to his graduating class, Logan anticipated that when the American soldier, "the black and the white," returned home from France, the nation might "raise her head even higher, unsullied, unblemished, untarnished" by adherence to white supremacy.[22] After graduating, he returned to his native Washington, D.C., and enlisted in the First Separate Battalion of the D.C. National Guard. His unit joined midwestern draftees and other Guard units from Ohio and New England to form the 372nd Infantry regiment of the 93rd Division. Logan felt sure he would rise to the top. Fancying himself a "soldier, statesman, and scholar"—as an older, angrier Logan ruefully recalled—the young man had believed the war could build fraternity among the most worthy men of the AEF, black or white.[23]

That dream of interracial fraternity died when Logan joined the 372nd Infantry. Logan considered himself a race leader, part of the "Talented

Tenth" of "exceptional men" that W. E. B Du Bois had singled out at the turn of the century as the potential saviors of "the Negro race."[24] However, in the Army, Logan's white commanding officer Colonel Glendie B. Young made it clear that he saw no worthy black men, only "god-damn black sons of bitches." Young expressed his reluctance to lead African Americans by treating them with the contempt he felt they deserved.[25] Unlike the graduates of Fort Des Moines who went on to serve as captains and lieutenants in the 92nd Division, the African American officers of the 93rd came from within the National Guard. Logan, who had trained as a junior cadet while in high school and done a brief stint in the Student Army Training Corps while at Williams College, rose quickly through the noncommissioned officer ranks. He received his commission in January 1918, after taking a qualifying exam that he dubbed "the most unfair examination I have ever taken," but the accomplishment afforded him no respect from his regiment's commanding officer.[26] During their April 1918 voyage across the ocean, Glendie Young destroyed a roster assigning cabins to all officers based solely on their rank and issued a revised one that gave white officers preferential treatment. Lieutenant Logan, who called the colonel an "s.o.b." when he referred to him politely, recollected that the African American officers consequently were "so cramped in quarters that they walked on trunks to move about the room."[27]

For Lieutenant Logan, whose upbringing in Washington, D.C., and academic accomplishments at Williams had left him confident that he was more of a gentleman than most of the white people he encountered, Jim Crow's daily assaults on his dignity proved almost unbearable.[28] Several days into the 372nd's voyage, Colonel Young ordered a group of African American soldiers to put on a show for the other passengers and instructed the rest of the black soldiers to preserve the same segregated seating during recreation that they did during meals. An incensed Logan responded by telling his fellow officers that any "damn fool" who attended the show and suffered the indignity of Young's order "ought to be hanged."[29] Logan had enlisted in the Army because he had "naively" taken "at face value" President Wilson's democratic rhetoric, but Colonel Young crushed his naiveté. The pettiness of Young's actions and the resulting absurdity of black officers' position in his unit offered up to Logan "a perfect example of the American democracy in war."[30] The swells across the Atlantic wrested Logan from his imaginary war. He surfaced to face the ugly realities of his service abroad.

Between Shores and States

Floating between shores and states, ships placed soldiers in interim spaces. As Rayford Logan began to cross the boundary from Talented Tenth patriotism to disaffected antinationalism at sea, so, too, did others begin to question their fixed identities, expectations, and self-conceptions. However, not everyone did so with the embittered assurance that graced Lieutenant Logan. For men like William Dyer and Henry Berry, who both sailed to Brest in summer 1918, the discomfort that nagged at them arose from the uncertainty of their positions. Departing on the *Covington* from Hoboken, New Jersey, Dyer watched the Statue of Liberty wave "a passing farewell" to his ship and the 5,000 soldiers on board. Once the ship lost sight of the coast, troops began grappling with a "semi-enthusiastic" feeling that Dyer described as being comprised "half of anxiety, half of dread." Unmoored, apprehensive, and Jim Crowed, they spent the evening "trying to console" themselves "with expressions of hopes for a bright future even though the beginning seemed" to them "quite dark."[31]

The normally upbeat Henry Berry registered the surreal quality of the Atlantic crossing. His journey from Virginia to France evoked for him "some great magnificent dream" in which the "astounding" persistently abutted the routine. On his boat, soldiers alternated between submarine drills and card games, gossip and training. Struggling to bring their minds "around to the realization of danger," they often treated the voyage "more like some gay picnic" than a passage to war.[32] Despite the surface gaiety, Berry noted that most men spent the bulk of their time "moodily gazing out over the sea, wondering how long" it would be before they once again saw land. Even Berry, who persisted in viewing his ship and the soldiers aboard it as embodying "the very might and power of America," could not fully shake a sense of dislocation and dread. He impatiently observed that, despite seemingly endless days at sea, his steamer never appeared to gain any ground, and he confessed himself unable to envision "what in the world" awaited him in France.[33] Surrounded by "eternal ocean," Berry and his shipmates felt so distant from any shore that some of them suspected that the ship was lost.[34] Only when they caught sight of the Brest harbor on the western tip of France did they regain their equanimity.

Ships detached black soldiers in the AEF from their landed identities and spurred an inchoate political reformation among many, but the process of politicization would continue in France. For black soldiers, ships were sites of anticipation and expectation—of becoming rather than being. To Lieutenant Osceola McKaine, the liminality experienced by his fellow African American soldiers at sea mirrored the double consciousness and dual sentiments experienced by blacks back home. According to McKaine, the "strange and perilous journey" undertaken by the 367th Infantry carried them away from "the terra firma . . . which they hated and loved" to "a strange, semi-mythical region" across the sea. France struck him as more ethereal than real, a "terrestrial heaven" where French "national idealism" freed African Americans from the sense that they were "an abnormality in the body" of civic life.[35]

A native of Sumter, South Carolina, Lieutenant McKaine had left his terra firma behind years before the volunteers and draftees who sailed to France alongside him. In 1908, at the age of sixteen, McKaine had harkened to a wanderlust that he self-consciously dubbed "the nomadic spirit of his migratory ancestors" and abandoned South Carolina to work as a stevedore aboard a merchant ship.[36] Reversing the forced journeys of his captive ancestors, he sailed from the southern Atlantic coast to the West Indies. He later made his way to Washington, D.C., and then on to Massachusetts where he studied at Boston's segregated Sumner High School and took courses at Boston College. In contrast to the celestial imagery he used to describe France, he referred to his migration from South Carolina as the "first chance" he had "to get out of the jungle."[37]

Staying out of the jungle meant going to the tropics. After a two-year stint working as a reporter for a Bookerite newspaper in Boston, he joined the 24th Infantry, lured by a veteran trooper whom he described as a "marvel" at recruiting.[38] McKaine shipped out to the Philippines in late 1914 and, alongside troopers who would later meet their fate in the Houston mutiny, earned accolades from Governor General Francis Burton for his part in the colonial occupation. McKaine and the 24th earned similar plaudits in subsequent service along the Mexico border where they guarded General Pershing and joined in the 1916 Punitive Expedition intended to rout Mexican revolutionary general Pancho Villa.[39] With the U.S. entry into the Great War, then-Corporal McKaine transferred out of the 24th and into the Officer's Training Camp. Upon receiving his commission, he joined the 367th Infantry of the 92nd Division. Unlike many of the northern draftees who made up the bulk of the enlisted men in the regiment, McKaine was a seasoned veteran with a record of international military service by the time war broke out.

He was also a practiced hand at presenting to a white public the most pa-triotic face of African American manhood. Like Ely Green or Henry Berry, Lieutenant McKaine saw martial service as an affirmation of that manhood. Moreover, he saw the centuries-old record of black fighting men as formative of "the Negro's . . . traditions, honor, and prestige."[40] Writing in the pages of a national weekly magazine while waiting to sail for France, McKaine traced black military contributions from Hannibal's victories over Rome, to freed-man Peter Salem's participation in the American Revolution, through Tous-saint L'Ouverture's besting of Napoleon, and on to the contribution of black regulars at San Juan Hill. He used a historical trajectory to invoke a "Negro" identity older and broader than America itself—while still emphasizing black men's foundational place in the American nation and their "blind, unswerv-ing, and undivided loyalty to the flag." At the same time, he cautioned that "the principles of democratic government" differed so greatly from the poli-cies of the "Democratic party" currently in power that black soldiers' will to fight might suffer. For the sake of morale and the war effort, McKaine appealed to white Americans to embrace the "esprit de corps" that made African American men good soldiers and solid citizens.[41]

To some extent, military esprit de corps worked. After checking in to a Red Cross hotel in Toul, France, a white Southerner, Corporal Clarence Trotti, fell asleep in his eight-man bunk. Looking over the next morning, Trotti wrote his nephew back in the United States, that he "saw a great big black negro sleeping along side of me." Sharing the bunk with the black sol-dier was "all right I suppose," he conceded, but he could only imagine "what would have occurred [sic]" if "a thing like that had happened in Atlanta or down South." Still, although Corporal Trotti accepted having a black bunk-mate in the topsy-turvy of wartime France, he later observed that other viola-tions of Jim Crow went too far. Complaining that too many French people welcomed African Americans on equal terms, Trotti warned folks back home that when black soldiers returned home, "we all are going to have trouble on our hands." He instructed his family to "get my two guns ready" because they would "come in handy" in settling down "Mr. Negro."[42]

Osceola McKaine celebrated the openness that threatened Clarence Trotti. In the United States, McKaine had to implore whites to think of Af-rican Americans as comrades, if not as brethren. In France, by contrast, he could argue that he felt "really free." Commenting on his regiment's "won-derful reception everywhere" they traveled throughout France, he wrote to

African American soldiers made welcome by French children. Kautz Family YMCA Archives, University of Minnesota Libraries.

white artist Orlando Rouland that for the first time he got to "taste real liberty," to enter unself-consciously into French people's "most intimate affections" and "in a phrase, 'to be a man.' "[43] Unlike his Philippines service where African American soldiers established their position in contrast and kinship with other people of color, service in France involved making war against white Germans, making friends with other white Frenchmen, and—although McKaine played down physical intimacy in his letter to Rouland—making love to white French women. Far more than when fighting for empire, fighting in France offered African Americans the opportunity to blur the boundaries so critical to maintaining white supremacy.

Indeed, the opportunity represented by France conceptually took on more importance than the actual social relations and political realities of the country. Even as they walked, fought, and died on French soil, black soldiers viewed the country through the obfuscating haze of their own experiences in the United States. For McKaine and countless other African Americans, "France" came to stand as America's promise fulfilled, a truer and more open democracy. Using language implicitly sexual and explicitly Biblical, McKaine painted France as the promised land. Black soldiers who landed there, he argued, felt as "Elijah must have" when he first "penetrated the inner portals of the heavenly gates."[44]

Henry Berry and William Dyer echoed Lieutenant McKaine's sense of awe over their new surroundings. Berry thought Brest, the Breton port town where he landed, a "rambling, strange-looking city" populated with even "stranger looking people." Although first struck by the traditional Breton dress and wooden clogs of its inhabitants, Berry could not help but also notice that most of the people he saw "were women and girls, old men and children."[45] In Brittany, devastated by war, few young men remained. William Dyer noticed it, too. The reverie that enveloped him as he passed through "the oldest and oddest" city that he had ever seen dissipated upon seeing the "sadness on the faces of the inhabitants."[46] Women working outside clad in mourning and children begging and performing for pennies drove home the toll—personal, economic, and demographic—exacted by four years of war.

Arrival at the barracks, after a three-mile hike down what an American visitor labeled "one of the bleakest roads in Brittany," offered an unwelcome distraction from previous sights; for conditions at Camp Pontanezen indicated that the war would exact a toll on American soldiers as well.[47] "Terrible

and dirty," the "horrid old" Pontanezen barracks retained an aura of the
prison camp it had once been under Napoleon.[48] Although the ground was
not nearly as treacherous as it would become several months later when the
mud would get knee high, as it had done—a reporter later noted in an exposé
of the camp's miserable conditions—every winter "since the days of the late
Charlemagne," it still caused problems.[49] Trying to pitch his tent on the rain-
saturated ground, Berry found himself stuck in a "slippery, soggy scene of
mud." Filthy, exhausted, and "to some extent disgusted," he found that his
enthusiasm for France had temporarily waned.[50]

Ely Green marked his landing at Brest as the moment when his "dreams"
of garnering a man's respect began to come true, but he observed also that
the barracks, located on more than six hundred acres of swampy land, seemed
more fit for animals than men. To Green, they resembled "barns, cold and
damp" and inhospitable. For all their talk of manhood and glory, the "first
night of warfare living" left the soldiers in Green's unit feeling "a bit blue."
The battalion's funk only deepened after the majority of them contracted
food poisoning from the canned salmon fed them their first few days ashore.[51]

Nevertheless, the shock of their initial encounter with French terra in-
firma would quickly give over to the excitement of new experiences. Of the
two million American troops who came to Europe either to fight or to toil,
750,000 passed through the camps at Brest, but for the majority of those
troops, the ports of entry functioned simply as gateways to the rest of the
country. Many black stevedore regiments stayed in Brest, but other labor
battalions joined a multiracial throng of workers in busy ports such as St.
Nazaire, Le Havre, Bordeaux, and Marseilles. Some of the labor battalions
headed inland, charged with building the infrastructure that carried mate-
riel from the ports to the front lines. The 365th, 366th, 367th, and 368th Infantry Regiments who made up the 92nd Division were sent off for further
combat training in the Haute Marne in northeastern France, while the National Guard units became the four regiments of the 93rd Division, the 369th
through the 372nd, and joined the French Army.

A Tough Deal

All the African American men who served in France engaged the war on different fronts, in different ways. Working on the docks in St. Nazaire, for example, Sergeant Ely Green would not run up against the same troubles that

weighed upon the combat officers who had graduated from Fort Des Moines and joined the 92nd Division. Likewise, Haywood Hall, who held no pretense of patriotism or aspiration to status, would sidestep the soul-crushing disillusion that nearly drove Rayford Logan mad. Yet for all their diversity of perspective and experience, these men's war stories contributed to a cohesive picture of the disaffection that would radicalize a generation of African American men.

Having made it to France, Ely Green repeated his vow to "be a man at any cost," and he would have stuck to his guns if anyone had proven willing to issue them to him.[52] Green tried in vain to receive a transfer to the infantry, but Judge Dunlap had used the long reach of his power and patronage to keep his favorite servant away from the front. More concerned with Green's physical safety than his quest for manhood, the Judge wanted to ensure that Green stayed out of harm's way even if it meant confining him to the service battalions. Denied entry into a combat division, Green became a noncommissioned officer in a company of stevedores in St. Nazaire. The exchange, Sergeant Green noted simply, "was a tough deal."[53]

For the duration of the war, the camps around St. Nazaire would set the boundaries of the lives of Ely Green and twenty thousand other black and white soldiers stationed there with the SOS. Like Brest to its north, St. Nazaire struck the African American troops as "odd but picturesque."[54] Nestled in the crook of the Atlantic coast and the Loire Rver, its narrow streets and clay houses, cafes and little shops made the town seem quintessentially French. However, the soldiers who passed through this second largest port of American embarkation found themselves in an environment dramatically transformed by the American presence.

St. Nazaire during the war grew into the "greatest freight port of the Expeditionary Forces."[55] In the process it became one part France and one part Old West. So many prostitutes descended on the city after the creation of the American camps that a local paper declared the town, "infested" with "women of loose morals."[56] American troops, delighted to find the wicked French women that reformers had warned them about, provided enough business to keep at least 300 brothels afloat. The paper decried the American-spurred boom, claiming that it put at risk "honest women" who had to endure the "filthy proposals" of overstimulated soldiers and innocent children who had to witness the scandalous behavior.[57] French observers noted that the American presence endangered the public in more direct ways as well. American troops—"Sammies," they were called—showed an unnerving fondness for firearms. Soldiers carried their pistols like playthings, brandishing them to threaten café owners and farmers or simply to startle passersby in the street. Even the military policemen, civilians complained, whipped out their guns "with excessive ease" whether they wanted to frighten a suspect, kill him, or simply signal for other MPs to come help.[58] The streets of St. Nazaire became an American playground, with many troops on their worst behavior.

Herded into camps surrounded by barbed wire, with passes into town "as hard to secure as American gold," African Americans in the SOS missed much of the frontier-style lawlessness that overwhelmed the city.[59] Moving in an orbit that circled from camp to dock with only an occasional foray into town, African Americans stationed at St. Nazaire engaged one another and their white fellow soldiers more than they did the civilians around them. Mostly, though, they just worked. Laborers in France found themselves in only marginally better conditions than the laborers they had left behind in Newport News. While the engineer battalions around them built the docks, railroads, roads, and warehouses that made up the infrastructure of the nine camps near St. Nazaire, black stevedores unloaded supplies.

Largely considered the dregs of the military forces—and in the case of black men, a servant class for white soldiers—laborers were driven to the brink of emotional and physical exhaustion. A sympathetic white captain in Bordeaux was appalled to realize that his company of black stevedores had received only two days off in six weeks, and that his men on the night shift had to work fourteen hours without food. When he protested on their behalf, he found that "the sentiment seemed to be everywhere that the men were 'only niggers.'"[60]

In both St. Nazaire and Brest, an investigator on conditions of black soldiers reported, "the hardest work on the docks was done by exclusively by black soldiers." Gangs of workers coaled ships and unloaded cargo, moving in one instance 30,000 tons of cargo in a day.[61] They put in sixteen-hour days and, Ely Green recalled, sometimes pulled twenty-four-hour shifts. They were "gluttons for work," white reporters wrote, "shuffling, grinning, happy-go-lucky" plantation Negroes too simple and sturdy to mind the effort.[62] German prisoners of war got right to the point, mocking the stevedores in Green's squad as "slaves" and noting in one instance that the Army had black soldiers toiling in the rain while the Germans stayed dry under tarps. When Sergeant Green tried to preserve morale among his bitter crew by reminding them that they were "fighting for democracy," one of his fellow noncoms shot back, "Dont you say a word about democracy. There isnt any dam democracy."[63]

Overworked and undersupplied, men found it hard to believe in Ely Green's or Woodrow Wilson's democracy. Despite occasional public focus on the "tremendous and unprecedented" scale of their work, black stevedores often toiled without proper clothing, equipment, or respect.[64] Working with troops in Young Men's Christian Association (YMCA) camps near St. Nazaire, Addie Hunton and Kathryn Johnson heard accounts of the first harsh winter, when black stevedores "plunged through the deep mud" on their way from camp without the oilskin boots issued to others. Once at the docks, they "handled the cold steel and iron without gloves."[65] The labor battalions' efforts, which appeared "superhuman" given the "constantly unfair attitude" displayed by their white officers, strengthened Hunton's and Johnson's conviction "that the colored man was in the war to justify his plea for democracy."[66] Looking around the camps at St. Nazaire, at the "cruel injustice" that was often black soldiers' recompense, the two women fumed at the sight of democracy denied. On the faces of soldiers who had once thought the war would bring opportunity, Hunton and Johnson saw only the stoic "endurance of an outraged manhood."[67] In St. Nazaire in the midst of war, democracy seemed as far off as New York or Ohio.

Ely Green clung to his faith in the meaning of military service, nevertheless, like a drowning man clutching a life preserver. Months after their arrival in France, Sergeant Green and his men still lacked basic supplies. As crew leader, he requested boots and gloves for his platoon, telling his captain that after ten straight days of rain, their hands had begun to bleed and that, while they were unloading a shipment of meat the night before, "we had to use our socks for gloves." When the captain dismissed him with vague promises and little concern, Green gritted his teeth and reminded himself that his allegiance lay with the uniform the officer wore, no matter how he felt about the man who wore it.[68]

Other black troops in the SOS struggled to balance loyalty and disillusion. James Crawley, a railroad worker from central Virginia who served near Brest, considered himself as "patriotic as any man" but described his overseas experience as "deplorable." As a member of the 538th Engineers, he had "worked all the time," yet he "felt as if my country did not appreciate my service as a true American." Although he continued to believe in "the principles for which we fought," he thought African Americans had given "all to gain for everyone except ourselves." For Crawley, the take-home message of his overseas service was not one of national identity or military affiliation. The Army "lack[ed] the true democratic spirit," he realized, but "God made all men to live on the earth dependent on each other" nevertheless.[69]

God might have made all men interdependent, but the Army made some more subject than others. Sergeant-Major Charles Williams traveled to Marseilles with the 811th Pioneer Infantry expecting the "good feeling of brotherhood and fair play" he had found at camps in England. Instead, he found "an intense race feeling" rampant "among our own Americans, supposed to be our comrades in arms." Williams tried to reassure readers of the *New York Age* that "even amid trying circumstances," most labor troops outwardly "remained loyal to the Stars and Stripes," but for many troops the encroachment of Jim Crow had drained that loyalty of any substantive meaning. While Williams expected "to note the growth of democracy in America" on his return to the United States, service abroad convinced other soldiers that white men would never share power willingly.[70] To Dean Mohr, a first sergeant in the 329th Service Battalion, it seemed instead that whenever white noncommissioned officers oversaw African American soldiers, they would "take more than their authority."[71] Military service did not offset racial hierarchies, it entrenched them.

Military service also made racial tensions worse. After five months in France, the men of the 506th Engineer Service Battalion stationed at Camp St. Sulpice near Bordeaux had begun to chafe "under the yokes of homesickness, racial propaganda, lack of incentive . . . and the woman question." By the time their chaplain E. M. M. Wright joined their unit, they had come to believe, as one black captain informed him, "that the only good white man is a dead one with the marble slab securely fastened."[72] Army authorities gleaned enough of African Americans' discontent to worry that "practically every member of the Negro labor battalions" who returned to the United States would have "secreted somewhere about their person" a "revolver" for use in the "race war" they believed was being fomented by African Americans at home. A white officer with the 112th Ammunitions heard similar rumors.[73] Upon returning home to Marietta, Georgia, he wrote to warn Military Intelligence that "the Pioneer Negro Infantry who were working in [the] salvage ammunition and small arms dumps were all in possession of Government automatic pistols or revolvers." He cautioned the authorities that "[p]ractically every man" had one.[74]

Although officers in the United States who oversaw black soldiers' return dismissed the idea that there was any "revolutionary spirit" among African American troops, labor troops did consider arming themselves for the ongoing conflicts in the American Army.[75] Back in St. Nazaire, the stevedores under Green's command felt that they needed weapons to protect themselves from white soldiers. While loading a hospital ship, the men of his company salvaged and hid seventy guns that they removed from packs left by soldiers killed at the front. When Green and a fellow sergeant learned of the stored weapons, they convinced their platoons to go out to the docks and drop the guns in the water—just hours, it turned out, before their company captain ordered a surprise search of their barracks. The men sang the hymn "I Couldn't Hear Nobody Pray" as they marched to the docks, with one of the sergeants belting the line, "the dungeon has shaken and the chains fell off" as they lowered the arms down to the water.[76]

Even without guns, Green's crew did not always settle for spiritual release. Following several instances of police brutality, including the shooting of one of their squad for crossing the street to approach a French prostitute, the men of Green's platoon eventually snapped. After a white marine guard drove a bayonet through an African American soldier who had tried to take a piece of candy from a broken crate, Green's men grabbed their cargo hooks and rushed to retaliate. The crew ignored Green's pleas to halt, stopping only when they realized that two squads of marines had their guns trained on them. Ironically, the captain of the marine guard had Green arrested, claiming that he had been "encouraging the niggers to attack the guards." Green went to the marine stockade where he watched white guards "torment" twenty-six prisoners, all African Americans who seemed either too young or too old for Army service, by beating them and forcing them to drink a vomitous combination of Epsom salts and castor oil. Although his company commander quickly arrived to secure his release, Green still weathered a cruel thrashing from the marines in charge of the stockade. Lying silently on the stockade floor after a guard threatened to "beat his brains out" with a rifle if he so much as made a sound, Green began "cursing the day" he "had thought of coming to France."[77]

Green's days too often passed like this, with mundane scenes turning violent and his mood oscillating between faith and despair. With his confidence in the democratic potential of the nation shaken, his old ideal of black manhood offered little comfort. The black troops of the Regular Army, whom he had lionized when he first met them in Houston before the war, turned out to be the terrors and bullies of the service units in St. Nazaire. Harder and more experienced, the Regulars transferred into the service battalions and took many of the top noncom spots. They had the favor of their white commanders and the run of the company. They treated the greener soldiers as if they were rookies, and those soldiers took to "honoring" them as if they were gods.[78]

In careers spent making war, the black Regulars had internalized the brutality, their manhood predicated on their ability to make violence. The day after his run-in with the white Marine guards, Green saw a black mess sergeant, formerly of the 10th Cavalry, commit an act as vicious as anything that had occurred in the stockade. In line for dinner, in front of Green and his men, the old soldier emptied his gun into a member of another company who had taken a loaf of bread without permission. As the dead soldier sat keeled over a mess table, the mess sergeant resumed his conversation with another black Regular as casually, Green noted in horror, "as if he had killed a cock roach." The second Regular instructed the other men in the mess hall to take the shooting as a warning "not to monkey with an old soldier." Looking directly at Green, he added, "there are several niggers in this company who should have gotten what that nigger got." The two black soldiers left confident that there would be no repercussions from white authorities.[79]

The experience with the Marines followed by the mess hall shooting underscored for Green the misery of the labor battalions' position. "The only difference in us and the men on the front is they die quickly," Green informed his outraged crew after the shooting. "We are dying slowly."[80] With the arbitrary enforcement of laws and regulations alongside "a triditional program" for controlling black laborers, the camps at St. Nazaire resembled "the black belt of the South," only with white northerners as hateful as any men found below the Mason Dixon line. As Green saw it, in an environment created and sustained by the white soldiers around them, the labor battalions occupied the status of "slaves."[81] The Regulars who had become their noncoms had found a way to maneuver in the confined space of the camps, but only by striding atop other black soldiers; they used the greener soldiers as counterpoint to their authority and their manhood. In the world constructed by the AEF in St. Nazaire, white supremacy not only shaped how black and white soldiers interacted, it also affected how African Americans treated one another.

As some of the lowest men in camp, Green worried that if members of his squad went into the stockade, nothing could guarantee that they would come out alive. For their own safety, he urged his company to obey all Army regulations. More than he had in the past, Green echoed his men's skepticism about talk of democracy. "I am not fighting for the Government men," he told them, "I am fighting for your and my servival."[82]

Survival meant weathering the Jim Crow Army with soul intact. It also meant reaching the end of the day in one piece; accidents on the docks frequently left men injured or killed, including a young sergeant that Green saw die when a hatch cover sliced him in half at the waist. Additionally, for Green, survival meant holding on to his sense of himself as a man so that he could continue to believe himself entitled to citizenship rights. He continued to believe that if they worked hard enough, if they overcame white soldiers' tendency to dismiss them as what the camp newspaper called "the ordinary run of colored labor," the men of the SOS could exchange accolades for recognition as American citizens.[83] He held fast to the belief that black men could be in a position to demand their rights, whether or not white Americans wanted to grant them. Sustaining that faith, cushioning it from the body blows of fellow soldiers intent on destroying it, also sustained the rest of his beliefs—in justice, in social change, and in God. Unlike his men, Green could not insulate himself with a steadying cynicism. The only alternative to his hope was nihilism.

Imagining France saved Green from despair. Enclosed in a Jim Crow "hell" in the American camps, Ely Green and other African Americans constructed the France outside of their camp as the promised land. On that truly foreign soil, "where free men lived and died," Green believed that there was none of the crippling prejudice that infected the camps at St. Nazaire.[84] To him, beyond the limits of the American camps lay Osceola McKaine's "terrestrial heaven." Others felt the same way. Marching through the French countryside, Henry Berry took a moment to appreciate that among the French he was "not a savage, not a mere educated dog, but a human being . . . having the right to live and be happy in the beautiful world."[85] The country was "too proud to be other than just" and "too liberty loving to deny freedom to even the darkest skin," black war correspondent Ralph Tyler rhapsodized. Establishments opened their doors to anyone who could pay and "deport themselves as people of culture."[86] Issuing a challenge to America upon his return from the war, a former Lieutenant declared in the pages of the socialist *Messenger* that "France has solved and exemplified" to African Americans "the world-long struggle for freedom."[87]

A World Ruled by White Americans

Even if France remained black Americans' grand illusion, they could never actually escape the hard reality of segregation. For men like Rayford Logan, raised on uplift and the doctrine of the Talented Tenth, the disjuncture between France's promise and America's betrayal produced a form of Jim Crow shell shock. Surrounded by white supremacists in the Army, Logan fought his own "private war" alongside the Great War, and he admitted later that even as a veteran he never grew able to discern what the war had done to his personality "or which war had done what."[88] As an officer "and a gentleman"—a point he stressed vigorously—Logan brooked no offense.[89] When he overheard some white officers in his quarters complaining that African American soldiers "were being 'spoiled' by the French people in general and French women in particular," he erupted. Logan waited long enough for one of them to vow to put African Americans "back in their place" when they all got back to the United States before he furiously entered the room and "cussed them out."[90] Logan also threw a book at a Red Cross nurse who shrieked when she found him in a hospital room, dressed down a white junior officer he overheard berating a black stevedore, and ordered the arrest of enlisted white men who refused to salute him in the street.[91] By the time he received his honorable discharge in Brest, Logan had grown exhausted from his arrow-backed defense of his status and uniform. His struggle against "discrimination, humiliation, embarrassment" ultimately left him convinced that he "hated white Americans." Having enlisted in 1917 flush with patriotic fervor, Logan refused in 1919 to consider leaving Europe for home.[92]

Some soldiers had never believed long enough to share Logan's or Green's crisis of faith. The men in Haywood Hall's unit fought because they were brave, because it was their job, or because survival required it. Even as they faced the Central Powers on the Western Front, they voiced what Hall dubbed the "now familiar" refrain: "what are we doing over here?" It was American "crackers," not Germans, that they "should be fighting."[93]

In Charles Houston's experience with the 92nd Division, it felt like black and white Americans *were* fighting each other and not the Germans. Houston spent the war in field artillery training at Camp de Meucon in Vannes, Brittany. There, German prisoners of war passed on the "propaganda" they had heard from their white guards: that the Fort Des Moines graduates "were an inferior grade of officer," that "white soldiers did not have to obey" them, and that they were in field artillery school "merely to learn how to take care of the equipment." Lieutenant Houston had gone into the Army with enough skepticism about Woodrow Wilson and European empire to know that the "war was just not [his] fight." He had joined to avoid the draft and because he believed that citizenship, having a "say about how [the] country was run," required "sharing every risk the country was exposed to." Even so, "the hate and scorn showered on" black officers by their "fellow Americans" further convinced Lieutenant Houston "there was no sense in my dying for a world ruled by them."[94]

African American soldiers could barely step outside the world ruled by white Americans, and encounters in France—with German prisoners, white nurses, or white soldiers—often underscored the evanescence of the terrestrial heaven. With its medieval spires and high stone walls, Vannes resembled something from a French storybook. For black officers, eager to learn French and willing to reach out to civilians, the picturesque coastal town came as a delight. Charles Houston and his friends got on well with the *Vannetais,* especially "the ladies of the town" who displayed "a keen interest" in the young officers. But within weeks of the Des Moines graduates' arrival, "American race prejudice had got itself organized" to end their Breton idyll. Segregation signs went up in dining rooms, and black officers were shunted to the worst corners of the American officers' hotel. White officers warned hotel maids that black soldiers would likely try to assault them and that white men would protect them as they did women in the United States. Such claims "fell on deaf ears," Houston found; he and his friends continued building relationships with Vannes shopkeepers, families, and young women even as they moved warily around white Americans.[95]

As segregationists faltered in attempts to inculcate foreigners with the American strain of white supremacy, they strove even harder to remind soldiers that black men's place remained fixed no matter where they traveled. In Vannes one Saturday night after the Armistice, white soldiers' disapproval of interracial liaisons hardened into rage and then erupted into a near riot. Houston termed it a near lynching. He had gone out with three other officers and bumped into a pair of French "sporting girls," camp followers, who had become the "special pets" of two white captains from the American Army. The women flirted enough with Houston's friends to incense the white captains, who called in a "mob" of officers and enlisted men to put the black officers "back in their places."[96]

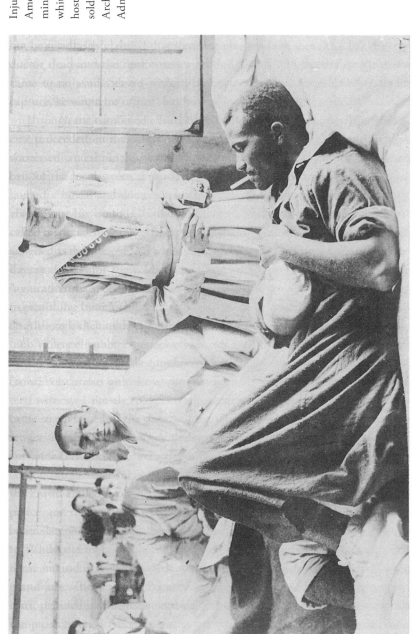

Injured African American receiving ministrations from white nurse and hostility from fellow soldiers. National Archives and Records Administration.

No townspeople stood in the plaza where the mob had gathered. They "were all locked down in their houses" where they retreated when American soldiers took over their streets. The four black officers faced enlisted men "milling around" and an officer "yelping" about " 'niggers' forgetting themselves just because they had a uniform on." The four men countered that they "had done as much for America as anybody" and challenged the white officers in the group to come forward and fight like men. Houston did not feel too frightened; he figured the enlisted men would not risk hitting a superior officer, even a black one, and he felt sure his group could take the officer in a fair fight. All the same, he found the whole situation "messy." At one point, a French guard squad appeared in the plaza, and Houston hoped they would be "the answer" to his predicament. When the French squad cut right through the crowd "oblivious" or indifferent to the Americans' fight, he "had a feeling of being deserted by friends."[97]

French friends could not save black soldiers from the violence that undergirded Jim Crow. Eventually the captain of the military police came and broke up Charles Houston's confrontation in the Vannes plaza, but conflicts continued between the black and white soldiers until his group rejoined their division and left for home.[98] South of Vannes in Brest, a black sergeant from Kentucky got a bottle smashed over his head for venturing into a café that white soldiers had declared segregated space. The soldier, Sergeant William Cox, had frequented the café enough to know the proprietor "well," and he continued toward the counter even after the white men had ordered him out. "I have as much right to be here as you have," Cox stated right before white soldiers struck him. Either during the altercation or after, two of the white men were shot, and while the Army did nothing about the bottle attack, it charged Cox, who maintained his innocence, with assault and battery with intent to kill. Cox found the "environments of the army" so "bad that it is almost impossible to keep straight." American "Anglo-Saxons" were "trying to start segregation and prejudice in this far away land," he wrote home to his family, noting that officers called him "all kinds of 'Niggers' " as they investigated the fight.[99]

As chilling as black soldiers found physical attacks in the Army, they found the legal structure that bolstered Jim Crow even more disheartening. Sergeant Cox begged his father to pray for him as he awaited court martial, since they both knew how African Americans suffered when they "face[d] the court all on one side."[100] Ely Green knew that suffering, too. He warned his men in St. Nazaire to steer clear of the stockade because the "brutish wolves" who guarded it would torture black stevedores to secure racial control. Green and his squad were, practically speaking, "in a helpless position."[101] Haywood Hall's brother Otto bounced from guard house to guard house while serving with labor battalions in St. Nazaire and Le Mans. Haywood described Otto's guards as "sadistic" and his brother as "bitter and disillusioned."[102] Guards did not reserve all their abuse for black soldiers—white veterans told plenty of tales of beatings inside the stockade—but the systematic blurring of legal and extralegal violence bound African Americans more deliberately.[103]

Lynching offered the most graphic reminder that Jim Crow trailed black soldiers in France. Veterans traded accounts of what they had seen: decomposing black bodies with nooses still on them dug up by the Graves registry; mutilated black bodies in St. Nazaire, identified only as victims of "the nigger killer"; pleading men begging for their lives when white engineers sought vengeance for a riot in Gièvres.[104] Senior Army officials denied most allegations of lynchings, but soldiers held fast to their claims. The terror did its work under the cover of official denials.

Legal executions, those hangings that came after a trial, still had a vicious and demonstrative edge. Haywood Hall's unit walked into the lingering shadow of a hanging in the Lorraine village, but other African American soldiers witnessed hangings more directly. A chaplain with the 356th Engineers recounted to a black YMCA worker in St. Sulpice details of the execution of a "green country boy" for attempted assault on an elderly French woman. The soldier, a nineteen-year-old South Carolinian, spoke no French but wanted to pay the woman to have sex with him. When "the woman accepted his money," the chaplain explained, "he thought this opened the way for him." They boy "never should have been hanged," the chaplain felt. In contrast, the chaplain recounted another tale where a white soldier in the camp committed rape but only received twelve years. In another case, the Army tried to pin rape of a nine-year-old girl on "some light colored" African American even though a French witness identified the suspect as a white marine.[105]

Lieutenant William Dyer also attested to the travesty of Army justice. During the last month of the fighting, Dyer had come to run an infirmary in the "dreary little village" of Belleville. Tucked in a valley with hills all around, Belleville sat within shooting distance of Belgium and Germany and just past French villages already abandoned to the war. Dyer worked amidst desolation—fending off the flu in the face of "constant cold and rainy weather" during the day and staying up listening to air raids and artillery fire at night. Yet, for all the devastation around him, the most "terrible" thing that he named in Belleville was the hanging of an African American soldier in an open field near his building. The soldier had been convicted of a grim deed, raping a sixty-year-old French woman, but Dyer considered the order "so openly and poorly carried out that it was rightly termed a lynching."[106] Between illness and accident, Dyer and his fellows doctor would see countless more deaths, all "pitiful" and tragic, but it was the soldier's execution, they felt, that most "dampened our ambitions."[107] Dyer found, as had Ely Green and Charles Houston, that for all its supposed grandeur and ghastliness, the violence that characterized the Great War could be eclipsed by the prosaic devastations of Jim Crow.

African American soldiers navigated the porous borders between the front and the homefront, the foreign and the domestic. If white supremacy acted as a form of gridding—creating spaces within spaces—in the AEF, then both black and white soldiers used French streets to test the boundaries of those spaces. That constant friction would embitter many African American men and harden others. It would force them either to clutch their sense of nationalism even more desperately, as Ely Green did, or to abandon it, as Rayford Logan seemed to. Such friction would also move them to find validation and elaboration of their manhood in other quarters—in French homes and French arms—but it would never be enough. Freedom in the United States could not come through the French imaginary.

Still, serving overseas offered its own kind of grace. It gave black soldiers "the world's experience," as the aptly named Christopher Columbus Watts explained upon coming home to Virginia with a medal from the French Army and a disability from gas attacks on the Western Front. Watts felt certain that "the Negro deserve[d] much different" than what he had received from America, but he did not regret volunteering. Somehow, in the midst of his travails, he managed to glimpse the world.[108]

Fighting Jim Crow could only obscure, not occlude, the world that existed beyond the bounds of American military life. African American soldiers' ordeals and expectations mediated their encounter with France, but encounter it they nevertheless did. Even as the war amplified American and African American nationalism, the interactions among African Americans, Europeans, and French colonials would begin to spawn a new, more international consciousness. Freedom struggles in the months after the Armistice would demonstrate the developing ways in which African American soldiers viewed themselves in relation to other broader communities of color. With changes wrought by World War I, internationalism—or, more in the case of many black soldiers, particular forms of internationalized nationalism—would cease to be the provenance simply of intellectuals. As President Wilson arrived in France to secure international peace on American terms, African Americans sought to use the world stage to secure freedom in America.

5

The World's Experience

Sergeant Christopher Columbus Watts had called it "the world's experience," the privilege of seeing beyond the insistent borders of the United
States. His fellow Virginian, James Royal Steptoe, articulated the same sense
of discovery. Steptoe had traveled from his home in the Shenandoah Valley to
fight with the 367th Infantry on the Western Front. A barber by trade before
and after the war, Steptoe came back feeling weaker in body but "broader" in
mind. While other soldiers documented the insults and injuries of fighting
Jim Crow abroad, Steptoe proclaimed his overseas service "the greatest experience" he would "ever have."[1]

In Europe, African Americans sat nested between international visions
and domestic ambitions. If toiling in St. Nazaire forced Ely Green to refract
notions of manhood and citizenship through the prism of a Jim Crow army,
for example, then it also enabled him to refine those notions through limited
interactions with both white Europeans and foreign people of color. During
a shift spent unloading a meat ship just two days before the November 1918
Armistice, Ely Green struck up a conversation with the boat's Belgian captain. He had sought out the captain because a fellow stevedore had advised
him always to meet the commander of any ship he worked; they could

benefit from ship captains' worldliness, Green and his friend figured, because "all men that went from country to country had to be smart."[2] With a bottle of wine as a way of introduction, Green sat down with the Belgian sailor.

Green got an earful in his conversation with the man he referred to as "The Captain of the Belgium Flag" who mistook the light-skinned Green for a white American. After raising a toast to the Armistice that he assured Green was but days away, the Belgian proceeded to give the American soldier his analysis of wartime and postwar politics. In the course of their one-hour conversation, the captain decried American economic imperialism, fretting that European nations would "be obligated to Wall Street for the next quarter of a century." He derided Woodrow Wilson's vaunted statesmanship and anticipated that Wilson's proposed League of Nations would fail "to have any effect on wars," spurred as world conflict was by "greed." Arguing that the United States had entered the war "strictly for political and financial gain," the captain likened Wilsonian "propaganda" to the story of "Little Red Riding Hood": after Europeans witnessed the spread of segregation to French soil in the summer of 1918, they had begun to discern "what big ears Grandma has, and what sharp teeth."[3]

To the Belgian captain, the evangelical American gospel of "democracy and humanitarian relief" rang false. "You Americans," he told his assumedly white drinking companion, aimed "to enforce white supremacy and dominate where you can with financial force." The captain saw the two things, white supremacy and financial force, as interrelated. Though more self-consciously radical than Green, his ideas resonated with the stevedore's own belief that Jim Crow kept down poor whites—who Green had once described as being enslaved to that "propaganda word 'white supremacy'"—as much as it did black people. Stating it more materially, the captain argued that the American government, through law and economics, had made "free slaves" out of African Americans to "control the wage scale of the white layman." When a dubious Green asked him how he knew so much about American law and labor, the captain responded, "Hell, I lived there six years." He had toiled as a machinist in Terre Haute, Indiana, and in steel mills in Pittsburgh, Pennsylvania, and he counted himself a proud member of the Industrial Workers of the World (IWW). Working the docks in France, Green had befriended a Wobbly.[4]

More than merely a haven for black soldiers bruised by Jim Crow, France supplied a field of encounter for African Americans curious about the world beyond Waxahachie or Washington. St. Nazaire exposed stevedores to more than hardship or heartache; there, a Texas chauffeur could break bread with a roving anarcho-syndicalist. Likewise in Bordeaux, African Americans weathered the frustrations and humiliations that Rayford Logan so relentlessly recorded in his diaries; but as Addie Hunton observed, the city also teemed with "Colonial troops, Chinese laborers" and "maimed French soldiers."[5] And on the Mediterranean coast in cosmopolitan Marseilles, Lieutenant William Dyer noted the legions of people from all over the world. Dyer did not connect with the Algerians, "many of whom were black as tar," or the "Hindus" whom he found "queer-looking," but alongside them he formed part of the "great conglomeration of the races" gathered in the port.[6] Black soldiers could not break out of the orbit of the American enclaves in France, but they nonetheless moved within a larger universe.

That expanded universe held emancipatory promise, not only for soldiers but also for the civilian activists who mobilized around them. Racial reformers endeavored to harness the broader minds black soldiers gained abroad to the task of combating white supremacy at home. Activists looked to the world both as a site of black soldiers' political transformation and as a stage for garnering international support; and they strove for solidarity with global communities of color while simultaneously focusing on the national frame of citizenship rights. Like the soldiers that they viewed as emissaries for them all, race reformers navigated the mixed terrain between the local and the global. Even as they took up the language of Wilsonian internationalism, revamping and reinvigorating it to make it their own, black civilians had their mind set on freedom in the United States.

In the opening months of 1919, amidst the clamor and celebrations marking the peace talks in Paris, African Americans of all sorts and backgrounds strove to represent themselves as central to any understanding of America and its democratic possibilities. Their efforts took many forms, some more overtly political than others. Through venues such as the Pan-African Congress, activists like W. E. B. Du Bois would work to articulate an expansive black internationalism that challenged President Woodrow Wilson's myopic view of democracy and self-determination. Claiming soldiers' experiences as their own, Du Bois and other reformers moved to construct a unified front, not only as one of many suffering and subjugated peoples but also as a vanguard agitating for real democracy.

In many ways, high political activists were staking a one-way claim, one that did not always elicit an amen from their rhetorical allies. In their haste to challenge President Wilson, African American protestors often spoke for Africa in the abstract without invoking or envisioning actual Africans. Their diasporic consciousness, nascent but not fully developed, oriented them toward the continent, but they saw it through the haze of their own domestic needs. Similarly, racial activists linked themselves to black soldiers in the months after the Armistice in order to strengthen their claims for belonging and civil rights. However, African American soldiers themselves—for whom the war had confounded their nationalism and wounded their patriotism—did not immediately reimagine themselves as citizens of the world or unabashedly embrace civilians' agendas for domestic reform.

Soldiers' responses came gradually and in a variety of ways. The dark absurdity of fighting a war for democracy in a Jim Crow Army yoked black soldiers to a citizenship bereft of much meaning. For some, like Rayford Logan, the disillusion would drive them out of the United States and into the cosmopolitan racial conglomeration of postwar Europe. Others returned, but with a burning resentment that would eventually flare into outright rebellion. Tacking between the local and the global, African American troops had to define their relationship to home: to the black communities they represented that celebrated them, to the country they served that rebuffed them, and to the wider world they inhabited that contained them. For black soldiers and their civilian allies, the process of social learning—of seeing the intransigence of American white supremacy, rethinking their relationship to the nation, and laying strategies to reform the state—reshaped their freedom struggle in the wake of World War I.[7]

All Over But the Shouting

President Wilson's quest for a peace that could, as he pledged, "lay the foundations for the freedom and happiness" of the world's "many peoples" set the stage for mass agitation in the wake of the Armistice. Wilson arrived in Brest a hero to the thousands who gathered to hear his words. The Fourteen Points Plan he had unveiled in the U.S. Congress promised to bring world peace by enforcing justice, and the crowds who greeted him in December 1918 hailed the American president as "The Champion of the Rights of Man."[8] Wilson had reached what one scholar would later dub his "apotheosis."[9] Not only in

Europe but in colonized territories in Asia and North Africa, people took Wilson's proclamation that national self-determination was "an imperative principal of action" as indication of his kindred spirit.[10]

Colonialism, especially in Africa, would test the limits of Woodrow Wilson's kinship. The French had turned to African colonization after their 1871 defeat in the Franco-Prussian war, licking their national wounds by seizing large swaths of territory across western Africa. "God offers Africa to Europe," author Victor Hugo asserted in urging his fellow Frenchmen to add to holdings in Senegal and Algeria, "Take it . . . and at the same time solve your own social questions!" To his own rhetorical question "From whom" was the land being taken, Hugo responded, "From no one!" Britain and the newly unified states of Germany and Italy also joined what came to be known as "the scramble for Africa" and invoked the civilizing mission to justify their jockeying for international stature and the continent's vast mineral resources.[11]

Western European powers met at a conference in Berlin in 1884 to establish spheres of influence, hastening Africa's partition. By 1914, France had grabbed land from North Africa through present-day Mali and into the center of the continent. Britain held large swaths of eastern and southern Africa in addition to outposts on the former Gold Coast. German-held territory included most of present-day Rwanda, Burundi, and Tanzania in eastern Africa, as well as present-day Namibia and Cameroon in the west. Belgium's King Leopold oversaw a notoriously brutal regime in the Congo while Italy claimed Eritrea, Somalia, and Libya. Playing out their national rivalries on African soil, European countries had wrested almost the entire continent from the nobodies, in Hugo's formulation, who lived there. Only Ethiopia and Liberia remained independent.[12]

Africa lay at the heart of the World War, Du Bois had started arguing back in 1915, and it needed to figure in the making of the peace. Competition for colonies had fed the secret treaties and open animosities that sparked the war, and as the conflict ground on, colonialists in Britain and France made clear that they intended to keep Germany's colonies upon victory. However, Woodrow Wilson had pledged to seek a magnanimous "peace without victory," and if he were to hold true to the principles of self-determination that had won him such acclaim, then he would have to challenge the British and French plans for Africa. To hold true, he would need to lead his imperial allies in seeing the Masai in German East Africa as equally deserving of the right to choose their own course as the Slavs of Europe's fallen Austro-Hungarian empire.[13]

To African American activists, who understood the limits that white supremacy placed on Wilsonian internationalism, this seemed unlikely. "The
danger to the Negro lies in the fact that the southern point of view will be put
forward at the peace table," AME minister and former Shorter College president William Byrd wrote in the pages of the black paper, the *Cleveland Gazette,*
"and not the point of view of the real square American." Byrd had arrived at
Shorter in 1914, eight years after the race riot that had terrorized Kathryn Johnson, but he had spent the previous seventeen years in Georgia watching white
supremacy consolidate, strengthen, and expand from its base in the Deep
South. Likening the rule of Jim Crow to the "revolting" abuses of "King Leopold toward the African colonies of Belgium," Byrd argued that African
Americans—the lone "real square" Americans—needed to descend upon Paris
with "vigorous and effective propaganda" to "carry out the essence of real democracy." The United States, Southernized by the Wilson administration and
as much a "culprit" in "ill-treating her peoples" as any colonial power, could
not negotiate a just peace without black intervention.[14]

Reverend Byrd and other African Americans saw as much threat as promise
in the spread of Wilsonianism. Attentive to the President's flowery rhetoric of
"new foundations of justice and fair dealing" but suffering under the thorny
realities of his administration's demonstrated commitment to white supremacy,
many African Americans viewed Wilson's formulation of a new, democratic
world order as corrupted.[15] Acidly noting that the President's "conception of
democracy" did not "extend beyond a *scheme* of government," and that he was
"pitiably clannishly [*sic*] ethnologically," black Missourian George Vashon expressed doubt in a December 1918 letter to W. E. B. Du Bois that any "actual
contribution to democracy can come to this nation from Versailles."[16]

The son of a leading clubwoman and an abolitionist lawyer and, according
to Kathryn Johnson, one of the National Association for the Advancement of
Colored People's (NAACP) most "ardent campaigners," Vashon believed that
African Americans could do a better job than Wilson of propagating world
democracy. He encouraged the *Crisis* editor in his plan to convene in Paris a
Pan-African Congress that would coincide with the peace talks. By Du Bois's
reckoning, pan-Africanism could offer an alternative to the stunted self-
determination that Wilson meant only for parts of Europe. Vashon saw an
even more immediate use of the Pan-African Congress: black activists could
take the opportunity to shame the President before the world. America's "national hypocrisy must be so vividly exhibited in France that its reflection here

will compel reform," Vashon urged. Otherwise, he wrote, explicitly linking domestic reform to black soldiers' labors, "our sacrifices in war will be fruitless." If black people wanted to secure their rights, they would have to "so impress the assembly of peace makers that" the United States delegation would be "forced to make confessions and concessions" in response to the pressure.[17]

Civil rights organizations expressed a similar determination to wrest the rhetoric of democracy and self-determination away from their President. During the National Race Congress that met in Washington, D.C., in December 1918, antilynching reformer Ida B. Wells-Barnett invoked the hanging of the Houston mutineers to discredit Woodrow Wilson.[18] Wells-Barnett and the members of the National Equal Rights League (NERL) who had convened the Congress decried the perpetuation of a "race autocracy" in the United States that stripped black people of "every civil, political, social, and judicial right." To follow the National Race Congress, they announced their intent to call a National Colored Congress for World Democracy. Like Du Bois's Pan-African Congress, NERL's National Colored Congress would take place in Paris. As conceived by newspaper editor Monroe Trotter, the all-black organization's fiery chair, the National Colored Congress would "make good the promise of the victors in the world war" by petitioning for "the discontinuance of color proscriptions, and all distinctions based on color, civic, political, and judicial IN EVERY NATION." Without a commitment to universal equality written into the peace accords, the members of the NERL argued, there could be no "dawning of a new day of democracy, nor of a new era of permanent peace."[19]

The League of Nations, the international association at the heart of Wilson's Fourteen Points Plan, laid out for black activists an avenue for reform. Jim Crow, along with "every denial of justice, humanity, and democracy" anywhere, had become "a matter for CORRECTION AND ABROGATION ON A WORLD BASIS BY A WORLD COURT," the members of NERL argued, and they hoped to make the League the authority that oversaw the correction.[20] During the war, African Americans had fought to upend white supremacy and alter the political landscape of the United States in Houston, as well as in extraterritorial spaces like Bordeaux and St. Nazaire. With the war ending and all eyes on Paris, African American rights groups wanted those contests over citizenship and access, entitlement and manhood to take place before a world audience. Having come through what Howard University dean Kelly Miller would soon label a "World War for Human Rights," they pushed to have American white supremacy considered an international injustice.[21]

Indeed, so many delegations, both elected and self-appointed, made plans to descend upon the peace deliberations in Paris in early 1919 that even some African Americans began to express consternation. George Vashon fretted to Du Bois that the "wisdom" of his Pan-African Congress might drown in the "deluge of blatant Negro ignorance" poised to flood France. "Is there anything we can do," Vashon asked Du Bois, "to check this promiscuous hegira?"[22] In print, writers for the *New York Age* announced that African Americans were "making themselves ridiculous" by agitating for representation in the Paris talks. Arguing that deliberations in the peace conference should best be left to actual diplomats, the *Age* correspondent excoriated preachers who, like William Byrd, misused "their pulpits to inflame well-meaning members of the race" by "vilifying and misrepresenting" the conference. While the writers supported black agitation within the limits of the Pan-African Congress, they thought that going any further constituted nothing but self-aggrandizement.[23]

Yet, the promiscuous hegira could not be checked by the counsel of a conservative few. Just as nationalist anticolonials had appropriated Woodrow Wilson's rhetoric and suffused it with democratic potential far more expansive than the President himself could imagine, so too did everyday African Americans broaden the notion of representation beyond select members of the Talented Tenth. The most populist reformers wanted was a "goodly number" of the race shouting loud enough—as Boston minister William Reed anticipated—to "make a lasting impression."[24]

Not content to leave the struggle to War Department advisor Emmett Scott, or even in the busy hands of Du Bois alone, black Americans opted "to choose their own" voices for the Paris talks.[25] As early as January 1918, A. Philip Randolph and Chandler Owen at the *Messenger* had advocated sending "Negro delegates to the peace conference" when the time came, and "to send men who are acquainted with the problems which the peace delegates will be called upon to settle." For socialists Randolph and Owen, this meant people—"men" specifically—who understood the roots of the war in "economic greed and national imperialism." After the Armistice, Randolph served as secretary of the short-lived International League for Darker Peoples dedicated to "the realization of common interests on the part of the darker peoples" against a "common evil," imperialism and white supremacy.[26] For Marcus Garvey, founder of the Universal Negro Improvement Association

(UNIA), the ideal representatives would be committed black nationalists who could ensure that "the Negro" take "proper steps to make his power felt" abroad. Chandler and Owen's working-class cosmopolitanism placed them more in line with Ely Green's Belgian Wobbly than with the UNIA and its dream of a black "Racial Empire" unfettered by white Europeans. But they all imagined a space in Paris to challenge Woodrow Wilson.[27]

Despite their droves and determination, however, African American activists would meet with only limited success in getting to France and, once there, getting their voices heard. Stonewalled by government officials unwilling to grant passports to folks they considered "more or less agitators," African Americans found themselves in a position similar to Vietnamese, Egyptian, and other people of color who attempted to journey to Paris to bend Wilson's ear: they seemed to be shouting into the wind.[28] Nevertheless African American advocates of self-determination and colonized racial subjects who agitated alongside them saw a value in the shouting, whether in Paris or in places closer to home. For them, representation bespoke more than a presence at the peace table; it signified a resolve to demonstrate their commitment to democracy, to "simple justice" as Reverend William Reed put it, to settling the race question both national and international.[29] If African American intellectuals had long considered their domestic struggle against white supremacy to be "but a local phase of a world problem," as Du Bois had declared in the wake of the Atlanta race riots in 1906, then in the postwar period, more African Americans had begun to imagine a new phase in which the world held the solution for their domestic dilemmas.[30]

The Difficulties of Double Consciousness

The high political activists who invoked black soldiers' wartime service moved forward with a clarity that many soldiers themselves lacked. As reformers rushed to represent African Americans *before* the world, black soldiers endeavored to figure what it meant to be *in* the world. They struggled to contend with their world's experience. At the same time, members of the Wilson administration, and the African American voices who spoke on its behalf, sought to cast those experiences in a nonthreatening light. They worked to constrain the world's experience.

Part of the question lay in how black soldiers would fold those experiences into their understanding of themselves as American. Robert Russa Moton,

Booker T. Washington's successor as head of Tuskegee, sailed to France in December 1918 at the behest of President Wilson and Secretary of War Newton Baker to settle that question. Covering one thousand miles on a speaking tour that took him from Brittany to Lorraine, he was both to investigate "conditions affecting Negro soldiers" and to offer "encouraging" words to soldiers in Brest, St. Nazaire, Bordeaux, and Gievres.[31] To Moton, the most notable product of his trip would be his campaign to squelch what he called "the whispering gallery," rumors propagated by racist white commanders of black soldiers' failure on the battlefield and allegations of widespread assaults and rapes of white women.[32] To Moton's many detractors, his most infamous action would be the speeches he gave to African American troops instructing them, as black war correspondent Ralph Tyler saw it, to "come back with your tail between your legs."[33]

Moton sought to domesticate black martial manhood—to reassure white Americans and notify African Americans that the war had not changed anything or anyone. After assuring African American soldiers that they would return home "heroes," the Tuskegee principal invoked a model of manhood already on the wane. He advised black troops to conduct themselves in a "modest, manly way"—to "find a job" and find a wife, to "marry and settle down."[34] Their new "more severe and important battle" was "not against Germans," Moton told his audiences. Rather, they had to expunge the effects of their overseas service and wage an "individual, personal battle—a battle for self-control, against shiftlessness, laziness, and willfulness." Moton urged his listeners not to let French social latitude—what Haywood Hall wistfully remembered as "the spell of freedom from racism"—go to their heads.[35] According to Moton, their "self-control" should commence in France. As they waited to demobilize, black troops needed to "leave such a reputation as to constrain our Allies, who have watched as with interest, to say forever that the American Negro will always be welcome not only because of his courage but because of his character."[36]

The most disaffected soldiers had little use for Moton's speeches. Lieutenant William Colson, a graduate of Virginia Union University and veteran of the 367th Infantry, claimed that Moton's attempt to "palliate the unrest among the soldiers and prepare them for homecoming" did "more harm than good." Having glimpsed the outlines of a "new politics" while in France, Colson anticipated that few African American veterans would prove willing to follow meekly the Tuskegee path.[37] Listening to Moton give his speech in St. Nazaire, Ely Green felt "so bitter" at hearing him speak of the "Negro"—a word he considered barely better than a racial epithet—that he called out, "Why in the hell did President Wilson send you over here to tell us how he honors the Negro?" On French soil, African Americans were "represented as black men," Green shouted. Moton could take his servile language "back to the States" and teach it "to the Halleluia Negro that dont know any better."[38]

The break between the modest Hallelujah Negro and the restive New Negro (or, in Green's case, the New Black Man) was not as clean as Colson and Green might have wanted. Black soldiers like those in Green's crew wrestled with their belief in Moton as "a smart man and a great leader" even as they derided Green's one-man campaign for civil rights. After a particularly spiteful encounter where a white officer from Georgia drowned his crew's pet dog and warned that the Klan had the same in store for black stevedores who forgot their place, one of Green's men taunted, "Is this the Democracy you have been preaching about?" Green retorted, "No, it is that nigger that Doctor Moton was telling you about that the white people was so proud of." A new politics could only come to those men willing to "rebuke" the terms and teachings of white supremacy. For most soldiers, that process of unlearning would happen in fits and starts.[39]

Self-making and social learning incorporated a broad spectrum of responses to the disjunction between a war for democracy and a Jim Crow army. Sergeant Green and Lieutenant Colson, along with other soldiers such as Rayford Logan, exemplified distinct strains of those responses. They developed along different trajectories, but Ely Green's willful nationalism grew out of his past ambitions and present circumstances as surely as did Rayford Logan's wounded cosmopolitanism. Other African Americans would go through the same processes in their own ways. Rethinking the parameters of their identity, as national subjects and citizens of the world, black soldiers reevaluated uplift strategies of earned citizenship and rearticulated the meaning and draw of home.

Old ties did not completely unravel. Ely Green, who had drunk the wine of the world with a Wobbly, would never embrace the radical internationalism of his new acquaintance. Although he agreed with many of the Belgian's critiques, Green did not initially like him: he considered him "too much of a hypothetical character," and he "resented" his "appraisal of the U.S." Having clung to a steadfast nationalism to brace himself against the daily disillusions of his military service, Green took on the United States' faults, successes, missteps, and motives as his own.[40]

Only after the captain offered a solution for stemming the rising tide of whiteness did Green begin to check his skepticism. Because "the U.S." had "placed their Government on trial to the world" by becoming the voice of democracy and self-determination, the Belgian called upon African Americans to use the war as leverage. If "these Negros would demand the U.S. Government to discharge them as black men of the flag," he told Green, they "would help all of the laboring classes." As the captain saw it, the problem for all workers was that Jim Crow kept the African American from being "a man" and "a citizen of the U.S."[41] Establishing black civic manhood would free black men from segregation and white working men from their devil's compact with white supremacy.

Manhood served as their shared idiom. Green heard in the captain's words an echo of his own resolutions to gain rights and respect through service, and he responded with tears of joy. He finally explained to the captain that he was "not a white man." But he also added that he was "not a Negro." Rather, he declared, "I am a black man to the French flag at present." His time in France had convinced him to escape his racial two-ness by doubling up on his national affiliations. He had "come to France to earn" his "citizernship to the U.S. Government" and ended up "serving over here a man to the French flag."[42] During his lowest moments, the biracial heritage that made him both races and neither to his fellow soldiers left him feeling that he "had been a misplace" in the world since "the beginning."[43] Yet, within his French imaginary, Green could claim multiple homes.

Green's vision had panned wide, creating in him a form of nationalism that was nestled in a broader world citizenship. Just as he long had claimed that he was both "a Texas man" and a citizen to the U.S. flag, he could now imagine himself both an American and "a black man to the respect of all flags of the world." As their conversation drew to a close, Green told the Belgian that when he got back to the United States, he planned to "live the rest of [his] life as a black man to both flags," France's and America's, even if it put him at odds with Jim Crow. "I may not live long in this attempt," Green told the captain, "but I am sure going to try."[44]

Ely Green's orientation was less cosmopolitan than it was multiple.[45] As his conversation with the Wobbly sailor indicated, he insisted on speaking of the people he met in France through the shorthand of their national (and gendered) signifiers; thus, the cargo ship's captain was a man "to the Belgium flag," even though he had traveled the world, spoke seven languages, and had lived for years in the United States. And when Green envisioned his own emancipation from his status as a "Negro slave," he saw it coming via a country-by-country recognition of his manhood and American citizenship, not through a unifying cosmopolitanism that cast him as a citizen of the world. Reaching out to the "officers of many nations" who increasingly passed through St. Nazaire in the winter of 1918–1919, Green never lost his focus on home.

Contact with black foreigners at once reinforced and rattled Green's nationalism. Even when he approached African soldiers, he did so as an American more than as a pan-Africanist or a member of a diaspora. Taking a walk beyond the bounds of the American camp in late December 1918, Green tried to initiate conversation with a group of *tirailleurs* standing outside the Senegalese armory. He offered up a jaunty *Bonsoir.* When the soldiers looked coldly back at him, he asked "Black man of France no compre Black man of America?"[46]

White Americans back in the United States had anticipated moments like these and had in fact lampooned them. In spring 1919, the white weekly *Literary Digest* ran a fictional piece imagining the "The Discovery of France" by a "Colored Doughboy" named Joseph Williams. Only three pages long, the story pithily diminished African American military service, African humanity, and the potential for Africans and African Americans to connect. The short story creates a comforting caricature of the what the magazine called "the typical Negro doughboy" in France; the title character is not just colored, he is "coal black" with teeth "china-white," and as he galumphs around the Normandy countryside, he greets Norman peasants with a grin that suitably stretches "from ear to ear."[47]

Peasants aside, the story's most meaningful encounter comes when the African American soldier rounds a corner and finds himself with a Senegalese soldier, described by the author as William's "own double—or very nearly." Having set them up as similar, the author then creates an insuperable barrier in the form of language, sketching the two soldiers' "tragedy" and "pathetic bewilderment" when they find they cannot communicate with one another. In the story, Williams responds to their difference with indignation: "Why nigger," he asks, "what so't of fancy nigger do yo' think yo' is?" The other soldier responds with a *Yakki-wakki-hikki-doolah!"* which causes Williams to realize that his double "ain't no nigger at all!" He dismisses the soldier as "only a A'fican."[48] The author of the *Digest* piece drew distinctions between "nigger"s and "A'fican"s, and seemed to expect African Americans to do the same.

Paternalist Floridian Lieutenant Karl Bardin developed his own comic narrative of diasporic encounters while serving with the 371st Infantry. Like the *Digest,* the white officer recounted an African American enlisted man's shock upon meeting a "tall black nigger," as Bardin reported the private saying, who "acted curious" and "couldnt talk United States." When the private enquired whether Bardin reckoned the other soldier "crazy," Bardin replied that the man was not crazy, only foreign. "That is one of your real brothers from Africa," Bardin explained, expressing a presumptive kinship based on his sense that the African and African American were "just the same." Their essential sameness was confirmed for Bardin half an hour later when he saw the black soldier and *tiralleur* deep in their cups, "arms around each other's shoulders, splitting a bottle of wine." Race and alcohol trumped language and experience.[49]

African Americans themselves portrayed moments of encounter as far more complex than Lieutenant Bardin or the *Digest* imagined. Ely Green's question—could the black man of France understand the black man of America?—created three different points for either rupture or connection: national origin, race, and gender. Despite his status as a disfranchised American and the soldiers' standing as French colonial subjects, Green still positioned them all in respect to the nations that held them, and held them down. His framing may have come from his ignorance of the mechanics of French colonialism in Senegal and the distinctions it drew between white citizens and most African subjects, or from a realization that many Senegalese hoped, as one veteran explained to an interviewer decades later, to "become citizens" by virtue of their service.[50] In Senegal, the French colonial state distinguished between *originaires,* the approximately five percent of the native Senegalese population who lived in the four communes of Dakar, Rufisque, St. Louis, and Gorée, and the rest of the largely rural *sujets* who lived in the interior. Prior to the war, *originaires* traditionally had received limited citizenship rights, and in 1916, as the French moved to conscript more *originaires,* Blaise Diagne convinced the Chamber of Deputies to encode their citizenship in law. The vast majority of Senegalese remained *sujets* but hoped that military service would reap rewards for them as well.[51] To Green such distinctions may have mattered little.

Green identified the West African soldier who finally responded to him as Sergeant Alphonso Clemitis. More interested in Green's racial affiliations

Colonial laborers in Brittany, France. National Archives and Records Administration.

than his national ones, he asked in fluent English why Green did not "support the word Negro like all the other black Americans in northern France." Green's account leaves ambiguous whether the other soldiers in the group snubbed him because they initially mistook him for a white American or because they had heard of his resistance to the term Negro and resented it, but Sergeant Clemitis seemed to sympathize. As Green recalled, Clemitis also claimed to "detest the words white supremacy and Negro," viewing them as opposed to his understanding of himself as a "black man to the black race." Although Green may well have translated the *tiralleur*'s words into his own vernacular, Clemitis conveyed a common understanding. He also knew as well as Green the sway that white supremacy held in the American encampment. When Green invited him to come visit the American camp, Clemitis refused and explained that in Green's camp, he would be just another Negro. He urged Green to come back to the Senegalese armory where they could "talk as men."[52]

As much as anything he had experienced in France, his conversation with Sergeant Clemitis shook Green's abiding nationalism. Clemitis had forged a solidarity with Green based on their shared emphasis on manhood, and he had reinforced it with racial pride by recognizing Green as a black man. He had laid out common terrain. However, his unwillingness to cross the threshold into the American camp set the boundaries of that common ground. It served to define white supremacy as a U.S. phenomenon and set Green apart as well. Green walked away from his conversation with Clemitis "feeling so small" that for once he regretted having "to say that I was any part of America."[53]

Green would experience this ambivalence time and again in the early months of 1919 as white American soldiers' behavior in France made him confront the "two unreconciled strivings," as Du Bois had labeled them, of forging an international identity based on race while seeking his political rights through American citizenship.[54] Clashes between black and white soldiers, frequent throughout the war in the American camp, became even more severe as soldiers started to anticipate return to the United States. White Services of Supply (SOS) crews, military police, and officers in St. Nazaire aggressively reminded black troops that "the Government" had not sent them abroad "to mess around with white women."[55] Many African American troops responded by flaunting their liaisons and friendships more defiantly or by retaliating through violence. Fed up with a particularly rabid commanding officer, Green answered a white lieutenant's racist taunt by grabbing him around the neck and shoving his head into the hull of a ship. When threatened with a firing squad as punishment, Green assured himself that he had done "what any sound man would do."[56] As another soldier expressed in a letter to W. E. B. Du Bois, "I did not get kill in the great battle, but I am willing to give my life for equal."[57]

African Americans felt the difficulties of double consciousness even more acutely when white Americans directed their antipathy toward foreigners. Throughout 1919, reports came back to the United States of white troops' run-ins with soldiers of color from different nations. In Winchester, England, in April, "ill feeling" erupted into violence as fighting broke out between black South Africans and white Americans serving in the British army. At least thirty people were injured.[58] Back in France, white American soldiers shot and killed a black Brazilian sailor on the streets of Brest. Amidst calls by the Brazilian congress for an investigation, military police defended their actions by saying that the sailor struck them as dangerous. Although the American military ruled their actions justifiable, skeptics continued to speculate that "race hatred was the only motive for the killing."[59]

Such incidents provided foreigners ample material for scorning the United States' self-appointed role as defender of international democracy—and to use that failed image strategically. Just as African Americans constructed their France as America's utopian other, French people of color painted the United States as France's dystopian possibility. In July in Paris, delegates from Martinique and Guadeloupe spoke out in the French Chamber of Deputies against American military policemen's widespread abuse of French troops of color, as well as against the "complicity" of French authorities in such incidents. Although the French Minister of the Interior asked the Caribbean deputies to abandon the subject for reasons of "diplomacy," a Parisian deputy took the opportunity to belittle the United State peace delegation, noting the irony that "it is America that wants a society of nations." The deputies passed a resolution affirming "the absolute equality of all men" and their "right to the benefit and protection of all laws."[60]

In pressuring the Chamber of Deputies to protect French troops of color, the Caribbean delegates most likely hoped to assert their constituencies' rights by underscoring their Frenchness (or at least their non-American-ness). Moreover, with rumors circulating in 1919 that the French meant to cede their holdings in the Antilles to the United States, Guadeloupeans moved to remind the metropole of the ties of service and obligation that bound France to the Caribbean, and vice versa. For the metropole, waving the banner of liberty and equality provided a welcome redirection from outright critiques of empire and exploitation. Adopting a position both principled and self-serving, the French legislature moved to position segregation, not democracy, as the quintessentially American export.[61]

The Caribbean French deputies identified white Americans in St. Nazaire as particularly egregious when racial conflicts rippled through the city in the spring of 1919.[62] Ely Green twice had to duck French mobs furious with Americans. In one instance, a white American officer's "profane and violent" remarks about a French woman eating lunch with a French man of color set off what Kathryn Johnson called a "tumult of dischord" with angry patrons demolishing the restaurant.[63] As fighting spilled out of the restaurant and took over the city, French rioters decided to go after all white Americans. "God help any American blanco in uniform," Green remembered his West African friend, Sergeant Clemitis, warning him. To get across town, Green had to flag down a dark-skinned member of his company to shield him from angry mobs intent on beating up white Americans. Every time a French person ran up to them out of the dark, the soldier would either shout, "He no blanco. He my sgt," or announce, "We black men!" Without the young soldier by his side, Green might well have died a white man.[64]

But if their race had saved African Americans from the wrath of the French mob, it did not forge strong ties to the *tiralleurs*. Green reassembled squads of African American laborers in the early dawn after the riot and marched them back to camp in formation. They moved through their section of town unmolested, but when they passed the Senegalese Armory, the hundreds of troops milling on the sidewalk turned their backs on the African Americans. "They despised both white supremacy and Negro," Green realized, and they viewed the two together.[65] The bounds of nation seemed to forestall the bonds of race. Not blanco but still American, black soldiers found themselves caught on the shoals between the two.

Despite the difficulty of establishing solidarity through racial internationalism, Green did differentiate himself and his own sense of nation from the mean-spirited parochialism of white American soldiers. Before the riot and after, he criticized white soldiers for casting "verbal slurs at the men of other nations" and acting as if the American "was the only man in the world." He understood that white soldiers' scorn for "Limies, Frogs, Fritzies, Poles, Bo-hunks, and Crawfishes" fed the sort of chauvinism that led inexorably to a hatred of "the nigger."[66] By way of contrast, he adopted an instrumental internationalism, striving to "learn every thing" he could about foreign countries' opinions "of the Negro and our government."[67] By insistently locating himself in the broader world, building a dockyard League of Nations as he unloaded cargo from ships, Green used the international stage to push the borders established during the war by American military authorities.

This self-conscious placement in the world reflected an international consciousness awash in local considerations. In the wake of the Armistice, Green experienced what Lieutenant William Colson had observed while billeted in French towns during the war: the "strange anomaly" that black soldiers abroad "became associated with the only class of persons" who acknowledged them as American citizens, "those foreigners who had never been to the United States."[68] This anomaly evinced strong responses in the soldiers who felt it, but not all soldiers responded in the same way. In contrast to the halting but persistent beat of Green's nationalism, Lieutenant Colson challenged African Americans to withhold their loyalty until the United States earned it. He excoriated black Americans' "nationalistic patriotism" given the difference between black soldiers' mistreatment at the hands of Americans and their fair treatment by foreigners, and he announced that "intelligent Negroes have all reached the point where their loyalty to the country is conditional."[69] Returning to the United States to write for the black socialist magazine the *Messenger,* he argued that African Americans had to fight for "national social enlargement"—for the social economic rights of all classes—before a "new patriotism" could take effect.[70]

Certainly, not everyone heeded Lieutenant Colson's call. Some soldiers, like North Carolinian artilleryman Ernest McKissick, managed to accept the contradiction of fighting in a hostile army by focusing on the most local of ties. McKissick fully understood that although he and fellow members of the 92nd Division "tried to make it safe for democracy," that much-vaunted slogan "wasn't working at all at home." White people spoke of democracy, McKissick observed, but they did nothing to dismantle Jim Crow. Instead, white supremacists "tried to put us down in every way: Street cars and buses and everything." Wherever McKissick looked, it was "Jim Crow! Jim Crow!"[71]

Nevertheless, McKissick "went and fought for America right on," and he gladly returned home. Less touched by French kindness than moved by French suffering, he compared "the poor conditions over there, that those people were in" to his circumstances at home in Asheville, North Carolina, and resolved,

"My God, I'd rather live at home, regardless of this prejudice and all." Indeed for McKissick, ties of community and kin—of *home* located in the institutions developed by the African American community in Asheville—stood in for the grander identifications of nation. He understood white supremacy and "took it as it was" because he wanted to "come back home to be with my people and see them and see what I could do." He took his stand against white supremacy quietly, by holding on to his own dignity and shoring up black civic institutions in Asheville. More rooted than Ely Green and less radically ambitious than Willliam Colson, McKissick felt that if he had "stopped and tried to fight" Jim Crow head on, it might have destroyed him. "I don't know where I'd be today," he commented decades later.[72]

Staging a one-man stand against white supremacy in the wartime military, Lieutenant Rayford Logan could attest to the toll it had taken on him. Young, handsome, and fluent in French, Logan had found succor in his ability to communicate and connect with French civilians better than most white soldiers and had taken perverse satisfaction in parading his white girlfriends in front of white American soldiers. Nevertheless, he realized that the humiliations and ironies of fighting combat in a Jim Crow army had altered profoundly his relationship to America. Unlike Ely Green, he had no interest in proving himself a man. Nor did he wish to reform the United States, be it gently like Floyd McKissick or fiercely like William Colson. Logan could not purge the "hate" for white Americans that had burgeoned as a product of his military service and had no desire to return home.[73] At war's end, he took his discharge in Europe and opted for the dislocation of an exile.[74]

Rage and expatriation had loosed Rayford Logan from the binds that held hopeful patriots like Ely Green and muted pragmatic loyalists like Ernest McKissick. For many of the black exiles who left the United States after the war—veterans, artists, musicians, and mixes thereof—Paris became the locus and the draw; in the city's Montmarte district, they created a Harlem in miniature where they could live, as historian Tyler Stovall put it, "as self-conscious refugees from American racism."[75] Before he settled in Paris, however, Logan chose to wander. He forewent home, any home, in favor of a loose cosmopolitanism that carried him across Europe. Trading against the dollar in the "halcyon days," as he would later describe them, when European currencies "were cascading towards zero," Logan sought refuge in well-financed rootlessness.[76] He traveled "extensively," through France, Belgium, and Lichtenstein as well as "Germany, Poland, Austria . . . Switzerland, Portugal, and

England."[77] Running across the white Americans who comprised a large part of the postwar tourist traffic, he was mistaken for a fellow white man, a German, an Indian, and once despite his protests, for a Polish prince.

Cosmopolitanism still left room for white supremacy. Looking back at the repeated moves to "de Negroize" him, as he would later put it, Logan could pick up on the pervasiveness of the notion of place in the "export of American prejudice abroad."[78] When Logan ventured outside his educationally, economically, and spatially "circumscribed milieux"—not only rising above his place but literally moving beyond it—white Americans in Europe failed to see him as "an American Negro."[79] The placelessness that whites found suspect when they imagined it in blacks in America became cognitively impossible when they saw it in Logan in Europe. His wanderings had de-raced him in ways that smacked of racial prejudice; in spite of his "African" features, "yellow" skin tone and curly hair, Logan ceased to be black in the minds of white American travelers because they did not find him where they felt black men should be. Logan countered by forcefully asserting his identity as a Negro and endeavoring to establish an internationalism that did not cloak Jim Crow in color blindness.[80] Within a couple of years of his discharge, Logan had based himself out of Paris and started to help W. E. B. Du Bois organize the second Pan-African Congress, held in Paris, Brussels, and London in 1921. No longer an "unwilling Nordic," he had begun to count himself as a vocal member of the African diaspora.

The Conscience of the World

The shift in African American soldiers' orientation, from a narrow focus on home to a broader imagination of kinship with colonial peoples, linked them to activists and intellectuals like W. E. B. Du Bois who had long looked beyond the nation-state for liberation. The pan-African movement that Rayford Logan came to embrace had its renaissance in the Paris conference pulled together by Du Bois in February 1919. Du Bois had been positing "the problem of the twentieth century" as "the problem of the colour line" since 1900 when he addressed the Pan-African Conference assembled in London by Trinidadian lawyer H. Sylvester Williams.[81] In the intervening two decades, he had worked and rearticulated his formulation of international racial politics in light of expanding colonialism, ascendant Wilsonianism, and after 1914, the terror and promise of the Great War. Three and a half years after arguing in the pages of the *Atlantic Monthly* that the roots of the conflict lay in Africa, he moved to convince the world that so, too, did the possibilities of a meaningful peace.

Civilian intellectuals' conceptions of black internationalism were as diffuse as those conceived by black soldiers. Indeed, other activists competed with Du Bois to offer more clear-eyed messages of international solidarity. Chandler Owen and A. Philip Randolph called upon African Americans to join the "Irish" guarding the "Emerald Isles," "Hindus" challenging Britain, "Chinese" saving China from "future ravage," and "Turks" safeguarding Constantinople.[82] Likewise, Hubert Harrison, a West Indian journalist and activist who scholars have celebrated as a "radical, race-first Renaissance man," pushed for "a self-governing Egypt, a self-governing India, and independent African states as large as Germany and France."[83] Wondering in 1918 why it was that when "white folk insist on the right to manage their ancestral lands" it was celebrated "as 'democracy' and 'self-determination,'" but when "Negroes, Egyptians, Hindus" sought the same, it was considered "impudence," Harrison described the "hundreds of millions" of people under colonial rule as a "seething volcano" set to blow.[84]

Du Bois's most famous rival of the early 1920s, Marcus Garvey, also put forth a competing vision of black internationalism. Through pomp and parade, Garvey and the UNIA used the man-centered militarism so prevalent in this period to mobilize black masses. Unlike the anti-imperialist Du Bois, Garvey embraced the "solidarity" promised by a counterempire, a black empire—figured, as one historian writes, "as a way of imagining racial empowerment . . . and statehood" across and beyond other political formations.[85] He offered up such a black empire as a counterweight to the League of Nations, which Garveyites like Haitian-born UNIA representative Eliezer Cadet considered a "sham."[86]

Even if Du Bois's expression of internationalism was neither the most spectacular nor the most militant, it was the most public. With the black monthly magazine *Crisis* as his mouthpiece, Du Bois could bring his perspectives into 100,000 homes by 1919, and he used his podium to sell his readership on his Pan-African Congress. Dismissing as "careless thinkers" the "few Negroes" who argued "that the Negro problem is a domestic matter to be settled" solely in places like "Richmond and New Orleans," he fashioned his Paris meeting as a necessary demonstration of African American politics. He informed his readers that "not a single great, serious movement or idea in

Government, Politics, Philanthropy or Industry in the civilized world has omitted to send and keep in Paris" a body of representatives. Black Americans would have been foolish to neglect the theater in favor of "Podunk" or wherever else they might set their limited sights.[87] Likening the worldwide phenomenon of racial subjugation to the spread of a house fire across a city block, Du Bois felt convinced that "the Negro problem in America will never be solved so long as Africa or the West Indies are seats of economic slavery and despotism."[88] White supremacy was a global problem, and they needed to treat it as such.

By the time he sailed for France on December 1, 1918, intent on resuscitating the pan-African movement, he had "been working for some months on the question of the African colonies." Just days earlier, on November 27, Du Bois had written Woodrow Wilson's secretary and gatekeeper Joseph Patrick Tumulty. He enclosed a "Memoranda on the Future of Africa" with the explanation, "We want to get this memoranda before the Peace Conference and before the Conscience of the world." Drafted by Du Bois and white philanthropist George Foster Peabody, the document echoed the sentiments of his 1915 *Atlantic* piece. Labeling colonialism "a fruitful cause of dissension among nations, a danger to the status of civilized labor, a temptation to unbridled exploitation," and "an excuse for unspeakable atrocities committed against natives," the memo urged Wilson to endorse a partial application of his own principles of self-determination in the disposition of the African question. Du Bois proposed a series of conferences to gauge the desires of African colonials, blacks in the United States, South America, and the West Indies, and "the independent Negro governments of Abyssinia, Liberia, and Hayti." Making an explicit link between the fact of diaspora and the acts of dispersal, he suggested that the keynote event be the tercentenary commemoration of the arrival of Africans in America.[89]

In the memo and elsewhere, Du Bois returned often to the concepts of culture and civilization. Africa represented to him a "world-old" wisdom, the fount of civilization older than history itself. This primordial timelessness, however, could not last.[90] To be civilized, or rather recivilized, Africa had to become modern. Du Bois suggested that this modernization come under "the guidance of organized civilization," the European and American influence of "science, commerce, social reform, and religious philanthropy," which would lead ultimately to an "International Africa" molded from the former German colonies. He looked to education as the main agent of reconstruction. "Within a generation," he predicted, "young Africa should know the essentials of modern culture" and be ready to establish an industrial democracy free of "private land monopoly and poverty, promoting cooperation in production and socialization of income."[91]

Unlike someone like Ely Green who developed his sense of Africa through the ground-level confusion and clarity of his encounters with Africans, Du Bois conceived of Africa from on high. Du Bois's memo reflected his intellectual investment in the Enlightenment, his own education at Harvard and in Berlin, and the Progressive moment in which he wrote. Despite the barbarities that Europe had visited upon other countries, civilization implied to him European influence, the thought and learning of the "world's great universities," and the high cultural products of the continents' great musicians, artists, and writers.[92] His faith in the leavening possibilities of education and the grand potential of an industrial democracy founded in the spirit of cooperation placed him in line with a good many social reformers of his day, including Woodrow Wilson. Although Du Bois was always among the first to critique the alienating aspect of industrialism and modernity as a conceptual terrain, the actual process of modernizing was both a practical necessity and an ultimate good.

Du Bois forwarded a copy of the memo to Secretary of State Robert Lansing as well as to Secretary of War Newton D. Baker and expressed his desire to present it formally to the President. He added a second wish, "to call in Paris at the time of the Peace Conference "a small Pan-African" meeting. He proposed that the gathering include "half a dozen" African Americans "of the highest type" along with an unspecified number of "representatives from Africa and the Islands." To that end, he requested help in securing passports for six men to sail "sometime in December."[93] Four days later on December 1, he boarded the USS *Orizaba* without approval from the State Department. Instead, he did some "quick and adroit" finagling to secure passage as a journalist on the advance press steamer.

"Paris is full and still more coming," Du Bois noted a few days after landing. The city seemed both giddy and brittle: "feverish, crowded, nervous, hurried."[94] In his letters back to the *Crisis,* Du Bois noted the "surging crowds" that threw things into disarray and then "jammed" the streets to hail American President Woodrow Wilson when he arrived for the peace talks on December 14.[95] Yet the haze of renewed vitality that hovered over Paris during these early weeks could not obscure the concrete fact of death: "Everywhere are evidences of war—cannons, protected buildings, soldiers of all nations." More striking than these virile traces of a yet unsettled war, he identified the sentimental emblems of ongoing mourning in "the women clothed in silent black!" who walked amidst the crowd.[96] He lingered on this image of the city "with its soul cut to the core" with "tears so intertwined with joy that there is scant difference."[97] In Du Bois's Paris, death and renewal moved together and convinced him that he was part of the rebirth of the world.

Along with his lofty visions of rebirth and renewal, Du Bois saw the practical exercise of power. In that winter of 1918–1919, away from the squares and the masses, "in a small room in the *Hôtel Crillon,*" Woodrow Wilson, Georges Clemenceau, David Lloyd-George, and Vittorio Orlando—four "unobtrusive" men—sat serenely at a table and held "the destinies of mankind" in their hands.[98] Du Bois wanted to diffuse that concentration by opening up both the subjects and theaters of debate. Styling himself the "unofficial and unselected" African American delegate in Paris, he moved "to see that the things" black people "wanted should be brought before" the Council of Four.[99]

Despite its rhetorical significance, the Pan-African Congress had more the air of improvised performance than orchestrated production. "It is quite Utopian," a reporter for the *Chicago Tribune* observed, "and it has less than a Chinamen's chance of getting anywhere."[100] Du Bois barely pulled the meeting together. He traversed the city "without credentials or influence" for weeks, first approaching the American peace delegation with his proposal.[101] They dubbed it "impossible" and told him that with the city still under martial law, the French government would crush the plan before its inception. Undaunted, Du Bois turned to "the ace up my sleeve," Senegalese statesman and designated president of the Pan-African Congress, Blaise Diagne.[102]

Just as the unlettered and unschooled Ely Green had projected on his West African friend a kinship based on their shared identity as black men, Du Bois—educated at Harvard and the University of Berlin—considered himself and Diagne both *exceptional* black men. As a deputy in the French parliament—representing "all Senegal, white and black," Du Bois was quick to point out—and a close friend of Prime Minister George Clemenceau, Diagne enjoyed a great amount of prestige in France.[103] He had recruited hundreds of thousands of African colonials to join the war, and in the 1930s, he would go on to become the Under Secretary of State for French Colonial Affairs.[104] In his eminence, he represented the greatest possibilities for Africans within the French empire—what Du Bois would have viewed as the benefits of civilization and political inclusion. Indeed, in the January weeks while Du Bois could gain no audience with President Wilson and Department of Justice agents trailed his every step, Diagne strode about Paris imbued with the prerogatives of state.

At the same time, Diagne also served as a compromised ally. His stature partially depended on the continued subjugation of Africa to France. An avowed assimilationist, he was implicated in French colonialism even as he tried to ameliorate its conditions; and while he increased the Congress's visibility, he also dulled its threat. His access to Clemenceau came with an assurance of moderation, and his conservatism reined in Du Bois's ideological excesses. Five years and two Pan-African Congresses later, Du Bois would dismiss Diagne as "a Frenchman who is accidentally black" and voice a suspicion that Diagne "despise[d] his own black Wolofs," but in the winter of 1919, Du Bois needed him.[105] Even with Diagne on his side, it took "two wet, discouraging months" for Clemenceau to grant his permission to hold the conference.[106] "Don't advertise it," he finally told Diagne at the end of January, "but go ahead."[107]

Du Bois sent a triumphant telegram announcing that "carefully selected delegates" were welcome to attend the Congress in mid-February, but there were more obstacles to come for his and other conferences. Insisting that the French government had not given and would not give its consent, the State Department refused to issue passports to "persons desiring to proceed to Paris" for this or any such meeting.[108] Landlocked African Americans included A. Philip Randolph, Ida B. Wells-Barnett, women's beauty mogul and International League cofounder Madame C. J. Walker, and NERL's William Monroe Trotter. Britain followed suit, barring passports for the liberal white Secretary of the Aborigines Protection Society and for indigenous South Africans.[109] For a while, it looked as though Du Bois ran the danger of hosting a Congress with no delegates. To get around the passport conundrum, he culled delegates from people already overseas and proceeded with his plans.

As Du Bois charged forward, members of the African American press began to denounce the Wilson administration. The *New York Age,* which had earlier warned "foolish" and "pathetic" race leaders against conflating the Peace Conference with the Pan-African Congress lest their humbuggery embarrass the race, now snorted at the State Department's refusal. Writers at the *New York Call* flatly stated that the denials resulted from "fear" that the delegates "would tell the story of Negro lynchings, 'Jim Crow' laws and discrimination against the black race in the United States." The *Crisis* gave a hearty amen.[110]

Nevertheless, Du Bois found delegates. Most of the fifty-seven participants "happened to be residing" in France, he recalled years later, "mainly for reasons of the war."[111] Fifteen countries had delegates, with Francophone countries making up the largest contingent after the United States. The French West Indies sent thirteen delegates, including deputy René Boisneuf. Haiti and France contributed seven each, French West Africa one, and Algeria one. Liberia sent three representatives and the Spanish colonies two. The other nine countries had one delegate apiece.[112] Americans formed a majority with sixteen representatives. They included Morehouse President John Hope, celebrated black orator Roscoe Conkling Simmons, and Baptist pastor William H. Jernagin who had told the State Department he was traveling to do "religious work" on behalf of the Federal Council of Churches to mask his plans also to attend an international "Conference of the Darker Races" as well as a meeting of the "League of Small Nations and Weak Peoples."[113] White NAACP Board members Joel Spingarn, William English Walling, and Charles Edward Wallace also attended, along with George Jackson, a black missionary who came to share his experiences in the Congo.[114]

Du Bois culled from the ranks of black clubwomen as well, inviting Addie Waites Hunton and Ida Gibbs Hunt to take part in the conference. Both Hunton and Hunt provided crucial links between the exalted orientation of Du Bois's pan-Africanism and the wretched, often claustrophobic, experience of African Americans in the American Expeditionary Forces. In her work with the YMCA, Hunton had furiously noted the "mean prejudice and subtle propaganda, of misrepresentation and glaring injustice" to which black soldiers were subjected. Once the Pan-African Congress ended, she would return to camp work, volunteering with black soldiers until August 1919.[115]

Ida Gibbs Hunt knew France and could map the diaspora better than most of the American delegates at the conference. The daughter of a former diplomatic consul and the wife of a current one, Hunt had lived in Madagascar and had spent the previous twelve years in St. Etienne, France. In the twelve years following the 1919 Pan-African Congress, the consular service would send her family to Liberia, Guadeloupe, and the Azores.[116] Her contacts both domestic and international made Hunt a sound choice to sit on the Executive Board of the Congress, alongside Diagne, Du Bois, and British Guiana's Edmund F. Fredericks. Her family connections, too, made her a valuable addition to a conference on the prospects for postwar reform: her brother-in-law, attorney Napoleon Bonaparte Marshall, attested to both internal and external wounds born by black soldiers. While stationed in Spartanburg as a Captain in the 15th New York National Guard, the Harvard Law School alumnus was called a "dirty nigger" and forced off the sidewalk by a white man. A month before the end of fighting, he suffered a spinal injury in a raid conducted with the 365th Infantry, south of Metz.[117] Hunt's internationalism, her emphasis on peace, and her commitment to racial justice grew out of her experiences and those of her loved ones.

With the State Department forestalling the possibility of having more representative bodies in France, Du Bois's Pan-African Congress became a sounding board for diverse, often competing, perspectives on black internationalism. E. F. Fredericks and his colleague John Archer came to the conference representing the African Progress Union, founded in Britain three months earlier. Diagne and the deputies from the West Indies represented France, but they had little desire that "Africa be ruled by Africans," as Du Bois proposed. When Du Bois submitted a resolution calling for African rule, they protested that they actually wanted to be treated as Frenchman "in the fullest sense that the term Frenchman implies."[118] Americans Hunt and Hunton wanted to be treated as Americans, with all the privileges that the term should imply, but they had to remind the assembled men "of the part that Colored womanhood" would play "in the redemption, not of Africa," Roscoe Conkling Simmons paraphrased, "but of Africans."[119] Embarking on what would turn out for both of them to be a decades-long commitment to the cause of pan-Africanism, Hunton and Hunt integrated their feminism with their commitment to race reform. They would bring the organizational networks they established through the National Association of Colored Women and international groups like the Women's Peace Party to the aid of the African diaspora.

The UNIA's Eliezer Cadet's reaction to Du Bois underscored the extent to which different groups competed to best perform their politics. Cadet had used his Haitian passport to get to Europe, but with other UNIA delegates barred from leaving the United States, he decided to go on a speaking tour of France and England. Designated by Garvey the "High Commissioner of the Universal Negro Improvement Association and African Communities' League," he wrote that "outrages" against blacks in the Americas and Africa "cannot be regarded as national or domestic questions, but as international violations of civilized human rights." There would be no peace without justice; black people were poised to fight back.[120] Unlike other black activists in France, the UNIA was less interested in persuading a white audience than it was in establishing its leadership among militant blacks. Although Cadet's overall critique seemed to complement Du Bois's and his participation in the Pan-African Congress passed without comment, Garvey and Cadet soon after labeled Du Bois a "reactionary" and accused him of hampering Cadet's mission.[121]

Although the UNIA surely overstated how much of a mission Cadet had to be hampered, it took little exaggeration for Garvey to argue that the Pan-African Congress could have pushed harder. The first day's speeches focused as much on responsibilities as on rights. Delegates gathered in the council room of the Grand Hôtel on Wednesday, February 19, 1919. Blaise Diagne served as the Congress's President, and he opened the ceremony by praising both racial unity and French colonial rule. Sitting in the audience, Roscoe Conkling Simmons rhapsodized that the deputy was "all mind" and that his opening remarks were "jewels of statesmanship." When Diagne challenged the audience to render "groundless" the claims "that we as a race are superficial both in thought and work," Simmons approvingly observed that Diagne reminded him of Booker T. Washington.[122]

Subsequent speakers continued to focus on rights and responsibilities. After a series of speeches calling for universal human rights and singling out the United States for "special deprecation," a Liberian delegate arose with a pointed reminder about the Congress's practical calling. "We are asking for rights," he told his listeners, "but let us not, therefore forget our duties." He informed the Congress that they had an obligation to help his struggling independent republic to "be considered a home for the darker races" if they were going to make a valid claim for African self-governance. Group identity entailed mutual support. He concluded with the admonition that "wherever there are rights, there are duties and responsibilities."[123]

The next morning, the mayor of London's Battersea borough, John Archer, revisited this theme, infusing it with a dose of manly bravado. The first black man ever to hold public office in Britain, Archer was also the newly elected president of the African Progress Union. Born in Britain to a Barbadian father and Irish mother—"born in trouble," he told his audience in the Pan-African Congress as nod to both Irish and Caribbean struggles—Archer had married a black Canadian woman and had circled the world three times while working as a seaman. A true child of the diaspora, he also embodied its militant potential. In his November 1918 presidential address to the African Progress Union, he had inspired cheers by declaring that he would "not ask" for the equal rights of citizens in the British Empire: "I am not asking for anything, I am out demanding."[124] He brought the same message with him to France: "We must fight for our just rights at all times."[125]

The last sessions of the Congress addressed the place of women in black world politics, with Addie Hunton outlining the significant contributions of women "in the world's reconstruction and regeneration of today." France's Jules Siefried voiced the support of the International Council on the Rights of Woman. Eschewing Du Bois's sentimental invocations of motherhood, birth, and mourning, Siefried made her claim in republican terms: "No one could appreciate better than women the struggle for broader rights and liberties."[126] Ironically, the *New York Evening Globe*'s coverage of the event the next day included a description of the "Negroes in the trim uniform of American Army officers, other American coloured men in frock coats or business suits," and "polished French Negroes who hold public office."[127] The account erased women delegates from view even as it lingered over the outer trappings of black male citizenship. The picture of the delegates included in the May 1919 issue of the *Crisis* did not make the same mistake. Ida Gibbs Hunt conspicuously sat directly next to Du Bois.

The Congress's proposals were better documented and more heated than its speeches. Most items echoed Du Bois's earlier suggestions for Africa. The Congress asked for a trustee period of indeterminate length with eventual autonomy for native Africans, public education and public health initiatives, and cultural freedom, all under the supervision of the League of Nations. If the proposal sounded disconcertingly like the mandates system of oversight that the Big Four did put in place as part of the Versailles Treaty, Du Bois at least added two caveats to forestall the colonial exploitation of the prewar period. The first called for the universal application of rights "wherever persons of African descent are civilized and able to meet the tests of the surrounding culture." The second would have provided a valuable tool for policing in U.S. race relations: it insisted that the League of Nations publicly censure a country whenever it found "that any State deliberately excludes its civilized citizens or subjects of Negro descent from its body politic and cultural."[128] Steeped in the language of liberation as well as social evolution, the two points show both the scope and the limits of Du Bois's pan-African proj-

ect. "The world-fight for blacks rights" was indeed "on," as Du Bois exuber-
antly wrote upon returning from Paris, but he would need the bottom-up
engagement of people like Ely Green to help pitch its battles.[129]

In politics high and low, the Great War opened up the world for African
American soldiers and the civilians who laid claim to them. Stepping out, they
might reach beyond the boundaries of Jim Crow, begin to hold the United
States accountable to its own stated ideals, or commence the world fight for
black rights. In all its forms—from Rayford Logan's cosmopolitan exile to the
idiosyncratic self-positioning of Ely Green to W. E. B. Du Bois's romantic re-
embrace of pan-Africanism—internationalism offered analytical and emotional space for black people to see themselves as more than Woodrow Wilson's
"dusky" wards of the European diaspora. And for the African Americans who
explicitly challenged the President's right to speak for the ideal of democracy,
black internationalisms offered alternatives and correctives to "the danger," as
one minister labeled it, of Wilsonian internationalism.[130]

Their vision was by no means perfect: W. E. B. Du Bois had not rid himself from the threads of white supremacy weaved into his civilizationist discourse around Africa any more than Ely Green had examined the ways that
his emphasis on manhood might reinscribe white paternalism. Nevertheless,
the perspectives espoused by black activists, embodied by black soldiers, and
anticipated by black civilians began a broad process of reimagining black political subjectivity that would only gain strength in ensuing decades. Reaching out toward an international humanity grounded in a national citizenship,
African Americans had begun to develop "a racial consciousness and racial
strength," as Addie Hunton wrote, "that could not have been gained in a half
century of normal living in America."[131]

This racial and global consciousness connected the African Americans
fighting abroad to those struggling in the United States—and made the war
a catalyst for social change. Despite Addie Hunton's ringing formulation,
there was no "normal living" in America during the era of World War I, as
black civilians strove to buttress their racial strength with the state-based
guarantee of citizenship rights. In the weeks after the Armistice, a former
member of the 24th Infantry Regiment would give Americans a new opportunity to wrangle with African American manhood and black citizenship.
Over the course of 1919, a fight on a streetcar near the coal hills of Alabama

would grow steadily from a localized confrontation into a grand struggle over African American soldiers and the protection owed them by their federal government. Determined to avoid the summary execution that closed the Houston riot, African American Alabamans strove to make the federal court system work on behalf of their race. Despite previous setbacks, they refused to turn the nation back over to Jim Crow.

6

Saving Sergeant Caldwell

The ride from Hobson City, Alabama, to neighboring Anniston would carry Edgar Caldwell to the gallows. On a Sunday afternoon about a month after the Armistice and ten days before Christmas in December 1918, Caldwell boarded a streetcar on the Alabama Power Company's Constantine line. A sergeant at Camp McClellan, he carried a pass that allowed him to leave his post located eight miles outside of Anniston to spend an afternoon in Hobson City, the all-black town on the city's southern outskirts. He wore the khaki and wool uniform of a noncommissioned Army officer—"nice clothes," a witness would later call them—chevron stripes indicating his rank, and a military-issue hat. Unseen, tucked in his clothes, he carried a pistol.[1]

Even as racial activists and white supremacists speculated on what to expect from soldiers returning from service in Europe, a black soldier in Alabama lashed out against Jim Crow at home. An everyday argument between the soldier and a white transportation worker in Alabama would lead to a murder trial that became a *cause célèbre*. It began when Sergeant Caldwell, a former member of the 24th Infantry then serving in an Alabama labor battalion, boarded the streetcar and immediately butted heads with the conductor, Cecil Linten. Their Jim Crow argument grew into a fight, and the fight ended with Linten dead and white motorman Kelsie Morrison wounded. Within a month, civilian authorities had tried Caldwell in Alabama state court and convicted him of murder. They sentenced him to death by hanging.

In the months that followed, Sergeant Caldwell's murder case wended a path through the state and federal court systems, resulting in the April 1920 Supreme Court ruling Caldwell v. Parker on military power and federal jurisdiction. As it traveled from Calhoun County to the nation's capital, the case allowed African Americans to pull back from their international imaginaries and give shape to the national realities in which their internationalisms were rooted. Through *Caldwell* African Americans engaged questions of federal citizenship, state's rights, criminal procedure, and the limits of white supremacy in wartime; they pushed the Wilson administration to define Caldwell's citizenship in such a way that the state of Alabama could not confine him.

Caldwell's case captured the spirit of both returning soldiers and the African American troops who had served in stateside camps. Just days after Caldwell's arrest, a fellow sergeant in the 157th Depot Brigade wrote on open letter to his "Comrades" mustering out of the Army at Camp Gordon near Atlanta, Georgia. Lauding the troops' development into "the equal or superior of any troops that ever wore the khaki uniform," he anticipated that after having realized their manhood through military service, they would never again consent to "sit aside while the neighboring white man gets possession of all the spoils." The sergeant, Wellington Dixon, predicted a competition between black men and white men "for the wealth, the education, and the political rights of the country."[2]

Wealth, education, and political rights provided the foundations for an active citizenship, one that could allow for African American participation in public politics, but with the *Caldwell* case, they fought for something more elementary. If even passive citizens enjoyed "the right of protection of their person, of their property, of their liberty, etc." set forth in nineteenth-century liberal doctrine, then blacks had not yet cleared the first hurdle.[3] By defending Caldwell, African Americans defended their own freedom not to be lynched in the town square or railroaded in the courtroom; they fought for what Ely Green would have called "the right of law." Using arguments over military jurisdiction that suggested that Sergeant Caldwell's rights should have been his to keep no matter where he traveled, Caldwell's defenders looked to the Army to protect black citizenship.

Like the activists in Paris who claimed black soldiers' efforts for all the race, African Americans involved in the *Caldwell* case linked their fate to his.

Edgar Caldwell's solitary act of self-defense served only as prologue. What followed was a grander story of community vision and mobilization, as black people in cities across the country used the circumstances created by the war to push the federal government to protect one of their, and its, own.

The First Racial Trouble of Any Kind

Stepping out on that Sunday afternoon, December 15, 1918, Caldwell must have found his day off a welcome respite. Troops in Caldwell's labor battalion worked just as hard as those in Virginia or St. Nazaire, and things did not slack off with the Armistice. Since their transfer from Camp Gordon to Camp McClellan earlier in the fall, the Army had worked him and the other 5,000 African American troops assigned to the 157th Depot Brigade to the bone. Now that the war had ended, they were no longer given military training. Instead, they worked from dusk to dawn doing heavy labor: hauling lumber, building roads, and cleaning up debris. Exhausted at day's end, they piled into tents plagued by shoddy construction, crowded conditions, and poor sanitation.[4]

The soldiers at Camp McClellan may have comforted themselves with the knowledge that things could have been worse. In colder camps, for example, men reportedly "died like sheep" when poor quarters and inadequate clothing exposed them to the excesses of winter.[5] When weather did not kill black soldiers in other camps, excessively cruel treatment often did. Complaints of African American soldiers in Anniston could barely rival those of troops in Camp Humphreys, Virginia, where sergeants were armed and told "to shoot the 'damn niggers' if they [could not] rule them any other way," or of the service battalion working at a warehouse in Schenectady, New York, whose dictatorial major dragged sick men out of the hospital to unload supply cars.[6]

Still, conditions at Camp McClellan took their toll on morale. In the stockade in the winter of 1918, a black civilian lay dying of pneumonia, held without charge or trial for allegedly "making disloyal remarks" in violation of the wartime Sedition Act. Local authorities had turned him over to the military with no regard for habeas corpus. And just days before Caldwell took his fateful ride on the streetcar, an African American draftee compared his own condition to incarceration. He wrote to W. E. B. Du Bois that African American soldiers were "being held" at Camp McClellan "to do all the fatigue work, while thousands of white soldiers" were sent home. He asked that the National Association for the Advancement of Colored People (NAACP) help them procure honorable discharges. "We don't want to disgrace or mar our fine record," the weary soldier stated simply, "but we must have relief."[7] As a sergeant, Caldwell stood somewhere between the enlisted men who labored in the worst conditions and the handful of black commissioned officers whose lighter load and superior quarters were offset by the contempt of troops who scorned them as accommodationist. An experienced soldier, he might have reconciled himself to the discomforts of military life, but as events would show, he had not yet come to accept the daily injustices of Jim Crow.[8]

Neither experience nor rank could cushion Caldwell from the tedium that overlay life in Camp McClellan. Soldiers stationed stateside had no Paris to which they could escape, or imagine escaping; they had little to help them push back on the closing walls of white supremacy. Apart from a handful of baseball teams, camp life provided black soldiers in Anniston with few recreational outlets. They had little access to the corn liquor produced by moonshiners in the nearby hills and, given their distance from the city, even less opportunity to meet black civilians. When they could get to town, they found that the area's African American churches had organized few programs for their benefit. Soldiers might approach young women in Anniston's African Americans neighborhoods, but with eighty girls arrested for "immoral conduct" between July and November 1918, prostitution and public courting came under harsh regulation. The influenza pandemic that spread in late 1918 isolated the troops even more, as a campwide quarantine kept most soldiers on base and most visitors off.[9] Occasionally soldiers still made it downtown to attend the social club half-heartedly established for them by the War Camp Community Service. Run by a Baptist minister, the club had writing tables and stationery but no piano or record player. All the same, by December, soldiers would have craved even the small diversion this provided.[10]

For all its hardships, Sergeant Caldwell's Army service had brought its rewards. Unlike some of the lower-ranked enlisted men who went for months before receiving a clothing issue of fatigues, Caldwell could sport his non-commissioned officer's uniform when he went to town. Though there were no fights over white girlfriends to spark racial showdowns, the same tensions that animated black soldiers' interactions with white soldiers in Europe guided encounters here, and in Anniston, the civilian population enforced Jim Crow as forcefully as the Army did, if not more so. Yet as Caldwell boarded the streetcar, he dressed as if no one had a claim to him except for Uncle Sam himself. The hat, the uniform, the pistol functioned as armor for a black officer aboard a segregated streetcar. As a principal "theater" for the performance and enforcement of racial mores, public transportation repeatedly served to remind African Americans of their assigned place in the Southern caste system. Yet at the same time, streetcars also provided African Americans with an opportunity to challenge publicly, through gestures small and large, white supremacist notions of that place.[11]

Edgar Caldwell. *Crisis,* March 1920.

Born in 1889, into the Greenwood, South Carolina, landscape where Populism failed and Ben Tillman triumphed, Caldwell knew the circumscription and denigration that set the boundaries of black life in the Progressive Era South.[12] However, having served as a soldier both in the present war and five years earlier as a member of the proud 24th Infantry stationed in the Philippines, he also knew places and possibilities more expansive than those presented by Jim Crow. Cloaked in the uniform of the United States Army, Caldwell gestured toward an identity as a citizen, and toward the honor and respect denied him merely as an African American man.[13]

For just this reason, the sight of dark brown Caldwell in his Army khakis must have appeared to a white country boy from Alabama like a red flag to a bull. Older white Annistonians had the memory of the black troops stationed near Anniston during the Spanish-Cuban and Philippines Wars to help them adjust to uniformed African American men in their city. Streetcar conductor Cecil Linten, young and newly arrived in town from rural Lineville, did not. Whether Caldwell truly waltzed aboard and "insisted" on sitting at the head of the car "in the section set aside for the use of white passengers," as the white newspapers claimed, or had simply refused to let Cecil Linten cheat him of his fare, as some black commentators later insisted, his dress and manner flouted the tenets of white supremacy that gave order to Linten's world.[14] To Caldwell's silent, glaring provocation, the young conductor responded by striking the soldier twice in the face.[15]

As passengers watched, Caldwell fought back. "I heard the window crash," a white witness recalled later, "and I jumped up on the seat to see what it was."[16] He stood up in time to watch Linten, aided by his motorman Kelsie Morrison, force Caldwell to the back of the car and shove him out the rear and on to the street. Having harshly reminded Caldwell of his place, the crew proceeded to punish him for forgetting it. As the motorman Morrison moved to strike—one newspaper claimed "with a heavy piece of iron"—Caldwell allegedly drew his pistol from his pocket and fired twice with lethal precision.[17] The first bullet entered Linten's chin and "crashed through the top of his head." The second passed close to Kelsie Morrison's heart leaving him alive but "desperately wounded."[18] With passengers charging from the streetcar to apprehend him, Caldwell fled the scene heading south, toward the hills outside the city.

*   *   *

By late 1918, white Alabamans like the field secretary for the state Council of Defense had turned their attention to the threat of returning black members of the American Expeditionary Forces who might rouse "laboring people, especially the colored people" into violence. Yet they fretted, too, about the African Americans among them. White Annistonians had worried when the Great War brought African American troops back into the state. Old memories of the 1898 Battle of Anniston at Camp Shipp and fresh concerns from the Houston riot arose across Alabama in late summer 1917 as inhabitants prepared for the black soldiers to arrive. In an attempt to ease the irritations that had led to clashes in the past, military and civilian authorities assigned the African American community responsibility for the black soldiers. Montgomery led the way, sending a white brigadier general and delegation of the state capital's "leading colored citizens" to instruct black troops on the etiquette of white supremacy.[19] Anniston followed suit. Ministers and local leaders from Calhoun County's black community met with the troops from Camp McClellan to outline the social and cultural resources on their side of the color line.[20]

For a time, the alternate civic and social space available in all-black Hobson City and among Anniston's African Americans ameliorated the pain of Jim Crow without directly challenging its hegemony. Yet, when Sergeant Caldwell broke the fragile, year-long calm by instigating what the papers labeled "the first racial trouble of any kind," civilian and military officials immediately looked to Hobson City.[21] Like the defiance of African American troops that Army authorities blamed on French wine and women, fault for Linten's death lay in the city's drinking holes known as "blind tigers," on African American "immoral women," and on "other things of like nature" that authorities dared not call by name.[22] The war had barely ended, and already African Americans were troubling the waters. To stem the tide, white supremacists would have to redouble their efforts to defend Jim Crow.

If need be, white Annistonians would try to uphold it through force. Coming as it did in the weeks after the Armistice, the streetcar workers' fight with Caldwell should have struck a blow for the continuing dominance of white supremacy. Instead, the limp bodies of Linten and Morrison added fuel to white supremacists' smoldering unease.

Tension grew as word of the incident swept through the county. As evening turned to night, a mixed posse of soldiers, military policemen, sheriff's deputies, city police, and civilians combed the surrounding area for Caldwell.[23]

Downtown, other white soldiers took to the Anniston streets with white civilian men to form a vengeful and volatile crowd. Waiting for Caldwell, the downtown mob turned its fury on an African American porter who ill-advisedly wandered their way around 7:30 in the evening.

The mob's rationale for attacking the hapless porter demonstrated how quickly the alchemy of white supremacy turned individual acts into collective threats and blurred the lines between violence, sex, and politics. The attackers, who purportedly numbered in the hundreds, chased and shot at the man based on an unfounded rumor that he had "cursed a white woman" elsewhere in town.[24] He survived only because the police pulled him from the crowd and placed him in the jail for his own protection.

As the Anniston authorities blamed immoral black women for contributing to Caldwell's transgression, the Anniston mob, by their turn on the black porter, reconstituted the soldier's act of armed self-defense as part of a larger attack on white womanhood. Wartime mobilizaton had carried the specter of Negro domination to France, and the prospect of demobilization would bring it home again. White supremacists read the political threat of African American veterans as a sexual one, and following in this mold, Annistonians told the story of Caldwell's crime as an assault on innocent white womanhood. Coincidentally, the fight occurred just blocks from Linten's home, and several newspapers brought the war home by focusing on white women's deprivation. Papers piteously noted that "the wife of the dead conductor heard the shots that made her a widow" as she sat at her hearth with the couple's young child.[25] The night of the shooting, rumors circulated around Anniston that Mrs. Linten had fallen dead from shock upon hearing of her husband's murder. Although the press reassured the public that she had not died, the *Anniston Star* did note that she was "prostrated" and "pitiful" with grief.[26] When Sergeant Caldwell killed Cecil Linten, he left the conductor's baby without a father, his wife without a husband, and both with neither provider nor protector. When he wounded Kelsie Morrison, he left a father of five on the brink of death. He wrought havoc on the white family and in so doing, endangered one of the most fundamental institutions in Southern society. By the time a military police officer apprehended Caldwell in the mountains and brought him to the county jail, the mob had begun calling for his head.

If many white people in Calhoun County seemed determined to refortify white supremacy in the wake of the streetcar shooting, members of the county's African American community seemed equally committed to resist it. A contingent of African American ministers attempted to quell the fury of white Anniston with a prayer that "peace and harmony" might "continue to prevail among the two races." Issuing a formal statement from the Negro Ministers Union of Anniston and Hobson City, Reverends Roland Williams, W. M. Leak, and C. H. Brown diplomatically expressed their regret for Caldwell's crime. They deplored the "sad occurrence" and extended their sympathies "to the bereaved families of the two street car men."[27]

Yet, what looked like accommodation soon took shape as resolve. Even as they reassured the public of their respect for the white family, the ministers neither distanced themselves from Caldwell nor advocated his merciless prosecution. Instead, they urged authorities "to do everything in their power" to try Caldwell in the courts and "in a manner," they added suggestively, "which will insure full justice for all involved." Although the local paper viewed their statement as a pledge of support for "the constituted authorities, civilian and military" to prosecute Caldwell, the Ministers Union resolution actually read like a velvet-gloved demand. They not only intended to see Caldwell survive to go to a trial, they wanted to see him receive full justice.[28]

"Justice" would be the concept that determined Edgar Caldwell's fate. Black troops had labored and fought for justice, and racial activists and intellectuals had agitated for it at home and abroad. African Americans had performed their citizenship for public consumption during the war, and they had clashed with whites to preserve their sense of entitlement and belonging. With the war at an end, they needed to protect their links to the nation and the state by securing equal protection under the law. In spite of the experience of soldiers in Houston and France, the Army offered Caldwell's best hope.

Although the Army's idea of justice surely differed from that of the area ministers or racial activists, military officials could ill afford to allow an Anniston mob to lynch their soldier. Although the military policeman who found the sergeant placed him in civilian custody—"incorrectly," as Camp McClellan's Colonel J. H. Lewis would later admit—Colonel Lewis also sent an additional military police guard into town to protect Caldwell from the growing crowd.[29] Only the extra guard, the driving rain that soaked the town the night of Caldwell's arrest, and in the reproving words of the *Anniston Star,* "the lack of determined leadership" among the members of the crowd managed to stave off a lynching.[30] In the short run, the Army saved Caldwell's life.

Plenty of African American soldiers would run up against white mobs in the first year of the peace. On December 28, just over a week after Caldwell's case went to the grand jury, a group of white men in Bartlett, Texas, jumped and stabbed a soldier discharged from the 165th Depot Brigade after the soldier, a professor friend, and the professor's wife got in an altercation with a white man on the sidewalk. The soldier, Joy Warren, reported that he and his friends had tried to walk around the white man, who had not moved out of the middle of the sidewalk as they approached, when the man turned and shoved him off the walk. The federal agents who investigated the incident surmised that "that these negroes got 'biggety' and tried to shove the white man off the sidewalk whereupon the white man and his friend retaliated." Local sheriffs must have concurred with speculation that the veteran had gotten his friends all biggety and worked up. They kept him in the jailhouse for seven hours, charged him a fifteen dollar fine upon his release, and sent him on his way out of town in the middle of the night. Though Warren's stab wound was not serious, witnesses reported that his eyes were bruised and discolored and that he "smelled like a walking drug store from the amount of iodoform and antiseptics he had on him."[31]

Compared to others, Joy Warren got off easy. At least ten African American soldiers and roughly seventy-seven African American civilians were lynched in the year following the Armistice. Just one day after Caldwell's streetcar fight, on December 16, a mob of seventy-five to one hundred men "swarmed"—as an eyewitness characterized it—into the county jail in Hickman, Kentucky, broke the locks with sledge hammers, and lynched Charlie Lewis, a discharged soldier accused of robbing two African Americans.[32] Although Lewis's crime was not enough to rile up a mob, he and his accomplices attacked a sheriff's deputy who came to arrest them. Holding him at gunpoint, Lewis and friends repeatedly knocked the deputy to the ground, "striking him in the face every time," and told the officer that he "had no right to arrest a soldier." A posse caught them just over the state line in Tennessee, and once they returned Lewis to Kentucky, "infuriated citizens," as a black Cincinnati paper described them, demonstrated what rights they believed white folks still had.[33]

Nine months later in Bogalusa, Louisiana, "a mob of more than a thousand men" hunted down a discharged soldier named Lucius McCarty, named him the attacker of a local white woman, and killed him.[34] With the lynching done, they dragged his body "through the principal streets of Bogalusa" and burned it on the lawn of his alleged victim.[35] If Caldwell had died at the hands of an Alabama mob, he simply would have been another statistic.

What We Do Must Be Done Quickly

Yet Sergeant Caldwell's status as a soldier still in uniform, rather than a discharged veteran, affected what might happen to him. Camp McClellan's Colonel Lewis surrendered Caldwell and then protected him because the colonel and his fellow officers had to strike a difficult balance in dealing with the shooting, their own soldiers, and the civilian community. Their camp had already weathered a few scandals. During Camp McClellan's construction in 1917, workers purportedly organized by the Industrial Workers of the World had put a local face on wartime labor unrest.[36] In the late days of 1918, some troops, too, had given in to their restlessness by purchasing fake discharges from a corrupt junior officer. Others, like white Georgian Thomas Goble, simply went AWOL, slipping into the Georgia mountains and disguising himself as a woman to elude civilian posses.[37] African American soldiers also yearned for release. Even without the violence on the streetcar, Camp McClellan experienced taut social relations.

Given the tension outside of camp, the Army had to tread lightly. On the one hand, Army officials recognized the suspicion with which some Southerners viewed the intrusion and upheaval of a national army and military camps throughout the South.[38] With peace as yet unofficial, the Army could little afford to alienate local people over a black soldier who had shot two white men—especially when white soldiers who shared Annistonians outrage roamed the streets alongside civilians. At the same time, however, Army officials could not cede all of their authority to a mob, civilian or military. To allow Alabamans to lynch a soldier on active duty would mock the principle of discipline so critical to military order and lessen the authority of the Army itself.[39] By bringing in Caldwell, but guarding him until he could go to civilian trial, Colonel Lewis appeased the mob while asserting the Army's power. Throughout the war, military and federal officials would repeatedly seek to manage the competing demands of local interest, federal power, and international clout. In Anniston, they did so by helping to rush Caldwell's case to trial.

Over the next few days, the streetcar shooting remained "the main topic of conversation in the city" as authorities moved to deal with Caldwell before the mob could.[40] Frankly and formally, Caldwell described his position in a letter to his commanding officer. "It gives me great pleasure to write you," he announced the morning after his arrest, "that I am in trouble." Stripped of his uniform and outfitted in overalls, he wrote back to camp from a cell in the county jail.[41] The night before, he had admitted to his military interrogators that he had fought with Linten and Morrison on the Oxford line car, but he steadfastly claimed that someone else fired the shots that left the conductor dead and the motorman wounded.[42] Caldwell knew that his denial came to no avail. Served with an arrest warrant on the morning after his capture, he wrote his officer that he was "to be tried for murder."[43]

Through the combined efforts of the military, city, and county police, the case proceeded, in the words of an impressed reporter, "with a speed seldom witnessed" in criminal investigations.[44] The day after the shooting, as members of the local streetcar workers' union accompanied Linten's body back home for burial and doctors announced that Morrison would probably survive despite his wounds, Calhoun County circuit court judge Hugh Merrill called a special meeting of the grand jury for Thursday, December 19.[45] He assigned as defense counsel a local lawyer, Charles D. Kline, and set Wednesday as the day of the soldier's preliminary hearing. The whites took this "assurance of a speedy trial" as a sign that there would "be no dillydallying" in punishing Linten's killer.[46]

Although the rapid response of local authorities lessened the potential for mob violence, public fascination was at a peak by the time Caldwell arrived for his bail hearing on Wednesday morning. The initial hearing pulled a "big crowd" of curious onlookers who "thronged the courtroom" to watch as fifteen witnesses, mostly soldiers, recounted Sunday's events.[47] The crowd became so engrossed in the drama of the trial that when the first streetcar passengers identified Caldwell as the man who shot Cecil Linten, some people applauded. At the end of the day, after Judge Merrill declared that he could "do nothing less than hold the defendant for the grand jury without bond," the crowd trailed Caldwell and his protective guard of sheriff's agents, city police, and military men back to the jail.[48] If anything happened to Caldwell before he made it to trial, they wanted to be there to see it.

While the mob watched over Caldwell in the street, Alabama government and industry came together in the courthouse to build their case for the grand jury. The Alabama Power Company, employer of Caldwell's two victims, retained its Anniston counsel, Knox, Acker, Dixon, and Sterne, to aid the prosecution.[49] An eminent lawyer and Yale Law School alumnus, Niel

Sterne served as the big gun in a three-man prosecutorial team rounded out by the county attorney and a state solicitor sent up from Talladega to assist in the proceedings. Vowing to the public that "no effort would be spared" to ensure "that full justice was done in the case," Sterne and his associates entered the fray over the meaning of justice for Edgar Caldwell.[50]

In many ways Sterne, praised by his peers as a man of "much courage, good sense, and humor," represented the most benign face of Anniston's white supremacist elite.[51] A local boy, his roots in Anniston dated back almost to its opening as a public town in the early 1880s.[52] In 1887, four years after Anniston ceased being a closed, factory settlement, Sterne's father Anselm moved his wife and children—including three-year-old Niel—to the fledgling town in the Alabama hills. To the elder Sterne, himself a Jewish immigrant from the German state of Westphalia, the move from Albany, Georgia, to northern Alabama would have seemed short but significant. As a veteran of the ravaged Confederate Army, he could have found in industrial Anniston, founded in 1872, the promise of a revitalized South.

Indeed, the Sternes would prosper as the city grew. Anselm became a wealthy grocer, a city alderman, a Mason, and a life-long member of the United Confederate Veterans. As he wove the family into the fabric of the city through business and community networks, his wife Henrietta extended their ties through public service and participation. A dedicated clubwoman and founder of the Anniston's Ladies Hebrew Benevolent Society, Henrietta acted as a leader in the town's small Jewish community while becoming the honorary life-president of the local chapter of the United Daughters of the Confederacy (UDC).[53] His parents and their civic activities provided Niel Sterne with a model of Southern place and race making, as they regrouped from the Civil War's material devastation, sanctified the Lost Cause, and firmly ensconced themselves in the Anniston community as Jews certainly, but first and foremost as white Southerners.[54]

If the elder Sternes harkened back to the Old South, Niel Sterne unquestionably evoked the New. Unlike his father who had fought in Stonewall Jackson's army, Niel served under a more successful defender of white supremacy. Prior to law school, he worked as a secretary and stenographer to Colonel John B. Knox, railroad lawyer and president of the 1901 Alabama Constitutional Convention, who laid out the "question of Negro Domination" as the issue driving state constitutional reform.[55] "What is it we want to do?" Knox rhetorically asked the gathered delegates, answering "Why it is within the limits imposed by the Federal Constitution, to establish white supremacy in this state."[56] Although Knox justified past acts of fraud and terror against African American voters as acts "of necessity for self-preservation" against "the menace of Negro domination," he recognized that the times called for new stratagems.[57] With an eye toward their "duty to posterity," Knox rallied the delegates to establish white supremacy by law.[58] From John Knox, Sterne would receive his early lessons on law and politics in Alabama.

In addition to receiving Knox's guidance, Sterne, like many other young, well-to-do Southern white men, benefited immensely from the world that Knox helped to create. By quelling the ferment that came from black and dissenting white voters, disfranchisers like Knox created an illusion of order that made Southern politics more palatable to Northern observers. White elites could rely less on force or fraud because they had embodied "in fundamental law such provisions" as would "protect the sanctity of the ballot."[59] Disfranchisement allowed Southern Democrats to masquerade as democrats. Moreover, the romantic haze in which groups like the UDC suffused memories of the antebellum South and the War also helped the region seem more noble than lawless. Thus, Sterne could dare venture North to attend such a bastion of Yankee education as the Yale Law School because his parents and his mentor had effected the cultural and political coup that fostered regional reconciliation and assimilation: Sterne, in short, was a child of Reunion, and he could wear the mantle of white supremacy without ever uttering its name.[60]

Upon returning home to Alabama, Sterne continued to reap the benefits of his association with Knox and his established membership in the white ruling class. In 1911, three years after graduating summa cum laude from law school, he became a junior partner in Knox's firm and a prominent citizen.[61] He joined the Rotary Club, served on the board of Anniston's Carnegie Library, and began a lauded "ever endless effort to better the community."[62] By the time Edgar Caldwell tangled with the crew on his client's streetcar, Niel Sterne was well on his way to becoming the irreplaceable "contributing influence in the business of [the] city" that his friend Governor Thomas Kilby would one day eulogize him as having been.[63]

Niel Sterne was not the only well-connected legal official Caldwell would face in the court. Like Niel Sterne, Judge Hugh Merrill was the son of a Georgian Confederate soldier; and like the Sternes, the Merrills had moved from Georgia to northern Alabama during the political upheaval of the

1880s. They settled in neighboring Cleburne County, where Merrill's older brother Walter became head of the county's Democratic party and a state senator. After graduating from the University of Alabama law school in 1898, Hugh Merrill followed his brother into politics. He represented Cleburne County in the state house of representatives from 1900 to 1901, the year of the constitutional convention.[64] After his term in the Birmingham legislature, he moved to Anniston and took a job at John Knox's corporate law firm.

Merrill's fortunes flourished in Anniston. He stayed at the Knox firm until the year after Sterne left for law school. In 1906, he began a two-year stint as Anniston's city attorney, working under the authority of then-mayor Thomas Kilby. Five years later he began his first of three terms as a state circuit court judge. After the Caldwell case, Merrill would return to politics. He went on to become speaker of the Alabama House and, during the early Depression years, the state's lieutenant governor.[65] Both Merrill and Sterne belonged to a local elite, linked by ties of kin and community, in which law, business, and politics closely intermingled. An outsider, a "stranger in the city," Edgar Caldwell had run afoul of some of the most powerful men in northern Alabama.[66]

The Negro Ministers Union and other members of the black community watched with consternation as the "full justice" they had requested following the streetcar shooting got trampled in the authorities' lockstep march toward reprisal. On Thursday, the day after his preliminary hearing, Caldwell returned to the courthouse for a special convening of the circuit court grand jury called solely to hear his case. He only stayed for a few hours. After a ninety-minute period of deliberation that even the *Anniston Star* found "remarkably short," the grand jury returned an indictment charging the soldier with first-degree murder.[67] According to Reverend Roland Williams, one of the signers of the Ministers Union petition, the court later "boasted" of the grand jury's perfunctory consideration.[68]

The court's behavior made it apparent that African American leaders could no longer balance assertion and accommodation if they wished to save Caldwell's life. "Sure" that the soldier could "not get a fair trial" in Anniston with "the passion . . . so high," a group of local African Americans resolved to better his chances by using their own networks to counter the informal and institutional ties that united white authorities against him.[69] If black soldiers had languished in Anniston because of the "lack of unselfish leaders" among Calhoun County's fifteen black churches, the emergency occasioned by the streetcar shooting now moved area ministers to action.[70] Banding together with small businessmen, they formed a legal committee to advocate for Caldwell. The Anniston committee hired additional defense counsel, Basil Allen and Charles Kline, and launched a fundraising drive to pay the legal fees incurred. Recognizing that it had a significance that reached far beyond the Alabama hills, the committee also began pleading Caldwell's case to the NAACP in New York and to Special Assistant to the Secretary of War Emmett Scott in Washington, D.C. From his house on Brown Avenue in downtown Anniston, the forty-one-year-old Reverend Williams became the committee's spokesperson.[71]

The alternate public sphere that African Americans developed under Jim Crow provided the networks that linked the area's black middle class to each other and to the rest of the African American community. Although they could match white Anniston's upper classes neither in pedigree nor wealth, they could nevertheless surpass them in ingenuity and resolve. Even those folks without independent employment—people who could not afford to speak out publicly on behalf of Caldwell—could walk over to Tenth Street and chat about his circumstances with their neighbors in Thomas Jackson's dry goods store. Domestics who worked for white people in Anniston or laborers who did custodial work for the white-owned iron works company could keep their mouths shut, but still place a little money for Caldwell in the offering plate at the Mt. Zion Baptist Church. In the places where black public life happened, the shops and church halls and barbershops, people mulled over the Caldwell case. As Reverend Williams told the NAACP, they "organized."[72] The class divisions that normally stratified even small African American communities could compress or extend depending on circumstances. Although they might normally go their separate ways within the community, for Caldwell, the county's African Americans united.

Long decades of resistance had taught African Americans to improvise a variety of tools to use in the fight against white supremacy, but the war supplied them with new ones. In addition to the discursive advantage presented by Wilsonian rhetoric and its disconnection from social realities, wartime mobilization helped to extend African American community networks out of their local setting and into the nation at large. Established civil rights groups such as the NAACP gained new branches and members during the war—growing in numbers from 9,282 people in 80 branches in 1917 to 91,000 people in 310 branches by the end of 1919—while public campaigns for war funds and food production created new organizational infrastructures.[73] To garner African American support for the Liberty Loan drives, for example, the government-organized Committee of One Hundred brought together men from black churches, educational institutions, fraternal organizations, and commerce agencies. Moreover, these new networks also encouraged interracial cooperation in men and women's civic groups. Niel Sterne, for example, sat on the board of Anniston's Liberty Loan committee. Roland Williams served in its ranks.[74]

On Christmas Eve in Anniston, Roland Williams moved to harness, on behalf of Edgar Caldwell, these resources of war-related community organizations. In wavering handwriting, on stationery he took from the United War Work Campaign, Reverend Williams informed the NAACP national office that down in Anniston they faced "a serious case" that was "being rushed through the courts for fear of mob violence." The defendant, Williams made sure to mention, was an active-duty soldier, "not discharged," with "a fine record" and a long history of military service. Using wartime service as shorthand, he positioned himself as a community leader and transformed Caldwell from a common criminal to a worthy cause.[75]

Williams spoke in shorthand because, as he curtly informed the NAACP in his letter, "What we do must be done quickly."[76] As the court "rushed through the preliminery proceedings," Caldwell's local defenders had little time to waste wooing outside help.[77] The urgency only increased with the coming of the new year. Following the arraignment, where Caldwell entered a plea of not guilty, Judge Merrill scheduled the trial for January 17, 1919.

The defense team twice moved for a continuance, arguing that the court had placed "the case too early for the defendant to properly prepare for trial." Specifically, they needed time to seek out "a soldier, who was with the defendant at the time of shooting whom the defendant had not yet been able to locate" but who they suspected might have returned to camp. They also sought a second eyewitness, a soldier named Nathaniel Phillips who had been demobilized in the three weeks since the shooting. Caldwell and his defense team continued to maintain that someone else had shot the transportation workers. The court denied both motions to delay the trial but granted the defense permission to summarize the testimony of the discharged soldier.[78]

In January 1919, while dozens of African Americans endeavored to get to France to perform and reinforce black citizenship during the peace conference, African American Annistonians looked to the courthouse as the next theater of the struggle. "I feel," Rev. Williams wrote after Caldwell's arraignment, "like this is [a] test case of what is coming to us after war."[79] The black and white citizens of Calhoun County who thronged the courthouse a week later felt much the same way. African Americans "coming from all parts of the county" pressed into the courtroom "until it was practically impossible to get in or out." When Judge Merrill ordered the court cleared of anyone without a seat, insistent spectators stooped at cracks in the door to continue listening to the muffled proceedings. Under Merrill's orders, the police cleared them away as well.[80]

The trial remained a public event despite the restricted access to the courthouse. African Americans barred from the building gathered on the road in front, creating an impromptu open-air forum for discussing the trial. Most could have agreed with Reverend Williams statement that "the rase here sees Prejudice in the court here."[81] Looking around the courtroom, they would never even have expected to see a jury of *their* peers. Despite the best intentions of the 14th Amendment, the broad discretionary powers given to judges, prosecutors, and local administrators would keep Southern trial juries and the right of law in the hands of white men until well into the 1950s.[82] They might well have noted, also, that there were no "good white folks" on the jury, as "the men free from race prejudice were easily struck by the state" early in the process.[83] Some optimists in the crowd might have speculated about whether the legal committee's attorney Basil Allen, former judge and reputedly "one of the best lawyers in the state," could improve Caldwell's odds.[84] Given the animosity that the county's white communities radiated toward the soldier, few people likely held out much hope.

The more observant in the audience might have reported glimpsing Tressie Ford Caldwell sitting next to her husband in the court room. Contrary to some angry white Annistonians' claims that "a damn Yankee Negro soldier had come down south to start trouble," Caldwell had lived in Atlanta before he reenlisted in the military. His wife came to Anniston from their home on Auburn Avenue to see him through the trial.[85] With Cecil Linten's widow seated not far away, observers who understood the gender codes of white supremacy would have shown no surprise in seeing the two women contrasted in the next day's paper: the faceless "woman alleged to be" Caldwell's wife versus Mrs. Linten "in widow's weeds" with "her sad face clearly indicating her suffering."[86]

Whether or not she showed it, Tressie Caldwell must have suffered also. As the trial unfolded, witness after witness came forward to help paint her husband's actions as murder and foreclose any possibility of claiming self-defense. Prosecutors Sterne and Matthews presented Caldwell as the aggressor, maintaining that he chased the conductor through the streetcar and that the crewmen threatened to kick him only if he tried to board the car again.[87] Yet the prosecution appeared to condemn Caldwell equally for his violence and his skill. Over the objections of the defense, the prosecution lingered on the details of the shooting. Kelsie Morrison showed the court precisely where the bullet entered the his neck. Another witness demonstrated how Caldwell held the pistol as he fired.

Tressie Caldwell watched as prosecutors performed a juggling act, presenting her husband as both crazed murderer and calculating marksman. In so doing, they drew upon the tropes that shaped white supremacists' articulation of civic manhood, but they added a twist. Whereas in Houston, the mutineers of the 24th Infantry had been vilified for succumbing to passion over mastery and savagery over civilization, Caldwell—himself a veteran of the 24th—had demonstrated an excess of manhood. Whereas the prosecution might refer to his act of murder as brutal, mastery Caldwell had in full, and his aggression combined with his self-possession made him too dangerous to go free. In the figure of Caldwell, Sterne and Matthews underscored the potential threat to white supremacy posed by black veterans returning from the Great War; now the crazed beasts had been trained to kill and given guns to do so.

As if mindful that portraying the shooting as an act of self-defense might incite the jury as much as would deliberate murder, the defense took a different tack. Attorneys Allen and Kline conscientiously refuted the prosecution's claims that Caldwell instigated the assault. Then they went further, claiming as Caldwell had when he was arrested that someone else had shot the streetcar crew. Caldwell had fought both men, they admitted, but he had killed no one. For his part, Caldwell said nothing. Outside the courtroom, he steadfastly maintained his innocence, but he never took the stand in his own defense.[88]

Judge Merrill's refusal to admit anyone without a seat kept curious African Americans from returning in the same numbers on January 18, the trial's second day. Those who stayed away missed little. With a silent defendant and an absent eyewitness, the defense limped into the afternoon before resting its case. In the closing arguments that followed, Basil Allen summarized the testimony of ex-soldier Nathaniel Phillips, the would-be witness for whom

Judge Merrill refused to delay the trial. In the prosecution's subsequent close, county attorney Matthews dismissed the missing Phillips as a "paper witness," and Sterne followed with a forceful recap of the state's case.[89]

Merrill closed the trial with his charge to the jury. The defendant "had no right to take the life of Cecil Linton unless a necessity to take his life existed at the time," the Judge instructed the jury on the law, "or unless there was apparent necessity" to take Linton's life. In considering whether Caldwell had committed a first-degree murder, Merrill told the jury that they could make a broad reading of premeditation. It did "not mean that" the killer had to "sit down and reflect over" his crime "for an appreciable length of time." Rather, the premeditation could "exist before and while he pressed the trigger that fired the fatal shot, even if it be only for a moment or instant of time." Had Caldwell wanted to kill Linten? Could he, as a "reasonable man," have believed "that there was danger to his life"? Merrill went on to remind the jury that "no prejudice" should influence them "one way or the other"—neither "prejudice against his [Caldwell's] race" nor "sympathy for the dead man." "On the other hand," Merrill also told them, "the State of Alabama and its citizens have rights and their rights should be respected in making your decision." Telling them to use, "cold reason and the law as I have given it to you," Merrill sent them out to deliberate.[90]

The jury applied their powers of cold reason for two hours before deciding Caldwell's fate. No local African Americans remained in the courtroom by the time the jury returned, for "seeing the prejudise as it existed in the entire court," most people grew "discouraged."[91] Stoic, Caldwell sat amidst his attorneys, "a dozen or more" white soldiers, and "two or three dozen" white civilians. "Betraying no perceptible emotion," the soldier listened as the jury found him guilty of first-degree murder and sentenced him to death by hanging.[92] Six days after that, Judge Merrill scheduled his execution for a month later—February 28, 1919.

Parens Patrie

As the local paper celebrated the "closing of the drama," Caldwell's defenders geared up for the second act.[93] "We have put up a thousand dollars and we are willing to put up a thousand more," the legal committee told the still-lukewarm NAACP leadership. Although they had already contacted Emmett Scott at the War Department, they asked the NAACP to redouble their efforts to involve the government in the soldier's case. This was not a local concern, the committee nudged the Association, "this matter means much not only to Sergeant Caldwell but to the whole race."[94]

For the people who supported Caldwell, it came as no surprise that the test case for postwar civil rights grew out of a criminal trial. Looking at the Caldwell case, they saw clearly a systemic reality that a Mississippi judge would concede only years later: that the sort of retributive impulse that drove cases like Caldwell's through court so rapidly constituted a "fictitious continuation of the mob," with legal authorities doing the dirty work.[95] By trying to ensure him full justice, Caldwell's advocates asserted that the legal system owed every African American more options than simply the lynching bee versus the kangaroo court. Their push for due process, rightly observed, overtly challenged a criminal justice system that had historically served as a pillar of institutional Jim Crow. In making his cause their own, Caldwell's defenders took aim at the power that buttressed men like Linton and Morrison, as well as Sterne and Merrill, as squarely as had Caldwell himself.

As the case garnered national attention, commentators explored the promise and problems of pursuing racial justice through the law. On the one hand, the militant black *Cleveland Advocate* editorialized, "to take a life is a serious thing," and in "shooting the two 'crackers' Sgt. Caldwell broke the bonds of sanity and sound judgment," and placed himself at the mercy of the law. However, like the legal committee in Anniston, the *Advocate*'s editor could not separate the soldier's criminal act from the legal system to which he reacted: the law itself was the crux of the problem. By codifying the degradation of African Americans, it reified the cultural practices of white supremacy. By disproportionately criminalizing African American behavior, it enforced white supremacy's political and economic program. Caldwell may have broken the bonds of sanity and sound judgment by shooting the two men who were trying to kill him, but in providing no quarter for a black man to defend himself, the law strained them. "Those shots from Caldwell's pistol were not aimed merely at the men who attempted to jim-crow him," the editor explained, "but they were aimed at THE POWER those men represented."[96] In short, when Edgar Caldwell shot Cecil Linton and Kelsie Morrison, he had also taken aim at Jim Crow. Whether Caldwell had delivered a mortal wound remained anyone's guess.

In the shooting, the *Advocate* editor saw an act of "courage and daring," of physical and psychological self-defense. If Caldwell had not fired his pistol, he would have ended up just another black man beat down on a Southern street-car, and the law would have provided little recourse. Yet gauging the conse-quences, the editor could not help but question the "wisdom and expediency" of Caldwell's behavior.[97] As a symbol for "all those who believe in Negro man-hood," as W. E. B. Du Bois would later label him, Caldwell provided a quick, visceral satisfaction.[98] As an attempt to extricate himself from the South's web of white supremacy, Caldwell's action had resoundingly failed.

The question for Caldwell's supporters, then, became one of how best to use the law to overcome a system that was itself bound up in law. To his de-fenders in Anniston, Caldwell's wartime military service seemed the key to the prison gates. Because Caldwell "was an honored sergeant in the U.S. Army when he was tried," the legal committee held, the federal government had a "duty" to "see to it that he got a fair trial."[99] The notion of mutual ob-ligation that African Americans had articulated during mobilization and ex-tended to the streets of France had firmed for Annistonians defending Caldwell. Having helped to shine what President Wilson called "the light to lead men down the path of liberty," they now expected concrete protections of their rights as citizens.[100] The committee understood that staking a claim to federal citizenship was the clearest path out of the prison of states' rights and back into the full light of "humanity, or Human rights which" they had "fought for in the world war."[101]

With the cooperation of the federal government, they could lift Caldwell above the reach of Alabama law. Even as the legal committee prepared the soldier's appeal to the Alabama Supreme Court, Reverend Williams explained to the NAACP that their efforts would "avail nothing" unless the federal government "takes hold" of the case. Williams urged legal titan and NAACP President Moorfield Storey to "kindly get busy at all hazard" and bring the Attorney General, A. Mitchell Palmer, into the case.[102] Williams also used the understanding of duty to apply pressure to government officials. "In view of the fact that this man was a Soldier," Reverend Williams informed War Department advisor Emmett Scott as the case progressed through the sum-mer, "I know you will stand by us."[103]

Across the country African Americans expressed the belief that Caldwell's position as a soldier gave him a special standing. An NAACP member in Pennsylvania demanded to know whether "in the name of our God and the name of this branch, cannot something be done at once to stay this execu-tion?" If nothing else, the writer asserted, his military service should "at least fine [*sic*] him the attention of the Chief Executive."[104] In Chicago a delegation of black ministers and politicians took it upon themselves to wire Woodrow Wilson as "citizens of the United States" and humbly "beg him" to convince Alabama governor Thomas Kilby to give Sergeant Caldwell a brief reprieve. In their telegram the Chicago contingent argued that there was "reasonable doubt" as to whether Caldwell had committed first-degree murder. Although they did not overtly challenge the President to act as steward over a soldier in his Army, their use of Caldwell's rank when referring to him gently reminded the president of his status.[105] The *Advocate* reported that similar letters and telegrams "from every part of the country" also flooded the offices of Alabama officials.[106]

Even African Americans uninterested in staid venues of political pressure drew inspiration from Caldwell's position as a soldier. In lieu of stately appeals to Woodrow Wilson or Alabama officials, an anonymous man from St. Louis wrote Judge Hugh Merrill directly. Calling him a "Southern dog," the letter writer informed the judge that there were men in Anniston who would sacrifice their lives to avenge Caldwell. More specifically, the author informed Merrill that if Caldwell died, someone would shoot the judge through the heart two weeks later. The writer closed the letter with his initials and a black hand labeled "Death" drawn at the bottom of the page.[107]

Caldwell's defense committee in Anniston succeeded in making the case a national concern, and the many forms of public pressure succeeded in prolonging his life. The day before Caldwell's scheduled execution, Secretary of War Newton Baker—urged by Emmett Scott—composed a telegram for Woodrow Wilson to send to Alabama's Governor Thomas Kilby explaining that they wanted the attorney general to look into the case. The reasoning that had driven African American protest of the Caldwell case found its way from Roland Williams to Emmett Scott, and from Scott to Baker to Wilson. Using Baker's words to ask whether "in view of the fact that this man was a soldier of the United States" Kilby might "be willing to grant a brief reprieve," the President echoed black Annistonians' long-argued position. In response, Kilby wired Wilson that the Alabama Supreme Court had already issued a stay of execution pending their hearing of the case. The federal government would have time to review the case without Kilby, a friend of prosecutor Niel Sterne and a former mayor of Anniston, looking too sympathetic toward the defendant.[108] States rights and federal authority remained in balance.

On the ground in Alabama, Caldwell's legal committee continued their exhaustive efforts to save him. Anticipating a setback in the state Supreme Court, they resolved to "wait quietly until a dissition is made" and then "push our claim [for] all it is worth to get it out of the state courts into U.S. courts."[109] They organized an Anniston/Hobson City NAACP branch to lobby more effectively for Caldwell and to pull the NAACP national office more completely into the fight. With some financial help from the Montgomery branch and working with the branch office in Washington, D.C., the Anniston/Hobson City chapter kept up pressure on the attorney general, the Army's judge advocate general, and the U.S. attorney in Birmingham.[110]

The Alabama Supreme Court ruling in July 1919 underscored—to Caldwell's followers—the necessity of getting Caldwell's case out of the state courts. Looking at Judge Merrill's denials of continuance, his charge to the jury, his tortured interpretation of first-degree murder, the unorthodox convening of the grand jury, and the composition of the petit jury, the justices reaffirmed "the power of the court to control the business of the court." What appeared arbitrary or biased to Caldwell's defense attorneys easily fell within the bounds of Judge Merrill's authority and Alabama law, the justices ruled.[111] The state Supreme Court upheld Caldwell's conviction and his death sentence. If Caldwell's advocates wanted to save him, they would have to rely on higher authorities and federal laws.

Federal authorities, however, proved themselves reluctant allies. "The Caldwell case is a mighty difficult case to handle at the War Department," Washington branch president Archibald Grimke complained in a progress report back to NAACP headquarters. "It is like butting one's head against a stone wall." Grimke rightly suspected that both the War Department and the Department of Justice would rather "evade" the Caldwell case than deal with the questions it raised.[112] In fact, as members of the legal committee fired off heartfelt missives to race activists urging them to continue pressuring A. Mitchell Palmer, the attorney general, Palmer for his part sent the President a terse letter stating that he "could find no authority warranting interference by the Federal Government."[113]

Caldwell's advocates refused to be deterred. They pressed the NAACP national office for funds so that they could send their attorney Charles Kline to Washington, and they continued to press the organization to work in concert with Emmett Scott in the War Department and with James Cobb, a lawyer on the Washington branch's legal committee. Cobb, who would become one of the greatest assets in the fight for Caldwell, served as a crucial bridge between the Jim Crow South and the high politics of Washington. Born on a plantation near Shreveport, Louisiana, in 1876, Cobb was an orphan by the age of eight. Through a combination of luck and enterprise, he managed to work his way through Straight University in New Orleans and Fisk in Nashville, Tennessee. After college, he made his way to Washington, D.C., to attend Howard Law School.[114]

Cobb built his legal career from within the federal government. He joined the Department of Justice during the Roosevelt administration, rising to the rank of assistant U.S. Attorney in D.C. Displaced by the changing of the guard under Wilson, "the mutations of politics"—as the *Washington Bee* genteelly described the Wilson administration's elimination of posts for black

James Cobb, Caldwell's lawyer. Scurlock Studio Records, Archives Center, National Museum of American History, Behring Center, Smithsonian Institution.

federal employees—he joined the faculty at Howard Law School.[115] During
the Coolidge administration, Cobb would replace Judge Robert Terrell on the
D.C. municipal court. Later, as a law professor at Howard, he would teach
alongside former lieutenant Charles Hamilton Houston.

In July 1919, Cobb wrote NAACP Secretary James Weldon Johnson in New
York to tell him that he had read the court record and thought the Caldwell
case "should be pushed to the limit."[116] Cobb's memo, dated July 21, came in
the midst of a season of racial violence that surpassed anything seen in the
United States since the end of Reconstruction. A minimum of thirty-eight
riots broke out during the Red Summer, as Johnson labeled it, in places like
Longview, Texas; Charleston, South Carolina; Omaha, Nebraska; Elaine,
Arkansas; Chicago, Illinois; and in Washington, D.C.[117] Many of the riots
involved soldiers, black and white. In Charleston in May, for example, after
an African American shot a white man in a poolroom, hundreds of white
sailors ran riot through the city. The mob destroyed some black-owned businesses and killed two African Americans, one of whom they shot after
snatching him off a streetcar.[118]

For the committee working on behalf of Caldwell, July's riot in Washington, D.C., would hit the closest to home. On Saturday, July 19, "several hundred soldiers, sailors, and marines" joined with "more than a thousand"
white civilians to launch attacks on African Americans.[119] Fired by reports
of a "Negro Crime Wave" and purported attacks on white women, mobs went
after African Americans in the streets, in parks, and on public transportation—
dragging men off of streetcars, as rioters had in Charleston the month
before.[120]

Without serious intervention, Cobb predicted in his July 21 memo, "the
city [would] be drenched in blood." Events proved him correct: mobs ram-
paged until Tuesday, with "women . . . beaten, men shot, and even young-
sters hurled from windows of moving cars." In one white district, four white
men ripped the clothes off of a black woman and made her walk naked out of
their neighborhood. Such violence directed at black men and women, the
headlines in the *Bee* observed, was the " 'Colored Americans' reward for
fighting for 'world democracy.' "[121]

In the midst of the rioting, James Cobb joined William Houston and a
delegation of prominent black men who urged D.C. government leaders to
protect African Americans in their districts. However, African Americans on
the ground in riot-besieged districts did not wait for government protection

that might never come; they fought back. Of the fifteen people killed or critically wounded during the riots, at least ten were white.[122] Messengers on bicycles rode through black neighborhoods warning when white mobs were approaching. While some people stayed home to protect their property from marauders, the black weekly *Washington Eagle* noted with a touch of satisfaction, others took to the streets "armed to the teeth."[123]

Often, black Washingtonians targeted soldiers and the police. Four black men fired on the entrance of the Naval Hospital the day after white soldiers instigated the first round of rioting. That night, authorities literally had to call in the cavalry on an African American man in the northwest section of town who was leaning out the window shooting at white soldiers. The cavalry rode up to the apartment building with sabres drawn, but the shooter had disappeared out his back door. Elsewhere in northwest D.C., a young African American woman held police off at gunpoint while she fired off rounds out the window of her second-floor apartment. When a policeman forced his way in, she shot him before other officers could subdue her. In many parts of town, the *Washington Bee* crowed, "Ethiopia reigned supreme."[124]

Just a week later at the end of July, in Chicago, when the stoning of a black child by whites protecting their segregated beach ignited the most deadly riot of the summer, blacks would fight again. African American veterans rushed to the streets to prevent the wholesale massacre that had defined the East St. Louis riot two years earlier. A returned Haywood Hall joined with other veterans of the Eighth Illinois to defend their neighborhood from the "racist gangs, organized by city ward heelers and precinct captains," whom he blamed for the tensions underlying the riot. Hall and his friends used Army-issue Springfield rifles and a submachine gun that he presumed came from the regiment's Armory to "setup watch" for white "invaders." Although no one came their way, Hall heard that another group of black veterans had successfully ambushed white rioters sixteen blocks down the road.[125]

Black militancy came at a cost. African Americans had stood up to white mobs, Hall noted with pride, but they had also lost much. Twenty-three black people died in the Chicago rioting that lasted from July 27 until August 2, 1919. Another fifteen white people died, and five hundred people, black and white, suffered injuries. Somewhere near a thousand people were left homeless. Hall came out of the riots sobered by the death and destruction and determined that "racism . . . and the bombings and terrorist attacks" that had marked the riot "must be eliminated."[126]

As riot followed riot in the summer, Cobb and the legal committee focused their efforts on saving Caldwell to reclaim the justice system for all African Americans. With the Red Summer underscoring the gruesome toll of large-scale racial violence, justice through law seemed, to them, imperative. In a meeting with a representative of the Justice Department, Cobb explained that, in this instance, the federal government held responsibility for guaranteeing that justice. "While the state had jurisdiction," he stressed to the assistant attorney general, Robert Stewart, "it only had that jurisdiction by virtue of the fact that the United States Government had surrendered Caldwell to it." Thus, "it was incumbent upon this government to see that he got a fair and impartial trial."[127]

After "travelling completely and fully over the situation," Palmer's assistant attorney general Robert Stewart came to agree that "the record disclosed peradventure that a fair and impartial trial had not been granted." By the time Cobb, Scott, and Kline left, Stewart had consented to file an amicus curiae brief in the second state Supreme Court hearing.[128]

Less amenable to the idea, A. Mitchell Palmer turned the decision over to the president. The attorney general expressed his reluctance and simultaneously validated the claim previously made by Caldwell's supporters. "The only excuse, of course, for going this far," he grumpily echoed Cobb and the Anniston legal committee, "is the fact that the defendant, at the time of the commission of the crime, was a soldier and the War Department might have tried him for the offense but did not." Palmer laid out the options: they could file a brief and field accusations of interfering with the state courts, or they could do nothing. If they chose the latter, he wrote to the president in the wake of the Chicago riots, "I presume Negroes generally will feel that the Government is not interested in its Negro soldiers."[129] After quick consideration, Wilson instructed Palmer to write the brief.[130]

The amicus brief forcefully asserted the federal government's ownership of, and right to protect, Sergeant Caldwell. Military service effects a soldier's complete withdrawal "from civil life," the Justice Department explained, making the United States responsible for "his housing, clothing, medical and other requirements." In other words, the brief continued, "the soldier dwells in a realm of unusual exactions and discipline, subject to laws and tribunals exerting no authority elsewhere." Thus "the United States truly becomes the soldier's *parens patrie*." Soldiers, celebrated as the ultimate men in the civilian community, were reconstrued as children as the federal government insisted upon its responsibility for them. The federal government would "not suffer a wrong or injustice done to" a soldier because both his "restricted and exacting life" and the need to "keep his mind 'staid' upon" military tasks made the soldier worthy of protection. Convicting Edgar Caldwell of anything more than manslaughter seemed to the Justice Department an injustice worthy of intervention.[131]

Not even the reassuring paternalism of the Justice Department's brief could sway the justices of the Alabama Supreme Court. Upon rehearing the case in October 1919, the high court stuck to its guns. Justices dismissed the contention that "the public mind was inflamed against the defendant because of his race through newspaper articles" because the defense could not demonstrate that any jurors had read the paper. After twice giving the case the scrutiny that "the importance of the cause demands," the court remained "convinced" that the "appellant was given a fair and impartial trial in the court below."[132] With his conviction affirmed and rehearing denied, Caldwell was sentenced to hang on December 5, 1919.[133]

"This is the biggest case in the U.S.," black Annistonians informed the NAACP national office in the wake of the state court's decision. "The Dread Scott case was not more famous and did not [do] more disgrace to Democracy than this one."[134] Hyperbolic though they sounded, Caldwell's champions touched on a measured political argument. The same questions drove the *Caldwell* case that had animated *Dred Scott* in 1859: "Can a negro, whose ancestors were imported into this country and sold as slaves become a member of the political community formed and brought into existence by the Constitution?" Was the black man entitled to the rights of a citizen?[135]

Justice Roger Taney had based part of his ruling against African American citizenship on the fact that black people could not serve in state militias. "In New Hampshire," he pointed out, black people formed "no part of the sovereignty of the state and [were] not therefore called on to uphold and defend it." Congress had passed a similar law, he argued, effectively excluding "the African race . . . from the duties and obligations of citizenship."[136] Yet the 14th Amendment had made African Americans citizens, and conscription had ratified Sergeant Caldwell's obligation to uphold and defend the United States. On what basis, then, could the court deny him protection? Moreover, just as abolitionists believed that Dred Scott's free status should have carried over from the free territories to the slave state of Missouri, Caldwell's defenders held that Caldwell's rights—as a soldier, man, and citizen—traveled with him regardless of region. Sixty-two years and three wars after Roger Taney ruled against African American citizenship, the black community in Anniston prodded the U.S. government to stand behind the federal citizenship of Edgar Caldwell and thereby protect "the rights and privileges and immunities guarantied" to all its citizens.

Nothing Short of Judicial Murder

Caldwell's advocates kept on pushing. Caldwell's wife, Tressie Ford Caldwell, traveled the South soliciting aid for her husband's case.[137] Closer to home the legal committee struggled to raise the money to petition for a writ of habeas corpus, a request to remove the case from state courts and place it in the federal jurisdiction. In Washington, Cobb, Scott, and Kline continued to lobbying the federal government for legal aid.

In mid-November, James Cobb emphatically told Secretary of War Newton Baker that if Caldwell died it would "be nothing short of judicial murder." Recapitulating the arguments presented in the Justice Department's Alabama court brief, Cobb asked Baker "with all the emphasis that within" him lay, to put his support behind Caldwell.[138] He asked again in face-to-face meetings with Baker and Assistant Attorney General Stewart. When Stewart resisted the idea that the federal government had jurisdiction over the case, Cobb countered with another case in which a white Kentucky national guardsman who had been indicted for murder in civilian court received a habeas writ returning him to military jurisdiction. Cobb made the same point to Stewart that he had made in his letter to Baker. "If it be true in that case" where a guardsman only became a United States soldier because the Army had taken over the National Guard for the war, "how much more so is it true" for Caldwell "who was a United States soldier in the regular army" and who had "risen to the dignity of Sergeant."[139]

Cobb's reasoning pacified Stewart and won over Baker, who "had manifested a very sympathetic interest from the beginning."[140] The strongest objections to federal intervention came, ironically, from the acting judge advocate general (JAG) who noted that the Army had dishonorably discharged the soldier following his arrest. The habeas writ would oust the state jurisdiction if approved by the district court, but since Caldwell was now technically a civilian, the Army would not be able to prosecute him. He would go free. Cobb urgently "tried to impress upon" the military lawyer that Caldwell "was cast in that position by no election of his" and that to execute him "upon a sentence with no legal standing" would "be nothing short of lynching."[141] Secretary Baker sided with Cobb over the acting JAG and asked the Justice Department to help with the habeas petition.

The Justice Department ordered the U.S. attorney for the Northern District of Alabama to join as amicus curiae on the habeas petition despite holding "serious doubts of the merits of the petitioner's contention."[142] As the assistant attorney general saw it, the amicus brief would satisfy Caldwell's advocates who had been hounding the department for well nigh a year. Whatever happened with the petition, Stewart reasoned to President Wilson's powerful presidential secretary Joseph P. Tumulty, "there will be no possible criticism but that the United States has exercised every known legal method to safeguard" Caldwell's rights.[143] After that, they could walk away.

Filed two weeks before the scheduled hanging, the petition laid out in legal terms what Caldwell's supporters had maintained from the outset: "By reason of the Constitution and Laws of the Government of the United States of America the state court was without jurisdiction and authority to indict or try or convict a soldier of the United States Army for the offense of murder" while the country was at war. The petitioners requested that the federal judge set aside the conviction and free Caldwell.[144] The court denied the request but issued a certificate of reasonable doubt that stayed the execution and entitled him to an appeal.[145] Marching forth on their earlier vow "to fight to the highest court in the land," Caldwell's legal committee prepared to carry the petition to the U.S. Supreme Court.[146]

As James Cobb readied a brief for a March 4, 1920, appearance before the Supreme Court, the NAACP finally launched a fundraising and publicity campaign in the *Crisis*. "We want 500 Negroes who believe in Negro manhood," editors wrote in the March 1920 issue, "to send *immediately* one dollar each" to fund the defense effort.[147] By spring 1920, "Negro manhood" had weathered several storms. With the Red Summer behind them and the final soldiers returned from war by fall 1919, the promise of a New Reconstruction had given over to retrenchment and defense in the face of overwhelming white reaction. The *Crisis*'s photograph of Caldwell somber faced in his Army khakis seemed to symbolize white America's unyielding will to exclude African Americans from the state and nation more than the inevitable triumph of black public service. Still, African Americans pushed on. Donations for Caldwell's case came from men and women all over the map: from Americus, Georgia, to

Thermopolis, Wyoming; Colusa, California, to Cotton Plant, Arkansas. Even members of the far-flung 24th Infantry in which Caldwell had served from 1913 to 1915 contacted the NAACP to express their desire to help him.[148]

The patchwork assemblage of Caldwell supporters faced a powerful adversary in the state of Alabama. With the case on its way to the Supreme Court, Roland Williams noted with dismay, "the political wires" were "being pulled" by influential white men in Alabama in a craven attempt "to defeat justice."[149] The state's attorney general, bolstered by a bevy of high-powered Washington and Alabama lawyers, paid a visit to A. Mitchell Palmer to discourage him from further participating in the Caldwell case. With one eye on the 1920 presidential nomination, a twitchy A. Mitchell Palmer bowed to their wishes. Removing his assistant attorney general from the case, he turned it over to the Solicitor General Alexander King, who flatly told James Cobb that the "United States would be stultifying itself if it interfered."[150]

Once again Cobb endeavored to reengage the Justice Department. To the NAACP national office, he observed that King, "who is from the state of Georgia," came across as "in perfect sympathy with what was done in Alabama." As racial activists endeavored to use the federal government to overcome white supremacy, Southern Democrats in the Wilson administration repeatedly threw up barriers. Undeterred, Cobb reminded King that the Justice Department had already interfered. When the solicitor general grudgingly agreed to write a brief even though he did not agree with Cobb's position, Cobb told him not to bother unless his "heart and head were at one that this man had not been fairly dealt with."[151]

Ultimately, King produced a brief which Cobb deemed "very good." In the brief, the solicitor general's office disavowed "any desire to interfere with the asserted jurisdiction of the courts of Alabama to try and convict" a United States soldier "if such jurisdiction shall be made to appear." However, prior court decisions showed that that the state's jurisdiction might not exist. King cited the case previously mentioned by Cobb in which a Kentucky district judge had conceded exclusive jurisdiction to the federal government. Reviewing case law, King queried whether "Congress in the Articles of War has taken over the Government and control of the soldier in such a manner as to forbid the attaching of State jurisdiction except in the time of peace."[152] In wartime, could no one stake a claim to Caldwell besides Uncle Sam himself?

In their brief for the appellant, James Cobb, Charles Kline, and fellow lawyer Henry Davis argued that, indeed, Uncle Sam *did* have the primary claim on Edgar Caldwell. Their argument emerged from an understanding of nationhood and citizenship molded by America's Great War experience. They began with the assertion that "the United States is—no longer 'are'—a nation in all that the word imports." Through a decades-long process that culminated during the war, the American nation had become a nation-state, singular and strong, "and within its sphere its authority is complete and supreme."[153] They conceived of the nation less as an imagined community of shared history and lineage than as one titanic body, vast and ravenous, which subsumed the people born and naturalized within its territory.[154] The appellant counsel proffered a version of the nation-state in which the South could not continue its selective enforcement of the Civil War amendments. The logical end of their argument was with a robust enforcement of the protections guaranteed by the 14th Amendment.

Central to this conception of the nation-state was its compulsory power. National citizenship, which history had revealed as "primary, paramount, and dominant" over state citizenship, marked individuals as organs of the nation-state, more than of the individual states, and made them subject to the nation-state's will. Military service increased the dominance of national citizenship. In times of war especially, "the human as well as material constituents" of the military existed "beyond any other reach than" that of the nation itself. Soldiers were the ultimate national citizens.[155]

Paring away the many layers of affiliation and belonging that marked African American political consciousnesses in the period after the war, Caldwell's lawyers hooked their hopes for his salvation on a straightforward military nationalism. Whereas in normal circumstances an individual might have multiple identities and citizenships, the transformation of the national body during war made this impossible. War rendered the national body in two, the appellant counsel argued, creating a civil citizenry that retained its multiple jurisdictions and a military citizenry that did not. They remained as separate "as though the two were composed of members of different races of men." To Caldwell's case, his lawyers applied the one-drop rule: his military service made him a military citizen. Since the courts-martial in times of war had exclusive jurisdiction on murders committed by soldiers in the United States Army, they argued, the State of Alabama could lay no valid claim to Edgar Caldwell.[156]

Niel Sterne and the remaining counsel for the state of Alabama presented a simple but effective rebuttal. Where the appellant's brief had been ornate and theoretical, theirs was spare. Where Caldwell's lawyers had suffused their brief in racialized arguments, they mostly avoided reminders of race. Because Caldwell's team had not challenged their laws, only their ability to enforce them, the Alabama lawyers could best defend white supremacy through circumspection.

Ignoring the arguments over citizenship that would have pulled the question of Caldwell's status out into the open, the Alabama legal team took a more narrow approach to the question of jurisdiction. Through a close reading of the Articles of War, they argued that nothing in the law expressly excluded trying soldiers in civil tribunals. Exclusive jurisdiction, they warned, would "remove from civil tribunals the right to punish a large class of offenses against the civil sovereignty" even when "the civil sovereignty would have a greater interest in the prosecution than the military establishment." It would "compel the abdication" of what a Supreme Court justice had once labeled "'that supremacy of civil power which is a fundamental principle of the Anglo-Saxon polity.'" The state's lawyers felt sure that Congress had never meant to pass a law "so obnoxious to the feelings and beliefs of the American people."[157] After his oral argument, Justice Louis Brandeis would send Niel Sterne a note congratulating him on the forcefulness of his presentation.[158]

The oral arguments lasted two days, and as James Cobb noted, "the Court and all the lawyers in attendance" showed "unusual interest" in the case.[159] The solicitor general and assistant attorney general told Cobb that they considered the case "one of the most important" to have gone before the Court "in a long time." With the publicity campaign still going, "people from all over the country" wrote to question Cobb and the NAACP about the case. Although they had a month to wait before the Court's decision, Cobb declared himself "quite sure the case will do good in many directions."[160]

Cobb's optimism proved misplaced. Like the lower courts before it, the Supreme Court ruled against Edgar Caldwell in an April 1920 decision authored by Chief Justice Edward Douglass White. A former slaveholder and "hidebound reactionary in every sense of the word"—as the *Messenger* unlovingly described him—White focused on the question of jurisdiction.[161] Rejecting the arguments of Caldwell's attorneys and the solicitor general, he ruled that the phrasing of the 1916 amendments to the Articles of War did not mandate exclusive jurisdiction on murder cases in war time. Because Caldwell was off base in a town not directly involved in military conflict, the military shared its jurisdiction with the state of Alabama. If the Army had claimed Caldwell from the outset, perhaps his reading might be different, but as it stood, White the ex-

Confederate soldier could not countenance the "destruction of state authority" that would result from "the enlargement of military power" to an exclusive jurisdiction "as the mere result of a state of war."[162] Mobilization for war may have aided the Progressive-Era project of consolidating power into the federal government, but White would choose states' rights over Caldwell's rights. He affirmed the district court's decision to deny the habeas corpus writ, closing the door on Caldwell's last hope for a legal remedy.

The Supreme Court ruling seemed to come as little surprise to the members of the African American press who had been following the case. The *Houston Informer* and *Cleveland Advocate* had jumped the gun and reported his execution months before.[163] Right after the ruling, the Montgomery-based *Emancipator* reported that the Supreme Court had dismissed "Caldwell's Appeal," but made little comment on the substance of White's ruling. Like the *Defender* and *Advocate* that ran articles closer to Caldwell's July date of execution, the *Emancipator* skirted around the case's legal issues to return to the dramatic story of Caldwell's initial stance. For those African Americans who wanted the sergeant to symbolize the apex of defiant African American manhood rather than have him evoke the tribulations that followed that first retaliatory impulse, the beginning of Caldwell's story mattered less than the ending.

Even for those who continued to try to fight for Caldwell, hope would finally peter out. Advocates for Caldwell continued to press the governor and the president to commute the soldier's sentence, and people continued to mail funds to the NAACP national office for months to come. The legal committee appealed to the state's American Legion, the "white women of Anniston," and, "confidentially, the dead man's wife" to help them wrest clemency from the Alabama governor.[164] Their efforts came to naught, however, and over the next few months the letters slowly stopped issuing from Williams's house on Brown Avenue. James Cobb, who felt that "everything humanly possible should be done" on Caldwell's behalf, came to "hope for little" in terms of actually saving him.[165] The people who had put up a valiant fight for Edgar Caldwell's life began to work to come to terms with his death.

For the final time, an Alabama judge sentenced Caldwell to hang. Granting him the latest date allowable by law, the judge set the execution for July 30, 1920. With the support of the Bible and his "good little wife," Caldwell kept his chin up.[166] At his sentencing hearing in late May, the local paper noted, he stood in military position "with the clasping and unclasping of his left hand the only indication of his excitement or nervousness."[167] Almost to the end, he seemed convinced that he would escape death. As late as July, Caldwell expressed his expectation to a friend that he would be going to the state penitentiary rather than the gallows, but it was not to be.[168]

With telegrams requesting executive clemency still coming in from across the country, Edgar Caldwell went to his death. On July 30 at noon, after speaking briefly with the widow and son of Cecil Linten, he gave his longest, and last, public statement. "I am being sacrificed today upon the altar of passion and racial hatred that appears to be the bulwark of America's civilization," he told the 2,500 people gathered in front of the jail. If his death could "alleviate the pain and sufferings" of other African Americans, he would have counted himself "fortunate in dying." However, the war and its aftermath had showed the futility of heroic sacrifice. Caldwell counted himself as "but one of the many victims among my people who are paying the price of America's mockery of law and dishonesty in her profession of an American democracy."[169] After thirty minutes of speaking, reading scripture, and singing hymns, the Calhoun County sheriff took him back into the jail enclosure. About 200 people watched the execution while outside the jail his supporters wept. Twelve agonizing minutes after the sheriff sprang the trap, physicians pronounced him dead. James Ballard, undertaker and member of the legal committee, turned Caldwell's body over to his wife for burial.[170] "Never before" had "such a fight been made in the state of Alabama to save a man's life," the Birmingham *Age* marveled when it was all over.[171]

It took nineteen months for Edgar Caldwell to travel the long path from Hobson City to the gallows. Along the way he became both an emblem and tactic of black resistance, as race activists sought to use his status as a soldier to change his status as a citizen—and thereby save his life. The people who propelled and funded the Caldwell case were not simply interfering "Northern negroes" as the *Anniston Star* tried to paint them.[172] Rather, they were local people who learned to organize nationally and saw Caldwell's cause as part of their own. With acumen, ingenuity, and a resolve that set them a pace ahead of the NAACP, and several strides ahead of the federal government, African Americans in Calhoun County chose the criminal justice system as the field on which to wage this battle in the long-standing struggle to pry American democracy free from the lock-grip of white supremacy.

Sergeant Caldwell's "legal lynching," as the *Crisis* denounced it, did not diminish the efforts made by his defense committee or the countless people who sought to uphold Negro manhood by supporting his cause. "His end," the *Crisis* argued, supplied "but one more reason for a more unbending and relentless fight" on the part of antiracists to "end this farce which allows color prejudice to blind justice."[173] As the NAACP moved on to more criminal defense cases—defending the Elaine, Arkansas, rioters in the Supreme Court in 1923, Ossian Sweet in Detroit in 1925, and with the International Labor Defense the Scottsboro rape cases of 1932–1935, for example—their victories built on their experiences defending Caldwell.[174]

The fight would have to take other forms as well. With Southern courts hiding behind the threat of lynching to justify doing the work of the mob in the courtroom, racial activists realized that they would have to turn their attention to the problem of unequal justice at the street level. The *Caldwell* case underscored the need for Congressional antilynching legislation, for the federal government to interpose itself between the individual and the Southern states to protect African American lives in any meaningful fashion. After *Caldwell*, the NAACP and its membership would focus its efforts on passing the Dyer Anti-Lynching Bill and continue to press for a full citizenship that combined liberty and life, political and civil rights.[175] With the 1923 defeat of the Dyer bill, and time and again in the postwar period, the federal government would fail African Americans, but they kept pushing all the same.

With organizational strategies developing alongside their political consciousnesses, African Americans at war with Jim Crow carried the freedom struggle to the halls of Paris and the hills of Alabama. They continued fighting after demobilization, taking on white supremacy whether it appeared in a Klansmen's robe or dressed in a fascist's uniform. In the NAACP, the UNIA, the club movement, and the radical left—or through the idiosyncratic self-positioning of someone like Ely Green—African Americans drew on the experiences of World War I to shape their subsequent activism. Embracing a sense of diaspora and militant struggle, they survived the Jazz Age and weathered the Depression years to bring their knowledge and resolve to the next great war. If African Americans were ready to fight for a Double Victory during World War II, it was because they had begun training for that fight twenty years earlier.

7

Forewarned Is Forearmed

In 1919, disabled white veteran Richard Roberts, fresh back from France, entered a "Negro Shoe Shop" not far from Camp Meade, Maryland. On the wall, he saw a large poster picturing "an army of negro men in uniform and 2 Negro Officers" looking down at them from a hilltop. Twenty-three years later, as World War II raged, Roberts still recalled the text that accompanied the picture. "'What do you see'?" one officer in the poster asked the other. Gazing down at what Roberts called "the body of negro soldiers," the second officer in the poster replied: "'What we couldn't do, if they only knew their strength.'" In the Great War, many African Americans explored and expanded their strength. The vicious white backlash that followed the war reflected and diagnosed that black power, though scholars have usually remembered the venom of the reaction against them rather than the self-assertion that made it necessary.[1]

Segregationists remembered. Such hints of militancy after World War I boded ill for World War II, Roberts wrote to Mississippi Senator Theodore Bilbo. After commending Bilbo for his "wonderful work" blocking the 1942 Geyer-Pepper anti-poll-tax bill in the Senate, Roberts described to him the poster he had seen upon his return from the front. "This was in 1919," he warned, "what do you suppose they think to-day?" With two more decades under their belt of organizing, recruiting allies, and campaigning against Jim Crow, Africans American had come to know their strength. If they marshaled it against white supremacists, at home and abroad, Jim Crow might well have a problem.[2]

Segregationists like Bilbo and Roberts were not the only ones regarding World War II through the lens of past experience. In 1940, more than a year before the United States declared war on Germany or Japan, Charles Hamilton Houston recorded his memories of service in the pages of the *Pittsburgh Courier*. He did so, he explained, "so that our white fellow citizens may learn

Charles Hamilton Houston presenting a brief, 1930s. Scurlock Studio Records, Archives Center, National Museum of American History, Behring Center, Smithsonian Institution.

they must treat Negroes as equals." More important, he told his story so that "this generation of Negro boys may have their eyes opened" to the struggles that lay ahead. "Forewarned," he wrote simply, "is forearmed."[3]

World War I had set Charles Houston's course. As a new soldier stationed at the same Camp Meade where Richard Roberts had seen his nightmare picture of the future, Lieutenant Houston had served a brief stint as a judge advocate with nothing to aid him but his undergraduate training and quick mind. The son of a lawyer, before the war Houston had chosen to teach English at Howard rather than follow his father into the family practice. But his experience with military courts-martial and the capricious exercise of power by Army officials led him to resolve that he would "never get caught again without knowing something about [his] rights." If he lived through the war, he vowed to himself, he "would study law" and dedicate himself to "fighting for men who could not strike back." And so he did. By 1940, Lieutenant Houston had earned a J.D. from Harvard. He had served as the first black editor of Harvard's law review and then joined James Cobb, Edgar Caldwell's lawyer, on the faculty of the Howard Law School. Houston had followed Cobb into work with the National Association for the Advancement of Colored People (NAACP); he became mentor to a generation of black activist lawyers and the architect of the NAACP's strategy to undo white supremacy through litigation.[4]

World War I permanently altered African American lives. The war did not generate the New Negro; African American men and women had appealed to and anticipated a resurgent black fighting spirit long before troops ever shipped to European shores. Rather, the war supplied a new theater for Americans to wage old battles over nation and state, color and access, power and rights. Set against the backdrop of colonial rivalries and international devastation, the war placed American white supremacy in sharp relief even as it steeled black people's resolve to grab for the democracy they had talked so much about. The war also exposed white supremacy as part of a larger system. Neither purely personal nor limited to the local, white supremacy linked economic and political exploitation of black people in the United States to the racial regimes of European empires. The New Negro had kin in Africa.

What did these New Negroes do with themselves after the war? They soldiered on. Veterans of the World War I–era struggles, military and social, met the political reaction of the 1920s and the economic devastation of the 1930s with a fearsome resiliency tempered in battles fought from the Argonne to Anniston. How they met the challenges of those years differed from person to person and moment to moment; yet many navigated using the nascent internationalism and deepened skepticism about the promise of American democracy that they had learned in war. As the clouds of a second great war gathered on Europe's horizon, these African Americans denounced European imperialism from the outset and started to formulate strategies for demanding concessions from another Democratic administration. As Richard Roberts and Theodore Bilbo anticipated, and as Charles Hamilton Houston knew, the generation of black Americans that came of age during World War I entered World War II knowing the pitfalls of purported wars for democracy and knowing, as well, their strength. Their work in the interwar years left them forearmed, ready to create a mass civil rights movement out of the shards and ruins of the next war.

Lead Thou Me On

The final Sunday of the Universal Negro Improvement Association's 1920 International Convention of Negroes began with all the pomp and proclamation that had come to characterize the month-long gathering. As they had at previous meetings in the August convention, the officers of the organization's "Legion of Honor" marched into the hall dressed in their paramilitary uniforms. Behind them came a church choir outfitted in white ecclesiastical garments and, in the rear, the association's newly elected officials "garbed," as the UNIA publication the *Negro World* described, "in the robes of their office." Where Marcus Garvey had launched the event with a grandiloquent roust of black people globally—"insane and bombastic rhodomontades," participant Hubert Harrison opined—the bishops and ministers who opened the Sunday meeting mixed Garvey's bluster with the fiery eloquence of the Good Book. A soloist sang a hymn that begged "Lead Kindly Light / Amidst the tumult and gloom / Lead Thou me on." As if in answer, Baptist theologian R. H. Eason urged the thousands gathered to do their "duty" by God and Ethiop, adding that Garvey preached a "new religion that saves your body as well as your soul." Mood and hopes ran high. Onto the stage, into this mélange of black power, military symbolism, and Christian striving, walked Kathryn Johnson.[5]

A year earlier, Johnson had returned from France, fighting. She had run up against Jim Crow before she had even made it to solid ground, clashing with white women aboard the return steamer *Noordam.* After one volunteer had chastised her and other black aid workers for "trying to get away from" their "race" by avoiding segregated seating in the dining room, Johnson sought out her supervisor to see if the segregation order stood. "Why yes," she remembered the woman saying, "You don't think we're going to treat you like the French people treated you!" Choking on her wrath and impotence, Johnson "felt like challenging her to a duel" but said nothing. She joined three Asian passengers and the rest of the black camp workers for the next meal and thought to herself that it was little wonder that "world's darker citizens" did not like white Americans.[6]

Upon reaching the United States, she immersed herself in activism on behalf of the world's darker peoples, mixing insistent respectability with the "righteous and indignant"—sometimes self-righteous and quite brazen—"protest against injustice" that she felt they needed to pursue. Moving into a Young Women's Christian Association (YWCA) dormitory in New York, she began lecturing on the necessary role of the YWCA in community life, on African American history, and on her experiences in the Great War. In collaboration with Addie Hunton, she set about documenting black soldiers' heroics and hardships because she "knew" that no history of the war would do justice to their experiences "unless some colored person wrote it." They paid a Brooklyn press to publish their memoir, *Two Colored Women with the American Expeditionary Forces,* intending it as a testament to black women's courage and black men's devotion. A teacher by training and temperament, Johnson wanted African Americans to know themselves and to believe themselves capable of greatness.[7]

The theater and substance of the UNIA's August 1920 convention offered a fitting platform for Kathryn Johnson's message of black pride, uplift, and solidarity. Speaking to the crowd in Garvey's Liberty Hall, she repeated a complaint she had expressed as an NAACP organizer—that "colored people are lacking in racial self-respect." She conceded that African Americans were "not altogether to blame" for their lack of race pride. Rather, white supremacy had "been imbedded" in black people for centuries, teaching them that "they come from nowhere and are going nowhere" and that any accomplishments worth mentioning "belong to the white race." Jim Crow had colonized them.

Johnson used her experiences in the war to disrupt that belief. First, she offered *Two Colored Women* as "the truth" about black soldiers' accomplishments in France; wartime sacrifice could instill racial self-respect. Second, she called upon African Americans to reject the internalized color prejudices that led them to distinguish between "high browns, chocolate browns, and other kinds of browns." Color gave no measure of "the quality of a man," she told the crowd after reminding them that "a house divided against itself cannot stand."[8]

To help make her argument that all black hues were beautiful, Johnson offered a glimpse of something she had seen in France. Holding up a picture of the Madonna and Jesus, she explained to the group that it depicted a statue placed by the Spanish in a village church in France's Savoie region hundreds of years before. Johnson described the statue as "ebony black" and explained that it represented "the Moorish conception of a dark-skinned Savior and his mother." In France, Johnson had noted how this Black Madonna had moved African American soldiers who had been degraded and denied because of their color. In Liberty Hall, she used the statue to give the crowd "food for thought" and speculated on what it might it mean if the Son of Man were "related to the darker nations of the earth by ties of blood." For Johnson, it promised to unite the "teeming millions who so far outnumbered" white Americans and Europeans. What the colored world might accomplish, Johnson implied, if they would only know their strength.[9]

She believed in black power. Johnson, who had found herself out of her job at the NAACP because she would not always accommodate interracialism, appreciated the UNIA's emphasis on black independence and entrepreneurial pan-Africanism. In her speech at the August convention, she declared herself a fellow traveler: fully behind Garvey's proposal to create a shipping fleet, the Black Star Line, to traverse and link the Black Atlantic and in "hearty sympathy" with his plan to establish a black state in Africa. However, she pursued black liberation through outlets other than the Garvey movement. Like much of the UNIA's base membership, Johnson plucked her notion of black power from a dense thicket of black political traditions. Her years on the road as a field agent had taught her the importance of the grassroots even as her YMCA work and Methodist church membership reinforced the power of institutions. Moreover, both her social work and her training as a teacher led her to use education as organizing, a strategy that placed her with generations of women in the African American freedom struggle. Johnson stood comfortably with one foot on Garvey's stage and another in the NAACP, her religious faith and clubwoman's service bolstering her militant politics.[10]

Yet if a long tradition of African American resistance shaped her as an activist, the Great War crystallized her efforts. She claimed that the war, and especially venturing abroad, had given African American troops "a broader view of life" and "vision of freedom" that brought clarity, hope, and inspiration. It had done the same for her. From Europe, she could see both the provincialism of America's system of racial subordination and its ability to travel beyond American borders. The personalized humiliations of Jim Crow stood out starkly against the backdrop of a War for Democracy, but the war had also revealed how much more the ideology of white supremacy encompassed. Increasingly, Johnson made those same links. If she had "all [her] interest in Africa," as she told the audience at the UNIA conference, it was because her dedication to the cause of African Americans had led her there.[11]

In the decades between the first World War and the second, Johnson continued tacking between an American-centered emphasis on African American pride and uplift and a more diasporic vision of black solidarity. During the 1920s, she would devote the bulk of her attention to blacks in the United States. Building from the sense she had gotten in publishing *Two Colored Women* that African Americans needed to see themselves in popular and historical literature, she assembled along with her book a "small library of other books on the history of the colored people" that she referred to as the "Two-Foot Shelf of Negro Literature." As she had with *Crisis* and the NAACP in the early 1910s, she brought her drive and determination to the service of Carter G. Woodson's Association for the Study of Negro Life and Literature in the early 1920s. She took to the road to sell these works by Woodson, Du Bois, Benjamin Brawley, James Weldon Johnson, and others. For Kathryn Johnson, the Two-Foot Shelf served a dual purpose: it got people reading, and more importantly, it helped "the Negro to understand his honorable place in the United States." Indeed, NAACP cofounder Mary White Ovington referred to Johnson's efforts as "Selling Race Pride."[12]

Promoting race pride was no small task in the years after World War I. The race wars of the Red Summer had illustrated the lengths white Americans would go to secure the strictures of place, causing one veteran of the 92nd Division to write to W. E. B. DuBois in despair of postwar circumstances for African Americans. "In stead of getting better," the soldier lamented, "it grows worse." The riots in ensuing years—1921 in Tulsa, Oklahoma, 1923 in Rosewood, Florida, and 1927 in Coffeyville, Kansas, for example—only reinforced the lesson.[13]

From Wilmington to the Meuse Argonne, racial violence had secured Jim Crow throughout the new century, but the reactionary temper of the 1920s created new obstacles for African Americans. They watched with concern as the Ku Klux Klan spread like smallpox in the first half of the decade, expanding out from Atlanta where it revived in 1915 to overrun the Midwest, West, and North. By 1924, the Klan claimed roughly four million members who rallied around a cry of "100 Percent Americanism." They pledged "to keep forever inviolate the Constitution," in the words of a Texas Klansman, "and make this a white mans Country." Protecting the nation for white people involved securing it against immigrants, Jews, and Catholics, as well as against African Americans; the Constitution may have been inviolate to the members of the Klan, but they defined its jurisdiction narrowly.[14]

Kathryn Johnson and other African Americans drew on their wartime service to defend against the Klan and other assaults on black people's "Americanism." Early in 1921, Johnson and her fellow YMCA volunteer Helen Curtis put back on the uniforms they had worn as camp workers in France to picket a New York showing of *The Birth of a Nation*, D. W. Griffith's film about the founding of the first Ku Klux Klan. Based on Thomas Dixon's novel *The Clansman,* the film had served as a propaganda tool for the resurgent Klan since its premiere in 1915 and had inflamed audiences across the country with its depiction of a murderous black rapist, celebration of lynching and mutilation, and lampooning of black Union soldiers as buffoons and incompetents. Johnson considered the movie a "slander upon the Negro people." The NAACP organized a national campaign against the film, using the publicity to label the "reviled Ku Klux Klan" as the true threat to America.[15]

In New York, the Association took direct action. Johnson and Curtis joined Laura Jean Rollock, another black YMCA volunteer who had come overseas after the armistice, in front of the Capitol Theatre on Broadway. Standing silently, they wore sandwich boards that demanded, "We represented America in France. Why Should 'The Birth of a Nation' Misrepresent Us Here?" Laura Rollock's brother-in-law, Llewelyn, and a graduate student named E. Franklin Frazier distributed pamphlets denouncing the film as Klan propaganda. An ex-sailor, Llewelyn Rollock wore his uniform. Another twenty-five black veterans in uniform also came out to lend support. Representatives of the NAACP leadership rounded out the crowd. Policemen interrupted the protest, charging Rollock, Frazier, and the three middle-aged clubwomen with the illegal distribution of handbills and circulars. The NAACP had come prepared for legal action, bringing along Harlem businessman John Nail to post their bail and black veteran-turned-lawyer Aiken Pope to defend them in court.[16]

The Capitol Theatre protests both fed the NAACP campaign and set off alarms for white authorities. Aiken Pope and the Association would make the arrests a "test case" for the right to distribute political matter, and they would eventually prevail on appeal. In the meantime, however, Johnson faced a night court judge and three hours in a holding cell. As she paced in her cell, Johnson overheard people in the corridors asking, "What are they? Bolsheviks?" In the wake of the Red Scare and Attorney General A. Mitchell Palmer's raids on suspected radicals across the country, the question carried both an insult and a menace for the church-going, middle-class Johnson. Indeed, when confronted with these embodiments of black womanhood and manhood, the magistrate who convicted them accused all the defendants of wanting "to start the war all over again." The judge did not understand, Johnson thought to herself. For all the work she and others had put into the War, white people still looked past them; her uniformed respectability, and the veterans' uniformed dignity, represented a challenge to social order, not a demonstration of social status. She felt "glad the war was over" in Europe, but she had to keep fighting Jim Crow because, as she later remarked, "I hated the prejudice that I was compelled to face in this, my native land." As the NAACP carried on its campaign against *The Birth of a Nation*, Johnson relocated to Chicago and began to turn her attention to other fights, on other fronts.[17]

The war had not altered the reality of life under white supremacy in the United States. If anything, the will to "normalcy," as 1920 Republican candidate Warren Harding put it, dampened white Americans' ardor for even the limited Progressivism of the prewar era. Nevertheless, many returning veterans followed Kathryn Johnson in pushing for civil rights, even as postwar antiradicalism shored up the status quo.[18]

As Johnson drew on organizations like the NAACP and the UNIA to fight prejudice in the United States, others in the World War I cohort found new outlets for their activist energies. Lieutenant Osceola McKaine, the ex-Southerner who once had appealed to white Americans' esprit de corps in the pages of mainstream magazines, returned from the war in 1919 convinced that African Americans could not trust the federal government to do right by them just because they had proved themselves faithful or worthy. The idealism of his precombat writing had dissipated, replaced by a busy determination to force the government to acknowledge black citizenship. "Only a thoroughly coordinated, organized effort" of veterans and their families, he argued alongside other returning soldiers, could gain black people the equal status "we merit, deserve, and desire." With other veterans, he formed the League for Democracy to pressure the federal government for civil and economic rights. Lieutenant McKaine became National Field Secretary. Aiken Pope, Kathryn Johnson's lawyer, served as the president of the New York chapter.[19]

Combining an old-fashioned emphasis on reputation and honor with a self-consciously New Negro emphasis on spirited resistance, members of the League for Democracy made it their task to exemplify and uphold black manhood in the dawning Jazz Age. Like the UNIA, the League celebrated black military manhood, foregrounding veterans of the war and work in "essential war industries" as well as denouncing the Army's treatment of African American soldiers. Indeed, one of the group's first tasks was to counter white officers' claims that black combat units had, in the words of 92nd Division Chief of Staff Colonel Allen Greer, "been dangerous to no one but themselves and women." McKaine and the League assailed Greer's "malicious venom," saying he had exceeded "even that peerless Bourbon Secessionist, Thomas Dixon" and his *Birth of a Nation.* The French Croix de Guerre, earned by two African American regiments, should say more about black soldiers' courage than Greer's "vile, vile, vicious and premeditated insult."[20]

Led by McKaine, representatives of the League traveled to Washington, D.C., to denounce Greer as a slanderer and traitor and to call for his dishonorable discharge. The protest rallied indignant African Americans but failed to deter an Army bent on discrediting black officers and shrinking the number of African Americans in the four standing Regular Army units. Demobilization, the transition from a wartime to peacetime military force, proved as racialized as mobilization had been. By the mid-1920s, African American soldiers would figure more as memory and symbol than they would as visible or actual uniformed service members.[21]

Both the League for Democracy and the UNIA endeavored to give meaning to soldiers in the abstract. Yet where the UNIA embraced spectacle and ceremony, McKaine's League concentrated on organization and order. The

League kept its focus strictly domestic. Envisioning branches throughout the United States—"camps," it called them—at the city, state, and regional levels, McKaine and his compatriots sought to create a mass protest organization similar in structure to the federal government but more democratic in practice. Although returned soldiers founded the organization and shaped its agenda, the League welcomed "both sexes," fashioning itself as "a representative self-governing body" in which "every active member" had a vote. The League actively supported voting and workers' rights and opposed lynching and segregation, and as editor of the League organ the *Commoner,* McKaine joined rent protests, mixed with other members of the black press, and helped to plot strategies for getting black representation in Congress. Their veteran's identity gave shape and substance to their politics.[22]

Moreover, that identity fueled their militancy. In the wake of the Charleston riot and other Red Summer attacks on African American soldiers and civilians, McKaine openly advocated armed self-defense. He informed an assembly that "no Negroes anywhere should ever let a white mob take a black man to lynch him without using all possible force to prevent it." As his audience applauded, he added, "The only thing with which to meet force is force." Months later in the pages of the *Commoner,* McKaine ordered African Americans to take the enforcement of the Civil War amendments into their "own hands," and he continued to hold that "force is the only reason the stupid, barbarous White Huns of the South know or respect."[23]

The League for Democracy's quick emergence demonstrated the will to fight among many veterans and their supporters, but its story also underscores the tenuous nature of early postwar efforts. Organizing helped to train the generation mobilized by World War I. After its founding in 1919, the League caught the attention of the NAACP and Urban League, who worked with the organization to petition President Harding to free some members of the 24th Infantry still imprisoned after the Houston Riot. However, McKaine's militancy also caught the eye of Military Intelligence and J. Edgar Hoover in the Bureau of Investigation, who monitored it closely. Like the older, more-established NAACP, the organization grew quickly in the immediate flush of postwar civil rights agitation, but its numbers declined dramatically in the early 1920s. By the mid-1920s, the League had disbanded. With "no stomach for what was going on," as his brother recalled, and his first attempt at organizing over, Osceola McKaine left New York and the United States, just as he had once escaped from South Carolina and the Jim

Crow South. Seeking freedom in a strange land, he moved to Ghent, Belgium, and opened a supper club.[24]

Revolution and Recognition

Osceola McKaine and the founders of the League for Democracy were not the only ones seeking new ways to overcome Jim Crow. An anonymous member of the 24th Infantry vented his rage and expressed his ambitions in a letter to the *El Paso Herald*. "All colored men in the 24th who has been in France and are now in the United States wants to get it," he wrote in early 1920. Announcing that veterans of military service "dont like the United States any longer," he hinted at a plot "which will surprise the World." Blood would spill, the letter writer promised, with white men, women, and children getting shot "like dogs." If it took joining with the Japanese—the ascendant power of the colored world—or going over to Pancho Villa, the writer and his compatriots would do it. Anything "to pull down your damn flage."[25]

Up north in Chicago, Haywood Hall also returned home seething. But where Osceola McKaine and Kathryn Johnson sought paths for reform and the anonymous 24th infantryman dreamt of retaliation, Hall would chart a course for revolution. He had returned from the galling experience of fighting American racists abroad to the maddening continuation of white hostility in Chicago. Many of the veterans of the Eighth Illinois displayed a "widespread dissatisfaction bordering on bitterness," government observers noted with concern. Hall was no different. He always "had been hot-tempered," he admitted, but after the war he grew even less likely to "take any insults lying down." Thus, when Chicago erupted in a Red Summer "holocaust" three months after his April 1919 discharge, Hall raced toward the fight.[26]

Chicago laid everything bare. "The frothy bloody wake of the Great War revealed many things in our civilization that shook our faith in God, in Christ, and in the divine purpose of mankind themselves," Wobbly and clandestine Communist Party member Harrison George wrote after the summer of 1919. "Nowhere" he added, was the "sickening" spectacle of inhumanity "more vivid and unescapable" than in Chicago. For Hall, so far from faith, the riot crystallized the discontent he had felt during and since the World War. Between the riot and the Army, the young veteran had grown "totally disillusioned about being able to find any solution to the racial problem through the help of the government." Official agencies, he felt, "were among the most racist and most dangerous" to the African Americans who needed them.[27]

Hall wanted nothing to do with the traditional ideals of black manhood and citizenship that Johnson and McKaine sought to reclaim and redeem. "Restless, moody, and ill-tempered," he steadily shed any ties to an aspirational model that relied on achievement or government good will. In 1920, he had married a young society woman determined to climb the economic and social ladder. Hall found her ambition stultifying, and he chafed at "the drab, lower middle-class existence," their union seemed to promise. Even worse, he gleaned that fulfilling the conventions of middle-class manhood in one way—protecting and providing for his new family—would undercut his sense of himself in another way. At work, he realized, his marriage meant that his employers "had me where they wanted me"; he would have to conform. Ultimately, Hall chose to maintain his independence and nurse his rage. He quit his job and dissolved his marriage and began "trying to figure out how best to maladjust." He drifted first toward the Nietzschean cynicism of newspaper critic H. L. Mencken before turning to Marx, Engels, and the revolutionary internationalism espoused by Harrison George and the Russian Bolsheviks.[28]

Looking back, Hall would frame his journey as one of political education and self-discovery. His confrontations with war and racial violence had left him as much curious as bitter, certain that he "could never again adjust to the situation of Black inequality" and bent on figuring out "who was responsible" for its perpetuation. Bouncing from job to job—on the rails, in kitchens, and at the post office—he read prodigiously, often taking suggestions from his older brother and fellow veteran Otto. While working a contract job at the post office, he joined a discussion group with other black employees and began wrestling with the literature of white supremacy and the few intellectual works that countered them. "Blacks have no history," Hall read in mainstream academia, but in the pages of Herodotus and Franz Boas he saw a black culture and a black past. As Kathryn Johnson worked to propagate black history from the trunk of her car back in New York, Hall endeavored to absorb it all in Chicago.[29]

For Hall, however, black pride was not the end point. He soon moved on from the post office discussion group and its reading list. Otto, who as a stevedore had labored in the Army's proletariat during World War I, ran with both Wobblies and Garveyites, and he added economic critiques to Haywood's readings on whiteness and culture. As Hall read, what he later called "the racial fog" lifted, and he "began to see that the main beneficiaries of Black subjugation also profited from the social oppression of poor whites, native and foreign born." At the same time, he became more attuned to other peoples of color and their struggles for liberation. He followed postwar nationalist movements in India, China, and Turkey and tuned his ear to the "rumblings in black Africa" manifested as "strikes and demonstrations against colonial oppression." Injustice internationally seemed to him connected to Jim Crow domestically; he had grasped the compact between capitalism and white supremacy. Having once enlisted in the National Guard in search of a fraternity of race men, he now saw an interracial proletariat, primed to replace "the state power of the dominant class," as his chosen fraternity. Black equality, he came to believe, "would prove an inevitable by-product" of a socialist United States. Three years after mustering out of the Army, he had journeyed "from being a disgruntled Black ex-soldier to being a self-conscious revolutionary looking for an organization with which to make revolution."[30]

Hall turned first to the African Blood Brotherhood (ABB). He had wanted to join the Communists, but Otto (himself a Communist Party member) urged him to begin with the ABB, a radical all-black organization whose Chicago chapter Otto had helped to establish. Founded in New York in 1919 by Caribbean-born intellectual and journalist Cyril Briggs, the ABB had snuck onto the scene of black wartime organizing. Shrouded in secrecy and determined to stay underground, the organization recruited approximately 3,000 members and reached tens of thousands more through the Briggs-edited publication, *The Crusader*. Branches of the organization spread South and West, reaching as far the Rockies with one outpost in San Francisco. A "disproportionate number" of the membership, historians have noted, were African American and West Indian veterans of the war.[31]

The ABB's appeal lay in its radical politics for some and, for others, in its professed willingness to "go the limit" to protect black people. Dedicated to "African Liberation and Redemption" as well as "the immediate protection and liberation of Negroes everywhere," the ABB combined a liberatory pan-Africanism with an enthusiasm for the Bolshevik Revolution. "Negro Salvation," Briggs argued in the pages of the *Crusader,* would only come "through the establishment of a strong, stable, independent Negro State" and "the establishment of a Universal Socialist Co-operative commonwealth." This pairing

seemed to Briggs "the most likely and feasible solution." Before salvation, however, came self-preservation. Although Briggs would later deny involvement,
many African Americans credited the ABB with organizing resistance to white
rampagers in the 1921 Tulsa riot. And while papers like the *New York Times*
denounced the ABB as instigators, members of the black press hailed them as a
welcome and worthy counter to the invisible empire of the Ku Klux Klan.[32]

Hall found his sojourn in the ABB "stimulating and rewarding," but after
six months he wanted to move on. The ABB itself had begun to drift toward
the Communist Party; Briggs and other members of the organization's leadership had joined, and they "began," Briggs would later say, "seeking a close
relationship between the two." Hall's brother Otto counted himself as a
Communist, too. By late 1923, the Brotherhood had fused with the Party,
and Hall had joined the Young Workers' League, a Communist youth organization. He joined the Party proper in 1925 and, adopting the alias Harry
Haywood to avoid federal scrutiny, departed for Moscow to study.[33]

Hall's trajectory was striking but not singular. Other veterans, too, traveled from the disillusion of the American Army to the chill of a Soviet dormitory. Oliver Golden, a Tuskegee-trained agronomist and former cook in the
92nd Division, had migrated north from Mississippi, passing through Memphis, New York, and Chicago before landing in Moscow. A handsome ladies'
man with a fierce independent streak, Golden went to Moscow to get out of
his job as a Pullman porter. "I would have done anything to get off those dining cars," he told Haywood Hall when they became friends in Moscow.
Golden's Army buddy James W. Ford had followed a similar path, only hail-
ing from Alabama rather than Mississippi and attending Fisk rather than
Tuskegee. Ford served as a signal corpsman in the 92nd, but his training and
service had done him little good in job-strapped Chicago. Like Haywood
Hall, he eventually secured a position in the post office, and from there he
became active in labor politics. Ford joined the Communist Party in 1926.[34]

The war, the riots, and the world color line all made sense when scruti-
nized through the logic of Marxism. For Golden and Ford, sons of the Jim
Crow South adrift in the segregated North, Soviet communism offered a new
light on white people and a read on white supremacy that situated the Negro
problem within the dilemmas of capitalism. For all the African American
veterans who turned to it, communism offered a way of encountering and
comprehending the world that their overseas service had only begun to open
up for them. Capital and empire, they realized, economic exploitation and

racial subjugation knotted together to form the tangle of their lives. Equally as promising, communism offered a way out. Those who pledged themselves to the party could channel their discontent into revolution.

A world away from Moscow, physically and politically, Ely Green aspired less to revolution than to recognition. Never an activist in the institutional mode of Johnson and McKaine, Green shared with Hall a more rough-scrabble form of individual rebellion. Yet where veterans like Hall ultimately directed their disillusion into organizations, others like Green carted their world's experience back to hamlets like Waxahachie and tried to live the lives their service had earned them. In and of itself this became a political act, one amplified by white supremacists' attempts to quell veterans' spirits and crush their bodies. The refusal to be disrecognized—to borrow a term from an Alabama sharecropper—and to root their citizenship claims in their military service characterized these veterans' efforts throughout the postwar decade. World War I became the touchstone by which they defined who they were.[35]

If the war had changed Ely Green, it had done so by making him more supremely himself. More dogged, more resourceful, and more certain that he deserved respect, Green came home determined to secure the "right of law" for himself and all African Americans in the South. He left the Army demanding that right, insisting on a discharge that listed his race and nationality only as "American," not Negro. When the clerk recording his information declared him an upstart who needed his "ears pinned back," Green challenged the clerk to go ahead and try. To the Colonel who came up and demanded to know why he would cause such a ruckus, Green replied, "I am a representative of the A.E.F., as you are." He had fought for an American flag, not a Negro flag, and he wished the Colonel to acknowledge that "God made both [black and white races] as men." As the recording clerk grumbled about Green's trying to "change the laws of the Government," the Colonel ordered him to let Green have the discharge on his own terms.[36]

To Green, the triumph felt enormous. It did not change his reception in Waxahachie, where white lawmen viewed him with renewed hostility, but it did boost his sense that the war had won him something that those lawmen could not take away—acknowledgment of his manhood and citizenship. He supplemented the Army's acknowledgment with his own visual cue; while waiting for a tailor to sew him some civilian clothes, he spent his first two weeks back home walking around in his military uniform. Irritated, the marshal instructed Green to hurry up and take off "that dam stuff of the Army," and warned him that he did not want any trouble from Green or any other "young nigger bucks" left in town.[37]

Green's symbolic triumph threatened white supremacists in postwar Waxahachie. Like Green, Waxahachie had changed during the war in part by becoming more resolutely itself. The paternalism and brutality that Green had grown accustomed to now weighed more heavily on its denizens, with brutality providing the bulk of the weight. Town leaders enriched and entertained themselves in central Texas's ongoing cotton boom, while white lawmen both preserved the status quo and expressed their own class resentments by preying on African Americans. "The ex-soldier are slain more than any," Green's friend, a prosperous doctor, warned after urging him to follow the stream of the Great Migration to less hostile territory. The doctor planned to sacrifice his practice and move to California because he wanted his children to "walk above fear of being mobbed."[38]

From Houston to Longview, and in scores more smaller confrontations, Texas had erupted into race war during World War I. The Klan, growing ever stronger and bolder, sought to carry that war into the next decade, and African Americans had organized and armed themselves in response. In nearby Fort Worth, the NAACP branch had grown from 117 members at its founding in spring 1918 to 267 members in late 1919, and over in Dallas, those numbers had grown from 169 members in September 1918 to 1,152 a year later. Green had not allied himself with the Association, but in a climate where white Texans viewed NAACP members as insurrectionists, Green with his Army uniform and talk of citizenship seemed to wear his affiliations on his sleeve.[39]

He was in the fight, whether he wished it or not. Green had planned a peaceful return and had even packed away his guns, vowing not have any more trouble with white people "unless I was struck by one of them." France had appealed to him with its "freedom of all men," but he could not fathom life outside the South, in a land that had "no ice cream, or ice tea." He wanted home: the affectionate embrace of the Dunlap family and other white patricians; the companionship of the town's black folks; and the ability, enhanced by his position as a returned veteran, to broker between the two communities. However, the changes in both Green and Waxahachie made his plans impossible. Many of the African Americans he knew had packed up and headed north. Most of the veterans had gone, Green noted, not only because the police targeted them, as his doctor friend stated, but also because Waxahachie had grown too small for them. "It was like the slogun," Green observed, "How are you going to keep them on the farm after seeing Paree?"[40]

More significantly, local law enforcement decided that Green, too, had grown too big for Waxahachie. A few months after his return, a deputy stopped him, accused him of speeding down Main Street, and placed him under arrest. Green pleaded, "I came back home to live as a citizen. Will you please let me do that?" The deputy scoffed at his pretensions and, as the two men approached City Hall, threw a punch while announcing, "I am going to beat the hell out of you." Green returned the punches, pummeling the deputy until, he recalled, "it seemed like the City Hall fell on me." Lawmen, "at least fifty men" it felt like to Green, piled on top of him, beating him until he nearly choked on the blood in his throat.[41]

Green fought for his life. He ducked a punch from the town marshal and then managed to kick the marshal in the face before the marshal pulled out a gun. "We wont have time to hang the black sonofabitch," the marshal explained to the crowd of officers, "I am going to kill him now." As he spoke, one of the Judge's friends, Charlie Penn, drove by and saw the gun drawn from its holster. Penn ran to the scene and kicked the marshal's firing hand off target. Green "heard the shot" and thought he "had been killed," but the marshal had missed his target. Penn had taken the gun and threatened to kill anyone who tried to lay another hand on Green.[42]

For his part, Green raced home intent on unpacking his guns and returning to "kill every cracker in town." When Judge Dunlap saw his chauffeur, crusted in blood with one eye swollen shut and the other seeping water, he began fuming. The marshal and his men had tried to nullify Green's citizenship claim, opting to kill him rather than cede him any kind of right at all. But as far as the Judge was concerned, they had created a far greater sin. By attacking his man, they had challenged his authority. They had violated Green's manhood, but they had impugned Dunlap's, too. Taking Green's rifle, the Judge vowed to show the lawmen "who can defend what belongs to a man" as well as "what law a man can have and shall have." He meant to teach them a lesson about place and authority. Only the intervention of friends and family kept him from trying to shoot someone.[43]

The marshal's ambush made it clear that Green could not stay in Waxahachie. His liminal position as broker between, and traverser of, the two

communities proved untenable in a climate where the lines between black and
white grew ever more rigid. Military service and national belonging had promised a certain degree of inclusion in those communities, but they had also disrupted the paternalism that kept Waxahachie in stasis. Green could not be
Dunlap's Negro and his own man at the same time, and he could not survive
in town without Dunlap's protection. As one of the Judge's friends explained in
the tortured language of the South, "You are too fine a boy to be killed when
you can go some other place where you can live like the man you want to be."[44]

Green concurred; Waxahachie "wasnt a healthy place for me to be," he
realized as he was recovering from his fight with the lawmen. In late 1919,
despite the Judge's opposition, he left town. He moved to Fort Worth, where
he worked as a driver for a Yankee couple who had moved to Texas to exploit
the oil boom. They proved indulgent employers, but even in Fort Worth,
Green fell "back into the same custom," as he described his ongoing run-ins
with Jim Crow, "Today smiles, tomorrow tears." The Klan wanted him out of
his job, warning him in a letter left in his car to find a position that did not
pay "a white man's salary."[45]

Like all "Kikes, Koons, and Katholics" in Texas, Green had good reason
to fear the Klan. The organization had indulged in what a California paper
described as an "orgy of whitecapping" throughout 1920 and 1921. In Dallas,
they kidnapped a black bellhop they suspected of wooing a white woman and
branded "KKK" across his head in acid. They whipped a black man in Belton
and then made him walk the streets carrying a sign that read, "Whipped by
the Ku Klux Klan." Green heard of Jewish businesses getting bombed and
saw an Italian man dropped from a car coated in tar and feathers. The Klan
tarred and feathered more men in Houston, Waco, and Fort Worth, and did
the same to a white woman in Tenaha. In 1922, Klan-backed candidates
"swept" elections in Texas cities and settled into public office. When Green
kept receiving letters that instructed him to get out of town—dropped, a witness observed on one occasion, by a policeman—he had good cause to feel,
as he said, "a bit anxious."[46]

In the end, Green decided to go on to California. He could not stay and
play "the diplomatic Negro," kowtowing enough to not threaten white supremacists. And he finally accepted that he would not convince other African Americans to do away with the word "Negro," especially not mainstream
black leadership. The term and identity, even the history that Green perceived as one of injury and subservience, formed part of the negotiation that

African Americans made with cooperative whites. Interracialism, and with it segregation, relied on Negroism. Green was, a friend from Waxahachie advised him, charging ahead of the crowd: he did not want interracialism, he wanted equality. In 1922, he left Texas behind, and with it his dreams of liberating African Americans in the South. He would continue his solitary quest for equal rights, but he would do so out West. Living as a citizen in Texas had proved too mighty a task.[47]

The Negro Studies War Some More

During the 1920s, black and white Americans carried the battles of World War I back from Europe to the home front. The lessons and processes that they wrangled with overseas—of black identities, reformulations of manhood, and the potential for social mobilization—traveled back as well, altered from the aspirations and imaginations they had carted off to war. Still, if the war offered African Americans an opportunity for social learning, it had left their visions and strategies for placing themselves in the nation and the world as yet inchoate. Through trying and failing as Osceola McKaine had done, or through standing firm and surviving as Ely Green had, African Americans developed the sophistication they would need for later battles. The steady move toward a second World War and the speculation about the terms on which Americans would join that war, allowed the World War I cohort to refine their stance on what it would take to gain equal rights.

In August 1935, Kathryn Johnson once more donned the YMCA uniform she had worn as an Army volunteer and took to the streets in protest. This time, she also draped the black, red, and yellow of the Ethiopian flag across her arm, and pinned a poppy, a remembrance of disabled veterans of her World War, to her dress. She marched in Chicago, where she had moved in 1924, amidst banners instructing fascist Italy to get its "Hands Off Ethiopia" and others urging Americans to "Force Congress to Act." A member of the Chicago Society for the Aid of Ethiopia, she joined students from the University of Chicago, popular front members of the American League Against War and Fascism, and Communist Party members—Haywood Hall included—in protesting Italian designs on Ethiopia. By summer 1935, invasion seemed imminent, and "the Negro people of Chicago," protestors explained in pamphlets, would not "sit idly by while the fascist tyrant Mussolini moves to enslave the last independent Negro country of Africa." Allied in a Joint Conference for the Defense of Ethiopia, they sought to follow up the "Hands Off Ethiopia" parades organized during the preceding months in Harlem by the UNIA, the Elks, Communists, and other groups.[48]

Ethiopia increasingly captured African Americans' attention. Throughout 1935, Italian dictator Benito Mussolini and his fascist party had adopted an ever more bellicose stance toward the East African nation, and Ethiopian Emperor Haile Selassie repeatedly appealed to the League of Nations to diffuse the growing crisis. The member states of the League "procrastinated" and "dilly-dallied," Kathryn Johnson bitterly recalled, declaring Ethiopia innocent of the transgressions Italy had conjured but refusing to come to the country's aid or to lift an arms embargo that would have allowed them to aid themselves. Selassie put up a brave front. "We are not looking for war," he responded to Italian threats, but if war should come, "we are willing to die to the last man." Mussolini, however, *was* looking for war and determined to make Ethiopia part of a Mediterranean empire that included holdings in Eritrea and Somaliland. Italy intended to "take her pound of flesh by force," W. E. B. Du Bois announced with his usual acumen on the eve of the October 1935 invasion. If Mussolini were to succeed, he added, "does anyone suppose that Germany will not make a similar attempt?"[49]

Many African Americans saw Mussolini's beating the war drums as a retread of the colonial jockeying that had spurred the Great War. The *Defender* made Ethiopia a stand-in for the entire continent, flatly stating that the Italians meant to "Grab Africa." Likewise, Du Bois declared that "increased colonial exploitation of Africa" had caused the World War and "heightens the danger of another similar conflagration." As people like Du Bois pressed Ethiopia's case in print, preachers advanced it in the pulpit. Noah Williams, a chaplain during World War I and Bishop in the AME church, described Italy's designs on "Christian Abyssinia" as "ungodly." He wrote a letter to Haile Selassie advising the emperor to "Trust God and give them hell." Churches sponsored days of prayer and fundraising drives. They petitioned the Roosevelt administration to intervene and sent members to populate the various Ethiopian aid societies that sprung up across the country. The threat of invasion, what Kathryn Johnson denounced as Italy's "war of aggression," raised the specter of war more broadly.[50]

Moreover, African American responses reflected the expansion of Du Bois's and the UNIA's pan-African visions. The Italian advance on Ethiopia revealed the extent to which black Americans had come to invest in diasporic identities and the sharpness with which they felt the sting of the League's failure in Africa. Kathryn Johnson referred to the invasion as "the rape of Ethiopia," an evocation both of the "rape of Belgium" that had mobilized anti-German sentiment in 1914 and of the centuries-old violation of black bodies that had marked black people's experiences in the New World. Years later she still railed at how the League let Italy get away with murder. "Right was crucified at Geneva," she wrote, expressing herself as a Christian and an African, "and the great powers sat by and consented to the lifting of the Cross."[51]

The Italian invasion mobilized black Americans. In Boston, Johnson's fellow YMCA volunteer, North Carolina–born African American Matthew Bullock, led a delegation committed to picketing and protesting the Italian consulate in Boston. Others went farther. Would-be volunteers in Louisiana, New Jersey, Florida, Ohio, and Oklahoma, among other places, offered themselves to fight for "Our Emperor Haile Selassie," as a group in West Virginia dubbed him. In Fort Worth, World War veteran Walter Davis drafted a letter to Selassie asking permission to "to organize a company of men by voluntary enlistment for military enlistment for military duty in your country." Positioning himself and the other attendees at a 600-person rally as children of Africa, broadly, he announced them all "ready to spill their blood in behalf of our native land, Ethiopia." Ethiopia stood in for Africa, and so, for their native land.[52]

Kathryn Johnson had long situated herself as a member of the diaspora, announcing her "interest" in Africa at the UNIA conference back in 1920. Since 1929, she had been receiving smuggled documents from Benjamin Nxumalo, a Swazi royal whom she had met in Chicago through their work in the Methodist church. Johnson would slowly piece those documents together into a booklet, *Stealing a Nation,* which chronicled the British exploitation of Nxumalo's homeland, Swaziland. Yet *Stealing a Nation* was ten years in the writing, and the Italo-Ethiopian crisis arose in the midst of it. This fight for Africa had a mass following, with thousands of African Americans articulating the internationalist consciousness that she had gained from her experiences in World War I. They needed people like her on the lines, drawing on those experiences and that consciousness to guide them toward a global struggle for rights.[53]

Thus, Kathryn Johnson joined the fray once again, and once again she was arrested. "Unexcelled police ferocity" quelled the protest in Chicago before it ever really got underway, the black press reported, adding that "more than

500 uniformed and plainclothes policemen" hauled in "about 450" people. Johnson described the police action as "an invasion," noting that the police arrested many unlucky passersby who had nothing to do with the parade. "In practically every case, the police plied their clubs heavily" on the bodies of those they arrested, the newspaper observed, whether those people had wittingly joined the protest or not.[54]

For the protestors, police repression reinforced the connections between their struggles and those of victims of fascism elsewhere. The affinities between white supremacy and fascism had hung in the air for at least a decade, with the *New York Times* pointing out as early as 1922 how "strikingly similar" Italian Fascisti sounded to the Ku Klux Klan. The Ethiopian crisis simply enhanced the sense that fascism was on the march and allowed African Americans to point the finger at Jim Crow justice stateside.[55]

Back from Moscow and organizing for the Communist Party under his alias Harry Haywood, Haywood Hall worked to raise Americans' awareness of the fascist menace. Like Kathryn Johnson, he served as a guide for African Americans ready to engage world phenomena. Linking domestic concerns to international campaigns, Haywood Hall saw the protest, and the city's ensuing crackdown, as a "fight for the streets of Chicago" as much as a defense of Ethiopia. He associated the rise of fascism abroad with "the growth of fascism right in Chicago . . . Jim Crow degradation, misery, and discrimination." The police response helped make his case; officers beat him so badly during his arrest that his legs gave out beneath him and he walked on crutches for a month afterwards. When a couple of policemen fumed that "there oughta be a Hitler over here" to take care of the agitators, one of the jailed protestors retorted, "He's already here."[56]

Kathryn Johnson the social worker did not receive the same manhandling as Harry Haywood the known Communist, but the police did tar them with similar brushes. Throughout her career, Johnson had shown herself willing to work with and within a variety of organizations from the UNIA to the AME church. Her coalition politics predated the Popular Front of communists, social democrats, and leftist labor and racial activists that had come together in the New Deal era, but she could join that front when the need arose. Packed into a jail cell with more than seventy other women—activists like her, along with more overt radicals and accidental detainees—she came to form part of it. Waiting for hours in the cramped space, the imprisoned women combined religious songs and protest songs until one of the guards "threatened to turn the hose on us," Johnson recalled, "if we did not stop singing." On the wall, a white woman scribbled out a call to arms for them all: "Black and White Unite and Fight." Eventually, the police released most of the protestors, pursuing charges against only nine of the women and twenty-six of the men. As he released her, an officer pointed to the poppy on her uniform and accused her of being "a red."[57]

More Republican than Red, Johnson nevertheless continued her own eclectic brand of politics throughout the 1930s. She kept working with the Chicago Society for the Aid of Ethiopia, even as Haile Selassie's troops fell to Mussolini's forces. In the thick of the Great Depression, however, she also had domestic concerns. She had inherited a "home for working women" from her friend and fellow clubwoman, Ezella Carter. Johnson ran it as a cross between a settlement house and a boarding home, opening the basement to young men students and the upstairs to women in need. With the Depression settled on the nation like a glacier, most of Johnson's charges did not have two nickels to rub together; she not only took them in, she found ways to feed them and get them back on a steady footing. She also served as president of her local community council, served on organizing committees of the AME church, and joined with the Anti-Saloon League to drive taverns out of her neighborhood.[58]

Fifty-six years old by 1935, Johnson had come of age in the era of Progressivism, women's club work, and early NAACP formation. Each had shaped her work as a volunteer with the AEF, just as her wartime experience in turn altered what reform, volunteer work, and racial justice meant to her. In the 1930s, a lifetime of abuse by the Democratic Party led her to regard Franklin Roosevelt's New Deal with skepticism, and she admonished those masses of African Americans who had abandoned the Republican Party in the 1936 election that they had "sold their birthright for a mess of pottage." After all, she reminded readers of the *Defender,* "the voiceless millions of Negroes in the Democratic South have been disenfranchised by the followers of this same New Deal." She felt sure that the road to real change lay in banding together and challenging the administration in power rather than relying on its mercy. "There is an old saying that we feed slaves," she wrote, "but freemen feed themselves."[59]

The genteel strain of black power that coalesced for Kathryn Johnson in World War I carried her through the interwar years and beyond. Whether she vied for the Republican nomination for a Congressional seat, as she did in 1940, or penned her own history of "a black African civilization in the Americas before Columbus," as she did with the 1948 pamphlet, "The Dark Race in the Dawn," she advanced from the position she had taken decades before: that African Americans must know themselves strong and trust themselves able in order to fight. And much like the soldiers she tended in World War I, Johnson invoked the trappings of her service to hold her claim on the United States while linking herself to "the Dark Race" of Africa. Even as an elderly woman, her niece Leota Singleton recounted, "Aunt Kathryn" would literally wrap herself in the mantle of her war work, pulling on "her big army cape" for warmth and reassurance. From the camps of western France to the streets of Chicago, it was the uniform of choice for the battle she waged her whole life long.[60]

Rayford Logan knew as well as Kathryn Johnson the power of a uniform and its signal of affiliation. He removed his uniform in 1919, turned his back on the United Sates and white Americans, and remained in Europe for more than five years following the Great War. Save for the occasional mortifying encounter, Logan's cosmopolitan wanderings kept him outside the orbit of white Americans, and free from the cutting reminders of Jim Crow, he slowly expelled the hate that had built up in him during the war. Yet expatriation did not divorce him from all the currents of African American life. Jessie Fauset, his former high school teacher and literary editor of the *Crisis,* arranged for him to work for W. E. B. Du Bois during the 1921 Pan-African Congress in London, Paris, and Brussels. More deft than Du Bois in French and more diplomatic in his dealings with Blaise Diagne, Logan interpreted for Du Bois and kept the peace between the increasingly acrimonious Anglophone and Francophone delegates.[61]

Diasporic solidarity would be hard fought and slow in coming. Logan continued working with the Congress of 1923 but steered clear of the 1925 and 1927 meetings as they succumbed to financial troubles and intragroup fighting. Du Bois's pan-African vision would not fully bloom until the fifth Congress, held at the end of World War II in Manchester, England. By then pan-Africanism would have reoriented toward anticolonial struggles in Africa and Asia, with Jomo Kenyatta and Kwame Nkrumah taking the helm. Despite its rocky path, however, the Du Bois–led movement provided a vital link from the World War I era to the independence movements of the Cold

War, and they in turn provided a training ground for people like Rayford Logan, eager to understand African Americans' home in the world.[62]

Indeed, for Logan, pan-Africanism became as much an intellectual as a political pursuit. He finally came home to the United States at the end of 1924, a veteran and wanderer determined to make his mark. He returned to school, teaching at Virginia Union and Atlanta University and studying at his alma mater, Williams College, and at Harvard University. Logan received is Ph.D. from Harvard in 1936. Delving into topics ranging from U.S. relations with Haiti, to the League of Nation's mandate system for governing regions in Africa, to the workings of German and European colonialism, his scholarship covered what he called in a 1933 essay "The International Status of the Negro." He served, in the words of his biographer, as a sharp critic of American and European empire and as an erudite and "effective polemicist and propagandist for Pan-Africa."[63]

By the late 1930s, Logan had emerged on the national scene, a Howard professor and established scholar. He would use his academic stature, along with his past military service, to gain a platform for addressing the war that he and other Americans could see on the horizon. As early as 1935, Logan had come to view another world war as "imminent," and in spite of the disillusion of his own experience, he believed that African Americans could leverage their support to advance the freedom struggle. He did not adopt this position naively. Rather, his survey of conditions in the United States, East Africa, and the "Hell Hole of Creation" that was South Africa convinced him that "nothing short of a considerable weakening of the white races by war" would improve life for black people across the diaspora. The key for African Americans was to set the terms of their loyalty ahead of time; they needed to change their song, he argued in the black press, "from 'Ain't Goin' to Study War No More' to 'Let's see what we can get out of this war.'" They could force the Roosevelt administration's hand by organizing before the war began.[64]

Logan sounded this call louder as war came nearer. At the NAACP's annual meeting in June 1940, nine months after the fighting had erupted in Europe, he asked members to think back to 1917, "when the United States went to war, ostensibly to make the world safe for democracy." Americans "are about to march on another crusade," he warned, "and I am scared because every time the crusade starts, some ideal is going to be crushed." To protect African Americans' ideals, they had to keep pressure on "the brass hats in the

War Department" determined to reduce black soldiers to "orderlies and flun-
kies" just as they had those men in the four units of the Regular Army.[65]

If the declaration of war in Europe capped the end of "a low, dishonest
decade," as British poet W. H. Auden wrote in disgust at the events of September 1939, then African Americans had faced the craven reality of the
postwar world for twice that long. Americans had "lynched 579 Negroes since
the Armistice," a writer pointed out in the *Pittsburgh Courier* three weeks
after the European war began. "What the Negro wants to know," he added,
"is what reward he'll receive after your next war?" In the lead-up to World
War II, African Americans rejected the faith in uplift and earned citizenship
that characterized black mobilization for World War I. Led by veterans of the
first war, civilian as well as military, they vowed to forestall the "first in war,

Rayford Logan, the internationalist, in the late 1940s. Scurlock Studio Records,
Archives Center, National Museum of American History, Behring Center, Smithsonian
Institution.

last in peace" doctrine that had previously guided the government's dealings with African American soldiers.[66]

To that end, black Americans organized. Logan joined with the *Courier* and what he characterized as "various religious, educational, fraternal, welfare, and civic organizations" to found the Committee for the Participation of Negroes in the National Defense Program (CPNNDP). He served as Chair, and Charles Hamilton Houston, by then Dean of the Howard Law School as well as the chief strategist behind the NAACP's legal victories in Murray v. University of Maryland and Gaines v. Canada, served as one of its "most active and helpful members."[67]

As a lawyer, Houston employed a gradual approach, dismantling the Jim Crow schoolhouse brick by brick. As an advocate for the CPNNDP, in contrast, he faced matters square on. He and Logan addressed the House Military Affairs Committee in August 1940, with Logan underscoring the ongoing discrimination against blacks in the armed forces and insisting that African Americans receive "equal opportunity to participate in the national-defense program, civil as well as military." In his statement, Charles Houston drew directly on wartime experiences "so bitter," he told the Congressional committee, that he "never even applied for a service medal." Stressing the need to maintain African Americans' morale to maintain the country's defenses, he argued that fifth columnists and communists posed less danger than did lynching and abuse. In short, "Negroes want some of the democracy they fought for in 1917," Houston testified, "and the sooner the better." Hope alone would not snare them.[68]

Forewarned and forearmed, African Americans used the CPNNDP as one part of a preparedness drive to shape the government's policy on conscription and service. With councils in twenty-five states, it provided a solid base for the Double V campaign, launched by the *Courier* after the war began. The Double Victory campaign joined the CPNNDP's lobbying to a more diffuse effort to boost black Americans' militancy. Rousing the black press and plastering their pages with the Double V logo, writers for the Courier worked to remind African Americans that "even in a democracy, freedom is not a bequest but a fruit of conquest." There would be no self-sacrificial closing ranks this time around; as Houstonian C. W. Rice put it, "Unless we ask for things at the proper time when someone needs our services, it is too late when it is all over."[69]

The lobbying and propaganda fed a mass movement. As the black press drummed up support for victory against white supremacy at home and abroad, and as Houston and Logan warned that anything less than parity in the armed forces would ignite racial revolt, A. Philip Randolph threatened to bring ten thousand African Americans out on to the streets. "Calling on the President and holding all those conferences are not going to get us any-where," he told a union organizer during a trip down South, "We are going to have to do something about it." Randolph proposed a March on Washington Movement (MOWM), a direct action certain to rouse the grassroots and give teeth to the general call for victory at home and abroad, and he asked Ray-ford Logan to head the D.C. committee. Although Logan begged off be-cause of other commitments, MOWM planning went charging ahead.[70]

Once the antiwar editor of the *Messenger,* A. Philip Randolph had moved away from socialism but not from agitation. He founded the Brotherhood of Sleeping Car Porters in the 1920s and spent the 1930s shepherding the all-black union through the Depression and using the Pullman porters' and maids' mighty organizational strength to back causes from Scottsboro to the National Negro Congress of 1936. Although Randolph had not served in the military, World War I, the racism and repression of the Wilson administra-tion, and the vehemence of white Americans' backlash provided the founda-tion of his political education as surely as it had Logan's or Houston's. What lessons he may have missed, he could glean from the veterans on the *Messen-ger* staff like William Colson, drama critic Theophilus Lewis, or Florida-born Communist Eugene Gordon.[71]

World War I had not resulted in dramatic change, but it had taught peo-ple like Randolph how to fight the battles of World War II. "Power and pres-sure are at the foundation of the march of justice and social reform," Ran-dolph stated in his January 1941 call to arms. This "power and pressure do not reside in the few, and intelligentsia, they lie in and flow from the masses." The MOWM showed no interest in the genteel demonstrations of middle-class decorum and manhood that had marked African Americans' parades in the lead-up to World War I. Limiting participation in the movement to black people only, Randolph intended to showcase organized African American power to force President Roosevelt to abolish discrimination in the national defense program. No waiting, no imploring, no hoping, he wrote, if African Americans wanted to work and fight on equal terms, "WE MUST FIGHT FOR IT AND FIGHT FOR IT WITH GLOVES OFF."[72]

Black Americans proved willing to fight. The MOWM set up thirty-six branches within about three months, building a broad base through the Brotherhood of Sleeping Car Porters and other labor groups, beauty shops and street corner talk, bars and churches. The 10,000 that Randolph had originally envisioned looked as though it might swell to 100,000. The FBI's J. Edgar Hoover, who had kept a baleful eye on Randolph since the early publications of the *Messenger,* warned against the "tremendous demonstration" planned for the nation's capital. First Lady Eleanor Roosevelt expressed alarm at the "trouble" that would occur when tens of thousands of black protestors encountered the Washington police, "most of them Southerners." Randolph refused to back down until the President banned discrimination in the defense industries, assuring Eleanor Roosevelt that there would be no violence unless her husband unleashed his Southern police force on the D.C. parade.[73]

The show of force worked. On June 25, 1941, Roosevelt issued Executive Order Number 8802. The order declared it "the duty of employers and of labor organizations" in the defense industry and government "to provide for the full and equitable participation of all workers in defense industries, without discrimination because of race, creed, color, or national origin." Moreover, it established a Fair Employment Practice Committee (FEPC) to safeguard that equal access. In return, Randolph cancelled the march and pledged African American loyalty should the United States enter the world war. "Never before in the history of the nation," the *Defender* crowed upon printing the order, "have Negroes ever been so united in an objective and so insistent upon action being taken."[74]

African Americans not only knew their strength, they used it to great effect in the lead-up to America's entry into World War II. The democracy hoped for in the first World War became the democracy demanded in the second, and those New Negroes anticipated before the Great War led the Young Turks of the 1930s and 1940s in the double battle against white supremacy at home and abroad. Freedom still would not come without a fight: Kathryn Johnson, for example, traveled to Washington, D.C., as part of a delegation pushing Congress to make the FEPC a permanent commission. And Ely Green spent much of the war years trying to enact Roosevelt's Executive Order in the defense plants of Los Angeles.

In the years since World War I, Green "had kept as posted as possible on world affairs" and with another war seemingly "imminent," he had written to the War Department to enroll in an officers training camp. With the War

"Mr. Prejudice" by Horace Pippin. Pippin's emphasis on a double V was influenced by his status as a veteran of the 369th Infantry. Philadelphia Museum of Art, Gift of Dr. and Mrs. Matthew T. Moore, 1984.

Department making no provision to train black officers in early 1941, Green simply waited. Thus when a woman approached him identifying herself as an "agent for Eleanor Roosevelt" and asking him to build relationships in three plants where the American Federation of Labor (AFL) had effectively barred black labor, Green responded in his usual patois of courage and paternalist identification. "You tell Mother," he said, "I will try to do my best." His struggles with the "Okie" migrants staffing the factories would echo his travails as a stevedore and in Waxahachie, but in the factories, as in the ports, he pressed on. Military service and his subsequent sense of recognition had convinced him of the necessity and the value of his efforts.[75]

Although Ely Green's story may seem extraordinary, he was but one of the near 400,000 African Americans to experience the mix of obligation, expectation, pride, and pain that came with wartime service. The nation was peopled with Ely Greens, African Americans who left for the Army and came back with bigger horizons and expanded senses of self and possibility. There were also countless indefatigables like Kathryn Johnson who applied their energies to everything from education to organization to street-level protest. For these members of the World War I cohort, the Great War set them on a path into activism and action. It shaped how they saw themselves as women and men, as Americans, and as citizens of the world. It refined their notions of gender, rights, and affiliation. It also shaped how they saw the freedom struggle, their position as individuals, and their potential as a collective.

Segregationists had good cause to worry about the legacies of World War I and its implications for World War II. For as much as the members of the World War I generation might differ from one another, they held a collective sense of the injustice they faced and the cause they shared that could and did spawn an efflorescence of movements, analyses, and strategies for change. The activists and veterans of the Great War did not simply prepare the ground for the freedom struggle in World War II. They showed their fellow African Americans how to walk that ground and pushed them to grasp the opportunities that a second war presented. The activism of World War I outlasted the repression of the 1920s and the Depression of the 1930s, kept alive by the watchfulness and willfulness of democracy's advance guard. And in the years after World War II, it would prove too strong for even Jim Crow's defenses.

Epilogue: The Fruit of Conquest

In 1940, Osceola McKaine came home. He had enjoyed his life as an African American in Ghent, "the most respected of all Negroes" under the Belgian typology of race and geography. Running a jazz club, Mac's Place, he bene-fited from his status as an American outside the dynamics of European col-ony and empire. Yet not even his American-ness could insulate him as the Nazis advanced on Belgium. Sixteen years after he had abandoned the United States, he traded the white supremacists of Germany for the segregationists of South Carolina.[1]

Despite his years in exile, McKaine's political mobilization had outlasted the immediate postwar flurry of organizational activity. Back in the South after thirty years away, he applied the lessons of the First World War to his organizing during the Second. As president of the Sumter, South Carolina, branch of the NAACP, he still sought to enforce the Civil War amendments to reclaim African American citizenship, albeit through the force of voter participation drives and teacher equalization lawsuits rather than the threat of violence. He challenged Jim Crow in other ways as well. Along with John McCray, his boss at the Columbia *Lighthouse and Informer,* McKaine founded the interracial Progressive Democratic Party (PDP) as an alternative to the white supremacist Democrats entrenched in state and national politics. In 1944, he ran for U.S. Senate on the PDP ticket, and in 1948 the PDP brought the party's commitment to defeat white supremacy into sharp focus when they vied for a seat at the Democratic National Convention. If McKaine had learned anything from his wartime service and activism, it was that America would not change for African Americans until they made it do so. He had entered World War I hopeful; he faced World War II determined.[2]

The veterans and civilian activists who pressed for civil rights after World War II were heirs of the men and women who had forged their political identities under the Wilson administration. Indeed, as Osceola McKaine's biography suggests, they were often the same actors. As Haywood Hall put it while considering his career as a communist, he had mustered out of the Army and "stepped into a battle that was to last the rest of my life." From the memory of his grandfather fighting off the Klan to his use of Malcolm X and Mao Tse Tung to analyze the freedom struggle in the United States, Hall's self-formation linked the Reconstruction of the mid-nineteenth century to the Cold War of the mid-twentieth. Within that long tradition of African American politics, it was in the crucible of war that his consciousness coalesced.[3]

Ely Green, too, linked the generations of the twentieth-century freedom struggle. Visiting Tennessee from California for the first time in almost forty years, Ely Green assured a white man in a Sewanee drug store that he was not with the interracial Freedom Riders who were challenging segregation laws during that summer of 1961. Green declared himself unaffiliated "with the racial program" and added, "My dog and I taken a freedom ride" of their own to observe the changes in the South. Still, although the sixty-eight-year-old Green disavowed the younger Freedom Riders' tactics and confrontational ways, the militancy of his youth and his continued hope for a "free nation" joined him to them, and them to him. Ever committed to gaining "a national respect of law and an international respect as a man," he had lived the rebellion that eventually brought down Jim Crow. Ely Green had been freedom-riding his whole life.[4]

Every life is at once singular and socially embedded, extraordinary and mundane. Not every soldier was Osceola McKaine nor every reformer Kathryn Johnson, but just like McKaine and Johnson, each of the hundreds of thousands of African Americans who engaged the war did so tacking between democracy's promise and Jim Crow's threat. And the 200,000 African Americans who went to Europe as part of the AEF shared the experience of anticipation, travel, travail, and return. Whether they turned to heightened protest or returned to their prewar patterns of living, they did so having shifted place in relation to their community, nation, and the world. For these soldiers and the reformers who tied their hopes to them, the war reconfigured boundaries both physical and psychological.

The struggle against white supremacy in the United States was comprised of the dreams, too often deferred, of people like Ely Green, Haywood Hall, Vida Henry, or Clara Threadgill-Dennis. World War I offered African Americans some opportunity to make those dreams a reality, even as it mobilized many white Americans to defend the status quo. The resulting conflict proved alternately disheartening and inspiring, destructive and instructive. African Americans found in the political and social ferment of the World War I era the material and resolve to forge the mass movements of the World War II era and after. If nationalism is born of fulfilling responsibility to generations that have passed and generations yet to come, then racial activists' will to make the United States do right and act justly served to strengthen and solidify the American nation.[5] We all should be such patriots.

Notes

Acknowledgments

Index

Notes

Du Bois Papers	*The Papers of W. E. B. Du Bois* (Sanford, N.C.: Microfilming Corporation of America, 1981).
FSAA	Theodore Kornweibel Jr., ed., *Federal Surveillance of Afro-Americans, 1917-1925: The First World War, The Red Scare, and the Garvey Movement* (Frederick, Md.: University Publications of America, 1985)
NAACP/LOC	*Papers of the National Association for the Advancement of Colored People,* Legal Files, Series D Box 49, Library of Congress Manuscript Division.
NAACP Papers	Randolph Boehm, August Meier, and Mark Fox, eds., *Papers of the NAACP,* Black Studies Research Sources (Frederick, Md.: University Publications of America, 1982)
NARA	National Archives and Records Administration, Washington, D.C.
NARA II	National Archives and Records Administration, College Park, Md.
OG	Old German File
RG	Record Group

TINCF   John W. Kitchens, ed., *Tuskegee Institute Newspaper Clippings File,
             1899–1966* (Sanford, N.C.: Microfilming Corporation of America,
             1976)
Wilson/LOC   Papers of Woodrow Wilson, Manuscripts Division, Library of
             Congress.
Wilson Papers Arthur S. Link, ed., *The Papers of Woodrow Wilson* (Princeton,
             N.J.: Princeton University Press, 1966).

Introduction

1. On the African American experience at Camp Gordon, see John Dittmer, *Black Georgia in the Progressive Era,* 1900–1920 (Urbana: University of Illinois Press, 1977), 195–196.

2. Ulrich B. Phillips, *American Negro Slavery* (1918; repr., Baton Rouge: Louisiana State University Press, 1966), viii–ix.

3. Ibid., ix.

4. Contemporary scholars began the work of framing World War I as a pivotal moment in the black freedom struggle, often glossing over hardships to emphasize heroism. See Kelly Miller, *Kelly Miller's History of the World War for Human Rights* (Washington, D.C.: Jenkins and Keller, 1919); and William Allison Sweeney, *History of the American Negro in the Great World War* (Chicago: Cuneo-Henneberry Co., 1919). W. E. B. Du Bois planned a history of the world war that would have mixed chronicle with protest. See David Levering Lewis, *W. E. B. Du Bois: Biography of a Race* (New York: Henry Holt and Company, 1993), 562; and Jonathan Rosenberg, *How Far the Promised Land: World Affairs and the American Civil Rights Movement* (Princeton, N.J.: Princeton University Press, 2006), 58.

5. The classic work on African American soldiers and World War I remains Arthur Barbeau and Florette Henri, *The Unknown Soldiers: African-American Troops in World War I* (1974; repr., New York: Da Capo Press, 1996). Other works that look at African Americans in World War I include Bernard C. Nalty, *Strength for the Fight: A History of Blacks in the Military* (New York: The Free Press, 1986); Jennifer Keene, *Doughboys, the Great War, and the Remaking of America* (Baltimore: Johns Hopkins University Press, 2001); and Richard Slotkin, *Lost Battalions: The Great War and the Crisis of American Nationality* (New York: Henry Holt and Company, 2005).

6. On African Americans and the wars for empire, see Willard B. Gatewood Jr., *Black Americans and the White Man's Burden,* 1898–1903 (Urbana: University of Illinois Press, 1975).

7. The work that follows is indebted to Mary Renda's elaborations on culture and politics, particularly her definition of American national culture as "a contested terrain on which people identifying themselves as Americans formulate, dispute, and reformulate structures of meaning and power associated with various forms of difference such as gender, class, race, and nation." See Mary A. Renda, *Taking Haiti: Military Occupa-*

tion and the Culture of U.S. Imperialism, 1915–1940 (Chapel Hill: University of North Carolina Press, 2001).

8. On African American history as international history, see Robin D. G. Kelley, "'But a Local Phase of a World Problem:' Black History's Global Vision," *Journal of American History* 86 (December 1999): 1045–1078; Brent Hayes Edwards, *The Practice of Diaspora: Literature, Translation, and the Rise of Black Internationalism* (Cambridge, Mass.: Harvard University Press, 2003); Michelle Stephens, *Black Empire: The Masculine Global Imaginary of Caribbean Intellectuals in the United States, 1914–1962* (Durham, N.C.: Duke University Press, 2005); Carol Anderson, *Eyes Off the Prize: The United Nations and the African American Struggle for Human Rights, 1944–1955* (New York: Cambridge University Press, 2003).

9. Ralph Ellison, "Going to the Territory," in John F. Callahan, ed., *The Collected Essays of Ralph Ellison* (New York: The Modern Library), 602.

10. On articulations of African American masculinity in the wake of the Civil War, see Earnestine Jenkins and Darlene Clark Hine, eds., *A Question of Manhood: A Reader in U.S. Black Men's History and Masculinity,* vol. 2 (Bloomington: Indiana University Press, 2001). On black soldiers, Jim Crow, and the 1898 wars, see Gatewood, *Black Americans and the White Man's Burden,* as well as Kristin L. Hoganson, *Fighting for American Manhood: How Gender Politics Provoked the Spanish-American and Cuban-American Wars* (New Haven, Conn.: Yale University Press, 1998). On manhood and white supremacy, see Gail Bederman, *Manliness and Civilization: A Cultural History of Gender and Race in the United States, 1880–1917* (Chicago: University of Chicago Press, 1995); and Stephen Kantrowitz, *Benjamin Tillman and the Reconstruction of White Supremacy* (Chapel Hill: University of North Carolina Press, 2000).

11. Martin Summers, *Manliness and Its Discontents: The Black Middle Class and the Transformation of Middle Class, 1900–1930* (Chapel Hill: University of North Carolina Press, 2004), 13. This perspective is also influenced by Glenda Gilmore's study of black women's activism in Jim Crow–era North Carolina. As she deftly illustrates, black manhood and black womanhood were mutually constitutive ideals, intended to reclaim lost political ground for African American men and women together. Black women's interventions in politics high and low would not allow for their relegation to a private sphere of apolitical domesticity. See Gilmore, *Gender and Jim Crow: Women and the Politics of White Supremacy in North Carolina, 1890–1915* (Chapel Hill: University of North Carolina Press, 1996).

12. Summers, *Manliness and Its Discontents,* 13.

13. Founded in 1908, the Bureau of Investigation became the Federal Bureau of Investigation in 1935. On the growth of the political surveillance, foreign and domestic, see Theodore Kornweibel, *Seeing Red: Federal Campaigns Against Black Militancy, 1919–1925* (Bloomington: Indiana University Press, 1998), and Mark Ellis, *Race, War, and Surveillance: African Americans and the United States Government During World War I* (Bloomington: Indiana University Press, 2001).

14. Kantrowitz defines white supremacy as "both a social argument and a political program." See *Benjamin Tillman and the Reconstruction of White Supremacy*, 2.

15. For an example of the African Americans' hopes for, and anxieties over, returning soldiers, see Mary P. Burrill, "Aftermath," in Kathy A. Perkins, ed., *Black Female Playwrights: An Anthology of Plays Before 1950* (Bloomington: Indiana University Press, 1989), 56–57. Originally published in *The Liberator,* April 1919.

1. World on Fire

1. Memoirs, Kathryn M. Johnson Papers, Schlesinger Library, Radcliffe College, 7, 25–27.

2. Ibid., 32, 37. Historian Carter G. Woodson described the founders of the school as "bold antislavery men" who stood firm against opponents of African American education. See Woodson, *The Education of the Negro Prior to 1861: A History of the Education of the Colored People of the United States from the Beginning of Slavery to the Civil War* (1919; repr., Whitefish, Mont.: Kessinger Publishing, 2004), 190.

3. Memoirs, Kathryn M. Johnson, 25–27. Additional information comes from James A. Padgett, "Ministers to Liberia and Their Diplomacy," *Journal of Negro History* 22 (January 1937): 87.

4. Memoirs, Kathryn M. Johnson, 24.

5. On Progressivism, see Robert Wiebe, *The Search for Order, 1877–1920* (New York: Farrar, Straus, & Giroux, 1966); William A. Link, *The Paradox of Southern Progressivism, 1880–1930* (Chapel Hill: University of North Carolina Press, 1992); and Daniel Rodgers, *Atlantic Crossings: Social Politics in a Progressive Era* (Cambridge, Mass.: Harvard University Press, 2000).

6. On segregation and white supremacy, see C. Vann Woodward, *The Strange Career of Jim Crow* (1955; repr., New York: Oxford University Press, 1974); and Stephen Kantrowitz, *Benjamin Tillman and the Reconstruction of White Supremacy* (Chapel Hill: University of North Carolina Press, 2000). For an exploration of how Progressivism fostered both white supremacy and black activism in the South, see Glenda Elizabeth Gilmore, *Gender and Jim Crow: Women and the Politics of White Supremacy in North Carolina, 1896–1920* (Chapel Hill: University of North Carolina Press, 1996).

7. See Alice L. Conklin, *A Mission to Civilize: The Republican Idea of Empire in France and West Africa, 1895–1920* (Stanford, Calif.: Stanford University Press, 1997); Eric Hobsbawm, *The Age of Empire, 1875–1914* (New York: Vintage Books, 1987), 56–83; and Ernest May, *American Imperialism, A Speculative Essay* (1968; repr., Chicago: Imprint Publications, 1991).

8. As historian Kevin Gaines points out, when African Americans sought to articulate their arguments for rights through the ideology of racial uplift, they often ended up reinforcing the "ostensibly universal but deeply racialized ideological categories of Western progress and civilization" from which white supremacy drew its power.

See Gaines, *Uplifting the Race: Black Leadership, Politics, and Culture in the Twentieth Century* (Chapel Hill: University of North Carolina Press, 1996), xiv.

9. W. E. B. Du Bois, "The African Roots of the War," *Atlantic Monthly* 115 (May 1915): 707–709.

10. Ibid., 712.

11. John Hope Franklin quoted in Rayford Logan, *The Betrayal of the Negro: From Rutherford B. Hayes to Woodrow Wilson* (1965; repr., New York: Da Capo Press, 1997), xxi.

12. Memoirs, Kathryn M. Johnson, 43, 47. On Wilberforce, see David Levering Lewis, *W. E. B. Du Bois: Biography of a Race* (New York: Henry Holt, 1993), 150–178. For a rich portrait of African American women as teachers and activists, see Katherine Mellen Charron, *Freedom's Teacher: The Life of Septima Clark* (Chapel Hill: University of North Carolina Press, 2009).

13. Memoirs, Kathryn M. Johnson, 63. On the state normal school in Elizabeth City, later the Elizabeth City Teachers College, see Nelson H. Harris, "Publicly Supported Negro Institutions of Higher Learning in North Carolina," *Journal of Negro Education* 31 (Summer 1962): 285.

14. Memoirs, Kathryn M. Johnson, 64.

15. "Degenerate sons of white race," from "Remember the Six" Handbill, n.d. North Carolina Collection, Wilson Library, University of North Carolina at Chapel Hill. Also see Le Rae Umfleet et al., *1898 Wilmington Race Riot Report* (Raleigh: North Carolina Office of Archives and History, 2006), 75.

16. "Chairman F. M. Simmons Issues a Patriotic and Able Address, Summing Up the Issues, and Appealing Eloquently to the White Voters to Redeem the State," *Raleigh News & Observer,* November 3, 1898.

17. Quoted in Glenda E. Gilmore, "The Flight of the Incubus," in David S. Cecelski and Timothy B. Tyson, eds., *Democracy Betrayed: The Wilmington Race Riot of 1898 and Its Legacy* (Chapel Hill: University of North Carolina Press, 1998), 75.

18. First labeled a coup in H. Leon Prather, *We Have Taken a City: Wilmington Racial Massacre and Coup of 1898* (Rutherford, N.J.: Associated Universities Press, 1984).

19. Alfred Moore Waddell and Thalian Hall, Wilmington, N.C., October 24, 1898, quoted in *1898 Wilmington Race Riot Report*, 82.

20. "'A Negro Woman' to President Wm. A. McKinley," 13 November 1898, RG 160, Box 117A, General Records of the Department of Justice, Year Files 1887–1904, in Appendix J, *1898 Wilmington Race Riot Report*, 372.

21. On the Philippines, see Paul Kramer, *The Blood of Government: Race, Empire, the United States, and the Philippines* (Chapel Hill: University of North Carolina Press, 2006). On the links between American racial ideologies and American expansionism, see Matthew Frye Jacobson, *Barbarian Virtues: The United States Encounters Foreign Peoples at Home and Abroad, 1876–1917* (New York: Hill and Wang, 2001).

22. Alfred Waddell, Speech at Thalian Hall, printed in *Wilmington Messenger,* October 25, 1898.

23. Presley Holliday to *New York Age,* 11 May 1899, in Willard B. Gatewood Jr., *"Smoked Yankees" and the Struggle for Empire: Letters from Negro Soldiers, 1898–1892,* 4th ed. (Fayetteville: University of Arkansas Press, 1987), 94; and Gary Gerstle, *American Crucible: Race and Nation in the Twentieth Century* (Princeton, N.J.: Princeton University Press, 2001), 38–39.

24. C. W. Cordin to H. C. Smith, editor, *Cleveland Gazette,* 21 December 1898, quoted in Gatewood, *Smoked Yankees,* 158.

25. C. W. Cordin to Hon. H. C. Smith, n.d., quoted in Gatewood, *Smoked Yankees,* 159; C. W. Cordin to Hon. H. C. Smith, 21 December 1891, quoted in Gatewood, *Smoked Yankees,* 157.

26. Allen S. Peal to *Cleveland Gazette,* 8 April 1999, quoted in Gatewood, *Smoked Yankees,* 175.

27. Robert L. Bullard, Diary, Robert L. Bullard Papers, Manuscript Division, Library of Congress, 93–94, quoted in Willard B. Gatewood Jr. "Alabama's 'Negro Soldier Experiment,' 1898–1899," *Journal of Negro History* 57 (October 1972): 346. Bullard served as the commanding officer of the Third Alabama and treated his men with a paternalistic goodwill. He would later become a notorious detractor of the fighting abilities of black infantrymen in World War I.

28. Gatewood, "Alabama's 'Negro Soldier Experiment,' " 347–349.

29. Ibid., 350.

30. "Southern Propagandists Are Now in the Saddle," *Baltimore Afro-American,* January 22, 1916.

31. Gatewood, "Alabama's 'Negro Soldier Experiment,' " 351.

32. Glenda E. Gilmore, "Black Militia in the Spanish-American/Cuban War," in Benjamin R. Beede, ed., *The War of 1898 and United States Interventions, 1898–1934, An Encyclopedia* (New York: Garland Press, 1994), vol. 2, 53–54.

33. See Richard Slotkin, *Gunfighter Nation: The Myth of the Frontier in Twentieth-Century America* (1992; repr., Norman: University of Oklahoma Press, 1998).

34. George Schuyler, *Black and Conservative: The Autobiography of George S. Schuyler* (New Rochelle, N.Y.: Arlington House, 1966), 28.

35. Max Weber, "Politics as a Vocation," in Max Weber, *From Max Weber: Essays in Sociology,* trans. and ed. H. H. Gerth and C. Wright Mills (1946; repr., New York: Oxford University Press, 1958), 78.

36. Walter White, *Rope and Faggot: A Biography of Judge Lynch* (1929; repr., New York: Arno Press, 1969), 231. On lynching, sexual politics, and struggles for political power, see Crystal N. Feimster, *Southern Horrors: Women and the Politics of Rape and Lynching* (Cambridge, Mass.: Harvard University Press, 2009).

37. On lynching as community ritual, see Trudier Harris, *Exorcising Blackness: Historical and Lynching Literary and Burning Ritual* (Bloomington: Indiana University Press, 1985).

38. As in Wilmington, the rape scare that initiated the riot was largely manufactured by Democrats campaigning on a white supremacist platform and promoted by a partisan press. See David Fort Godshalk, *Veiled Visions: The 1906 Atlanta Race Riot and the Reshaping of American Race Relations* (Chapel Hill: University of North Carolina Press, 2005).

39. Walter White, *A Man Called White* (New York: Viking Press, 1948), 11. Quote from "Atlanta Is Swept by Raging Mob," *Atlanta Constitution,* September 23, 1906, in Lewis, *W. E. B. Du Bois, Biography of a Race,* 333.

40. John Temple Graves, "Separation of the Races Is the Inevitable Solution," *New York World,* September 24, 1906, 2; and White, *A Man Called White,* 10.

41. *Illinois State Journal,* quoted in Lewis, *W. E. B. Du Bois: Biography of a Race,* 388.

42. Memoirs, Kathryn M. Johnson, 75.

43. "Dynamite Used to Rout Negroes, Blacks Kill Whites in Arkansas and Defy Officers," *Atlanta Constitution,* October 7, 1906, C1; and Memoirs, Kathryn M. Johnson, 73.

44. Memoirs, Kathryn M. Johnson, 73.

45. "Dynamite Used to Rout Negroes."

46. "Dynamite Used to Rout Negroes."

47. Memoirs, Kathryn M. Johnson, 69–71.

48. Ibid., 71.

49. Ibid., 71–75.

50. Ibid., 70–72.

51. Ibid., 72.

52. Ibid., 68.

53. William English Walling, "The Race War in the North," *Independent* 65 (September 3, 1908), quoted in Mary White Ovington, "The National Association for the Advancement of Colored People," *Journal of Negro History* 9 (April 1924): 109.

54. Kathryn Johnson to Roy Nash, 22 July 1919, in NAACP Papers, Part 1.

55. "The Standard Printed Version of the Atlanta Exposition Address," September 18, 1895, in Louis R. Harlan, ed., *The Booker T. Washington Papers,* vol. 3 (Urbana: University of Illinois Press), 584.

56. Gaines, *Uplifting the Race,* 37–38; Nikhil Pal Singh, *Black Is a Country: Race and the Unfinished Struggle for Democracy* (Cambridge, Mass.: Harvard University Press, 2004), 46–47.

57. Lewis, *W. E. B. Du Bois: Biography of a Race,* 256–262.

58. On alternate public spheres, see Evelyn Brooks Higginbotham, *Righteous Discontent* (Cambridge, Mass.: Harvard University Press, 1993), 9–11.

59. Gaines, *Uplifting the Race,* 3–5; Paula Giddings, *When and Where I Enter: The Impact of Black Women on Race and Sex in America* (New York: Bantam Books, 1984), 102–108.

60. Martin Summers, *Manliness and Its Discontents: The Black Middle Class and the Transformation of Masculinity, 1900–1930* (Chapel Hill: University of North Carolina Press, 2004); and Gilmore, *Gender and Jim Crow,* 62–63.

61. Emmett Scott to Booker T. Washington, 17 July 1902, in *Booker T. Washington Papers*, 6, 496. On the League, see Emma L. Thornborough, "The National Afro-American League," *Journal of Southern History* 27 (November 1961): 494–512.

62. On Wells, see Paula Giddings, *Ida, A Sword among Lions: Ida B. Wells and the Campaign against Lynching* (New York: Harper Collins, 2008). On Trotter, see Stephen Fox, *The Guardian of Boston: William Monroe Trotter* (New York: Atheneum, 1970). Quote from Ovington, "The National Association for the Advancement of Colored People," 108–109.

63. Ovington, "The National Association for the Advancement of Colored People," 113.

64. Dorothy Salem, *To Better Our World: Black Women in Organized Reform, 1890–1920* (Brooklyn, N.Y.: Carlson Publishing, 1920), 160.

65. Mary C. Nerney to Kathryn M. Johnson, 25 November 1913, quoted in Memoirs, Kathryn M. Johnson, 136–137.

66. Memoirs, Kathryn M. Johnson, 105–106.

67. Kathryn Johnson to Roy Nash, 1 May 1916, in NAACP Papers, Part 1, Reel 18.

68. Memoirs, Kathryn M. Johnson, 105–106, 129–130.

69. Elisha Green, *Ely: Too Black, Too White* (Amherst: The University of Massachusetts Press, 1970), 1, 5. Because he dropped out of grammar school rather than endure teasing for being mixed-race, Ely Green received only a few months of formal schooling. After a girlfriend left him for not having enough education, he taught himself to read and write at the age of twenty. His memory, ear for language, and colorful spelling reflect his early learning through oral tradition. I have chosen to leave Green's spelling mistakes unmarked.

70. Ibid., 123.

71. Ibid., 71.

72. Ibid., 71, 82.

73. Ibid., 114.

74. Ibid., 112.

75. Ibid., 134. "Sager" was a derogatory term for rural whites. See Lee Pederson, "Lexical Data from the Gulf States," *American Speech* 55 (Autumn 1980): 198–202.

76. Green, *Ely: Too Black, Too White*, 181.

77. Ibid., 176.

78. "Southern Propagandists Are Now in the Saddle," *Baltimore Afro-American*, January 22, 1916, 1.

79. Woodrow Wilson, *The New Freedom* (New York and Garden City, N.J.: Doubleday, Page, and Company, 1913), 13, 30. On Wilson as a Progressive, see John Milton Cooper Jr., *The Warrior and the Priest: Woodrow Wilson and Theodore Roosevelt* (Cambridge, Mass.: Harvard University Press, 1983).

80. Rev. William A. Byrd, "As to Mr. Villard," *Cleveland Gazette*, February 10, 1917.

81. Woodrow Wilson, "The Bible and Progress," in Papers of Emmett J. Scott, Special Assistant to the Secretary of War, 1917–1919, RG 107, Box 2, Emmett J. Scott Collection, NARA II.

82. Woodrow Wilson, "The Reconstruction of the Southern States," *Atlantic Monthly* 87 (January 1901): 6.

83. Henry Blumenthal, "Woodrow Wilson and the Race Question," *Journal of Negro History* 48 (January 1963): 2; John Morton Blum, *Woodrow Wilson and the Politics of Morality* (New York: Harper Collins, 1956), 43–45.

84. Blumenthal, "Woodrow Wilson and the Race Question," 13.

85. Ibid., 6.

86. Ibid.

87. Ibid., 13.

88. Brown quoted in Joel Williamson, *The Crucible of Race: Black-White Relations in the American South Since Emancipation* (New York: Oxford University Press, 1984), 360.

89. W. E. B. Du Bois, "My Impressions of Woodrow Wilson," *Journal of Negro History* 58 (October 1973): 454.

90. *Indianapolis Freeman,* August 9, 1913, quoted in Morton Sosna, "The South in the Saddle: Racial Politics during the Wilson Years," *Wisconsin Magazine of History* 54 (Autumn 1970): 35.

91. Cooper, *The Warrior and the Priest,* 229–247; "Bitterly Assails Wilson," *Baltimore Afro-American,* September 23, 1916.

92. Sosna, "The South in the Saddle," 33. Both Du Bois and Sosna suggest that the Bureau of Printing and Engraving was segregated at the request of First Lady Ellen Axson Wilson.

93. Woodrow Wilson quoted in Arthur S. Link, *Woodrow Wilson and the Progressive Era, 1910–1917* (New York: Harper Torchbooks, 1954), 66; and Kathleen L. Wolgemuth, "Woodrow Wilson and Federal Segregation," *Journal of Negro History* 44 (April 1959): 164. On the Wilson administration's systematic application of Jim Crow practices in the federal government, see Eric S. Yellin, "In the Nation's Service: Racism and Federal Employees in Woodrow Wilson's Washington" (Ph.D. diss., Princeton University, 2008).

94. Franklin J. Johnson, "German Agents Try to Start Rebellion," *Baltimore Afro-American,* April 7, 1917, 1.

95. *Milwaukee Free Press,* reprinted in "Wilson 'Father' of Segregation," *Chicago Defender,* April 29, 1916, 1.

96. Steven Hahn, *A Nation under Our Feet: Black Political Struggles in the Rural South from Slavery to the Great Migration* (Cambridge, Mass.: Harvard University Press, 2003), 465–466. See also Joe William Trotter, ed., *The Great Migration in Historical Perspective: New Dimensions of Race, Class, and Gender* (Bloomington: Indiana University Press, 1991); and Carole Marks, *Farewell—We're Good and Gone: The Great Migration* (Bloomington: Indiana University Press, 1989).

97. "Good for the South," *Atlanta Constitution,* July 27, 1914, 4.

98. Caroll L. Miller, "The Negro and Volunteer War Agencies," *Journal of Negro Education* 12 (Summer 1943): 417.

99. "President Wilson's Speech," *New York Times,* January 9, 1915, 4.

100. "The South's Silver Lining to Europe's War Cloud," *Atlanta Constitution,* August 6, 1914, 8.

101. Sydney Brooks, "The United States and the War: A British View," *North American Review,* quoted in Arthur S. Link, *Wilson: The Struggle for Neutrality, 1914–1915* (Princeton, N.J.: Princeton University Press, 1960), 25.

102. Booker T. Washington to Andrew Carnegie, 6 August 1914, in *The Booker T. Washington Papers,* vol. 13, 112; Washington to Robert Ezra Park, 5 August 1914, 111; Washington to Park, 14 August 1914, 116. On Europeans' enthusiasm for war, see John Keegan, *The First World War* (New York: Knopf, 1999), 71–75.

103. "Proposition de Loi par M. Pierre Massé et autres députés sur le recrutement d'une armée indigène," Chambre des Députés, Onzième Législature, session de 1915, C7537, Dossier no. 1461, Archives Nationales, Paris, France.

104. C. M. Andrew and A. S. Kanya-Forstner, "France, Africa, and the First World War," *Journal of African History* 19 (1978): 16; and Kimloan Thi Vu Hill, "A Westward Journey, An Enlightened Path: Vietnamese Linh Tho, 1915–1930" (Ph.D. diss., University of Oregon, 2001), 29.

105. Charles Mangin, *La Force Noire: Lieutenant-Colonel Mangin* (Paris: Hachette, 1910), 343, quoted in Joe Lunn, "'Les Races Guerrières': Racial Preconceptions in the French Military about West African Soldiers during the First World War," *Journal of Contemporary History* 34 (October 1999): 521.

106. Lunn, "Les Race Guerrières," 523.

107. Hyppolyte Langlois, *Temps,* November 12, 1909, quoted in Lunn, "Les Races Guerrières," 525.

108. "Africa's Untamed Black Men 'Civilized' by War," *Atlanta Constitution,* January 23, 1916, E5.

109. Ibid.

110. "'England Traitor to the White Race'—Dernburg," *New York Times,* January 2, 1916, SM3.

111. "Asiatics and Africans," letter to the editor, *New York Times,* January 6, 1916, 12. On disagreements with Dernburg, see "Germany's Colored Foes," letter to the editor, *New York Times,* January 4, 1916, 12; and J. M. Batchman, "The Imperial Government," *Cleveland Gazette,* January 27, 1917, 2.

112. See Joe Lunn, *Memoirs of the Maelstrom: A Senegalese Oral History of the First World War* (Portsmouth, N.H.: Heinemann, 1999), 65–80; and "Army Rights for Negroes," *New York Times,* July 11, 1915, 7.

113. Senator James K. Vardaman, "Recent Disturbances in East St. Louis," S. Res. 10, 65th Cong., 1st sess., *Congressional Record* 55 pt 6 (August 16, 1917), S 6063.

114. "An Address to a Joint Session of Congress," 2 April 1917, in Wilson Papers.

115. Ibid.

116. Johnson, "German Agents Try to Start Rebellion."

117. Green, *Ely: Too Black, Too White,* 311 and 315.

118. Kathryn M. Johnson, "The Negro and the World War," *Half-Century* 2 (June 1917): 13.

119. "Negroes Urged by Local Pastors to Fight for the Flag," *Atlanta Constitution,* April 2, 1917, 6. Late in the war, Proctor aided soldiers as a camp volunteer with the YMCA in France. See Emmett J. Scott, *Scott's Official History of the American Negro in the World War* (1919), 403

120. Johnson, "German Agents Try to Start Rebellion."

121. W. E. B. Du Bois, "We Should Worry," *Crisis* 14 (June 1917): 60–61.

122. "Pledge Loyalty on the Part of the Negro," *Baltimore Afro-American,* April 21, 1917, 1.

123. "In Re: Anonymous Communication Endeavoring Prevent Negro Enlistment: European Neutrality," April 30, 1917, OG 3057, RG 65, in FSAA, Reel 8.

124. "General European Neutrality Matters," May 7, 1917, OG 3057, RG 65, in FSAA.

125. "Alleged Disloyal Remarks in Texas," December 6, 1917, Casefile OG 105468, RG 65, in FSAA.

126. William Kelley to Newton D. Baker, Secretary of War, 1 August 1918, Casefile 10218-197, Record Group 165, in Correspondence of the Military Intelligence Division Relating to Negro Subversion, 1917–1941, NARA II. Spurred by rumors reported in the white press, many white Southerners believed that German and Mexican spies were traveling through Dixie attempting to recruit African American agents. See Theodore Kornweibel Jr., *"Investigate Everything": Federal Efforts to Compel Black Loyalty during World War I* (Bloomington: Indiana University Press, 2002), 40–47.

127. *The Messenger,* 1 (November 1917), 21.

128. Numbers come from Emmett J. Scott, *Scott's Official History of the American Negro in the Word War* (1919), 32. Thousands of Southerners of all races resisted the draft mightily. See Jeanette Keith, *Rich Man's War, Poor Man's Fight: Race, Class, and Power in the Rural South during the First World War* (Chapel Hill: University of North Carolina Press, 2004). On the draft, see Arthur Barbeau and Florette Henri, *The Unknown Soldiers: African-American Troops in World War I* (1974; repr., New York: Da Capo Press, 1996), 36.

129. Anonymous to R. M. Gates, n.d., File 10218-94, RG 165, NARA II; Captain GH Hill to HB Everett, 27 April 1918, Casefile 10218-145, RG 165, NARA II. I have left African American soldiers' spelling and misspellings in their original form, unmarked.

2. Fighting the Southern Huns

1. Testimony of Captain Haig Shekerjian, Acting Battalion Adjutant, RG 153, Records of the Judge Advocate General (Army), General Courts Martial, 1812–1938, 24th Infantry Regiment Court Martial 109045, U.S. v. Nesbit, William C. et al., Box 5384, NARA II. Also reported in "'Let's Clean Up!' Yell Soldiers Before Beginning Raid on Houston," *San Antonio Express,* November 3, 1917, 1.

2. Quotation from "Charge of Murder is Filed Against 34 Negro Rioters," *Houston Post,* 25 August 1917, 1. The most detailed treatment of the riot comes in Robert Haynes, *A Night of Violence: The Houston Mutiny of 1917* (Baton Rouge: Louisiana State University Press, 1976). Garna Christian also includes a thoughtful assessment of the incident in *Black Soldiers in Jim Crow Texas 1899–1917* (College Station: Texas A&M University Press, 1995), 145–172.

3. For a contemporary account of the Ell Person lynching, see James Weldon Johnson, "The Lynching at Memphis," *Crisis,* 14 (July 1917): 134. "Pogrom" quoted from an Eastern European immigrant in Herbert Shapiro, *White Violence and Black Response, from Reconstruction to Montgomery* (Amherst: University of Massachusetts Press, 1988), 115. See also Elliot Rudwick, *Race Riot at East St. Louis* (Carbondale: Southern Illinois University Press, 1964). Pennsylvania had a riotous summer; a race riot broke out in Chester in June, 1917, and the people of Homestead barely averted one. See Henderson H. Donald, "The Negro Migration of 1916–1918," *Journal of Negro History* 6 (October 1921): 439. For a general survey of outbreaks of racial violence, see Allen D. Grimshaw, *Racial Violence in the United States* (Chicago: Aldine Publishing Company, 1969).

4. Martha Gruening, "Houston: An NAACP Investigation," *Crisis,* 15 (November 1917): 14–15.

5. Gruening, "Houston," 15.

6. Lee Sparks, testimony before the Board of Inquiry in RG 393, Southern Department Headquarters Decimal File, 1916–1920, Houston Riot of 1917, General Correspondence File 370.61, Report of Colonel Cress, Adjutant Inspector General to Commanding General, September 13, 1917, NARA, hereafter cited as Cress Report.

7. Gruening, "Houston," 15.

8. Ibid.

9. Ibid.

10. Sparks testimony, Cress Report.

11. Ibid.

12. Gruening, "Houston," 15–16.

13. Statement of Corporal Charles Baltimore, RG 159, Office of the Inspector General, Correspondence 1917–1934, 333.9, Houston Texas, Boxes 802–803, NARA, hereafter cited as Chamberlain File.

14. Sparks testimony, Cress Report.

15. Gruening, "Houston," 16.

16. Sparks's version of the confrontation between him and Baltimore comes from Sparks Testimony, Cress Report, and from the testimony of Captain Haig Shekerjian in U.S. v. Nesbit, quoted in "Court Martial Witnesses Point Negroes," *San Antonio Express,* November 3, 1917, 2.

17. Account of the conversation comes from Sparks Testimony, Cress Report.

18. Baltimore statement, Chamberlain File.

19. Testimony of Haig Shekerjian, U.S. v. Nesbit.

20. Baltimore statement, August 31, 1917, Chamberlain File.

21. Sparks Testimony, Cress Report.

22. Gruening, "Houston," 16.

23. Sparks testimony, Cress Report.

24. Baltimore statement, Chamberlain Report.

25. Sparks testimony, Cress Report.

26. Glenda Elizabeth Gilmore, *Gender and Jim Crow: Women and the Politics of White Supremacy in North Carolina, 1896–1920* (Chapel Hill: University of North Carolina Press, 1996), 3.

27. African Americans quoted in James M. SoRelle, "Race Relations in 'Heavenly Houston,' 1919–45," in Howard Beeth and Cary D. Wintz, eds., *Black Dixie: Afro Texans History and Culture in Houston* (College Station: Texas A&M Press, 1992), 176.

28. McCray quoted in Danielle McGuire, "'It Was Like All of Us Had Been Raped': Sexual Violence, Community Mobilization, and the African American Freedom Struggle," *Journal of American History* 91 (December 2004): 909. On sexual violence and the African American freedom struggle, see McGuire, "At the Dark End of the Street: Sexualized Violence, Community Mobilization and the African American Freedom Movement," (Ph.D. diss., Rutgers University, 2007); Crystal N. Feimster, *Southern Horrors: Women and the Politics of Rape and Lynching* (Cambridge, Mass.: Harvard University Press, 2009); and Jacquelyn Dowd Hall, "The Mind that Burns in Each Body: Women, Rape, and Racial Violence," in Ann Snitow, Christine Stansall, and Sharon Thompson, eds., *Powers of Desire, The Politics of Sexuality* (New York: Monthly Review Press, 1983), 328–349.

29. Elisha Green, *Ely: Too Black, Too White* (Amherst: University of Massachusetts Press, 1970), 362.

30. Ibid., 362, 194.

31. Ibid., 362–363.

32. Ibid., 363.

33. Ibid.

34. Green, *Ely: Too Black, Too White,* 364.

35. Ibid., 367.

36. Ibid., 383.

37. Sparks testimony, Cress Report.

38. Beeth and Wintz, eds., *Black Dixie,* 89.

39. Letter, Houston, February 25, 1917, reproduced in Emmett J. Scott, "More Letters of Negro Migrants of 1916–1918," *Journal of Negro History* 4 (October 1919): 422. In his monograph on the riot, Robert Haynes cites the migration from Houston as one sign of African Americans' dissatisfaction with the region's racial politics. In discussing the migration, Haynes emphasizes the recruiting efforts of labor agents in convincing blacks to leave town. See Haynes, *A Night of Violence,* 32–34. However, letters collected by former Special Assistant to the Secretary of War Emmett Scott reveal how eager and anxious African American migrants were to depart for the North, labor agents or no.

40. Letter, Houston, May 16, 1917, 445.

41. Letter, Houston, April 20, 1919, 298.

42. Details of African American soldiers' experiences during the latter half of the nineteenth century come from Bernard C. Nalty, *Strength for the Fight: A History of African Americans in the Military* (New York: Free Press, 1986), 55–57; Monroe Lee Billington, "Buffalo Soldiers in the American West, 1865–1900," in Monroe Lee Billington and Roger D. Hardaway, eds., *African Americans on the Western Frontier* (Niwot, Colo.: University Press of Colorado, 1998), 54–72.

43. Private Henry McCombs quoted in Quintard Taylor Jr., "Introduction to the Bison Books Edition," in *Buffalo Soldier Regiment: History of the Twenty Fifth United States Infantry Regiment, 1869–1926,* by John Nankivell (1927; repr., Lincoln: Bison Press of the University of Nebraska Press, 2001), ix.

44. Billington, "Buffalo Soldiers in the American West," 70.

45. McCombs quoted in Taylor, "Introduction," ix.

46. On the tensions and overlaps between "civic nationalism" as a creed that celebrates heterogeneity and "racial nationalism" as one that creates distinctions and hierarchies based on racial and ethnic difference, see Gary Gerstle, "Theodore Roosevelt and the Divided Character of American Nationalism," *Journal of American History* 86 (December 1999): 1280–1307; and Gerstle, *American Crucible: Race and Nation in the Twentieth Century* (Princeton, N.J.: Princeton University Press, 2001), 3–47.

47. John W. Galloway, 24th Infantry, to Editor, *Richmond Planet,* November 16, 1899, in *"Smoked Yankees" and the Struggle for Empire: Letters from Negro Soldiers, 1898–1892,* 4th ed. (Fayetteville: University of Arkansas Press, 1987), 252.

48. Willard B. Gatewood Jr., "Blacks Americans and the Quest for Empire," *Journal of Southern History* 38 (November 1972): 559; Matthew Frye Jacobson, *Barbarian Virtues: The United States Encounters Foreign Peoples at Home and Abroad, 1876–1917* (New York: Hill and Wang, 2000), 251.

49. John W. Galloway to Editor, *Richmond Planet,* in Gatewood, *Smoked Yankees,* 252.

50. Quoted in Gatewood, "Black Americans and the Quest for Empire," 559. See also Paul Kramer, *The Blood of Government: Race, Empire, the United States and the Philippines* (Chapel Hill: University of North Carolina Press, 2006).

51. Quoted in Scot Ngozi-Brown, "African-American Soldiers and the Philippines: Racial Imperialism, Jim Crow, and Social Relations," *Journal of Negro History* 82 (Winter 1997): 50.

52. Ibid., 44.

53. Ibid., 50.

54. Kathryn M. Johnson, "East St. Louis," *Half-Century Magazine* 3 (August 1917): 8.

55. See Green, *Ely: Too Black, Too White* (Amherst: The University of Massachusetts Press, 1970), 467–468.

56. Statement of E. O. Smith, Chamberlain File.

57. After conducting a thorough investigation of the riot, Colonel G. D. Cress concluded that one of its main causes was "the incompatibility between the handling of the negro by the civilian authority of Houston and the training of the negro soldiers as pursued in the service." Cress cited the issue of respect, deference to federal authority, and the expectation of fair treatment as sources of tension. Conclusions, Cress Report.

58. In Re: S. H. Simpson, Seditious Remarks, 14 December 1917, casefile 107212, RG 165, FSAA.

59. The Third Battalion was comprised of the M, I, L, and K Companies. See Christian, *Black Soldiers in Jim Crow Texas,* 148.

60. Events in Brownsville are reviewed in Phocion Samuel Park, "The 24th Infantry Regiment and the Houston Riot of 1917," (master's thesis, University of Houston, 1971), 18–23. See also Nalty, *Strength for the Fight,* 85–97.

61. Harris County Local Option Committee advertisement, quoted in Haynes, *A Night of Violence,* 23.

62. Statement of John S. Green, U.S. District Attorney, Houston Texas, in Chamberlain File.

63. Park, The 24th Infantry Regiment and the Houston Riot of 1917," 83.

64. Ibid., 88.

65. Statement of J. F. Walters, Citizen, in Chamberlain File.

66. Major W. A. Trumbull, U.S.R., quoted in Park, "The 24th Infantry Regiment and the Houston Riot of 1917," 71.

67. H. G. French, testimony to the civilian Board of Inquiry, recorded in Cress Report.

68. Dunbar-Nelson discusses the problems of young women's infatuation with soldiers in her short history of women's war work. As she relates, organizations such as the Young Women's Christian Association (YWCA) and the War Camp Community Service (WCCS) tried to provide supervised outlets for men and

women's socializing "where the 'lure of the khaki' might find conventional self-expression." However, there was neither a YWCA-sponsored Hostess House nor a WCCS-sponsored Negro Community Service Center during the 24th's tour of duty in guarding Camp Logan. With the aid of the African American community in the city, soldiers had to improvise their own amusements. The night of the riot, they were supposed to go to a city-sponsored watermelon party in Houston's Emancipation Park. See Alice Dunbar-Nelson, "Negro Women in War Work," in Emmett J. Scott, *Scott's Official History of the American Negro in the World War* (1919), 374–397. On Alice Dunbar-Nelson's war work, see Nikki L. M. Brown, *Private Politics and Public Voices* (Urbana-Champaign: University of Illinois Press, 2006).

69. C. K. Green, testimony to the civilian Board of Inquiry, recorded in Cress Report; George Peyton, police officer, testimony to the civilian Board of Inquiry, recorded in "Time Had Been Set by Negro Soldiers for Start of Riot," *Houston Post,* 30 August 1917, 7.

70. C. K. Green testimony, Cress Report. The report that soldiers wore Jim Crow signs as badges at the dance hall comes from *Houston Post,* 30 August 1917, 7.

71. H. G. French testimony, Cress Report.

72. Lee Sparks quoted by Charles Baltimore in Baltimore Statement, Chamberlain File. Baltimore identified the speaker only as "the policeman who arrested me." As Sparks was more aggressive than Rufe Daniels in attacking and apprehending Baltimore, it seems most likely he was the speaker.

73. Text of Civilian Court of Inquiry Report in "Brock Criticised by Civil Board as Unfit for Job," *Houston Chronicle,* 12 September 1917, 1.

74. J. F. Walters statement in Cress Report.

75. Statement of Sergeant William C. Nesbitt, Co. I, in Chamberlain File.

76. James Z. George statement in Cress Report, quoted in Haynes, *A Night of Violence,* 80.

77. Nesbitt statement in Chamberlain File.

78. Gruening, "Houston," 16. Also quoted in Park, "The 24th Infantry Regiment and the Houston Riot of 1917," 81.

79. Gruening, "Houston," 17.

80. Captain J. A. Ross, 1st Illinois Engineers, Chamberlain File.

81. "Details Leading to Riot Given by Officer," *San Antonio Express,* November 2, 1917, 4. The Alabama national guardsman who answered the phone identified the caller simply as "some female voice." See Testimony of A. C. Moore, Chamberlain File. Presumably, the paper guessed her race by her neighborhood.

82. Testimony of Haig Shekerjian, U.S. v. Nesbit.

83. Ibid.

84. E. E. Ammons, Deputy Sheriff, Harris County, Chamberlain File. Also quoted in Haynes, *A Night of Violence,* 103.

85. Testimony of Ezekial Bullock, RG 153, Records of the Judge Advocate General (Army), General Courts Martial, 1812–1938, 24th Infantry Regiment Court Martial 109018, U.S. v. Washington, Cpl John et al., NARA II.

86. Testimony of Kneeland Snow, U.S. v. Nesbit.

87. Nesbitt statement, Chamberlain File.

88. Testimony of Bessie Chaney, RG 153, Records of the Judge Advocate General (Army), General Courts Martial, 1812–1938, 24th Infantry Regiment Court Martial 114575, U.S. v. Tillman, Cpl Robert et al., NARA II.

89. Testimony of Private J. C. Nelson, reported in "Negroes Who Took No Part Tell of Riot," *San Antonio Texas Light,* November 14, 1917, TINCF.

90. Testimony of Edna Tucker, in "Negroes Who Took No Part Tell of Riot."

91. Haynes, *A Night of Violence,* 106–107.

92. U.S. v. Nesbit. Soldier Henry Peacock, also a witness in the trial, attributed the statement to Corporal Baltimore.

93. Testimony of George Burrus, Company I, "Negroes Who Took No Part Tell of Riot."

94. Testimony of Robert Fitzsimmons to the Board of Inquiry, in Cress Report. The 9th and 10th Cavalries were not involved in the 1906 Brownsville incident, but they might have come to stand for all black soldiers for either Mr. Fitzsimmons or the soldier he overheard. The members of the 24th came from all over the United States and had spent the last few years in the west. It seems suspect for them to have referred to themselves as "Northern men" in front of Fitzsimmons.

95. Testimony of Haig Shekerkian, U.S. v. Nesbit.

96. Snow, U.S. v. Nesbit.

97. Baltimore, Chamberlain File.

98. Haynes, *A Night of Violence,* 119.

99. Haynes, *A Night of Violence,* 121, 122.

100. Snow, U.S. v. Nesbit.

101. Christian, *Black Soldiers in Jim Crow Texas,* 154. Historians disagree over whether a mob actually fired on the camp that night. Haynes dismisses the mob as a ruse, a "myth" created by a small group of soldiers who planned the riot and used the cry of an approaching mob as the signal for the violence to begin. In an article published in the *Griot,* C. Calvin Smith makes a viable case that a white mob did, in fact, attack the camp that night and could have been responsible for some of the injuries close to camp. Looking over Smith's evidence, Garna Christian concludes that the presence of fear does not preclude the possibility of a group of conspirators exploiting that fear. Conversely, it is equally important to recognize that some portion of the rioters thought they were acting in self-defense. Others went under pressure from fellow soldiers. See Haynes, *A Night of Violence,* 120–127; C. Calvin Smith, "On the Edge: The Houston Riot of 1917 Revisited," *Griot* 10 (Spring 1991): 3–12; Christian, *Black Soldiers in Jim Crow Texas,* 169.

102. Testimony of Sergeant Rhoden Bond, U.S. v. Nesbit.

103. Testimony of Sergeant William Fox, U.S. v. Nesbit.

104. Bond, U.S. v. Nesbit.

105. Testimony of Private Joseph Alexander, quoted in Park, "The 24th Infantry Regiment and the Houston Riot of 1917," 102.

106. "Weak minded fellows" taken from Green statement, Southern Department Decimal File. Second quote recorded in Park, "The 24th Infantry Regiment and the Houston Riot of 1917," 102. Despite their loyalty to the Army, military officials suspected that Fox and Bond still tried to shield some of the mutineers from punishment in the weeks after the riot. See Memorandum for Commander General of the Southern Department, Chamberlain File.

107. Bond, U.S. v. Nesbit.

108. Haynes, *A Night of Violence,* 128.

109. Ibid.

110. Snow, U.S. v. Nesbit; "Details Leading to Riot Given By Officer."

111. "Body of Corporal Brown, Executed for Part in Houston Riot, Given to Mother for Burial," *Chicago Defender,* March 30, 1918, 1; Haynes, *A Night of Violence,* 129.

112. Snow, U.S. v. Nesbit.

113. "Wild Night Scenes and Some Reflections, Cool and Otherwise," *Houston Chronicle,* August 24, 1917, TINCF.

114. Testimony of A. C. Cook, U.S. v. Washington.

115. See statement of Private Oliver Fletcher held in U.S. v. Nesbit; statement of Lark Jamison, "Negroes Who Took No Part Tell of Riot;" Isaac Deyo to Mr. John Haynes Holmes, NAACP Papers, 9A, Discrimination in the U.S. Armed Forces; statement of Risley Young in "Charge of Murder is Filed Against 34 Rioters," *Cleveland Advocate,* September 1, 1917, 1.

116. Testimony of G. W. Butcher, U.S. v. Nesbit.

117. Testimony of J. W. Kennedy, U.S. v. Nesbit.

118. Testimony of Fred Schofield, U.S. v. Nesbit.

119. Testimony of O. H. Reichert, Alma Reichert, U.S. v. Nesbit; "Victims of Rioters Give Details of Bloody Night," *San Antonio Express,* November 6, 1917, 4.

120. "Victims of Rioters Give Details of Bloody Night."

121. Testimony of Fred Schneider, U.S. v. Nesbit.

122. Ibid.

123. "Wild Night Scenes and Some Reflections, Cool and Otherwise"; Haynes, *A Night of Violence,* 173.

124. Testimony of Sam Navarro, U.S. v. Nesbit.

125. Colonel John Hoover, Commander 5th Texas Infantry, Chamberlain File.

126. "Quiet Restored After Night of Excitement and Terror," *Houston Post,* August 25, 1917, 4.

127. F. W. Sanker, Chamberlain File.

128. Testimony of Private Joseph Alexander, U.S. v. Nesbit.

129. Haynes, *A Night of Violence,* 158; Park, "The 24th Infantry Regiment and the Houston Riot of 1917," 145.

130. Alexander, U.S. v. Nesbit.

131. Closing statement for the prosecution, U.S. v. Nesbit.

132. Ibid.

133. Ibid.

134. Bessie Chaney, Cress Report.

135. W. R. Sinclair to Congressman Jeff McLemore, August 27, 1917, quoted in Park, "The 24th Infantry and the Houston Riot," 47.

136. On Jack Johnson and white ideas of black manliness and masculinity, see Gail Bederman, *Manliness and Civilization: A Cultural History of Gender and Race in the United States, 1880–1917* (Chicago: University of Chicago Press, 1995), 1-5. A native of Galveston, Texas, boxer Jack Johnson had defeated Tommy Burns and Jim Jeffries to become the first black heavyweight champion. A flashy athlete who brazenly dated white women, Jack Johnson was charged with violating the Mann Act in 1913. He fled to Europe where he stayed until 1920.

137. E. David Cronon, ed., *The Cabinet Diaries of Josephus Daniels, 1913–1921* (Lincoln: University of Nebraska Press), 195.

138. Quoted in Glenda Gilmore, *Gender & Jim Crow,* 103.

139. "The Houston Outbreak," *Macon Telegraph,* quoted in "What Some of the Southern Papers Had to Say about the Mutiny of the Negro Soldiers in the City of Houston," *Houston Post,* September 2, 1917, 10.

140. Ibid.

141. "The Houston Riot," *Nashville Banner,* in ibid.

142. Quoted in "Is Democracy Safe for the Negro," *New York Tribune,* September 2, 1917, TINCF.

143. "Herels Full Account of How the 13 Troopers Spent Their Last Hours," *Cleveland Advocate,* January 5, 1918, 1.

144. Corporal Charles Baltimore to Frederick Baltimore, December 10, 1917, in "Tells Part He Played in the Houston Riot," *New York Age,* December 29, 1917, 1.

145. Thomas J. Calloway to Archibald Grimke, March 25, 1918, in Archibald Grimke Papers, Moorland Spingarn Research Center, Howard University.

146. "Death on Scaffold Is Price Paid by Negroes Guilty of Rioting," *San Antonio Express,* December 12, 1917, 1.

147. Haynes, *A Night of Violence,* chapter 10. On the NAACP efforts on behalf of the 24th Infantrymen, see James Weldon Johnson, *Along This Way* (New York: Viking Press, 1933).

148. Douglass Lumpkins to Mr. E. A. Kreger, March 29, 1919, letter contained in file for U.S. v. Nesbit.

149. Isaac Deyo to Mr. John Haynes Holmes.

150. W. E. B. Du Bois, "Thirteen," *Crisis* 15 (January 1918): 14.

151. *Cleveland Advocate* quoted in Monroe Work, ed., *Negro Yearbook, 1917–1918,* 52.

152. "Tired of Wholesale Killing," *Cleveland Advocate,* January 12, 1918, 8.

153. "Negro Soldiers Hanged without Chance to Appeal to President," *Topeka Plain Dealer,* December 14, 1917, 1.

154. Ibid.

155. *Savannah Tribune* excerpted in *Negro Yearbook, 1917–1918.*

156. "Negro Soldiers Hanged without Chance to Appeal to President." In his book on the African American press in this period, William Jordan reveals how black newspapermen framed their responses to the Houston riot within an accepted discourse of liberty and democracy. Those who strayed too far down the path of critique faced suppression and the threat of prosecution by the Wilson administration, as Theodore Kornweibel amply demonstrates in his book on the federal response to African American dissent. See William G. Jordan, *Black Newspapers and America's War for Democracy, 1914–1920* (Chapel Hill: University of North Carolina Press, 2001), 92–98. Also, Theodore Kornweibel Jr., *"Investigate Everything": Federal Efforts to Compel Black Loyalty during World War I* (Bloomington: Indiana University Press, 2002).

157. "Brave to the Last!" *Cleveland Gazette,* December 15, 1917, 1.

158. *Baltimore Afro American,* September 1, 1917, 1.

159. "Denounces Killing of Colored Soldiers," *Brooklyn Standard Union,* December 17, 1917, TINCF.

160. W. E. B. Du Bois, "Houston," *Crisis* 14 (October 1917): 284–285.

161. Mrs. H. Lamartine to Archibald Grimke, February 15, 1919, Archibald Grimke Papers.

162. "Martial Law and Civil Justice," from the *Pueblo Chieftain,* December 14, 1917, reprinted in *Chicago Defender,* December 22, 1917, TINCF.

163. In Re: Lillian Smith, Negress, Disloyalty Matter, RG 165, Military Intelligence Division, NARA II.

164. Ibid.

165. United States v. G. W. Bouldin, RG 21, Records of the District Courts of the United States, in FSAA.

166. Ibid.

167. Ibid. Additional biographical information comes from *Polk's Morrison and Fourmy's Austin City Directory* (Houston, Tex.: Morrison and Fourmy Directory Company, 1918), 206.

168. U.S. v. Bouldin, RG 21, in FSAA.

169. In re: Lillian Smith, Negress, RG 165, NARA II.

170. Kornweibel, *"Investigate Everything,"* 170–175. Court records tracing the Bouldin story can be found in U.S. v. Bouldin, RG 21, FSAA.

3. Men in the Making

1. Elisha Green, *Ely: Too Black, Too White* (Amherst: The University of Massachusetts Press, 1970), 315, 372, 398.

2. Ibid.

3. See Jennifer Keene, *Doughboys, the Great War, and the Remaking of America* (Baltimore: Johns Hopkins University Press, 2001), 9.

4. Martin Summers, *Manliness and Its Discontents: The Black Middle Class and the Transformation of Masculinity, 1900–1930* (Chapel Hill: University of North Carolina Press, 2004), Introduction, esp. 8–9; Gail Bederman, *Manliness and Civilization: A Cultural History of Gender and Race in the United States, 1880–1917* (Chicago: University of Chicago Press, 1995).

5. LP McLendon to Mary Aycock McLendon, November 30, 1917, LP McLendon Papers, Southern Historical Collection, University of North Carolina at Chapel Hill; LP McLendon to Mary Aycock McLendon, April 6, 1917; LP McLendon to Mary Aycock McLeondon, November 30, 1917. For more on white manhood, love, and war, see Stephen W. Berry II, *All that Makes a Man: Love and Ambition in the Civil War South* (New York: Oxford University Press, 2003).

6. LP McLendon to Mary Aycock McLendon, November 27, 1918.

7. Quoted in the *Crisis* 15 (December 1917): 79.

8. Kathryn Johnson to Roy Nash, August 19, 1917, NAACP Papers.

9. Kathryn M. Johnson, "East St. Louis," *Half-Century Magazine* 3 (August 1917): 8. Poet, writer, and former diplomat James Weldon Johnson became Field Secretary after Kathryn Johnson left the NAACP staff.

10. Addie W. Hunton and Kathryn M. Johnson, *Two Colored Women with the American Expeditionary Forces* (1920; repr., New York: G. K. Hall & Co., 1997), 13–14.

11. Mrs. W. A. Hunton, "Colored Women Sail for France," *New York Post,* May 25, 1918 in TINCF.

12. Green, *Ely: Too Black, Too White,* 354, 390.

13. Ibid., 350.

14. Ibid., 348, 352. On the shift from manliness to masculinity, see Summers, *Manliness and Its Discontents,* 5–7, 155–end; William M. Tuttle Jr., *Race Riot: Chicago in the Red Summer of 1919* (Urbana: University of Illinois Press, 1996), 76. On similar evolving working class cultures and gender formations in the urban South, see Tera Hunter, *To 'Joy My Freedom: Southern Black Women's Labors After the Civil War* (Cambridge, Mass.: Harvard University Press, 1997), 145–186.

15. David Levering Lewis, *W. E. B. Du Bois: Biography of a Race, 1868–1919* (New York: Henry Holt, 1993), 530.

16. Henry Berry, "My Bit in the World War, or the Story of 2921486," in Berry Family Letters, Schomburg Center for Research in Black Culture, New York Public Library, 2.

17. Berry, "My Bit in the World War," 3.

18. Ibid., 2–3.

19. Alexandra Razdfkeriefo, "Introduction," in *A Pictorial History of the Negro in the Great World War, 1917–1918* (New York: Toussaint Pictorial Co., Inc., 1919), 5.

20. In his cultural history of the war, Modris Eksteins notes that "by 1917, there was no talk of glory and gallantry, fewer references specifically to duty, but a great deal of talk about holding out, determination, commitment, grit, and sticking to it" among French and British troops. See Eksteins, *Rites of Spring: the Great War and the Birth of the Modern Age* (New York: Anchor Books, 1989), 184. In Europe, as in the United States, the experience of war helped spur changes in the definition of manhood. Henry Berry held fast to an ideal of heroic manhood that was dying a slow death on the actual fields of battle.

21. Berry, "My Bit in the World War," 1, 3.

22. Emmett J. Scott, *Scott's Official History of the American Negro in the World War* (1919), 334. In an article based on a film put out by the Committee on Public Information, the periodical *Leslie's Weekly* concurred with Scott's appreciation of the practical skills that war training gave African Americans while agreeing also that the greatest effect of the war was "the negroes' awakened sense of citizenship." See "The Negro American in the War," *Leslie's Weekly,* November 9, 1918, in Du Bois Papers.

23. Berry, "My Bit in the World War," 6.

24. Ibid., 4; Henry Berry to Fanny Berry, December 20, 1918, Berry Family Papers.

25. Henry Berry to Fanny Berry.

26. Joshua E. Blanton, "Men in the Making," *Southern Workman* 48 (January 1919): 17–24. Blanton was the stepbrother of Tuskegee President Robert Russa Moton.

27. *The Negro Rural School and Its Relation to the Community,* quoted in Gerald Robbins, "Rossa B. Cooley and the Penn School: Social Dynamo in Negro Rural Subculture, 1901–1930," *Journal of Negro Education* 33 (Winter 1964): 49.

28. Blanton, "Men in the Making," 18–19.

29. Ibid., 18.

30. Summers, *Manliness and Its Discontents,* 152.

31. Harry Haywood [pseud. for Haywood Hall], *Black Bolshevik: Autobiography of An Afro-American Communist* (Chicago: Liberator Press, 1979), 43.

32. Willard Gatewood, "Alabama's 'Negro Soldier Experiment,' 1898–1899," *Journal of Negro History* 57 (October 1972): 334.

33. Bernard C. Nalty, *Strength for the Fight: A History of African Americans in the Military* (New York: Free Press, 1986), 88.

34. Haywood, *Black Bolshevik,* 43.

35. Ibid., 8.

36. Ibid., 45.

37. Reverend W. S. Braddan, "The Only Official or Authentic History of the Achievements and the Brilliant Military Record of the 'Old Eighth Regiment' of Illinois, or the Three Hundred and Seventieth United States Infantry on the French Battlefields," *Chicago Broad Ax,* May 3, 1919, 4. In contrast, see Haywood, *Black Bolshevik,* 45–46.

38. "The Diary of a Soldier," *Chicago Defender,* November 11, 1917.

39. Braddan, "The Only Official or Authentic History," 47.

40. "The Diary of a Soldier."

41. Haywood., *Black Bolshevik,* 48.

42. Ibid., 46.

43. Reverend W. S. Braddan, "Governor Frank O. Lowden Reviewed the Eight Regiment at Houston, Texas and Loudly Led off in the Cheering as it Passed . . ." *Chicago Broad Ax,* May 10, 1919, 4.

44. Braddan, "Governor Frank O. Lowden," 1.

45. Ibid., 4.

46. Haywood, *Black Bolshevik,* 50.

47. Braddan, "Governor Frank O. Lowden," 4.

48. Berry, "My Bit in the World War," 9.

49. "Newport News Is a Little Hell," *Baltimore Afro-American,* February 2, 1919, 4.

50. Charles H. Williams, *Negro Soldiers in World War I: The Human Side* (1923; repr., New York: AMS Press, 1970), 26. Williams investigated conditions of African American troops under the auspices of the Federal Council of Churches and the Phelps-Stokes fund. He originally published the results of his investigations in 1923 under the title, *Sidelights on Negro Soldiers.*

51. Arthur E. Barbeau and Florette Henri, *The Unknown Soldiers: African-American Troops in World War I* (1974; repr., New York: Da Capo Press, 1996), 51. In their monograph on discrimination in WWI, first published in 1974, Barbeau and Henri describe the conditions in Newport News as "particularly atrocious." While examining the creation of American citizen soldiers from a broad range of races and ethnicities, historian Jennifer Keene notes that although circumstances in Newport News may have been exceptional, the decision to dress African American soldiers in the blue overalls typical of black laborers across the South was part of a broad, conscious strategy on the part of Army officials to assure the white public "that these men were not really soldiers." See Keene, *Doughboys,* 40.

52. Keene, *Doughboys,* 40.

53. The portrait of life in the Newport News camps comes from Emmett Scott's reprint of Charles Williams's investigation, 107. See also Williams, *Negro Solders in World War I,* 25–27, and Barbeau and Henri, *The Unknown Soldiers,* 51–52.

54. Williams, *Negro Soldiers in World War I,* 27.

55. Colonel E. D. Anderson, Army General Staff, quoted in Barbeau and Henri, *The Unknown Soldiers,* 90.

56. Haywood, *Black Bolshevik,* 52.

57. Braddan, "Governor Frank O. Lowden," 4.

58. Autobiography, VI-6, Box 15, Rayford Logan Papers, Manuscript Division, Moorland-Spingarn Research Center.

59. Haywood, *Black Bolshevik,* 52.

60. Reverend W. S. Braddan, "The Eighth Regiment or the 370th U.S. Infantry Left Newport News Virginia, Saturday, April 6, 1918, on the Steamship George Washington," *Chicago Broad Ax,* May 17, 1919, 1.

61. Haywood, *Black Bolshevik,* 53.

62. Green, *Ely: Too Black, Too White,* 395.

63. Ibid.

64. Ibid., 396.

65. In his classic work on sexually transmitted diseases and social control, Allan M. Brandt writes that "the social hygiene campaign combined a high ideal of civilized sexual morality with a Progressive virility impulse." It also reflected the Progressive belief that a problem that could be identified was a problem that could be solved. See Brandt, *No Magic Bullet: A Social History of Venereal Disease in the United States Since 1880* (Oxford: Oxford University Press, 1987). In Jeffrey P. Moran's case in public education, he also traces the emergence of a moralistic discourse on social diseases and its affects on the making of citizens. See Moran, "Modernism Gone Mad: Sex Education Comes to Chicago, 1913," *Journal of American History* 83 (September 1996): 485–488. For a brief overview of the link between social purity and social hygiene in Britain, see Philippa Levine, " 'Walking the Streets the Way No Decent Woman Should': Women Police in World War I," *Journal of Modern History* 66 (March 1994): 39–42.

66. Dr. Albert H. Burr quoted in Brandt, *No Magic Bullet,* 15.

67. Morrow quoted in Moran, "Modernism Gone Mad," 486.

68. William F. Snow, M.D., "Social Hygiene and the War" (New York: American Social Hygiene Association, 1917), 422. The pamphlet, a reprint of an article in the association's *Journal of Social Hygiene,* provides a vivid example of the linkage between mobilization for war and mobilization for public hygiene measures.

69. Quoted in David M. Kennedy, *Over Here: The First World War and American Society* (Oxford: Oxford University Press, 1980), 186.

70. Quoted in Brandt, *No Magic Bullet,* 102.

71. Snow, "Social Hygiene and the War," 425. Daniels quoted in Brandt, *No Magic Bullet,* 58–59.

72. Quoted in Glenda E. Gilmore, "The Flight of the Incubus," in David S. Cecelski and Timothy B. Tyson, eds., *Democracy Betrayed: The Wilmington Race Riot of 1898 and Its Legacy* (Chapel Hill: University of North Carolina Press, 1998), 75.

73. First quote in Gilmore, "Flight of the Incubus," 75. Second quote in J. Morgan Kousser, *The Shaping of Southern Politics: Suffrage Restrictions and the Establishment of the One-Party South, 1880–1910* (New Haven, Conn.: Yale University Press, 1974), 76.

74. Brandt, *No Magic Bullet,* 16. As scholar Francis Dikkotter has pointed out, eugenics gave reformers and ideologues of varying stripes a vocabulary for portraying "society as an organic body that had to be guided by biological laws." Aggressively modern, it granted discriminatory practices against people of color, immigrants, the mentally ill, the working classes, and a multitude of other "others" the sheen of scientific validity. Although eugenics enjoyed global popularity during the early part of the twentieth century, eugenicists in each locale adapted its body of ideas to suit local concerns, assumptions, and cultural practices. See Dikotter, "Race Culture: Recent Perspectives on the History of Eugenics," *American Historical Review* 103 (April 1998): 467–478.

75. "Two Lieutenants Back from Front Tell of Fighting," *Cleveland Advocate,* October 26, 1918, 1.

76. "Southern Soldier on the Negro," letter of William D. Harris, Lieutenant, Battery F, 142nd Field Artillery to Editor, *Globe,* in NAACP Papers, Part 9A.

77. Ibid.

78. Memoirs, Kathryn M. Johnson Papers, Schlesinger Library, Radcliffe College, 208. Hunton and Johnson, *Two Colored Women,* 186.

79. Copy of memo in reproduced in Hunton and Johnson, *Two Colored Women,* 234.

80. Rayford Logan Autobiography, VI-15.

81. Long, "The Negro Soldier in the Army of the United States," *Journal of Negro Education* 12 (Summer 1943): 312.

82. Bullock quoted in Susan Kerr Chandler, "'That Biting, Stinging Things which Ever Shadows Us': African-American Social Workers in France During World War I," *Social Service Review* 69 (September 1995): 502.

83. Hunton and Johnson, *Two Colored Women,* 195–197; Ruby McEnglish to Addie Hunton, July 4, 1921, NAACP Papers, Part 1.

84. Memoirs, Kathryn M. Johnson, 216; Hunton and Johnson, *Two Colored Women,* 197. Ely Green made the same point. Upon watching his men line up to enter a cafe staffed by Algerian waitresses, Green realized that part of black soldiers' enthusiasm for white women arose "because they had no choice." If given their druthers, he believed most of his men would have sought the company of "brown babies." *Ely: Too Black, Too White,* 468.

85. Memoirs, Kathryn M. Johnson, 204. On YMCA programs for African American soldiers, see Scott, *Scott's Official History of the American Negro in the World War,* 407.

86. Nikki L. M. Brown describes Hunton as a surrogate mother or surrogate sweetheart in Brown, "'Your Patriotism is of the Purest Quality': African American Women

and World War I" (Ph.D. diss., Yale University, 2002), 166–167. See also Hunton and Johnson, *Two Colored Women,* 196–197.

87. Memoirs, Kathryn M. Johnson, 232.

88. Fred Parker to Addison Parker, November 20, 1918, in Addison B. Parker Papers, Kroch Rare Book and Manuscript Library, Cornell University. Fred Parker's father, Addison, was a prominent New York Democrat.

89. Colonel Linard, "Au Sujet des Troupes Noires Américaines," August 7, 1918, Mission Militaire Française pres l'Armée de Américaine, Série 16N, Côte 1698, Service Historique de l'Armée de Terre, Château de Vincennes, Paris. Du Bois published a translation of the memo in English in the *Crisis* 18 (May 1919): 16–17. For additional mention of the Linard memo, see Keene, *Doughboys,* 103, and Barbeau and Henri, *The Unknown Soldiers,* 114–115.

90. Ann Laura Stoler reads *métissage* as "a metonym for the biopolitics of empire at large." Stoler, "Sexual Affronts and Racial Frontiers: European Identities and the Cultural Politics of Exclusion in Colonial Southeast Asia," *Carnal Knowledge and Imperial Power* (Berkeley: University of California Press, 2002), 80. French pronatalists' consternation over population decline and subsequent concern with French women's sexual behavior predated the establishment of the Third Republic in 1870 and continued well past its fall in 1940. On pronatalism and its engagement with French republicanism, partriarchalism, and feminism, see Joshua H. Cole, " 'There Are Only Good Mothers': The Ideological Work of Women's Fertility in France Before World War I," *French Historical Studies* 19 (Spring 1996): 639–672; and Jean Elisabeth Pederson, "Regulating Abortion and Birth Control: Gender, Medicine and Republican Politics in France, 1870–1920," *French Historical Studies* 19 (Spring 1996): 673–698. My discussion of gender and nation in France's age of immigration, as well as the racial formulas for *métissage,* owes much to Elisa Camiscioli, "Reproducing the French Race: Immigration, Reproduction, and National Identity in France, 1900–1939" (Ph.D. diss., University of Chicago, 2000), 115–183.

91. "De la Repopulation," Le Commissaire Spécial à M. le Directeur de la Sûreté Générale," November 25, 1918, Affaires Internationales, WWI, Police Générale, Série F7, Côte 12396, Archives Nationales, Paris, France. The author of the report proposed that the French government might facilitate naturalization for some of the "beautiful American youth" who had come over with the AEF. Presumably, he meant white youth. For more on *métissage* and the French national body, see Claude Blanckaert, "Of Monstrous *Métis?* Hybridity, Fear of Miscegenation, and Patriotism from Buffon to Paul Bocca," in Sue Peabody and Tyler Stovall, eds. *The Color of Liberty: Histories of Race in France* (Durham, N.C.: Duke University Press, 2003).

92. Ludovic Naudeau, quoted in Camiscioli, "Reproducing the French Race," 140. Camiscioli notes that during the interwar years, especially, some social theorists actually promoted mixed marriages as the best way to "integrate foreigners into the national body."

93. Jean Bercovici, quoted in Camiscioli, "Reproducing the French Race," 144.

94. The phrase comes from Frederick Cooper and Ann Laura Stoler, eds., *Tensions of Empire: Colonial Cultures in a Bourgeois World* (Berkeley: University of California Press, 1997).

95. Tyler Stovall, "Love, Labor and Race: Colonial Men and White Women in France during the Great War," in Tyler Stovall and George van den Abbeele, eds., *French Civilization and Its Discontents: Nationalism, Colonialism, Race* (Lanham, Md.: Lexington Books, 2003), 314n3, 297.

96. Kimloan Hill, "Strangers in a Foregin Land: Vietnamese Soldiers and Workers in France during World War I," in Nhung Tuyet Tran and Anthony Reid, eds., *Vietnam: Borderless Histories* (Madison: University of Wisconsin Press, 2006), 273–274.

97. French documents quoted in Joe Lunn, *Memoirs of the Maelstrom: A Senegalese Oral History of the First World War* (Portsmouth, N.H.: Heinemann, 1999), 163.

98. Bernard Leocat, "La Prostitution à Brest aux 19e a 20e Siècles" (Masters thesis held in the Archives Municipales, Brest, France, 1988), p. 205. Numbers of French women in the work force come from Stovall, "Love, Labor, and Race"; for more on working women and colonial contacts, see 299–301. The racial violence that broke out between working class French men and colonial laborers often resulted from this inability to place or police working French women. See also Tyler Stovall, "The Color Line Behind the Lines: Racial Violence in France during the Great War," *American Historical Review*, 103 (June 1998): 737–769.

99. Maurice Donnay, *La Parisienne et la Guerre* (Paris, 1916); Berthem-Bontoux (1916) cited in Margaret H. Darrow, "French Volunteer Nursing and the Myth of War Experience in World War I," *American Historical Review* 101 (February 1996): 82.

100. Magnus Hirschfeld, *The Sexual History of the World War* (1930; repr., New York: Cadillac Publishing Company, 1941), 75–76.

101. Lunn, *Memoirs of the Maelstrom*, 173.

102. Stoler, *Carnal Knowledge and Imperial Power*, 41–78.

103. Green, *Ely: Too Black, Too White*, 428. The proprietor protected the club as African American space. When white soldiers approached, the English owner pretended to speak only French. She refused to let Ely Green enter until other soldiers reassured her that he was truly black.

104. See Fabio Paresecoli, "Bootylicious: Food and the Female Body in Contemporary Black Culture," *Women's Studies Quarterly* 35 (Spring 2007): 115; and Sterling Brown, "The Blues," *Phlyon* 13 (4th qtr., 1952): 288.

105. "Lieutenant Slyvanus Brown Writes of the Spirit of Colored Troops Overseas," *Cleveland Advocate,* November 11, 1918, 8. The *Advocate* lists him as Slyvanus, but the roster of officers included in Mason and Furr's appendix, he is listed as Sylvanus. See Monroe Mason and Arthur Furr, *The American Negro with the Red Hand of France* (Boston, Mass.: Cornhill Co., 1920), 163.

106. "Lieutenant Slyvanus Brown," 8.

107. Ibid.

108. Mason and Furr, *The American Negro with the Red Hand of France,* 140.

109. Osceola McKaine, "With the Buffaloes in France," *Crusader,* February 1919, 4. The article was a reprinted from the *Independendent* 97 (January 1919): 50.

110. Green, *Ely: Too Black, Too White,* 400. According to Green, the German POW turned out to be a member of the beer-producing Busch family who had resided in the United States for six years before returning to Germany to enlist when the war broke out.

111. "Moton off to France, Why?" *Baltimore Afro-American,* December 13, 1918, 4.

112. Rayford W. Logan Diaries, July 30, 1943, *The Papers of Rayford W. Logan,* Library of Congress, Manuscript Division; Rayford Logan Autobiography, VI-11.

113. Rayford Logan Autobiography, VI-29. In his biography of Logan, Kenneth Robert Janken covers his WWI experience in detail. See Janken, *Rayford W. Logan and the Dilemma of the African-American Intellectual* (Amherst: University of Massachusetts Press, 1993), 34–61.

114. Gable Finley, March 8, 1921, War History Commission, State of Virginia, Military Service Record, Library of Virginia, www.lva.lib.va.us (accessed May 2006).

4. At War in the Terrestrial Heaven

1. Harry Haywood [pseud. for Haywood Hall], *Black Bolshevik: Autobiography of An Afro-American Communist* (Chicago: Liberator Press, 1979), 60–61.

2. Arthur Little, *From Harlem to the Rhine: The Story of New York's Colored Volunteers* (New York: Covici, Friede, 1936), 146.

3. Haywood, *Black Bolshevik,* 61.

4. Ibid., 61–62.

5. Charles Taylor defines the social imaginary as the ways in which ordinary people "imagine their social existence, how they fit together with others, how things go on between them and their fellows, the expectations that are normally met, and the deeper normative notions and images that underlie these expectations." See Taylor, "Modern Social Imaginaries," *Public Culture* 14 (Winter 2002): 105.

6. One soldier writing to W. E. B. Du Bois in February 1919 compared Camp Pontanezen, Brest, to "a penal institution." See Du Bois, "The Negro Soldier in Service Abroad during the First World War," *Journal of Negro Education* 12 (Summer 1943): 333.

7. Bernard C. Nalty, *Strength for the Fight: A History of African Americans in the Military* (New York: Free Press, 1986), 112; Monroe Mason and Arthur Furr, *The American Negro Soldier with the Red Hand of France* (Boston, Mass.: Cornhill Company, 1920), 159.

8. Emmett J. Scott, *Scott's Official History of the American Negro in the World War* (1919), 316–317.

9. Louis H. Pontlock to W. E. B. Du Bois, April 26, 1919, Du Bois Papers, Reel 8.

10. Floyd G. Snelson, "Over There," *California Eagle,* November 16, 1918, 1.

11. William Holmes Dyer Memoirs, 1917–1918, Schomburg Center for Research in Black Culture, New York Public Library, 7.

12. William Maxwell, *Billie Dyer and Other Stories* (New York: Knopf, 1992), 9.

13. On Fort Des Moines, see Arthur E. Barbeau and Florette Henri, *The Unknown Soldiers: African-American Troops in World War I* (1974; repr., New York: Da Capo Press, 1996), 46–51.

14. Charles H. Houston, "Saving the World for Democracy," Part 2, *Pittsburgh Courier,* July 27, 1940. On Houston, see Genna Rae McNeil, *Groundwork: Charles Hamilton Houston and the Struggle for Civil Rights* (Philadelphia: University of Pennsylvania Press, 1983).

15. Du Bois quoted in William Jordan, "The Damnable Dilemma: African American Protest and Accommodation in World War I," *Journal of American History* 81 (March 1995): 1573.

16. On the debates over wartime protest strategies and the segregated officers' training camp, see Lewis, *W. E. B. Du Bois: Biography of a Race,* 528–532; and Jordan, "The Damnable Dilemma."

17. W. E. B. Du Bois, "Charles Young," *Crisis* 23 (February 1922), in W. E. B. Du Bois, *Writings* (New York: Library of America, 1987), 1195–1196. On Young, see Nalty, *Strength for the Fight,* 110–111.

18. Patterson quoted in Theodore Kornweibel Jr., *"Investigate Everything": Federal Efforts to Compel Black Loyalty during World War I* (Bloomington: Indiana University Press, 2002), 82.

19. Houston, "Saving the World for Democracy," Part 2.

20. William L. Houston to Charles H. Houston, August 27, 1917, William L. Houston Papers, Library of Congress.

21. Long, "The Negro Soldier in the Army of the United States," *Journal of Negro Education* 12 (Summer 1943): 310–311.

22. Rayford Logan Oral History, Rayford Logan Papers, Moorland-Spingarn Research Center, Howard University, 3.

23. Ibid.

24. W. E. B. Du Bois, "The Talented Tenth," in *The Negro Problem: A Series of Articles by Representative Negroes of To-day* (New York: James Pott and Company, 1903), 33.

25. Rayford Logan, Oral History, 5

26. Ibid., 4.

27. Ibid., 7; Rayford Logan Diaries, June 13, 1943, *The Papers of Rayford W. Logan,* Library of Congress, Manuscript Division.

28. Rayford Wittingham Logan did not come from the highest circles of African American D.C. society. His mother was a laundress and his father a butler. However

his prodigious intellect, light complexion, and family pedigree—traced through his maternal grandfather to a prominent white Virginia family—allowed him to develop his elitist sensibilities in spite of his material circumstances. On Logan's background, see Kenneth Janken, *Rayford Logan and the Dilemma of the African-American Intellectual* (Amherst: University of Massachusetts Press, 1993), 4–18.

29. Rayford Logan, Oral History, 7.

30. Rayford Logan Diaries, June 13, 1943.

31. Dyer Memoirs, 6. This reading of African American soldiers' displacement at sea owes much to sociologist Paul Gilroy's work on the black Atlantic. Arguing that ships were "microsystems of linguistic and political hybridity," Gilroy asserts that they were "mobile elements that stood for the shifting spaces in between the fixed places they connected." To Gilroy, ships offer "a means to conduct political dissent" as well as a "distinct mode of cultural production." See Paul Gilroy, *The Black Atlantic: Modernity and Double Consciousness* (Cambridge, Mass.: Harvard University Press, 1993), 12–17.

32. Henry Berry, "My Bit in the World War, or the Story of 2921486," in Berry Family Letters, Schomburg Center for Research in Black Culture, New York Public Library, 13.

33. Ibid., 16.

34. Ibid., 17.

35. Osceola McKaine, "With the Buffaloes in France," *Crusader,* February 1919, 3.

36. McKaine's nomadic spirit quote is cited in the introduction to two separate articles that he authored in 1918. See, "The Buffaloes: A First Class Fighting Regiment," *Outlook* 119 (May 22, 1918): 144 and " 'Death Does Not Matter' Writes Lieut. 'Over There,' " *Cleveland Advocate*, October 12, 1918, 1. Information on McKaine's travels comes from Miles Richards, "Osceola E. McKaine and the Struggle for Black Civil Rights, 1917–1946" (Ph.D. diss., University of South Carolina, 1994), 10.

37. Richards, "Osceola E. McKaine," 10.

38. McKaine, "The Buffaloes," 144.

39. Richards, "Osceola E. McKaine"; McKaine, "The Buffaloes," 144.

40. McKaine, "The Buffaloes," 145.

41. Ibid., 145–146.

42. Clarence Trotti to John, February 13, 1919, personal collection of Michael Trotti; Clarence Trotti to unknown, 1919, personal collection of Michael Trotti.

43. McKaine, "Death Does Not Matter."

44. McKaine, "With the Buffaloes in France," 3.

45. Berry, "My Bit in the World War," 19.

46. William Holmes Dyer Memoirs, 7–8.

47. George Rothwell Brown, "70 Yanks Toil in Mud while Waiting at Rest Camp," *Washington Post*, January 1, 1919, 1.

48. William Holmes Dyer Memoirs, 8.

49. George Rothwell Brown, "Navy Foresaw Brest," *Washington Post,* February 20, 1919, 1.

50. Berry, "My Bit the in World War," 20.

51. Elisha Green, *Ely: Too Black, Too White* (Amherst: The University of Massachusetts Press, 1970), 398.

52. Ibid.

53. Ibid., 404.

54. Monroe Mason and Arthur Furr, *The American Negro Soldier with the Red Hand of France,* 39.

55. *Organization of the Services of Supply, American Expeditionary Forces* (Washington, D.C.: Government Printing Office, 1921), 21.

56. Yves-Henri Nouailhat, *Les Américains à Nantes et St. Nazaire, 1917–1919* (Paris: Les Belles Lettres, 1972), 127.

57. Ibid.

58. Ibid., 125.

59. Memoirs, Kathryn M. Johnson Papers, Schlesinger Library, Radcliffe College, 227. Addie W. Hunton and Kathryn M. Johnson, *Two Colored Women with the American Expeditionary Forces* (1920; repr., New York: G. K. Hall & Co., 1997), 126.

60. Frank W. Harris, Captain of Engineers, U.S. Army to Editor, *Crisis,* June 26, 1919, Du Bois Papers, Reel 8.

61. Charles H. Williams, *Negro Soldiers in World War I: The Human Side* (1923; repr., New York: AMS Press, 1970)*,* 143–144.

62. Charles N. Wheeler, "Race Troops Winning Popularity in France," *Cleveland Advocate,* November 23, 1918; "The Colored Stevedore in France Receiving Special Attention from the YMCA," *Christian Chrendet* [?], October 31, 1918, TINCF.

63. Green, *Ely: Too Black, Too White,* 407.

64. George Rothwell Brown, "Task of S.O.S. Vast," *Washington Post,* February 10, 1919, 1.

65. Hunton and Johnson, *Two Colored Women,* 122.

66. Ibid., 124, 121–122.

67. Ibid., 126, 129.

68. Green, *Ely: Too Black, Too White,* 406.

69. James Waverly Crawley, n.d., "WWI History Commission Questionnaire," Library of Virginia Digitized Collections, www.lva.lib.va.us (accessed May 2006).

70. "'Y' Man Writes of Experiences Abroad," *New York Age,* March 3, 1919, 1. The Pioneer Infantry did double duty: they were primarily laborers but could be called into combat when necessary.

71. Dean Mohr to W. E. B. Du Bois, June 27, 1919, Du Bois Papers.

72. "Chaplain's Work as I Found It in France," Du Bois Papers. Although the manuscript in the Du Bois Papers lists the author as anonymous, a roster of "Colored

Chaplains in the United States Army" lists the chaplain of the 506th as E. M. M. Wright.

73. No. 254 Memorandum for Director of Military Intelligence, April 25, 1919, Casefile 10218-329, RG 165, NARA.

74. Chas D. Gordon, April 29, 1919, Casefile 10218-329, RG 165, NARA.

75. Confidential Report, John D. Austin to Commanding General, Port of Embarkation, Newport News, Va., Casefile 10218-329, RG 165, NARA.

76. Green, *Ely: Too Black, Too White*, 421–423.

77. Ibid., 408, 411. In 1922 hearings led by Georgia Senator Tom Watson, veterans recounted more hair-raising tales of abuse in military jails. See U.S. Senate, *Alleged Executions without Trial in France* (Washington, D.C.: Government Printing Office, 1923).

78. Ibid., 404.

79. Ibid., 415. In testimony before the Senate, Harry Gentry of the 92nd Division recounted another incident where a black officer killed a black enlisted man. The private had refused to go on kitchen patrol, and his superior officer responded by shooting him in the abdomen. See U.S. Senate, *Alleged Executions Without Trial in France*, 615.

80. Green, *Ely: Too Black, Too White*, 418.

81. Ibid., 418, 410. Green also attributed his unlikely release from the guard house to the arbitrariness of Jim Crow law enforcement, calling it "a case of the white man changing regulations to themselves." He recognized that, as with the judge in Waxahachie, he "was just lucky to have some of" them "as his friend" in St. Nazaire, 425.

82. Ibid., 418.

83. "Army Transport Service Made Famous," *Gangplank News*, April 6, 1919, 1. Put out by white soldiers in St. Nazaire, the *Gangplank News* also mocked black labor troops as backwoods halfwits with little interest in, or understanding of, the details of the war. See "Interviews with Little Known People II: Pvt Rastus Rhubarb, 897th Engineers," April 14, 1919, 5.

84. Green, *Ely: Too Black, Too White*, 442.

85. Berry, "My Bit in the World War," 24.

86. "Ralph W. Tyler Writes of the Spirit of France," *Cleveland Advocate*, October 26, 1918, 1.

87. William N. Colson, "The Social Experience of the Negro Soldier Abroad," *Messenger* 2 (October 1919): 26.

88. Autobiography, VI-25, VI-14, Box 15, Rayford Logan Papers, Moorland-Spingarn Research Center, Howard University.

89. Rayford Logan Autobiography, VI-30, VI-31. When he challenged white officers on their behavior, he sometimes did it on the basis of their shared status as gentlemen, as well. Logan's elitism left no doubt in his mind that he was a gentleman even as

he used the term derisively when he referred to the "crude Southerners" with whom he had conflict. Quote from Rayford W. Logan Diaries, June 30, 1943.

90. Rayford Logan Autobiography, VI-30.

91. Rayford W. Logan Diaries, July 30, 1943; Rayford Logan Autobiography, VI-31–VI-32.

92. Rayford Logan, Oral History, 8.

93. Haywood, *Black Bolshevik,* 57.

94. Houston, "Saving the World for Democracy," Part 9, *Pittsburgh Courier,* September 14, 1940.

95. Houston, "Saving the World for Democracy," Part 10, *Pittsburgh Courier,* September 21, 1940.

96. Ibid.; Houston, "Saving the World for Democracy," Part 11, *Pittsburgh Courier,* September 28, 1940.

97. Houston, "Saving the World for Democracy," Part 11. McNeil, *Groundwork,* 43–44.

98. Ibid.

99. Wm. Cox, Sgt. M.D., to Father, printed in "Soldier in Prison at Brest Tells of Insults Heaped upon Him by White Soldier," *Cleveland Advocate,* June 14, 1919.

100. Ibid.

101. Green, *Ely: Too Black, Too White,* 418.

102. Haywood, *Black Bolshevik,* 80.

103. See *Alleged Executions Without Trial in France,* 111–114.

104. "Soldiers testify to Lynchings," *New York Times,* January 5, 1922. Barbeau and Henri, *Unknown Soldiers,* 168–170.

105. Benjamin Seldon to W. E. B. Du Bois, n.d., Du Bois Papers, Series 5 Nonfiction Books, Reel 84.

106. *Alleged Executions Without Trial in France,* 614; Dyer Memoirs, 20.

107. Dyer Memoirs, 20, 22.

108. Christopher Columbus Watts, February 3, 1921, "WWI History Commission Questionnaire," Library of Virginia Digitized Collections, www.lva.lib.va.us (accessed May 2006).

5. The World's Experience

1. Christopher Columbus Watts, February 3, 1921, "WWI History Commission Questionnaire," Library of Virginia Digitized Collections, www.lva.lib.va.us (accessed May 2006); James Royal Steptoe, August 16, 1920, "WWI History Commission Questionnaire," (accessed May 2006).

2. Elisha Green, *Ely: Too Black, Too White* (Amherst: The University of Massachusetts Press, 1970), 434.

3. Ibid., 436–437.

4. Ibid.

5. Addie W. Hunton and Kathryn M. Johnson, *Two Colored Women with the American Expeditionary Forces* (1920; repr., New York: G. K. Hall & Co., 1997), 17.

6. William Holmes Dyer Memoirs, 1917–1918, Schomburg Center for Research in Black Culture, New York Public Library, 11.

7. On social learning and mass movements, see George Lipsitz, *A Life in the Struggle: Ivory Perry and the Culture of Opposition* (Philadelphia: Temple University Press, 1988).

8. Wilson Papers, vol. 53, 386–387; also quoted in Jonathan S. Rosenberg, *How Far the Promised Land: World Affairs and the Civil Rights Movement from the First World War to Vietnam* (Princeton, N.J.: Princeton University Press, 2006), 16. Descriptions of Wilson's arrival come from Rosenberg, 15–16, and from Erez Manela, "Imagining Woodrow Wilson in Asia: Dreams of East-West Harmony and the Revolt against Empire in 1919," *American Historical Review* 111 (December 2006): 1327–1328.

9. Manela, "Imagining Woodrow Wilson in Asia," 1327.

10. Woodrow Wilson, "Address to Congress," February 11, 1918, Wilson Papers, v. 46, 421. On Wilson's influence on nationalist movements, see Erez Manela, *The Wilsonian Moment: Self-Determination and the International Origins of Anticolonial Nationalism* (New York: Oxford University Press, 2006).

11. Ieuan L.I. Griffiths, *The African Inheritance* (New York: Routledge, 1995), 34–44; Mahmood Mamdani, *Citizen and Subject: Contemporary Africa and the Legacy of Late Colonialism* (Princeton, N.J.: Princeton University Press, 1996), 37–39; Victor Hugo quoted in Gilbert Rist, *The History of Development from Western Origins to Global Faith* (London: Zed Books, 1997), 51.

12. Griffiths, *The African Inheritance,* 34–44; Ieuan Griffiths, "The Scramble for Africa: Inherited Political Boundaries," *The Geographic Journal* 152 (July 1986): 204–205.

13. "German Colonies to be Divided Up," *New York Times,* February 23, 1917. On Wilson's "Peace Without Victory Speech, see Manela, *The Wilsonian Moment,* 22–25.

14. William A. Byrd, "The Peace Conference and the America Negro," *Cleveland Gazette,* January 25, 1919. Biographical information comes from Richard R. Wright, *Centennial Encyclopedia of the African Methodist Episcopal Church* (Philadelphia: Book Concern of the A. M. E. Church, 1916), 56.

15. Woodrow Wilson, "An Annual Message on the State of the Union," December 2, 1918, quoted in Wilson Papers, vol. 53, 276.

16. George B. Vashon to W. E. B. Du Bois, December 25, 1918, Du Bois Papers, Reel 7.

17. Ibid.; Kathryn M. Johnson to Roy Nash, February 26, 1916, NAACP Papers, Part 1. See also Paul N. D. Thornell, "The Absent Ones and the Providers: A Biography

of the Vashons," *Journal of Negro History* 80 (Autumn 1998): 284–301. On the limits of Wilsonian self-determination, see Manela, "Imagining Woodrow Wilson in Asia," 1331–1333.

18. Memorandum from W. H. Loving to Director of Military Intelligence, December 20, 1918, Casefile 10218-302,(3), RG 165, NARA II.

19. "Address to the Country and the World," printed in the *Chicago Broad Ax,* January 4, 1919. Reprinted as part of "Colored American Delegate Now in Paris Represents the Organized Action and Desires of Colored American People as a Race," *Boston Guardian,* 1919, TINCF. See also Mark Ellis, *Race, War, and Surveillance: African Americans and the United States* (Bloomington: Indiana University Press, 2001), 190–91.

20. "Address to the Country and the World." See also Rosenberg, *How Far the Promised Land,* 68–70.

21. Kelly Miller, *Kelly Miller's History of the World War for Human Rights; An Intensely Human and Brilliant Account of the World War; Why American Entered the Conflict; What the Allies Fought For; And a Thrilling Account of the Important Part Taken by the Negro in the Tragic Defeat of Germany . . .* (Washington, D.C.: Jenkins and Keller, 1919), also known as *Kelly Miller's Authentic History of the Negro in the World War.*

22. Vashon to Du Bois, December 25, 1918.

23. "Plan Pan African Congress in February; New York and Illinois Fighters Are Cited," *New York Age,* February 1, 1919.

24. "Nation's Platform at the Peace Conference," *New York Age,* January 25, 1919, 4.

25. Ibid.

26. "Negroes to be at Peace Conference in Europe," *Messenger* 2 (January 1918): 6; "The League of Darker Peoples" and "Japanese Representatives Urge Fight on Race Prejudice at Waldorf Astoria," *The World Forum,* in Casefile 10218-29, RG 165, NARA II.

27. "Editorial Letter by Marcus Garvey," November 29, 1918, in Robert A. Hill, ed. *The Marcus Garvey and Universal Negro Improvement Association Papers,* vol. 1(Berkeley: University of California Press, 1983), 300. Garvey most fully articulated his vision for a black "Racial Empire" to rival that of "the Jew . . . the Mongolian," or the Anglo-Saxon in a 1925 speech. See "Fundamental Thesis of the African Empire," in *The Marcus Garvey Papers,* vol. 10, 318.

28. "In re: Agitators, Peace Conference, Paris 1919," Casefile OG 36880, RG 65, in FSAA. On Vietnamese nationalists and the peace conference, see Kimloan Thi Vu Hill, "A Westward Journey, An Enlightened Path: Vietnamese Linh Tho, 1915–1930" (Ph.D. diss., University of Oregon, 2001). On Egypt, see Manela, *The Wilsonian Moment.*

29. "Nation's Platform at the Peace Conference," 4.

30. W. E. B. Du Bois, "The Color Line Belts the World," *Collier's Weekly* 38 (October 20, 1906): 30. On the long history of black internationalism, see Robin D. G. Kelley, "'But a Local Phase of a World Problem': Black History's Global Vision, 1883–1950," *Journal of American History* 86 (December 1999): 1045–1077.

31. Details of Moton's trip come from "Head of Tuskegee Sees Colored Units," *Stars and Stripes,* January 3, 1919, 5. Quotes come from his autobiography, *Finding a Way Out* (Garden City, N.Y.: Doubleday, Page and Company, 1920), 251.

32. Moton, *Finding a Way Out,* 252. Moton, "Negro Troops in France," *Southern Workman* 48 (May 1919): 219–224; Felix James, "Robert Russa Moton and the Whispering Gallery in France after World War I," *Journal of Negro History* 62 (July 1977): 235–242.

33. Ralph W. Tyler to George Myers, January 26, 1919, reel 7, Box 17, Folder 4, George A. Myers Papers, 1890–1929, memory.loc.gov/ammem/award97/ohshtml/myers/box17.html (accessed May 2009).

34. Moton, *Finding a Way Out,* 263.

35. Harry Haywood [pseud. for Haywood Hall], *Black Bolshevik: Autobiography of An Afro-American Communist* (Chicago: Liberator Press, 1979), 74.

36. "Head of Tuskegee Sees Colored Units," 5. Moton omitted from his autobiography this section of his speech in recounting what he said.

37. William N. Colson, "Propaganda and the American Negro Soldier," *Messenger* 2 (July 1919): 25.

38. Green, *Ely: Too Black, Too White,* 449. Other African Americans objected to the word "Negro" on the grounds that it masked their humanity and conveyed "to the intelligent mind but one thing, that of inferiority." See "Quit Saying Negro, Call Them Colored or Blacks," *Topeka Daily Call,* August 6, 1920, TINCF.

39. Green, *Ely: Too Black, Too White,* 450–451.

40. Ibid., 435.

41. Ibid., 436–437. Undoubtedly Green translated parts of the Belgian's words into his own phrasing of nationalism and masculinity, but he retained the spirit, if not the letter, of his words. As with racial politics, radical labor politics made central conceptions and embodiments of manhood in framing what workers would demand from the state. See for example Todd McCallum, "Not a Sex Question? The One Big Union and the Politics of Radical Manhood," *Labour/Le Travail* 42 (Fall 1998): 15–54.

42. Green, *Ely: Too Black Too White,* 437.

43. Ibid., 451.

44. Ibid., 438.

45. "Cosmopolitanism" is so over-defined as to be ill-defined. Throughout its many usages, however, there runs a common positioning of cosmopolitanism as a social imagining (or political positioning) that is somehow opposed to nationalism. For its practitioners (intellectual or otherwise), cosmopolitanism offers a worldliness and com-

mitment to universals that serves as an antidote to the exclusions and inequities of bounded nationalism. See *Public Cultures* 12 (Fall 2000), esp. Sheldon Pollock, Homi K. Bhabha, Carol A. Breckenridge, and Dipesh Chakrabarty, "Cosmopolitanisms," 577–589, and Walter Mignolo, "The Many Faces of Cosmo-Polis: Border Thinking and Critical Cosmopolitanism," 721–748. See also Paul Gilroy, *The Black Atlantic: Modernity and Double Consciousness* (Cambridge, Mass.: Harvard University Press, 1993).

46. Green, *Ely: Too Black, Too White,* 447.

47. "The Discovery of France by Jos. Williams, Colored Doughboy," *Literary Digest* 60 (April 12, 1919): 80. The story originally ran in *Metropolitan Magazine* as "The Promised Land."

48. "The Discovery of France by Jos. Williams," 82.

49. Karl Bardin, "My Most Unusual Experience while with the 371st Inf.," Record Group 120, Records of the AEF (WWI) Historical 371st Infantry, Box 2, NARA II. African American teacher Andrew Johnson described a similar encounter in which a member of his company expressed frustration with a group of soldiers in red fezzes for being "high hat" and speaking "gibberish" in response to questions. Johnson had to explain to the soldier that the men were "FRENCH Africans." Unlike in the accounts by white people, Johnson does not indicate that a natural racial affinity then brought together the African and African American troops. Andrew Johnson, "I Did My Bit for Democracy," 1938, manuscript in "American Life Histories: Manuscripts from the Federal Writers Project, 1936–1940," American Memory Collection, Library of Congress, memory.loc.gov (accessed October 2003).

50. Momar Cisse to Joe Lunn, in Lunn, *Memoirs of the Maelstrom: A Senegalese Oral History of the First World War* (Portsmouth, N.H.: Heinemann, 1999), 80.

51. Ibid., 17–19, 65–67.

52. Green, *Ely: Too Black, Too White,* 447.

53. Ibid. Clemitis was not alone in positioning white supremacy as first an American phenomenon. Responding to French Colonel Linard's infamous "Secret Memo on the Subject of American Negro Troops," Senegalese deputy Blaise Diagne painted Linard's endorsement of Jim Crow as decidedly un-French—a violation "of the intangible principles of colonial politics" and of the "noblest French principles in regard to civilization." An expert politician, Diagne spun the memo as an American encroachment on French values to prod the Chamber to acknowledge and appreciate colonial West African wartime sacrifices. See Le Commissaire Générale des Effectifs Coloniaux à Monsieur le Ministre de la Guerre (Cabinet), Série 6N Côte 97, Service Historique de l'Armée de Terre, Château de Vincennes, Paris.

54. W. E. B. Du Bois, *The Souls of Black Folk* (1903; repr., New York: Signature Books, 1982), 47.

55. Green, *Ely: Too Black, Too White,* 451. Military Intelligence agent Walter Loving anticipated racial friction between black and white troops focused on "colored men

mingling with white women in sporting houses and other questionable places" and recommended that "no discharges be given colored soldiers in France" and that the Army ship black troops out as early as possible to avoid any possible conflicts. Memorandum for General Churchill, November 18, 1918, RG 165, Casefile 10218-256, NARA II. Some soldiers, like Rayford Logan, did in fact receive their discharges abroad.

56. Green, *Ely: Too Black, Too White,* 458. Green, a former boxer, left the man bleeding from the head on the dock. He was threatened with court martial, but a sympathetic colonel and old friend of the judge arranged to have the charges dropped.

57. Private J. E. Williams to W. E. B. Du Bois, Du Bois Papers.

58. "Blacks Attack Americans," *Washington Post,* May 1, 1919, 5.

59. Cable message from American Consul at Brest, November 24, 1919, Casefile 10218-379, RG 165, NARA II.

60. "U.S. Color Line Stirs French Deputies," *New York Times,* July 26, 1919, 7; "Black Frenchmen Protest Treatment Accorded Poilu by American Military Police," *Houston Informer,* August 9, 1919, 1.

61. "Monuments to Madness? The Memory of the Great War and the Politics of Guadeloupe's Identity, 1919–1945," *French Historical Studies* 21 (Autumn 1998): 561–592, esp. 564–567. Holding American white supremacy up as particularly egregious also helped metropolitan French to perpetuate the myth of their racial egalitarianism while simultaneously exploiting ex-servicemen. Into the mid-1920s, the French government refused to return home African veterans of the Great War whom they suspected had succumbed to radical influences while in the metropole. See Iheanachor Egonu, *"Les Continents* and the Francophone Pan-Negro Movement," *Phylon* 42 (3rd qtr. 1981): 250–51. For coverage of the French government's mistreatment of colonial African troops during the war and after, see the Pan-Africanist paper, *Les Continents,* which served as the organ of the Afro-French Universal League for the Defense of the Black Race.

62. "American Soldiers Cause Trouble in French Cities," *Chicago Defender,* May 2, 1919. Memoirs, Kathryn M. Johnson Papers, Schlesinger Library, Radcliffe College, 235.

63. Memoirs, Kathryn M. Johnson, 235; Hunton and Johnson, *Two Colored Women,* 241.

64. Green, *Ely: Too Black, Too White,* 462–464. A couple of months later in June 1919, French and Americans again clashed, this time in Brest. French civilians and marines attacked American troops after an intoxicated American sailor tore down a French flag and trampled on it. Four people were killed and hundreds more wounded. "2 Yanks Dying, 2 French Killed in Brest Riots," *Chicago Daily Tribune,* July 1, 1919, 12.

65. Green: *Ely: Too Black, Too White,* 465.

66. Ibid., 460.

67. Ibid., 461.

68. William N. Colson, "Propaganda and the American Negro Soldier," 25.

69. William N. Colson, "An Analysis of Negro Patriotism," *Messenger* 2 (August 1919): 23–24. South Carolina congressman James F. Byrnes blamed the violence of 1919 on Colson's articles in the *Messenger* as well as on editorials like "Returning Soldiers" by Du Bois in *Crisis*. Citing militant editorials in the black magazines and newspapers, he called the violence of the Red Summer "deliberately planned" by African American leaders. "Blames Race Riots on Negro Leaders," *New York Times,* August 26, 1919, 14; "Reds Incite Negro Rioters," *Los Angeles Times,* September 1, 1919, I1.

70. Colson, "An Analysis of Negro Patriotism," 25.

71. Ernest and Magnolia Thompson McKissick Oral History, Louis D. Silveri Oral History Collection, Southern Highlands Research Center, D. Hiden Ramsey Library Special Collection, University of North Carolina at Asheville, 10. Hereafter cited as McKissick interview.

72. McKissick interview, 10–11. McKissick's son, Floyd, threw himself into the civil rights movement after returning from his own stint in the military in World War II. Floyd sued to become the first African American admitted to the University of North Carolina law school, and served as the national director of the Congress of Racial Equality (CORE) during the 1960s.

73. Rayford Logan, Oral History Interview, Rayford Logan Papers, Moorland-Spingarn Research Center, Howard University, 9.

74. Like Rayford Logan, Haywood Hall also found himself dismayed and "depressed" by the humiliations he witnessed in the Army. Hall "did not want to go back" to the United States, but ill health (he was suffering from a kidney ailment) and family ties convinced him to return home. Nevertheless, he wondered how he would readjust to "the conditions of blacks in the states," Haywood, *Black Bolshevik,* 74–75.

75. Tyler Stovall, *Paris Noir: African Americans in the City of Light* (Boston: Houghton Mifflin, 1996), 34.

76. Logan, "Confessions of an Unwilling Nordic," *The World Tomorrow* 10 (July 1927): 300.

77. Rayford Logan, Oral History, 9.

78. Rayford Logan Autobiography, VII-10, Moorland-Spingarn Research Center, Howard University.

79. Logan, "Confessions of Unwilling Nordic," 297.

80. Always a "Negro." Logan had an aversion to the term "black" that became venomous during the black power phase of the civil rights movement. See Kenneth Robert Janken, *Rayford W. Logan and the Dilemma of the African American Intellectual* (Amherst: University of Massachusetts Press, 1993), 230–232.

81. Literary historian Brent Hayes Edwards referred to Du Bois's famous phrase as both "a prophecy and a preface." See Du Bois, "To the Nations of the World," quoted in Edwards, *The Practice of Diaspora: Literature, Translation, and the Rise of Black Internationalism* (Cambridge, Mass.: Harvard University Press, 2003), 1. Details of the 1900 Pan-African Conference can be found in W. E. Burghardt DuBois, "The Pan-African Movement," in George Padmore, ed., *Colonial and Coloured Unity, A Programme of Action,* 2nd ed. (1947; repr., London: Hammersmith Bookshop, 1963), 13; as well as in David Levering Lewis, *W. E. B. Du Bois: Biography of a Race* (New York: Henry Holt, 1993), 246–251. For a broad history of Pan-Africanism, see Imanuel Geiss, *The Pan African Movement,* trans. Anne Keep (New York: Africana Publishing Co., 1974).

82. "Negroes to be at the Peace Conference," *Messenger,* 6.

83. Description of Harrison from Eric Arneson, "A Hubert Harrison Reader: Book Review," *African American Review* 37 (Spring 2003): 160. Kelley discusses Harrison's internationalism. Historian and journalist J.A. Rogers placed him ahead of both W. E. B. DuBois and William Monroe Trotter as "the foremost Afro-American intellect of his time." Quoted in Jeffery B. Perry, ed., *A Hubert Harrison Reader* (Middletown, Conn.: Wesleyan University Press, 2001), 1.

84. Hubert Harrison, "The White War and the Colored Races," *New Negro* 4 (October 1919), in Perry, *A Hubert Harrison Reqader,* 207–208.

85. See Michelle Stephens, *Black Empire: The Masculine Global Imaginary of Caribbean Intellectuals in the United States, 1914–1962* (Durham, N.C.: Duke University Press, 2005), 99–100. See also Stephens, "Black Transnationalism and the Politics of National Identity: West Indian Intellectuals in Harlem in the Age of War and Revolution," *American Quarterly* 50 (September 1998): 600–603. For a time, Hubert Harrison joined with the UNIA, serving as the editor of its organ, the *Negro World.*

86. "Eliézer Cadet to *L'Essor,*" *Marcus Garvey Papers,* vol. 1, 417.

87. W. E. B. Du Bois, "My Mission," *Crisis* 18 (May 1919): 7.

88. W. E. B. Du Bois to *New York Age,* draft, n.d., in Du Bois Papers.

89. "William Edward Burghardt Du Bois to Joseph Patrick Tumulty, with Enclosure," November 27, 1918, Wilson Papers, vol. 53, 236–238. See also W. E. B. Du Bois to Tumulty, Du Bois Papers.

90. "Always Africa is giving us something new or some metempsychosis of a world-old thing," Du Bois wrote in "The African Roots of the War," *Atlantic Monthly* 115 (May 1915): 701. He reworked the essay five years later for *Darkwater* (1920). In a separate essay in the same volume, he added that the darker people of the world regarded world war with clear, "world-old" eyes. See "The Hands of Ethiopia" in *Darkwater: Voices from within the Veil* (1920; repr., New York: AMS Press, 1969), 56; as well as "The Souls of White Folk," 34.

91. "Memorandum on the Future of Africa," Du Bois to Tumulty, 238.

92. Ibid.

93. W. E. B. Du Bois to Newton Baker, November 27, 1918; and W. E. B. Du Bois to Robert Lansing, November 27, 1918, Du Bois Papers.

94. W. E. B. Du Bois, "In France 1918," *Crisis* 17 (March 1919): 216.

95. "Letters from Dr. Du Bois," *Crisis,* 164. Newspapers accounts of Wilson's arrival describe a crowd waxing "madly enthusiastic" for the president. Uninterested in "what peace ideas were in the uncovered grey head" of Wilson, "hundreds of thousands" of French people came out to cheer him for sending the United States into the war effort." See Charles A. Selden, "Two Million Cheer Wilson," *New York Times,* December 15, 1918, 1.

96. "Letters from Dr. Du Bois," *Crisis,* 164.

97. Du Bois, "In France 1918," 216.

98. W. E. B. Du Bois, "My Mission," *Crisis* 17 (May 1919): 7.

99. "Dr. Du Bois Lectures on Impressions of Peace Conference: Says Color Question is International," 1919, TINCF.

100. *Chicago Tribune,* January 19, 1919, quoted in W. E. B. Du Bois, "The Pan African Movement," in *Colonial and . . . Coloured Unity,* 14. In this period, "Chinamen," as the reporter for the *Tribune* would have called them, had their own ambitions for the peace conference. Casting Woodrow Wilson as "spiritual, fair-minded, and firm in his determination" to protect the dignity of weak nations, they sought his support in restoring Chinese sovereignty and granting rights to Shantung province to China. When the conference turned Germany's former concession rights to Shantung over to Japan instead, critics referred to it as the "Rape of China." China, it seemed, also had about a Chinaman's chance of getting anywhere with Wilson and the Allies. Ironically, it was to imperial Japan that many African Americans looked to speak for the "colored" races at the peace talks. On Chinese nationalism in the postwar era, see Manela, "The Wilsonian Moment," 218–271; the description of Wilson comes from 218–219. On the American reaction to Japan, the rape of China, and African Americans' framing of domestic troubles in terms of international injustice, see "Here! Here! Is Your Shantung," *Cleveland Advocate,* July 26, 1919, 8; as well as Marc Gallicchio, *The African American Encounter with Japan and China: Black Internationalism in Asia, 1895–1945* (Chapel Hill: University of North Carolina Press, 2000), 15–29.

101. Du Bois, "The Pan African Movement," 13.

102. Du Bois, "My Mission," *Crisis,* 8; Du Bois, "The Pan African Movement," 15.

103. W. E. B. Du Bois, "Worlds of Color," *Foreign Affairs* 3 (1924–1925): 433.

104. George Padmore, *Pan Africanism or Communism* (Garden City, N.Y.: Doubleday and Company, 1971), 98–99. See also Lunn, *Memoirs of the Maelstrom,* 62–84, 194–205.

105. Du Bois, "Worlds of Color," 433.

106. Du Bois, "The Pan African Movement," 15.

107. Padmore, *Pan Africanism or Communism,* 99.

108. "The Denial of Passports," *Crisis* 17 (March 1919): 226. According to Ellis, NAACP secretary John Shillady "tactfully" omitted Du Bois's instruction to choose delegates "carefully" before he published the telegram in a press statement. See Ellis, *Race, War, and Surveillance,* 196; "Cannot Attend Conference to be Held in Feb'y" *New York Age,* February 8, 1919; and "Pan African to Meet: Reported Conference is a Mystery to Washington," *New York Times,* February 16, 1919, 23.

109. Du Bois, "My Mission," 8; David Levering Lewis, *W. E. B. Du Bois: Biography of a Race,* 575.

110. The *New York Call* is quoted in "The Denial of Passports," 226.

111. Du Bois, "The Pan African Movement," 15.

112. Attendees listed in Contee, "Du Bois, the NAACP, and the Pan African Congress of 1919," *Journal of Negro History* 57 (January 1972): 24. In his depiction of the Pan-African Congress, David Levering Lewis ruefully notes that it was more "pan" than "African." See Lewis, *W. E. B. Du Bois: Biography of a Race,* 574.

113. Ellis, *Race, War, and Surveillance,* 194. According to Ellis, Jernagin's other conferences never took place.

114. Contee, "Du Bois, the NAACP, and the Pan African Congress," 24.

115. Hunton and Johnson, *Two Colored Women,* 255. See Nikki L. Brown, "Your Patriotism is of the Purest Quality: African American Women and World War I" (Ph.D. diss., Yale University, 2002), 152. On Hunton, see Brown, "Your Patriotism," 151–178; and Kimberly Jensen, "Minerva on the Field of Mars: American Women, Citizenship, and Military Service in the First World War" (Ph.D. diss., University of Iowa, 1992), 404–417.

116. Biographical data on Hunt and her family comes from Benjamin Justeson, "African American Consuls Abroad, 1897–1909," *Foreign Service Journal* 81 (September 2004): 72–76; and Tom W. Dillard, "Golden Prospects and Fraternal Amenities, Mifflin W. Gibbs's Arkansas Years," *Arkansas Historical Quarterly* 25 (Winter 1976): 307–333.

117. Arthur E. Barbeau and Florette Henri, *The Unknown Soldiers: African-American Troops in World War I* (1974; repr., New York: Da Capo Press, 1996), 73, 157–158. Marshall described his injury and the battle in which he received it in "Brave Soldier Exploit Under Captain Marshall," reprinted in *A Pictorial History of the Negro in the Great War, 1917–1918* (New York: Toussaint Pictorial Co., 1919), 37. The 15th, known as the Harlem Hellfighters and famed for their jazz band led by James Reese Europe, became the 369th Regiment of the 93rd Infantry. They were brigaded with the French. Their experiences in Spartanburg are chronicled in Arthur W. Little, *From Harlem to the Rhine: the Story of New York's Colored Volunteers* (New York: Covici, Friede, 1936), as well as in Frank E. Roberts, *The American Foreign Legion: Black Soldiers of the 93d in World War I* (Annapolis, Md.: Naval Institute Press, 2004).

118. "Dr. Du Bois Lectures on Impressions of Peace Conference."

119. Roscoe C. Simmons, "Roscoe Tells of Pan African Meet," *Chicago Defender,* March 10, 1919.

120. "Mr. Eliezer Cadet's Address to the People of France," in "Editorial Letter by Marcus Garvey," *Marcus Garvey Papers,* vol. 1, 377–381. Garvey's editorial says Cadet delivered speeches before large audiences in France and England, but historian David Levering Lewis describes reports of Cadet's significant meetings as being greatly exaggerated. See David Levering Lewis, *W. E. B. Du Bois: The Flight for Equality and the American Century, 1919–1963* (New York: Henry Holt and Company, 2000), 60.

121. Described in David Levering Lewis, *W. E. B. Du Bois: The Fight for Equality and the American Century,* 59–61. Cadet's attendance at the Pan-African Congress was reported in Clarence Contee, ed., "The Worley Report on the Pan African Congress of 1919," *Journal of Negro History* 55 (April 1970): 141.

122. Simmons, "Roscoe Tells of Pan African Meet."

123. Du Bois, "The Pan African Congress," 272.

124. Peter Fryer, *Staying Power: The History of Black People in Britain* (London: Pluto Press, 1984), 292–294.

125. Du Bois, "The Pan African Congress," 272.

126. Ibid. The words belong to Du Bois, who paraphrased both Hunton's and Siegfried's speeches.

127. Du Bois, "Pan African Movement," 16.

128. Du Bois, "Pan African Congress," 272–273; Du Bois, "My Mission," 8.

129. Du Bois, "My Mission," 8.

130. William A. Byrd, "The Peace Conference and the Negro," 4.

131. Hunton and Johnson, *Two Colored Women,* 197.

6. Saving Sergeant Caldwell

1. "Negro Soldier Kills Conductor and Badly Injures Motorman of Anniston Street Car Sunday," *Anniston Star,* December 16, 1918, 1, in *Caldwell Case,* Vertical File, Alabama Room, Anniston Public Library, Anniston, Alabama. The witness testimony comes from the trial excerpt in the same vertical file.

2. Wellington G. Dixon, "A Letter to the Mustered Out Soldiers of the One Hundred and Fifty-Seventh," *Emancipator,* December 28, 1918, 1.

3. Abbé Siéyès quoted in Immanuel Wallerstein, "Citizens All? Citizens Some! The Making of the Citizen," *Comparative Studies in Society and History* 45 (October 2003): 651.

4. Charles H. Williams to Captain J. E. Cutler, Military Morality Staff, November 16, 1918, enclosure: "A Survey of the Social and Religious Conditions among Colored Soldiers at Camp McClellan and Anniston, Alabama," Charles H. Williams, November 7, 1918, FSAA.

5. Sergeant Bernard O. Henderson to W. E. B. Du Bois, December 18, 1918, Part 9A, NAACP Papers.

6. W. F. D. Bardeleben to Archibald Grimke, December 11, 1918, Archibald Grimke Papers, Moorland-Spingarn Research Center, Howard University; Mrs. E. H. Jefferson to Emmett J. Scott, December 19, 1918, Casefile 10218-27, RG 165, NARA II.

7. "Negro Prisoner Dies of Pneumonia," *Atlanta Constitution,* February 16, 1919, B3; Robert Gilbert to W. E. B. Du Bois, December 12,1918, Part 9A, NAACP Papers.

8. Williams, "A Survey of the Social and Religious Conditions among Colored Soldiers at Camp McClellan and Anniston, Alabama."

9. The flu affected 25 percent of the U.S. population and an estimated 20 percent of the world's population. Tallies of flu-related deaths range from 20 to 100 million, or roughly 2.5 percent of those who caught the virus. On the influenza epidemic of 1918, see Alfred W. Crosby, *America's Forgotten Pandemic: The Influenza Virus of 1918* (Cambridge, Mass.: Cambridge University Press, 1991). Ely Green lost a number of his white sponsors in Waxahachie and most of his black family in Sewanee to the flu. See Elisha Green, *Ely: Too Black, Too White* (Amherst: The University of Massachusetts Press, 1970), 444, 446.

10. Williams, "A Survey of the Social and Religious Conditions Among Colored Soldiers at Camp McClellan and Anniston, Alabama."

11. Writing about Birmingham in the 1930s and 1940s, Robin D. G. Kelley has characterized streetcars in Alabama and across the south as "moving theaters," martial sites and venues of performance. He sees them as crucial venues for enacting dramas of white supremacy and black resistance and notes that white conductors and white working-class passengers often turned to violence against black men and women to enforce Jim Crow. See Kelley, "Congested Terrain: Resistance on Public Transportation," *Race Rebels: Culture, Politics and the Black Working Class* (New York: The Free Press, 1994).

12. Caldwell's place and year of birth are recorded in *Registers of Enlistments in the U.S. Army, 1798–1914,* vol. 127, microcopy held at NARA. Although the *Register* lists September 7, 1889, as his birth year, it also gives his age as 21 in early 1913.

13. J. William Harris writes of WWI tensions that "A black man in uniform was a walking contradiction of the idea that only whites could enjoy full honor." See Harris, *Deep Souths: Delta, Piedmont, and Sea Island Society in the Age of Segregation* (Baltimore: The Johns Hopkins University Press, 2001), 235.

14. "Negro Soldier Shoots Anniston Conductor and Injures Motorman," *Birmingham Age-Herald,* December 16, 1918, 1; "Negro Soldier Kills Conductor, Wounds Motorman," *Atlanta Constitution,* December 16, 1918, 1. The *Cleveland Advocate,* an African American paper, exulted in Caldwell's behavior but initially carried the same explanation: "Soldier Defies Jim-Crowism, Shoots Two Men in

a Row," *Cleveland Advocate,* December 21, 1918, 1. W. E. B. Du Bois claimed that the fight stemmed from a fare dispute: "The Caldwell Case," *Crisis* 19 (January 1920): 131.

15. "The Caldwell Case," 131. A violent response to African Americans in uniform was not uncommon. A year earlier, the black papers ran a story about a black lieutenant who was forced to flee his hometown in disguise. Some white citizens in his town had declared that they would permit "no nigger to wear a uniform that a white man was bound to honor." See "Negro Officer Driven from Home by Southern Crackers," *Cleveland Advocate,* Saturday, November 17, 1917, 1; and "Negro U.S. Officer is Run Out of Mississippi," *New York Age,* November 15, 1917, 2.

16. Witness Testimony, Caldwell Case Vertical File.

17. "Sergeant Caldwell to Die on the Gallows," *Chicago Defender,* June 19, 1920, 1.

18. "Negro Soldier Kills Conductor," *Anniston Star.* Accounts of the altercation are given in Caldwell v. State, 84 So. 272; "Negro Soldier Shoots Anniston Conductor and Injures Motorman"; and "Alabama Colored Soldier's Death Sentence Affirmed by State's Highest Court," *Houston Informer,* July 26, 1919, 1.

19. Mrs. G. H. Mathis to Secretary of War Baker, November 21, 1918, File 10218-326, RG 165, NARA II; "Alabama is Willing to Receive Negro Soldiers—If Subservient," *Cleveland Advocate,* September 8, 1917, 1.

20. *Fort McClellan, A Cultural Resources Overview, Report Funded and Submitted to the Army Corps of Engineers, Mobile District* (Stone Mountain, Ga.: New South Associates, 1992), 118.

21. "Negro Soldier Kills Conductor and Wounds Motorman," *Atlanta Constitution.* Earlier in the fall, a white MP shot an African American soldier. None of the white papers who carried the Caldwell story mentioned the earlier shooting in their discussion of "racial trouble." Williams, "A Survey of the Social and Religious Conditions Among Colored Soldiers in Camp McClellan."

22. "Negro Soldier Kills Conductor," *Anniston Star.*

23. "Conductor Killed, Motorman Wounded," *Atlanta Constitution.*

24. "Negro Soldier Kills Conductor," *Anniston Star.*

25. "Negro Soldier Kills Conductor, Wounds Motorman," *Atlanta Constitution.* "Negro Soldier Kills Conductor and Badly Injures Motorman," *Anniston Star.* "Soldier Defies Jim Crowism, Shoots Two Men in a Row," *Cleveland Advocate,* December 21, 1918, 1.

26. "Negro Soldier Kills Conductor and Badly Injures Motorman," *Anniston Star.*

27. Ibid.

28. Ibid.

29. R. R. Williams to Mr. John Shillady, January 17, 1919, NAACP/LOC.

30. "Negro Soldier Kills Conductor and Badly Injures Motorman," *Anniston Star.*

31. "In re: Joy J. Warren Discharged Soldier Attacked in Texas," OG 343326, FSAA. The NAACP branch in Austin used the Warren incident to organize and start a defense fund for the soldier. Framing their agitation as a repayment for black soldiers' sacrifices, the branch president announced that soldiers "have returned to old homes but are not going to submit to old conditions." Quoted in Mark Robert Schneider, *We Return Fighting: The Civil Rights Movement in the Jazz Age* (Boston: Northeastern University Press, 2002), 30.

32. "In re: Charles Lewis," Casefile 10218-214, RG 165, NARA II.

33. "Grand Lynching Bee for Negro Soldier!" *Union,* December 21, 1918, 2.

34. "Lynching in Louisiana," *New York Times,* September 1, 1919, 14. A lumber company town, Bogulusa only had about 8,000 residents in 1919, 60 percent of whom were African American. Stephen H. Norwood, "Bogalusa Burning: The War against Biracial Unionism in the Deep South, 1919," *Journal of Southern History* 63 (July 1997): 597–598.

35. "Lynching in Louisiana," 14.

36. *Fort McClellan, A Cultural Resources Overview,* 118.

37. "Rule Record Finished," *Birmingham Age,* January 18, 1919, 11; "Caught Four Times after Deserting from Army Service," *Atlanta Constitution,* January 6, 1919, 3.

38. The most famous antiwar Southerners were demagogues such as Vardaman, Tom Watson, and Hoke Smith, who objected to the war because they feared either the increased centralization of federal power or the enhanced civic status of African Americans. Harris, *Deep Souths,* 227–228. Yet, as Jeannette Keith points out, rural and semirural whites demonstrated their own hostility to the war effort through draft evasion and organized political protest. Keith, "The Politics of Southern Draft Resistance, 1917–1918: Class, Race, and Conscription in the Rural South," *Journal of American History* 87 (March 2001): 1335–1361. In Oklahoma, black and white people came together to protest the draft in the Green Corn Rebellion of August 1917. Jack D. Foner, *Blacks and the Military in American History* (New York: Praeger Publishers, 1974), 112.

39. Different rules applied in France, where semisanctioned lynchings of African American soldiers as well as summary executions of white and black soldiers without court martial enforced a different sort of order and reflected a different unease with the civilian population. The investigation came to no definite conclusions. See U.S. Congress, Senate, *Alleged Executions without Trial in France* (Washington, D.C.: Government Printing Office, 1923).

40. "Linten Funeral Held Tuesday at Lineville," *Anniston Star,* December 17, 1918, 1.

41. "Caldwell Writes to Officer of His Arrest," *Anniston Star,* December 19, 1918, 5.

42. "Negro Soldier Kills Conductor and Badly Injures Motorman," *Anniston Star.*

43. "Caldwell Writes to Officer of His Arrest," *Anniston Star.*

44. "Calhoun Judge Has Called Grand Jury," *Montgomery Advertiser,* December 17, 1918, 1.

45. Ibid.; "Grand Jury Will Convene Thursday to Probe Killing," *Birmingham Age-Herald,* December 17, 1918, 3.

46. "Grand Jury Will Convene Thursday to Probe Killing," *Birmingham Age-Herald,* December 17, 1918.

47. "Caldwell Is Held Without Bail for Murder," *Anniston Star,* December 19, 1918, 5.

48. Ibid.

49. "Witnesses Tell of Shooting of Car Men," *Anniston Star,* December 18, 1918, 1.

50. "Negro Soldier Kills Conductor and Badly Injures Motorman," *Anniston Star.*

51. "Niel P. Sterne Praised," n.d., Sterne Family File, Alabama Room, Anniston Public Library, Aniston, Alabama.

52. Anniston was founded in 1872 as a closed, private town connected to the Woodstock Iron Company. It opened to the public in 1883. Grace Hooten Gates, *The Model City of the New South: Anniston, Alabama, 1872–1900* (Huntsville, Ala.: Strode Publishers, 1978), 32–55.

53. "Sterne Family Meant Much to Anniston," *Anniston Star,* 1957, 16.

54. On Southern Jews' struggles for acculturation and inclusion, see Leah Elizabeth Hagedorn, "Jews and the American South, 1858–1909" (Ph.D. diss., University of North Carolina, 1999).

55. "Sterne Rites Wednesday at Home on Drive," *Anniston Star,* February 14, 1939, 1. *Official Proceedings of the Constitutional Convention of the State of Alabama, May 21, 1901–September 3, 1901* (Montgomery, Ala.: Brown Printing Company, 1901), 8.

56. *Official Proceedings of the Constitutional Convention,* 8.

57. Ibid., 10

58. Ibid., 8, 10.

59. Ibid., 10.

60. On the cultural and political work that led to regional reconciliation and Northern acceptance of Southern white supremacy, see David Blight, *Race and Reunion: The Civil War in American Memory* (Cambridge, Mass.: Harvard University Press, 2001).

61. *Obituary Record of Graduates of Yale University Deceased during the Year 1938–1939,* in Mervyn Sterne Files, Department of Archives and Manuscripts, Birmingham Public Library, Birmingham, Alabama.

62. "Tribute Paid to Sterne by Many of his Friends," *Anniston Star,* February 14, 1939, 1.

63. Ibid.

64. Biographical data on Hugh Merrill comes from the Merrill Family File, Alabama Room, Anniston Public Library, Anniston, Alabama. See also Alabama Department of Archives and History, *Official and Statistical Register, 1931,* 33.

65. Ibid.

66. R. R. Williams to Mr. John Shillady, January 17, 1919, NAACP/LOC.

67. "Negro Indicted for Murder in 90 Minutes," *Anniston Star,* December 20, 1918, 1.

68. Williams to John Shillady, January 10, 1919.

69. R. R. Williams to Oswald Garrison Villard, December 24, 1918, NAACP/LOC.

70. Williams, "A Survey of the Social and Religious Conditions among Colored Soldiers at Camp McClellan and Anniston, Alabama."

71. Reverend James Brown et al. to Mr. John R. Shillady, June 12, 1919, NAACP/ LOC. Biographical information about Roland Robert Williams and the other legal committee members comes from their WWI Draft Registration Cards, held at NARA, Southeast Division, East Point, Georgia; copies also available on microfilm at NARA, Washington, D.C.

72. R. R. Williams to John Shillady, January 10, 1919, NAACP/LOC. In addition to the pastors who signed various letters to the NAACP about the Caldwell case, barber E. Julius Williams also wrote to the NAACP, as did merchant Thomas Jackson and undertaker James Ballard. For biographical data, see World War I Draft Registration cards as well as *Polk's Anniston City Directory, 1917–1918.*

73. *Tenth Annual Report of the National Association for the Advancement of Colored People for the Year 1919: A Summary of Work and Accounting,* January 1920, and Jonathan Rosenberg, *How Far the Promised Land: World Affairs and the American Civil Rights Movement from the First World War to Vietnam* (Princeton, N.J.: Princeton University Press, 2006), 71.

74. Emmett J. Scott, *Scott's Official History of the American Negro in the World War* (1919), 355–364. Williams wrote to the NAACP on Liberty Loan stationery with Sterne's name listed on the masthead. R. R. Williams to NAACP, n.d., NAACP/LOC.

75. R. R. Williams to Oswald Garrison Villard, December 24, 1918, NAACP/LOC.

76. Ibid.

77. R. R. Williams to John Shillady, January 10, 1919, NAACP/LOC. As with Ely Green and other voices, I am leaving the writer's spelling unmarked and uncorrected.

78. Supreme Court of Alabama, October Term, 1918–1919, 7 Div. 20, Appeal from Calhoun Circuit Court, Edgar C. Caldwell vs. State of Alabama, in *Supreme Court Records and Transcripts,* October Term, 1919, no. 636.

79. Williams to Shillady, January 10, 1919, NAACP/LOC.

80. "Caldwell Trial to Have Night Session," *Anniston Star,* January 18, 1919, 2.

81. R. R. Williams to John R. Shillady, January 17, 1919, NAACP/LOC.

82. Violations continued in spite of Supreme Court rulings. See Michael J. Klarman, "Is the Supreme Court Sometimes Irrelevant, Race and the Southern Criminal Justice System in the 1940s," *Journal of American History,* 89 (June 2002): 119–153.

83. Thomas Jackson et al. to John R. Shillady, July 12, 1919, NAACP/LOC.

84. R. R. Williams to John R. Shillady, January 17, 1919, NAACP/LOC.

85. Thomas Jackson et al. to John R. Shillady, July 12, 1919, NAACP/LOC; *Atlanta City Directory Company's Atlanta City Directory, 1916–1918,* Maloney Publishing Company.

86. "Caldwell Trial to Have Night Session," *Anniston Star.*

87. Supreme Court of Alabama, October Term, 1918–1919, 7 Div. 20, Appeal from Calhoun Circuit Court, Edgar C. Caldwell vs. State of Alabama, in *Supreme Court Records and Transcripts,* October Term, 1919, no. 636.

88. "Caldwell Guilty of Murder in the First Degree Says Jury of Cecil Linton's Slayer," *Anniston Star,* January 19, 1919, 1; *Houston Informer,* July 26, 1919, 1.

89. "Caldwell Trial to Have Night Session," *Anniston Star.*

90. Edgar C. Caldwell vs. State of Alabama; Caldwell vs. State, On Rehearing, October 23, 1919, 7 Div., 18 in *Supreme Court Records and Transcripts,* October Term, 1919, no. 636.

91. R. R. Williams to the NAACP, n.d.

92. "Caldwell Guilty of Murder in the First Degree Says Jury of Cecil Linton's Slayer," *Anniston Star.*

93. Ibid.

94. R. R. Williams to John Shillady, January 17, 1919, NAACP/LOC.

95. Justice J. Griffith quoted in Michael J. Klarman, "The Racial Origins of Modern Criminal Procedure," *Michigan Law Review* 99 (October 2000): 57. As with lynching, Klarman argues, the purpose of mob-dominated capital trial was to guarantee African American subordination rather than to establish guilt or innocence. He calls such trials a "formalization of the lynching process." Although Klarman focuses exclusively on the interwar years, a look at wartime criminal proceedings reminds us that at no point could white supremacists take black subordination as a given. There were no guarantees.

96. "Sgt. Caldwell, Martyr to Prejudice," *Cleveland Advocate,* January 25, 1919, 8.

97. Ibid.

98. "A Soldier," *Crisis* 19 (March 1920): 233.

99. R. R. Williams to Moorfield Storey, May 25, 1919, NAACP/LOC.

100. "Text of President Wilson's Speech in Boston," *New York Times,* February 25, 1919, 1.

101. Williams to Storey, May 25, 1919.

102. Ibid.

103. R. R. Williams to Emmett J. Scott, June 7, 1919, NAACP/LOC.

104. S. H. Kelly to John Shillady, February 25, 1919, NAACP/LOC.

105. Louis B. Anderson et al. to Woodrow Wilson, February 24, 1919, Casefile 4955, series 4, reel 376, Wilson/LOC.

106. "Sgt. Caldwell's Case Gets National Note," *Cleveland Advocate,* May 10, 1919, 1.

107. Ibid.

108. Woodrow Wilson to Gov. Thomas Erby Kilby, February 28, 1919, vol. 55, Wilson Papers.

109. Williams to Scott, June 7, 1919, NAACP/LOC.

110. NAACP branches sprouted all over Alabama in the postwar years. The Anniston branch was one of seven formed in the year 1919, and between 1918 and 1930, Alabamans formed thirteen new branches in towns like Gadsden, Florence, and Tuscaloosa. Sadly, most of the branches became inactive within about two years; only the Mobile and Montgomery branches would outlast the 1920s. See Dorothy Autrey, "'Can These Bones Live?': The National Association for the Advancement of Colored People, 1918–1930," *Journal of Negro History* 82 (Winter 1997): 1–12.

111. Edgar C. Caldwell vs. State of Alabama.

112. Archibald Grimke to Walter White, July 10, 1919, NAACP/LOC.

113. A. Mitchell Palmer to Woodrow Wilson, August 22, 1919, Wilson Papers, vol. 62. Palmer's refusal to interfere in the civil rights case came just as he launched the series of raids and deportations of suspected radicals that set off the Red Scare. On the Palmer raids and the Red Scare, see Stanley Coben, *A. Mitchell Palmer: Politician* (New York: Columbia University Press, 1963); and Theodore Kornweibel, *Seeing Red: Federal Campaigns Against Black Militancy, 1919–1925* (Bloomington: Indiana University Press, 1998).

114. Rayford Logan and Michael R. Winston, eds., *Dictionary of American Negro Biography* (New York: Norton Books, 1982), 116–119.

115. "James A. Cobb: Credit to Race, Bar, and Community," *Washington Bee*, n.d.

116. James A. Cobb to James Weldon Johnson, July 21, 1919, NAACP/LOC.

117. On the riots of the Red Summer, see W. E. B. Du Bois, *Dusk of Dawn: An Essay toward an Autobiography of a Race Concept* (New Hork: Harcourt, Brace, and Company, 1940), reprinted in *W. E. B. Du Bois: Writings* (New York: Literary Classics of the United States, 1986).

118. "Report Six Killed in Sailor-Negro Riot," *New York Times,* May 11, 1919, 31; Theodore Hemmingway, "Prelude to Change, Black Carolinians in the War Years, 1914–1920," *Journal of Negro History* 65 (Summer 1980): 223.

119. "Servicemen Beat Negroes in Race Riot at Capital," *New York Times,* July 21, 1919, 1.

120. Ibid. In his 1920 survey of newspaper coverage of the Red Summer, *Voice of the Negro,* Virginia Military Institute professor Robert T. Kerlin observed that African American periodicals paid a great deal of attention to the role of the white press in precipitating the summer's bloodshed. See Kerlin, *Voice of the Negro, 1919* (New York: Dutton, 1920), 4–9, 77–79. In its July 26 article about the riots, the *Washington Eagle* charged that the *Washington Post* had been deliberately inflammatory, depicting black men as the "Cretan Minataur devouring tender young white virgins." Pointing out that no white paper "cared to report" the "citations on the fields of honor of France," the *Eagle* lamented the white press's fixation on a criminalized version of African

American manhood. See "Marines and Negroes Start Riot: Negroes Protect Themselves," *Washington Eagle,* July 26, 1919, 1.

121. James A. Cobb to James Weldon Johnson, July 21, 1919, NAACP/LOC; "This Nation's Gratitude," *Washington Bee,* June 26, 1919, 1.

122. "Some Facts in the History of the Washington Race Riots," *Daily Herald,* July 29, 1919; Herbert Shapiro, *White Violence and Black Response* (Amherst: University of Massachusetts Press, 1988), 154.

123. "Marines and Negroes Start Riot: Negroes Protect Themselves," *Washington Eagle,* July 26, 1919, 1.

124. "Capital Clashes Increase: Armed and Defiant Negroes Roam about Shooting Whites," *New York Times,* July 22, 1919; "This Nation's Gratitude," *Washington Bee,* 1.

125. Harry Haywood [pseud. for Haywood Hall], *Black Bolshevik: Autobiography of An Afro-American Communist* (Chicago: Liberator Press, 1979), 81–82.

126. William M. Tuttle Jr., *Race Riot: Chicago in the Red Summer of 1919* (1970; repr., Urbana: University of Illinois Press, 1996), 10; Haywood, *Black Bolshevik,* 83.

127. James A. Cobb to James Weldon Johnson, August 28, 1919, NAACP/LOC.

128. Ibid.

129. A. Mitchell Palmer to Woodrow Wilson, August 27, 1919, Wilson Papers, vol. 62.

130. Woodrow Wilson to A. Mitchell Palmer, August 29, 1919, Wilson Papers, vol. 62.

131. Amicus brief excerpted in a letter from Cobb to Secretary of War Newton Baker, James A. Cobb to the Honorable Secretary of War, November 12, 1919, NAACP/LOC.

132. Caldwell v. State, 84 So. 272.

133. "Attorney General May Save Caldwell," *Cleveland Advocate,* December 6, 1919, 1.

134. James R. Ballard and Rev. R. R. Williams to John Shillady, November 18, 1919, NAACP/LOC.

135. U.S. Supreme Court, *The Dred Scott Decision: An Opinion by Chief Justice Roger Taney* (New York: Van Evrie, Horton, and Company, 1859), 17. For an extended discussion of Taney and *Dred Scott,* see A. Leon Higgenbotham Jr., *Shades of Freedom* (Oxford: Oxford University Press, 1996), 62–67.

136. U.S. Supreme Court, *The Dred Scott Decision,* 23, 26.

137. "Caldwell Will Not Be Hanged Here Friday," *Anniston Star,* n.d., in NAACP/LOC. Tressie Caldwell's national agitation for her husband anticipated later criminal justice campaigns in which black defendants' wives and mothers would travel on speaking tours on behalf of "their" men and boys. The most well-known is probably Mother Ada Wright's European tour—to Britain, Scandinavia, the Low Countries, France, Czechoslovakia, and elsewhere—on behalf of her son, one of the nine defendants in the Depression-era Scottsboro trial. Wright's tour was sponsored by the

Communist International Labor Defense (ILD). See James A. Miller, Susan D. Pennybacker, and Eve Rosenhaft, "Mother Ada Wright and the International Campaign to Free the Scottsboro Boys, 1931–1934," *American Historical Review* 106 (April 2001): 387–430.

138. Cobb to Baker, November 12, 1919, NAACP/LOC.

139. Ibid.

140. James A. Cobb to James Weldon Johnson, November 21, 1919, NAACP/LOC.

141. Ibid.

142. Assistant Attorney General R. P. Stewart to Charles D. Kline, Esq., January 30, 1920, NAACP/LOC.

143. Assistant Attorney General R. P. Stewart to Joseph P. Tumulty, Casefile 4955, Wilson/LOC.

144. Petition for Writ of Habeas Corpus, November 22, 1919, in *Supreme Court Records and Transcripts.*

145. James A. Cobb to Mary White Ovington, telegram, December 2, 1919, NAACP/LOC.

146. R. R. Williams to the NAACP, n.d., NAACP/LOC.

147. "A Soldier," *Crisis* 19 (March 1920): 134.

148. Sergeant Allen Brown and Corporal Henry W. Willis to J. E. Spingarn, telegram, April 27, 1920, NAACP/LOC.

149. R. R. Williams to Mr. John Shillady, February 4, 1920, NAACP/LOC.

150. James A. Cobb to John Shillady, February 14, 1920, NAACP/LOC.

151. Ibid.

152. Brief for the United States as Amicus Curiae, Edgar C. Caldwell v. W. E. Parker, Sheriff of Calhoun County, No. 636, Supreme Court of the United States, 252 U.S. 376, in *Supreme Court Records and Transcripts.*

153. Brief for Appellant, Edgar C. Caldwell v. W. E. Parker.

154. Benedict Anderson, *Imagined Communities: Reflections on the Origins and Spread of Nationalism* (London: Verso, 1983).

155. Brief for Appellant, Edgar C. Caldwell v. W. E. Parker.

156. Ibid.

157. Brief for Appellee, Edgar C. Caldwell v. W. E. Parker.

158. "Sterne Rites Wednesday at Home on Drive," *Anniston Star,* February 14, 1920, 1.

159. James A. Cobb to John R. Shillady, March 6, 1920, NAACP/LOC.

160. Ibid.

161. "Who's Who," *Messenger* 3 (July 1921): 221.

162. Opinion, Edgar C. Caldwell v. W. E. Parker.

163. "Sergeant Caldwell to Die August 15," *Cleveland Advocate,* July 26, 1919; "Alabama Colored Soldier's Death Sentence Affirmed by the State's Highest Court," *Houston Informer,* July 26, 1919.

164. R. R. Williams to Mr. John Shillady, May 13, 1920, NAACP/LOC.

165. James A. Cobb to John Shillady, April 24, 1920, NAACP/LOC.

166. Edgar C. Caldwell to John Shillady, March 26, 1920, NAACP/LOC.

167. "Caldwell Sentenced to Die on July 30," *Anniston Star,* n.d.

168. "Caldwell Thinks He Might Go to the Pen, Not Gallows," *Anniston Star,* n.d.

169. "Sergeant Caldwell Executed," *Crisis* 20 (October 1920): 282. "Edgar Caldwell Dies on Gallows," *Anniston Star,* July 30, 1920, 1. The *New York Times* did not record the speech included in the *Crisis,* but summarized Caldwell as having spent twenty minutes warning African Americans off of whiskey and playing cards. See "Doomed Man Warns Others," *New York Times,* July 31, 1920, 2.

170. "Negro Soldier Put to Death for Murder of Linten," *Birmingham Age,* July 31, 1920, 6.

171. Fred Gormley, "Edgar Caldwell Will Hang Today at Calhoun Jail," *Birmingham Age,* July 30, 1920, 2.

172. "Caldwell's Execution Contains Object Lessons," *Anniston Star,* July 30, 1920.

173. "Sergeant Caldwell Executed," *Crisis,* 282.

174. NAACP lawyers scored a victory for habeas corpus in Moore v. Dempsey, the Supreme Court case arising from the trials of sharecroppers in Elaine and Phillips County, Arkansas. On the Elaine riots, see Nan Woodruff, "African American Struggles for Citizenship in the Arkansas and Mississippi Deltas in the Age of Jim Crow," *Radical History Review* 55 (Winter 1993): 33–51. For details of the legal strategy in the Elaine riots of 1919, see Richard C. Cortner, *A Mob Intent on Death: the NAACP and the Arkansas Riots* (Middletown, Conn.: Wesleyan University Press, 1988). Cortner claims that marks the NAACP's first foray into criminal defense. Although the Arkansas cases reached the Supreme Court before Caldwell v. Parker, agitation for Edgar Caldwell began still earlier; on the Ossian Sweet case, see Kevin Boyle, *Arc of Justice: A Saga of Race, Civil Rights, and Murder in the Jazz Age* (New York: Henry Holt, 2004); on Scottsboro, see James Goodman, *Stories of Scottsboro* (New York: Pantheon Books, 1994).

175. On the fight to pass the Dyer Anti-Lynching Bill, see "Federal Antilynching Bill," *Crisis* 16 (June 1918): 76; as well as Schneider, *We Return Fighting,* 172–193.

7. Forewarned Is Forearmed

1. Richard H. Roberts to Honorable Senator Bilbo, November 24, 1942, Bilbo Papers, Box 1077, Folder 3, University of Southern Mississippi.

2. Ibid. On the anti–poll tax campaign, see Glenda Gilmore, *Defying Dixie: The Radical Roots of Civil Rights, 1920–1950* (New York: Norton, 2008), 336–341.

3. Charles Hamilton Houston, "Saving the World for Democracy," Part 1, *Pittsburgh Courier,* July 20, 1940.

4. Charles Hamilton Houston, "Saving the World for Democracy," Part 6, *Pittsburgh Courier,* August 24, 1940; Genna Rae McNeil, *Groundwork: Charles Hamilton Houston and the Struggle for Civil Rights* (Philadelphia: University of Pennsylvania Press, 1983), 34.

5. "Vast Crowds Jam Liberty Hall as Great Convention Draws to Close," *Negro World,* September 4, 1920, TINCF; The UNIA 1920 Convention, Hubert Harrison Diaries, in Jeffrey B. Perry, *A Hubert Harrison Reader* (Middletown, Conn.: Wesleyan University Press, 2001), 191.

6. Memoirs, Kathryn M. Johnson Papers, Schlesinger Library, Radcliffe College, 239–240. Suffragist and future New Dealer Gertrude Ely was the head of the Women's Division in France. See Susan Zeiger, *In Uncle Sam's Service: Women Workers with American Expeditionary Force* (Ithaca, N.Y.: Cornell University Press, 1999), 41.

7. Hunton and Johnson, *Two Colored Women with the American Expeditionary Forces* (1920; repr., New York: G. K. Hall & Co., 1997), 323; "YWCA Notes," *Chicago Defender,* October 4, 1919; "YWCA Notes," *Chicago Defender,* March 27, 1920; Memoirs, Kathryn M. Johnson, 255.

8. Speech reprinted in "Vast Crowds Jam Liberty Hall," *Negro World.*

9. Ibid. *Negro World* misidentified her as "Miss Catherine N. Johnson"; Memoirs, Kathryn M. Johnson, 209–210.

10. "Vast Crowds Jam Liberty Hall." On Garveyism and the UNIA as a social movement and the black organizing tradition, see Steven Hahn, *A Nation under Our Feet: Black Political Struggles in the Rural South from Slavery to the Great Migration* (Cambridge, Mass.: Harvard University Press, 2003), 469–476; as well as Judith Stein, *The World of Marcus Garvey: Race and Class in Modern Society* (Baton Rouge: Louisiana University Press, 1986). On education organizing and the black freedom struggle, see Barbara Ransby, *Ella Baker and the Black Freedom Movement: A Radical Democratic Tradition* (Chapel Hill: University of North Carolina Press, 2003); and Katherine Mellen Charron, *Freedom's Teacher: The Life of Septima Clark* (Chapel Hill: University of North Carolina Press, 2009).

11. Hunton and Johnson, *Two Colored Women,* 323.

12. Memoirs, Kathryn M. Johnson, 255–256; Elizabeth McHenry, *Forgotten Readers: Recovering the Lost History of African American Literary Societies* (Durham, N.C.: Duke University Press, 2002), 11; *The Correspondence of W. E. B. Du Bois: Selections, 1877–1934,* Herbert Aptheker, ed. (Amherst: University of Massachusetts Press, 1997), 334; Mary White Ovington, "Selling Race Pride," *Publisher's Weekly* (January 10, 1925), 111–114.

13. Sgt. Percy L. Jones to Mr. DuBois, August 6, 1919, Du Bois Papers, Reel 7. On the Tulsa riot, see Kimberly Ellis, "We Look Like Men of War: Africana Narratives of the Tulsa Race Riot of 1921" (Ph.D. Diss, Purdue University, 2002); on Rosewood, see Mark Robert Schneider, *We Return Fighting: The Civil Rights Movement in the Jazz Age*

(Boston: Northeastern University Press, 2002), 354–357; and on Coffeyville, see "Bullets Quell Kansas Riot, 10 Shot," *Chicago Defender,* March 26, 1927.

14. Klan membership comes from Kathleen Blee, *Women of the Klan: Racism and Gender in the 1920s* (Berkeley: University of California Press, 1991), 17. William Leuchtenberg estimated the Klan's membership at five million in *The Perils of Prosperity, 1914–1932* (Chicago: University of Chicago Press, 1958), 211; Klansman quote comes from "In the Name of Law and Order," *Dallas Express,* February 5, 1921.

15. Memoirs, Kathryn M. Johnson, 244, 247.

16. Memoirs, Kathryn M. Johnson, 248–249; "Negroes Picket 'Birth of a Nation,'" *New York World,* May 7, 1921, in NAACP Papers, Group I, Series C, Administrative File, microfilm Part 11, Series A.

17. Memoirs, Kathryn M. Johnson, 248–249; "NAACP Makes Test Case Protest of 'Birth of a Nation,'" May 13, 1921, NAACP Papers, Part 11, Series A.

18. Military Intelligence worried about soldiers banding together, but hoped that "men scattering" after demobilization would bring an end to nascent organizing. See "Organization among Negro Troops for Post Demobilization Activities," Casefile 10218-311, RG 165, NARA II. On the effect of federal antiradicalism on African Americans, see Theodore Kornweibel, *Seeing Red: Federal Campaigns Against Black Militancy, 1919–1925* (Bloomington: Indiana University Press, 1998).

19. Pamphlet, "Lest We Forget," FSAA, Reel 21; "War Workers Mass Meeting," *Chicago Defender,* April 5, 1919. For a thorough survey of African American veterans organizing in the League for Democracy, the Garvey movement, and other militant circles, see Chad L. Williams, "Vanguards of the New Negro: African American Veterans and Post-World War I Racial Militancy," *Journal of African American History* 92 (Summer 2007): 347–370.

20. "War Workers Mass Meeting"; Greer to Tennessee Senator Kenneth McKellar, December 6, 1918, quoted in Arthur Barbeau and Florette Henri, *The Unknown Soldiers: African-American Troops in World War I* (1974; repr., New York: Da Capo Press, 1996), 160, 171. See also Emmett J. Scott, *Scott's Official History of the American Negro in the World War* (1919), 438–440; Lieutenant Osceola McKaine to the Secretary of War, Press Release, in Casefile 10218-337, RG 165, NARA II.

21. "Goes to Capitol," *Chicago Defender,* June 21, 1919, 4.

22. "Lest We Forget." See also Miles Richards, "Osceola E. McKaine and the Struggle for Black Civil Rights, 1917–1946" (Ph.D. diss., University of South Carolina, 1994), 64–82; "Rent Protest Meeting," *Chicago Defender,* March 13, 1920; "Fight for Congress Seat Underway," *Chicago Defender,* December 13, 1919.

23. Walter H. Loving to James E. Cutler, June 11, 1919, FSAA, Reel 21; Osceola McKaine, "The Nineteenth Amendment," *New York Commoner,* March 28, 1920, quoted in Richards, "Osceola E. McKaine and the Struggle for Black Civil Rights," 80.

24. Richards, "Osceola E. McKaine and the Struggle for Black Civil Rights," 64–82; "League for Democracy," in Casefile 10218-337, RG 165, NARA II; quote from Patricia

Sullivan, *Days of Hope: Race and Democracy in the New Deal Era* (Chapel Hill: University of North Carolina, 1996), 196.

25. "Re: Anonymous Letter from Soldier in the 24th Infantry," Casefile 10218-392, RG 165, NARA II.

26. "Report from Director, Division of Negro Economics, to Secretary of Labor," September 12, 1919, quoted in William M. Tuttle Jr., *Race Riot,* 220; Harry Haywood [pseud. for Haywood Hall], *Black Bolshevik: Autobiography of An Afro-American Communist* (Chicago: Liberator Press, 1979), 83.

27. Harrison George, *Chicago Race Riots* (Chicago: Great Western Publishing Company, 1919), www.archive.org (accessed April 2008). The 1919 pamphlet was a socialist publication, but George is identified as a Communist in Harvey Kehr, John Earl Haynes, and Fridrikh Igorevich Firsov, *The Secret World of American Communism* (New Haven, Conn.: Yale University Press, 1995), 49; Haywood, *Black Bolshevik,* 83.

28. Haywood, *Black Bolshevik,* 90–92.

29. Ibid., 84, 92–101.

30. Ibid., 114–20. Biographical information on Otto Hall comes from Minkah Makalani, "For the Liberation of Black People Everywhere: The African Blood Brotherhood, Black Radicalism, and Pan African Liberation in the New Negro Movement, 1917–1936" (Ph.D. diss., University of Illinois, 2004), 144; and Theodore Draper, *American Communism and Soviet Russia* (London: Transaction Publishers, 2003), 133.

31. Haywood, *Black Bolshevik,* 122. Details on membership come from Cyril Briggs to Theodore Draper, March 17, 1958, Letter held in the Hoover Institute, Stanford, reproduced on www.marxisthistory.org (accessed May 2008). Claim about veterans comes from Winston James, *Holding Aloft the Banner of Ethiopia: Caribbean Radicalism in Early Twentieth Century America* (London: Verso, 1998), 168–169.

32. Haywood, *Black Bolshevik,* 124–125. The announcement of ABB came in *Crusader* 2 (October 1919): 27; "The Salvation of the Negro," *Crusader* 4 (April 1921): 8–9; Briggs to Draper, March 17, 1958; and "Denies Negroes Started Tulsa Riot," *New York Times,* June 5, 1921, 21. The *Crusader's* wire service sent out stories in which the ABB was credited with organizing in Tulsa; see "Klansmen Initiate with Pepper under Their Noses," *Chicago Defender,* December 23, 1922, 2.

33. Haywood, *Black Bolshevik,* 131, 147; Briggs to Draper, March 17, 1958. On African Americans activists in Moscow in the 1920s, see Gilmore, *Defying Dixie,* 43–51.

34. Gilmore, *Defying Dixie,* 47; Haywood, *Black Boshevik,* 166; Yelena Khanga with Susan Jacoby, *Soul to Soul: A Black Russian American Family, 1865–1992* (New York: W. W. Norton & Company, 1992), 45–50; "James W. Ford, 63, Red Leader Here," *New York Times,* June 22, 1957, 15.

35. See Theodore Rosengarten, *All God's Dangers: The Life of Nate Shaw* (1974; repr., New York: Vintage Books, 1989).

36. Elisha Green, *Ely: Too Black, Too White* (Amherst: The University of Massachusetts Press, 1970), 474.

37. Ibid., 479–480.

38. Ibid., 478–479.

39. Steven A. Reich, "Soldiers of Democracy: Black Texans and the Fight for Citizenship, 1917–1921," *Journal of American History* 82 (March 1996): 1502–1503.

40. Green, *Ely: Too Black, Too White*, 478–479.

41. Ibid., 487.

42. Ibid., 488.

43. Ibid., 489–490.

44. Ibid., 492.

45. Ibid., 496–497.

46. Ibid., 497, 503, 507, 531; "Tar and Feathers Sweep Texas," *Los Angeles Times*, August 7, 1921, III42. See also "My Act No Worse than Yours—Branded Man to Klansman," *Chicago Whip*, April 9, 1921; "Ku Klux Terror Runs Riot; Scores Flogged," *Chicago Defender*, July 30, 1921; "Klan Sweeps Texas Election," *Los Angeles Times*, July 24, 1922, I1.

47. Green, *Ely: Too Black, Too White*, 530–31. The 1930 census lists Green as a "caretaker" living with his wife, Tellie, in Los Angeles, California. The census taker did not ask if he was a veteran. U.S. Bureau of the Census, *15th Census of the United States Population Schedule, Los Angeles City*, NARA.

48. Memoirs, Kathryn M. Johnson, 390–392, 395; "Police Halt Big Protest Meeting Here," *Chicago Defender*, September 7, 1935, 2; "Harlemites Stage 'Hands Off Ethiopia' Parade," *Chicago Defender*, April 13, 1935, 4; "'Negro and White—Unite' Sign Used in Big Parade," *Atlanta Daily World*, August 15, 1935, 6.

49. Memoirs, Kathryn M. Johnson, 369, 370; "Ethiopia Defiant as Italy Makes Plans to Grab Africa," *Chicago Defender*, February 16, 1935; James H. Meriwether, *Proudly We Can Be Africans: Black Americans and Africa, 1935–1961* (Chapel Hill: University of North Carolina Press, 2002), 28–29; W. E. B. Du Bois, "Inter-racial Implications of the Ethiopian Crisis, A Negro View," *Foreign Affairs* 14 (October 1935): 86.

50. "Ethiopia Defiant as Italy Makes Plans to Grab Africa"; "Inter-racial Implications of the Ethiopian Crisis"; *Proudly We Can Be Africans*, 31; "'Trust God, Give 'Em Hell,' Bishop (Ex War Veteran) Tells Haile Selassie," *Atlanta Daily World*, August 3, 1935; Memoirs, Kathryn M. Johnson, 390.

51. Brenda Gayle Plummer, *Rising Wind: Black Americans and U.S. Foreign Affairs, 1935–1960* (Chapel Hill: University of North Carolina Press, 1996), 37–41; Memoirs, Kathryn M. Johnson, 389.

52. "Peace Meeting in Uproar," *New York Times*, October 23, 1935, 13; "War Notes: Texans Rally to Ethiopia," *Chicago Defender*, July 20, 1935; William R. Scott, *The Sons of Sheba's Race: African-Americans and the Italo-Ethiopian War, 1935–1941* (Bloomington:

Indiana University Press, 1993), 62–63; "Texans Aroused by Ethiopian War Beat," *Atlanta World,* July 26, 1935, 5.

53. Kathryn M. Johnson, *Stealing a Nation: A Brief Story of How Swaziland, a South African Kingdom, Came under British Control without the Knowledge or Consent of Its People* (Chicago: Pyramid Publishing Company, 1939); Memoirs, Kathryn M. Johnson, 359–362. On Nxumalo, see Hugh MacMillan, "Swaziland: Decolonisation and the Triumph of Tradition," *Journal of Modern African Studies* 23 (December 1985): 643–666.

54. "Police Halt Big Protest Meeting Here"; Memoirs, Kathryn M. Johnson, 390.

55. "The Klan in Europe," *New York Times,* July 29, 1922, 6. The Christian socialist monthly *World Tomorrow* made the link the year before; see "Italy's Ku Klux," *World Tomorrow,* September 1931, TINCF.

56. Haywood, *Black Bolshevik,* 451–456. On African American links between domestic oppression and Italy's designs on Ethiopia, see Rosenberg, *How Far the Promised Land: World Affairs and the American Civil Rights Movement* (Princeton, N.J.: Princeton University Press, 2006), 103–106.

57. Memoirs, Kathryn M. Johnson, 391–392; "35 Face Trial for Protest on Ethiopian War," *Chicago Defender,* November 2, 1935.

58. Memoirs, Kathryn M. Johnson, 400–406; "Mme. Ezella Mathis Carter Dies," *Chicago Defender,* June 2, 1934, 3; Leota Singleton Harris Interview, 1975, Black Community Project, University of Illinois at Springfield, Oral History Collection, 24–28, 134–135, www.uis.edu/archives/memoirs/HARRISL.pdf (accessed January 2007); "Suggest 3 AME Bishops for US," *Atlanta Daily World,* August 13, 1932.

59. Kathryn M. Johnson, "What the People Say," *Chicago Defender,* December 12, 1936, 16. On African Americans' move out of the Republican Party in the 1930s, see Nancy Weiss, *Farewell to the Party of Lincoln: Black Politics in the Age of FDR* (Princeton, N.J.: Princeton University Press, 1983); and Rita Werner Gordon, "The Change in the Political Alignment of Chicago's Negroes during the New Deal," *Journal of American History* 56 (December 1969): 584–603.

60. Bernice Hall, "Stage Hot for Cong. Mitchell's Seat," *Atlanta Daily World,* March 3, 1940; Lucius Harper, "Dustin' Off the News," *Chicago Defender,* February 11, 1950, 7; Kathryn M. Johnson, *The Dark Race in the Dawn: Proof of Black African Civilization in the Americas before Columbus* (New York: William Frederick Press, 1948); Leota Singleton Harris interview, 135.

61. David Levering Lewis, *W. E. B. Du Bois: The Fight for Equality and the American Century, 1919–1963* (New York: Henry Holt and Company, 2000), 37–38; Kenneth Janken, *Rayford Logan and the Dilemma of the African-American Intellectual* (Amherst: University of Massachusetts Press, 1993), 50–52.

62. Janken, *Rayford W. Logan,* 55–61, 176–77; George Shepperson, "Pan Africanism and 'Pan-Africanism': Some Historical Notes," *Phylon* 23 (4th qtr., 1962): 346–58;

Imanuel Geiss, *The Pan African Movement,* trans. Anne Keep (New York: Africana Publishing Co., 1974). 251–254.

63. Rayford Logan, "The International Status of the Negro," *Journal of Negro History* 18 (January 1933): 33–38; Janken, *Rayford W. Logan,* 74. For a sample of Logan's scholarship, see "The Operation of the Mandate System in Africa," *Journal of Negro History* 13 (October 1928): 423–477; "The Haze in Haiti," *Nation* 124 (March 16, 1927): 281–283; "The Anglo-Egyptian Sudan, A Problem in International Relations, *Journal of Negro History* 4 (October 1931): 471–481; and *The Diplomatic Relations of the United States with Haiti, 1776–1891* (Chapel Hill: University of North Carolina Press, 1941).

64. Rayford W. Logan, "The Negro Studies War Some More for New Angle," *Norfolk Journal and Guide* (September 28, 1935): 17.

65. Rayford Logan Statement to Business Session, Annual Meeting, June 20, 1940, NAACP Papers, Part I, reel 10.

66. W. H. Auden, "September 1, 1939," in *Another Time* (New York: Random House, 1940); "What About Negroes in Next War? Asks Writer," *Pittsburgh Courier,* September 23, 1939; "Nation's Negro Youth Wary as Europe's War Clouds Darken," *Kansas City Plain Dealer,* October 6, 1939, TINCF, Reel 64.

67. Statement of Rayford W. Logan, *Selective Compulsory Military Training and Service: Hearings before the Committee on Military Affairs, House of Representatives,* 76th Congress, 3rd Session, (Washington, D.C.: Government Printing Office, 1940), 585; Rayford Logan Statement to Business Session, NAACP Papers; McNeil, *Groundwork,* 131–151.

68. Statement of Rayford W. Logan, *Selective Compulsory Military Training and Service,* 585–589; Statement of Dr. Charles H. Houston, *Selective Compulsory Military Training and Service: Hearings before the Committee on Military Affairs, House of Representatives,* 76th Congress, 3rd Session, (Washington, D.C.: Government Printing Office, 1940), 589–590; "Charge Defense Heads with Jim Crow Policy," *Chicago Defender,* August 24, 1940. The *Defender* quotes Houston as saying that "Negroes want some of the democracy they fought for."; this does not appear in the official transcript of the hearings.

69. Janken, *Rayford W. Logan,* 116–117; Edgar T. Rouzeau, "Black America Wars on Double Front for High Stakes," *Pittsburgh Courier,* February 7, 1942; C. W. Rice to Business Session, June 20, 1940, NAACP Papers, Part I, reel 10.

70. Janken, *Rayford W. Logan,* 128; A. Philip Randolph to Milton Webster, quoted in Jervis Anderson, *A. Philip Randolph, A Biographical Portrait* (Berkeley: University of California Press, 1972), 247–248.

71. On Randolph and interwar activism, see Gilmore, *Defying Dixie.* On *Messenger* writers, see biographies in Tom Lutz and Susanna Ashton, eds., *These "Colored" United States: African American Essays from the 1920s* (New Brunswick, N.J.: Rutgers University Press, 1996) and Williams, "Vangaurds of the New Negro," 352–357.

72. Quoted in Anderson, *A. Philip Randolph*, 248–249.

73. Anderson, *A. Philip Randolph*, 250–251, 255; Gilmore, *Defying Dixie*, 358–360; Merl E. Reed, "The FBI, MOWM, and CORE, 1941–1946," *Journal of Black Studies* 21 (June 1991): 466.

74. Gilmore, *Defying Dixie*, 360–362. Anderson gives an in-depth account of Randolph's meeting with Roosevelt in *A. Philip Randolph*, 256–258. See also "Full Text of Executive Order," *Chicago Defender*, June 28, 1941; "FD's Order Kills Defense Bias," *Chicago Defender*, June 28, 1941.

75. "Two Delegations in Washington Urge Congress Backing for FEPC Bill," *Chicago Defender*, March 10, 1945; Green, *Ely: Too Black, Too White*, 538 and on his efforts in the factories, 539–567.

Epilogue

1. Miles Richards, "Osceola E. McKaine and the Struggle for Black Civil Rights, 1917–1946" (Ph.D. diss., University of South Carolina, 1994), 88.

2. Ibid., 97–156; Patricia Sullivan, *Days of Hope: Race and Democracy in the New Deal Era* (Chapel Hill: University of North Carolina Press, 1996), 170–197.

3. Harry Haywood, *Black Bolshevik: Autobiography of An Afro-American Communist* (Chicago: Liberator Press, 1979), 1.

4. Elisha Green, *Ely: Too Black, Too White* (Amherst: University of Massachusetts Press, 1970), 629, 631.

5. On nationalism and generational lineage, see Benedict Anderson, *The Spectre of Comparisons: Nationalism, Southeast Asia, and the World* (London: Verso Press, 1993), 360–68.

Acknowledgments

I think it was the late 1920s. My grandmother, Geneva Lewis, could not have been more than ten or twelve. With her parents and siblings, she lived in Ouachita Parish, Louisiana, in a segregated lumber camp where her father, James Lewis, cut wood for the Brown Paper Mill. Under Jim Crow, the state did not provide enough education funding to support black women teaching in segregated lumber camps, so the teachers who worked in the camp did odd jobs on the side to make money. One woman did hair, my Grandmother once told me, for ten cents a style.

Somehow, James Lewis and the other families made up the difference. Occasionally, my great-grandfather tried to pay the teacher's salary out of his own pocket. More often, he went around the camp and took up a collection, and everyone contributed what they could. After all, he was not the only one who wanted his children to get an education, to read and do figures, to know the world through learning. Jim Crow could deny them much—equal access, opportunities, institutions—but it could not deny them hope.

I hope that I have done all right by the Lewises, Smiths, Goinses, and all those who made this possible. I offer my greatest gratitude to my parents, Thomas and Carolyn Smith, for their strength, sacrifices, and unflagging support. I give the same thanks to my sisters. Alyssa, always capable, spent countless days on the phone walking me through the daily details of living. I may be older, but she is wiser. Karen picked me up at the airport when I started college and again when I began graduate school, sending me out both times into the alien world of academia with comforting protectiveness and fortifying pride.

This book and its author benefited immensely from the vibrant and generous intellectual community I found during my graduate studies. I give heartfelt thanks to my dissertation committee: Glenda Gilmore, Matthew Jacobson, and Jay Winter. Through example and advice, they have shaped me as a scholar and teacher. I could not ask for a better advisor, reader, editor, critic, or advocate than Glenda Gilmore. Her intellect, honesty, commitment, and panache never cease to astound me, and I am proud to call her a friend. Matt Jacobson repeatedly has challenged and encouraged me to think more rigorously and creatively, and he has never let me skirt by with an easy pun or rhetorical flourish. In many ways, this book is an ongoing attempt to answer the "simple question" about "nationalism, specifically black nationalism" that he asked me in 2001. Jay Winter taught me how elegantly a concise question can express a complex idea, and by encouraging me to visit sites of the war, he helped me to envision this project in the most essential ways. His nimbleness of thought and work on World War I have served as an inspiration. I also thank Robert Johnston and David Brion Davis for their invaluable encouragement, and John Demos who read parts of this manuscript with great care—and whose thinking and writing, graciousness and kindness make me glad to be part of this profession.

I wrote this book with my friends. Kat Charron is the heart of an extended kin network that has enriched my life intellectually and personally. She has read chapter upon chapter, always pushing me to think like a scholar and read like a poet. I would not have made it without her, and I am forever grateful. During Co-dependency Wednesdays and television binges, George Trumbull and Claire Nee Nelson helped me frame ideas and avoid mistakes; this book is filled with their insights. Tammy Ingram, my favorite South Georgian since Jimmy Carter, has graced me with her keen mind and good sense. Jason Ward generously shared sources from his own research. Jennifer Boittin helped me navigate resources on black France and, along with George, kept me from starving during my summer of research in Paris. I, and my stomach, thank them. I also thank Christian McMillen, Aaron Sachs, and Sandy Zipp; Aaron continually reminded me of the beauty in prose, Sandy the joy of ideas, and Christian the thrill of research. With Kip Kocek, Eric Grant, and Lien-Hang Nguyen, they formed the heart of my community near East Rock.

Years ago, Brett Flehinger (and his accursed green pen) and Jon Rosenberg (and his accursed sharp comments) made a writer and historian out a fairly unfocused undergraduate. More recently, Walter Hill at the National Archives in College Park guided me through NARA's vast holdings. Along the way, Steve Kantrowitz helped refine my thoughts through elegant edits, raucous laughter, and much valued support. Both Kathryn Ratté and Patricia McLaughlin allowed me to use their homes as my own, granting me valuable space to research and write, and encouraging me in the process.

In Ithaca, Ed Baptist and members of the American History Reading Group read an early draft of my Caldwell chapter and suggested new ways to approach the material. Through incisive feedback, Erin Lentz has encouraged me to find the same clarity of thought that graces her thinking; she is a wonder. Jason Cons has waded through more iterations of this project than he would probably care to count. His generosity, quick mind, and formidable wit make him a wonderful colleague and even better friend. Dia and Alex Da Costa humored me when I was not writing and advised me when I was. I thank Michael Trotti for allowing me to cite his family correspondence and for all the insight supplied by the members of the Beer 'n' History gang—Michael, Rob Vanderlan, Jeff Cowie, Derek Chang, Michael Smith, and again, Aaron Sachs.

Jennifer Guglielmo has been cheering me on for years now from Northampton, Massachusetts. She, Lisa Armstrong, Ginetta Candelario, and Daphne LaMothe each offer outstanding examples of intellectual creativity and curiosity, activist scholarship, and feminism in practice. I thank them for their attention and affection, and I thank the Five Colleges ABD Dissertation Fellowship and the Smith Mendenhall Fellowship for supporting the dissertation on which this project is based.

This project also has been supported by generous funding and institutional support from the Yale graduate school, the Beinecke Library, the Yale Center for International and Area Studies, the Howard Lamar Center for the Study of Frontiers and Borders, the Ford Foundation, and the Organization of American Historians. I owe especial thanks to friends and staff at Yale—Vicki Shepherd, Essie Lucky-Barros, Yvette Barnard, and Florence Thomas—who have saved my neck and sanity time and again. Florence has since passed on, but she lives in countless memories and in my affection.

The Carolina Postdoctoral Fellowship at the University of North Carolina allowed me time and energy to turn my dissertation into a book, as did the support of my colleagues in the Duke history department. I thank Lloyd Kramer and Bill Reddy, along with Bill Chafe, Gunther Peck, Dirk Bonker, Wayne Lee, Laura Edwards, Ed Balleisen, and the members of the Triangle seminars in military and legal history.

I have found a great community in the Triangle and have incurred many debts. Jacquelyn Dowd Hall was a model mentor during my time at Carolina. Perri Morgan and Tim Tyson brought me into their family, offering up delicious meals and gorgeous turns of phrase. Crystal Feimster and Heather Williams have provided guidance and grounding since my earliest days at Yale; if I ever grow up, I want to be just like them. Brett Whalen and Emily Burrill have taught me about everything from Francophone Africa to Medieval Christendom. Rhonda Lee offered the support and serenity that made thinking possible.

In addition, I would like to thank my colleagues who have engaged and improved my work at annual meetings of the Southern Historical Association, the Organization of American Historians, the American Historical Association, and the American Studies Association annual meetings. I also thank the anonymous readers who read my manuscript with great care. Their thought-provoking questions and measured feedback have made this a far better book.

Finally, I thank Christian Lentz, whom I love. He has carried a heavy load throughout this experience, and has remained caring, engaged, and inspiring. He has kept me laughing easily and living fully, even as he has enabled and encouraged me to be as curious and dedicated a scholar as he. I value his mind and his heart, and count myself lucky to know him.

Index